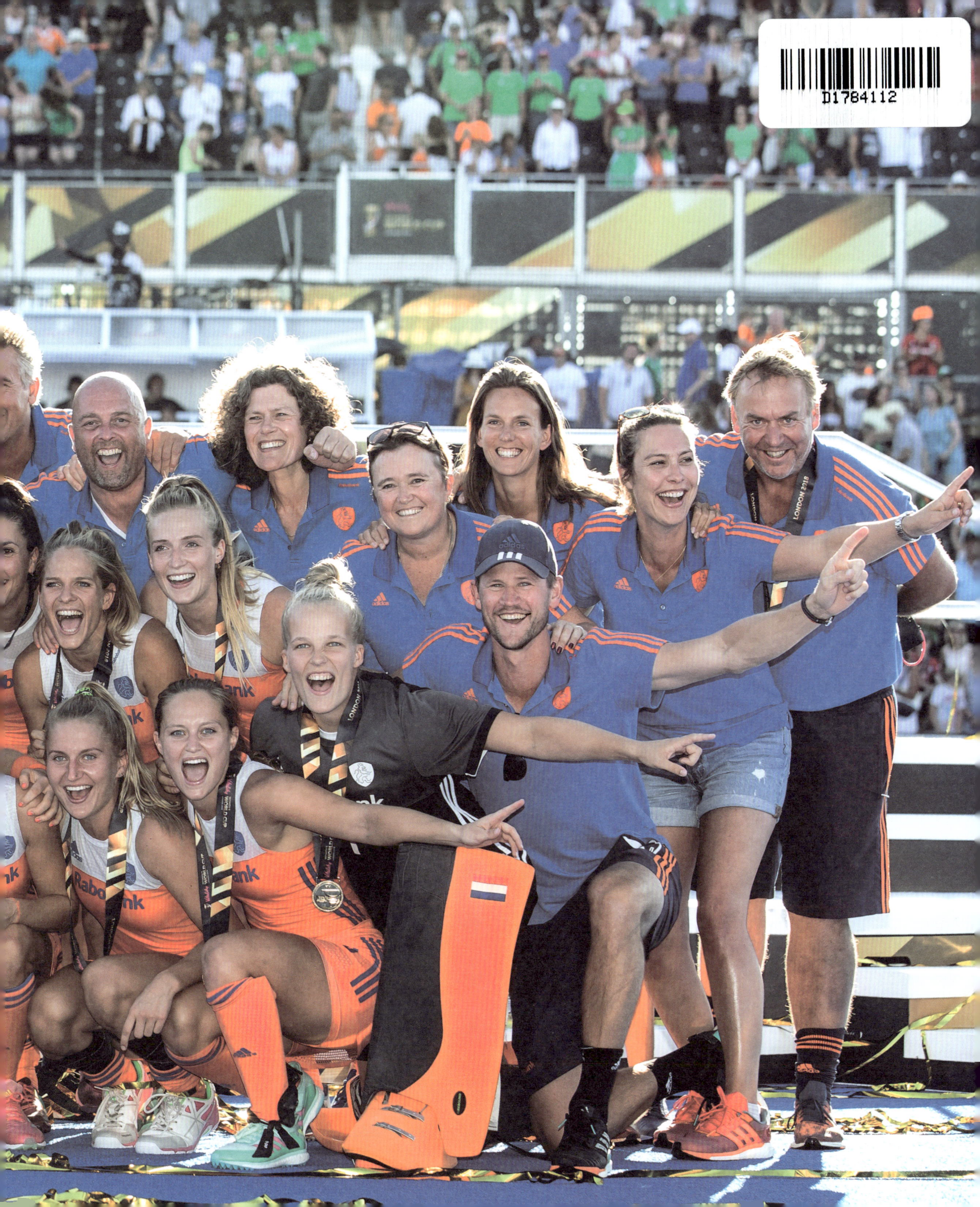

UNDER AN ORANGE SKY

Pitch Publishing Ltd
A2 Yeoman Gate
Yeoman Way
Durrington
BN13 3QZ

Email: info@pitchpublishing.co.uk
Web: www.pitchpublishing.co.uk

First published by Pitch Publishing 2018
Text © 2018 Sarah Juggins and Richard Stainthorpe

1

A CIP catalogue record for this book is available from the British Library.

13-digit ISBN: 9781785314926
Design and typesetting by Olner Pro Sport Media.
Printed in Turkey. Manufacturing managed by Jellyfish Print Solutions Ltd.

To Amy
Best of luck in all
your sporting endeavours
Sarah Juggins

UNDER AN ORANGE SKY

The Story of the
Vitality Hockey Women's World Cup
London 2018

Sarah Juggins and Richard Stainthorpe

Imagery by Frank Uijlenbroek and Koen Suyk,
with additional photography from Rodrigo Jaramillo

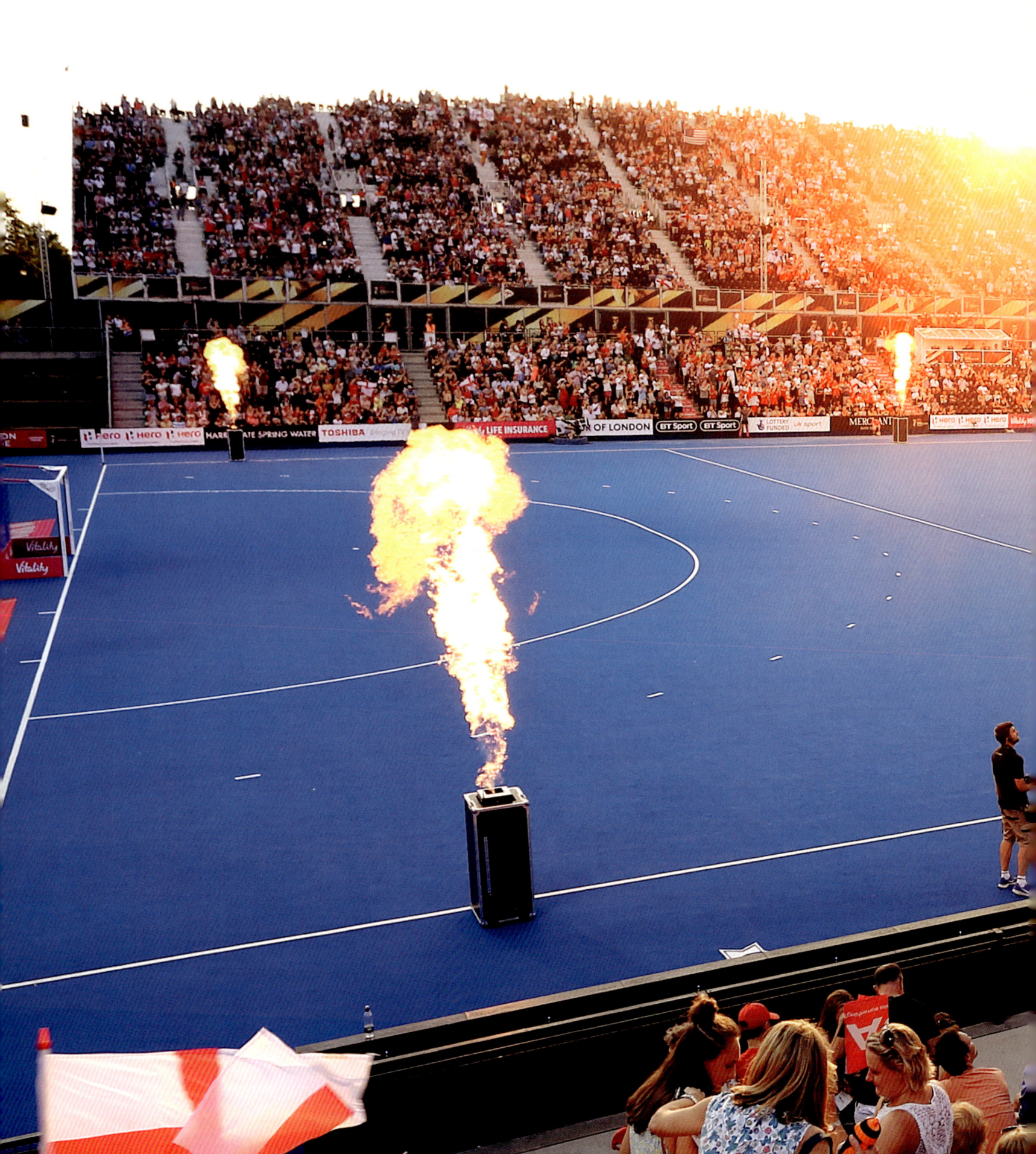

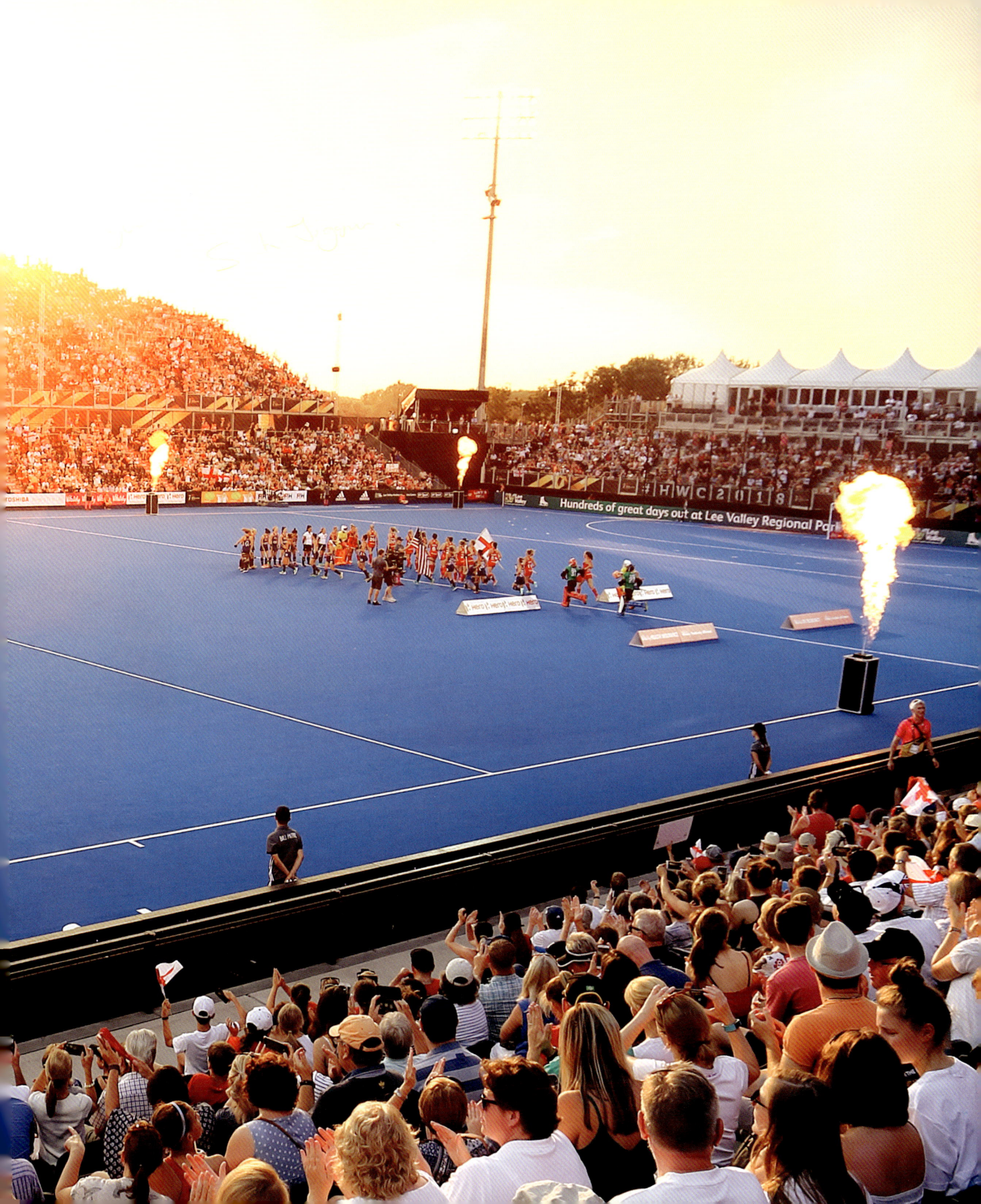

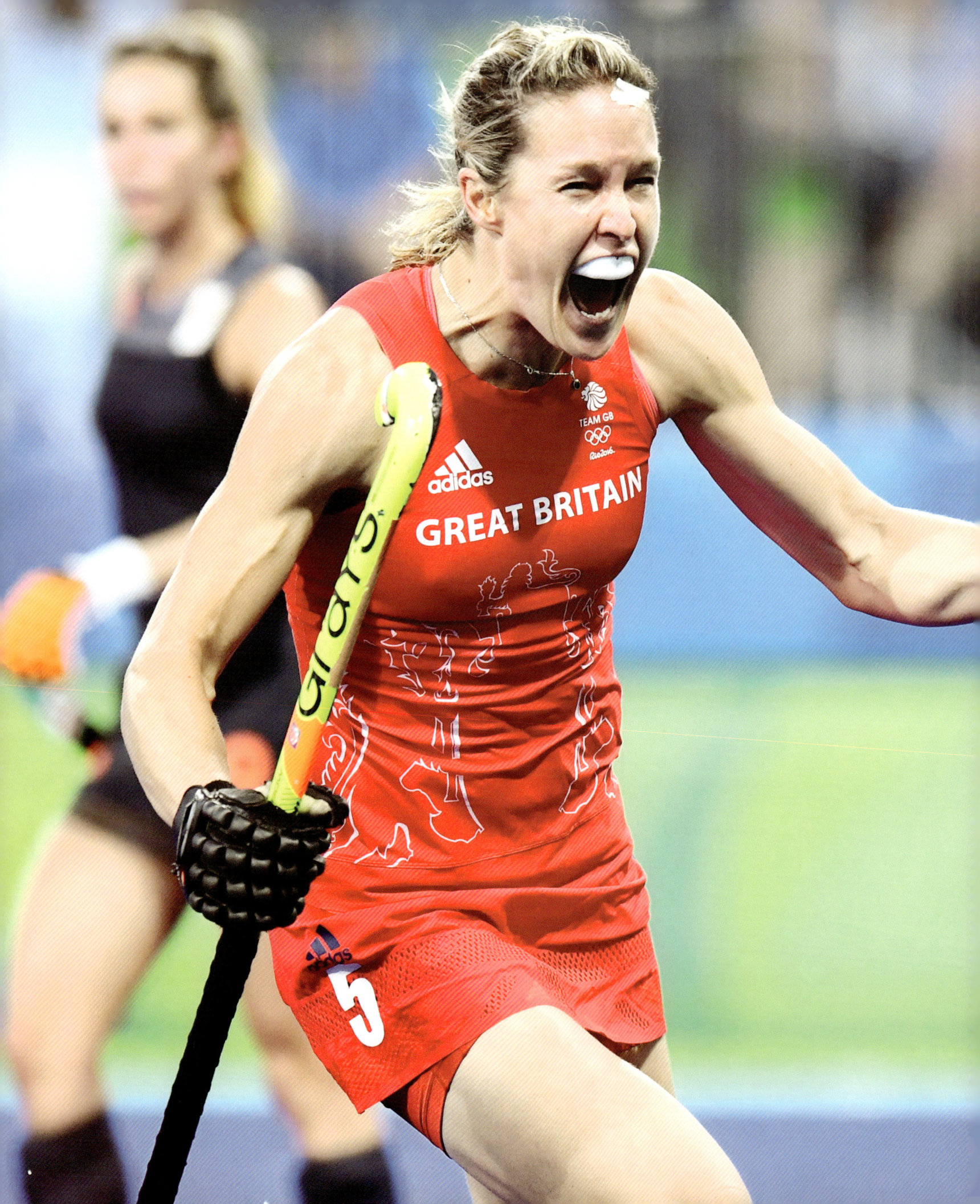

Foreword by Crista Cullen

Former England and Great Britain defender and triple Olympian and medallist at the London 2012 (bronze) and Rio 2016 (gold) Olympic Games.

A World Cup, in any sport, is something truly special.

t provides the opportunity for the best of the best to leave absolutely everything on the field, a chance to showcase years of hard work and gut-wrenching fitness and gym sessions, where athletes have pushed their bodies to their physical limits to give themselves the chance to lift the World Cup trophy.

For two weeks over the summer of 2018, London's Queen Elizabeth Olympic Park was electric, bringing back wonderful memories for those lucky enough to have been present at the Olympic Games in 2012. The revamped Lee Valley Hockey & Tennis Centre enjoyed sell-out crowds, with more than 120,000 fans attending what was a spectacular Vitality Hockey Women's World Cup London 2018.

The action on the field contained all of the flair, skill and determination that you would expect, but with it came a huge amount of unpredictability. The pool stage was certainly nowhere near as straight forward as some of the higher-ranked teams would have either wanted or expected it to be, and failure to hit form in the pool phase left many big teams facing the dreaded cross-over play-off matches. While the cross-overs would prove to be a graveyard for some big-name teams, for the audiences in the stands and watching back home, these additional play-offs lifted the excitement to another level. The cross-over play-offs were followed by more all-or-nothing contests as the knock-out matches continued to produce one shock result after another.

No World Cup competition is without drama, elation and, inevitably, heartbreak, and this event had all of those elements in abundance. We all love an underdog and, in London, this was undoubtedly the Irish. It was the first time in 16 years that the Green Army had qualified for the World Cup, and, while their ambitions were clear, it was the smiles on the Irish players' faces and the way they went about their business that captured the imagination.

A lasting memory for me involved stalwart Ireland player Shirley McCay. The defender was hastily leaving the field during one of the match intervals to join her fellow players for coach Graham Shaw's team talk. She was rudely interrupted by me, who, in my role working as a pitchside interviewer for host broadcaster BT Sport, thrust a microphone in her face and asked for her thoughts on the game. Ever the professional, she gave her answer, explaining about Ireland needing to take their opportunities while also being dogged in defence. My follow-up question related to the fact that moments earlier she had taken a ball to her cheek. The incident had drawn a huge gasp from the crowd, but McCay simply shook it off and got on with her job. Her smiling response to my question – which gave a good indication of how relaxed both McCay and her Irish team-mates were feeling in London – was: 'It just adds to the beauty.'

While it could be argued that lack of expectation played a big role, Ireland undoubtedly proved their worth many times over as they navigated their way through the competition. They answered all of the questions posed by the opposition teams and absolutely earned the right to compete in the World Cup Final.

Despite all of the shocks and surprises, nobody can dispute that this tournament was illuminated by the sheer brilliance of the team dressed in orange. Through their clinical nature and sublime skills, the Netherlands were sensational from start to finish as they claimed an eighth World Cup victory and completed a successful defence of the title that they won on home soil in The Hague in 2014. With 35 goals scored and only three conceded, the team coached by Alyson Annan truly stamped their class all over the World Cup in 2018, with only Australia getting near them before going down in a dramatic shoot-out. Yes, the fairy-tale story was undoubtedly Ireland's staggering journey to the final. But, ultimately, this World Cup was about excellence rising to the top. The Netherlands showed yet again that when it comes to top-class hockey, they have found a winning formula.

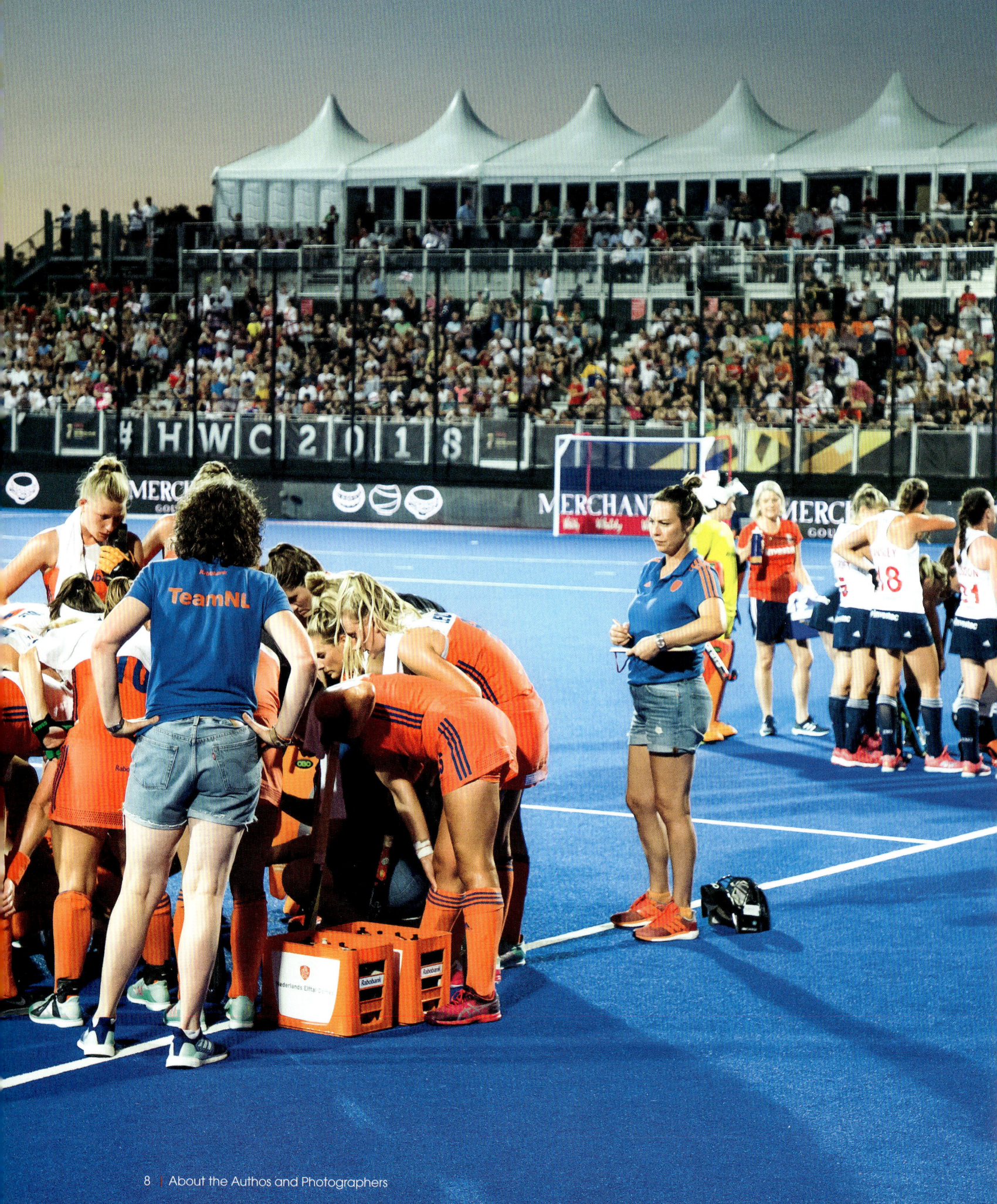

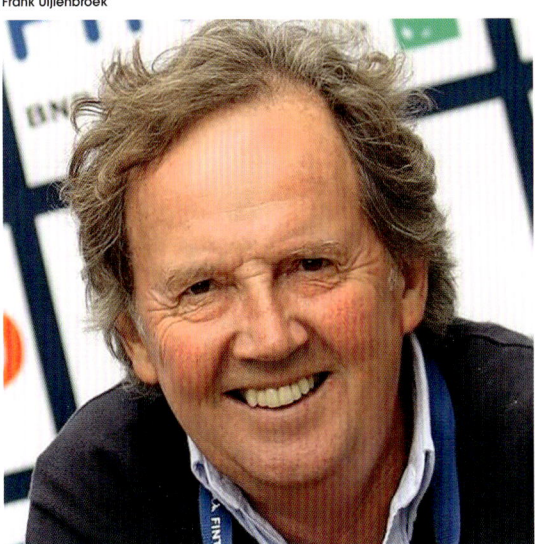
Frank Uijlenbroek

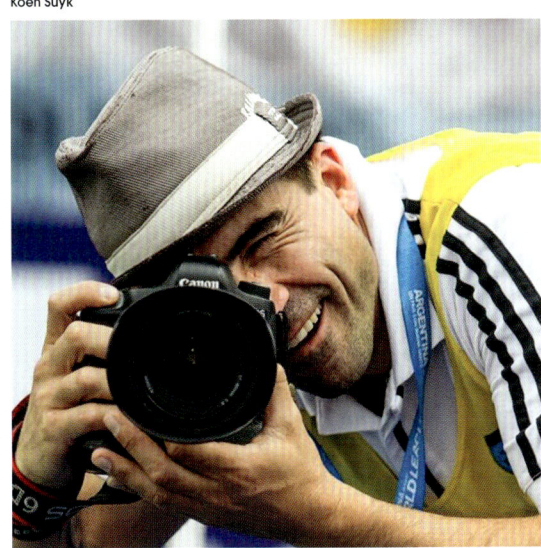
Koen Suyk

Rodrigo Jaramillo

About the Authors and Photographers

Under An Orange Sky: The story of the Vitality Hockey Women's World Cup London 2018 is the second collaboration between hockey journalists Richard Stainthorpe and Sarah Juggins. The two authors are uniquely placed as international hockey writers to tell the story of the Vitality Hockey Women's World Cup from an international perspective, due to their respective roles within the International Hockey Federation (FIH). Both Richard and Sarah write regular articles about teams from around the world and so have an in-depth understanding of the international hockey scene.

Richard Stainthorpe works for the FIH as writer, editor and media operations coordinator. He has covered many international events, including four hockey World Cups, two Olympic Games and numerous other international hockey tournaments.

Sarah Juggins is a freelance writer, working for the FIH, the Pan American Hockey Federation and Planet Hockey. She ran the Hockey Olympic News service at London 2012 and covered the 2014 men's and women's hockey World Cups in The Hague.

The majority of the images that appear in this book were taken by Dutchmen **Frank Uijlenbroek** and **Koen Suyk**, two of the world's leading hockey photographers. It is the second project in which Frank and Koen have worked in collaboration with Sarah and Richard, having also supplied the breathtaking imagery that featured in *The History Makers – How Team GB Stormed to a First Ever Gold in Women's Hockey*, which was named Thomson Reuters Illustrated Book of the Year at the Sports Book Awards 2018.

Frank has travelled the globe taking images of the sport, supplying various agencies, newspapers and major online news outlets as well as national associations, continental federations and the International Hockey Federation. He has almost 30 years' experience in the business and was on hand to capture the Beijing 2008, London 2012 and Rio 2016 Olympic Games. Frank is the owner of the FFU and World Sport Pics photo agencies.

Koen is a veteran of eight Olympic Games and has captured some of hockey's most iconic moments. Over a 40-year career he has earned a reputation as a world-class photographer working for agencies such as Reuters, ANP and ANEFO (Amsterdam). At the Rabobank Hockey World Cup in 2014 in The Hague, the Royal Dutch Hockey Association (KNHB) honoured Koen by creating a public display of some of his finest images. A famous shot of Alex Danson in full flight was named Best Photo at the 2015 EuroHockey Championships in London.

Frank and Koen are joined on this project by talented Argentinian photographer **Rodrigo Jaramillo**, who has also contributed some terrific images, thanks to his work with the World Sport Pics photo agency.

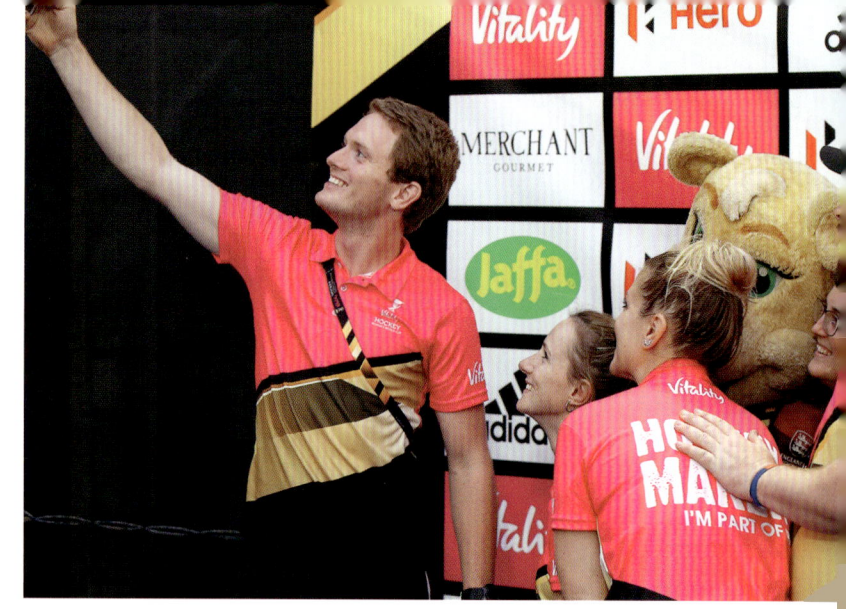

Acknowledgements

Although assembled by a small team of writers and photographers, a project like this is not possible without the assistance of a great many other people. We would like to thank all of the athletes and coaching staff for speaking to us before, during and after the Vitality Hockey Women's World Cup London 2018. In addition, the following people also offered invaluable help.

International Hockey Federation: Martyn Gallivan, Paula Jenkins, Danny Parker and Nikki Symmons.

England Hockey: Sally Munday, Sue Bodycomb and Sue Catton.

Statistics and proofing: B.G. Joshi, Sophie Stainthorpe, Ross Bone, Beth Moorley, Stephen Findlater, Mikhail Mokrushin/Evgeniy Lomov (Russian Hockey Federation), Park Myung Suk (Korea Hockey Association), Yan Huckendubler, Claudia Klatt, Craig Mortimer-Zhika, The Hockey Museum (Mike Smith, Katie Dodd, Kate Vermeulen and the team).

Special thanks to Andy McMenamin, Anna McInerney, Tracey Smedley and all Hockey Makers involved with the outstanding press operations team in London, who worked tirelessly to facilitate interviews and ensure that photographers could capture spectacular imagery from this wonderful event. Big thanks also to New Zealand photographer Ned Dawson who, through his website Planet Hockey, kindly supplied us with the stunning Red Arrows photo from the opening day. Finally, a huge thank you to photographer Antonella Garello Bonini and Leonhard Uijlenbroek for their wonderful efforts supporting the work of the World Sport Pics team. Their respective contributions have been immense!

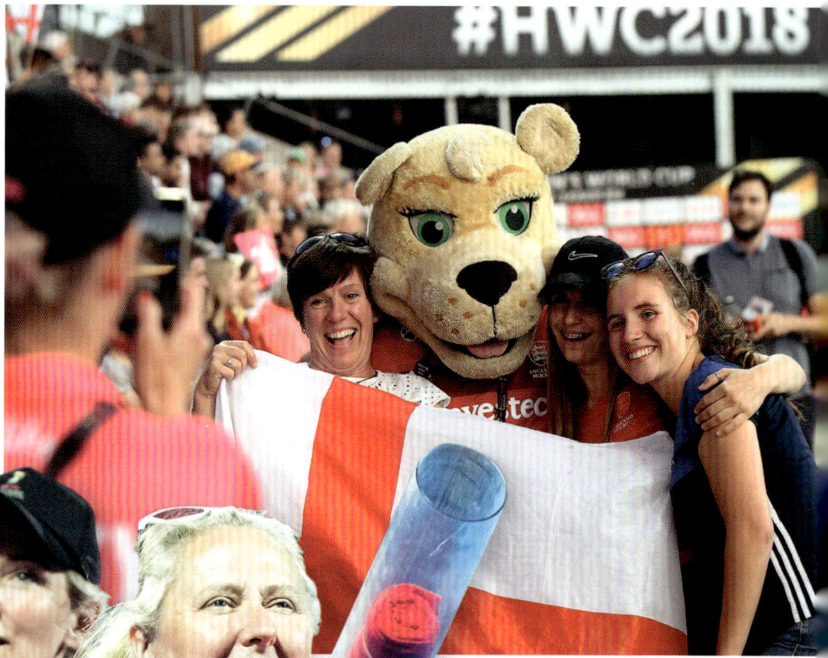

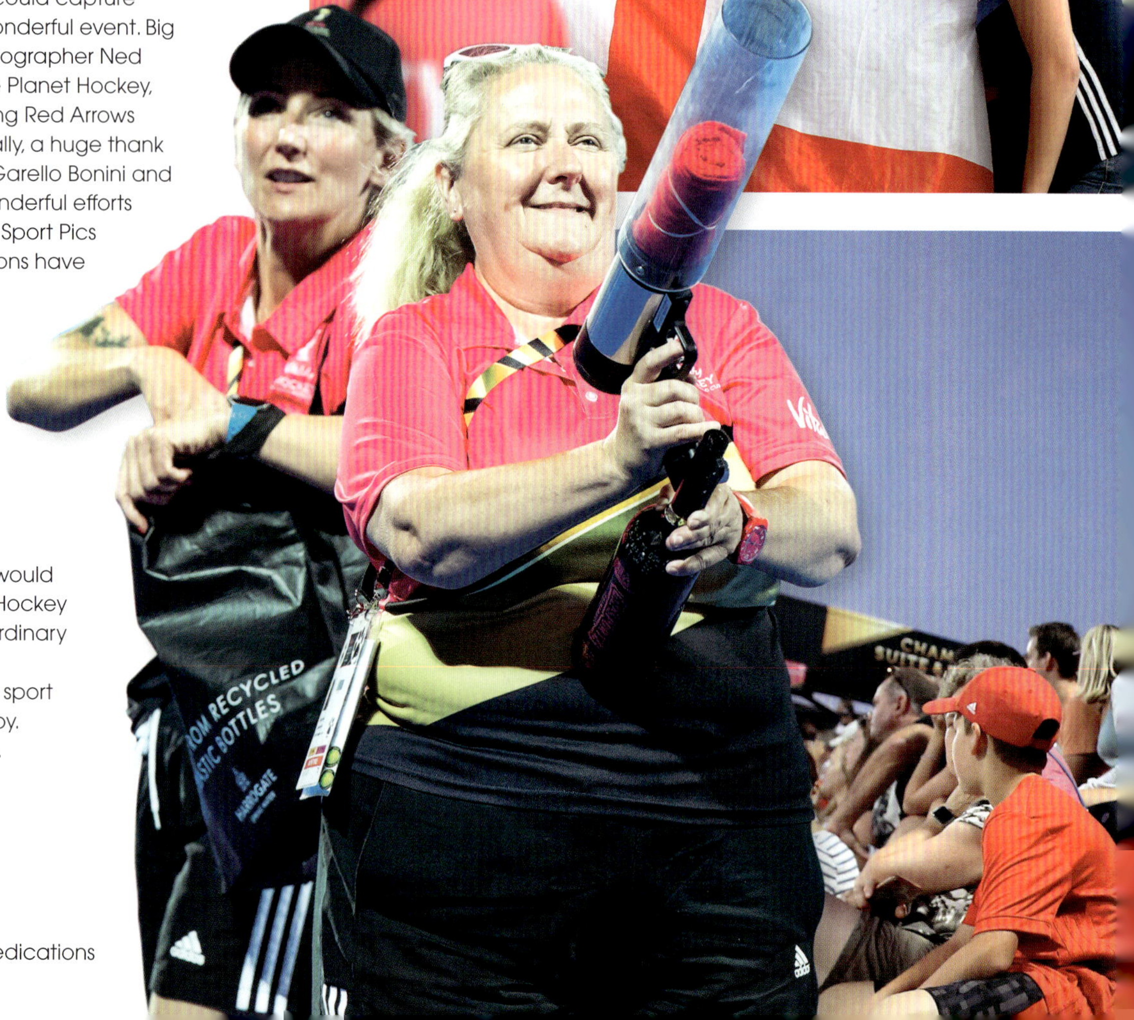

Dedications

The authors and photographers would like to dedicate this book to the Hockey Makers, England Hockey's extraordinary army of volunteers. Your passion, dedication and sheer love of the sport made every single day an utter joy. You made it happen – thank you.

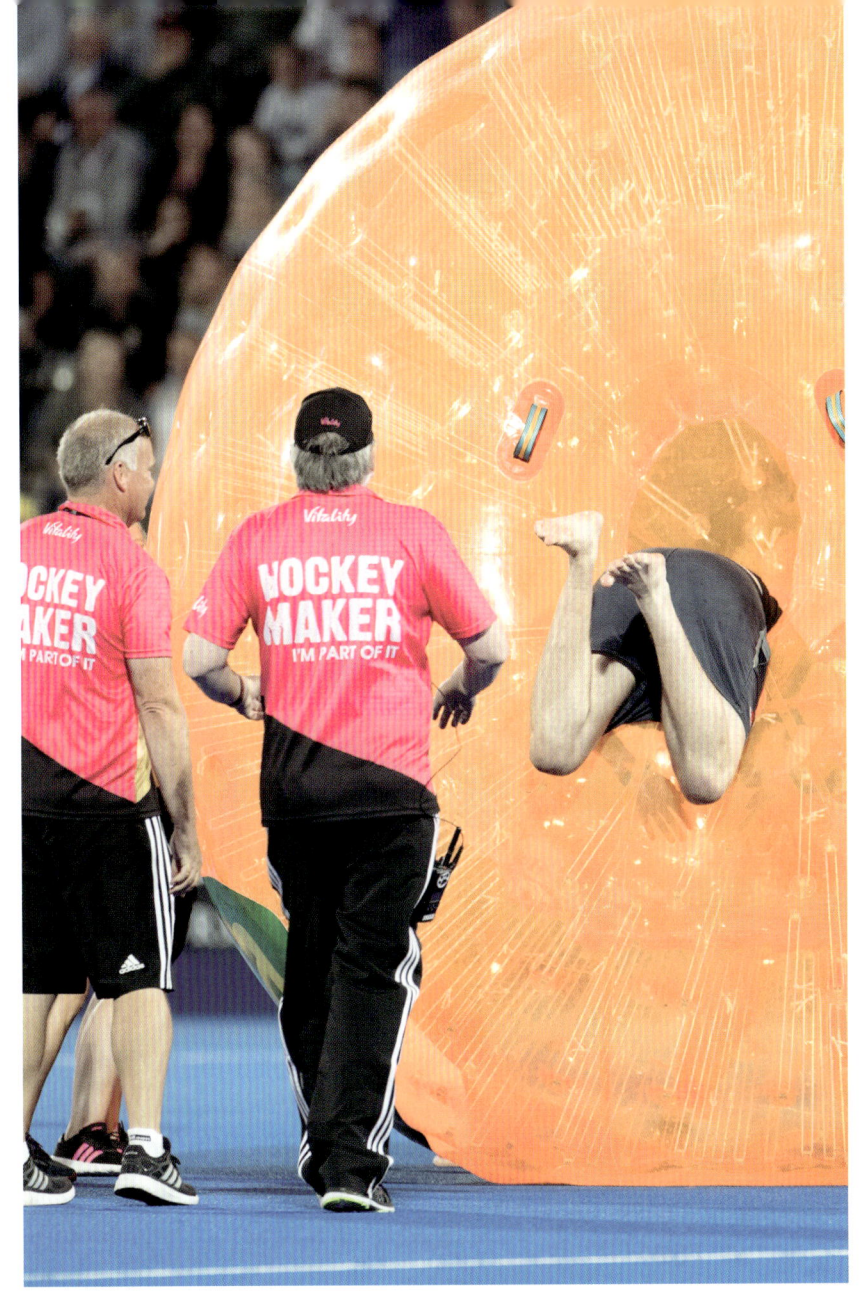

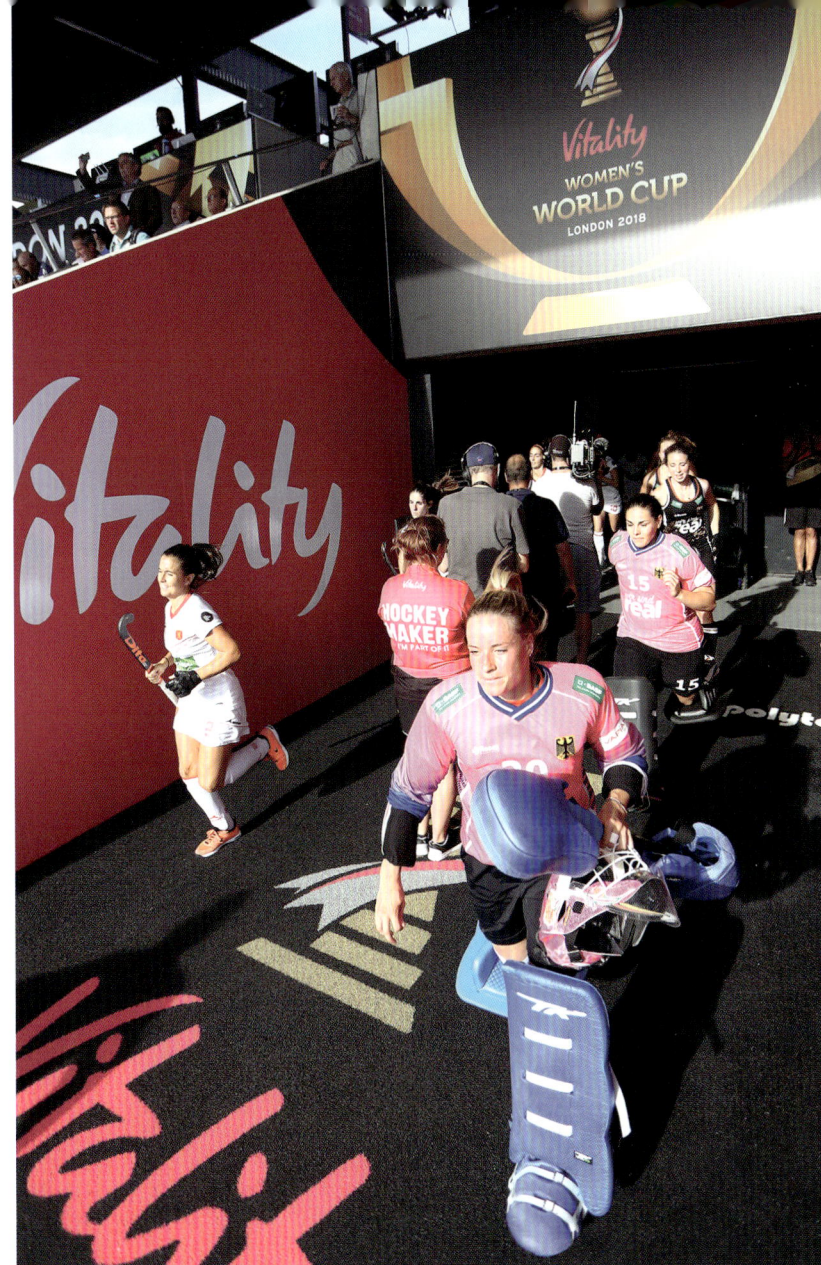

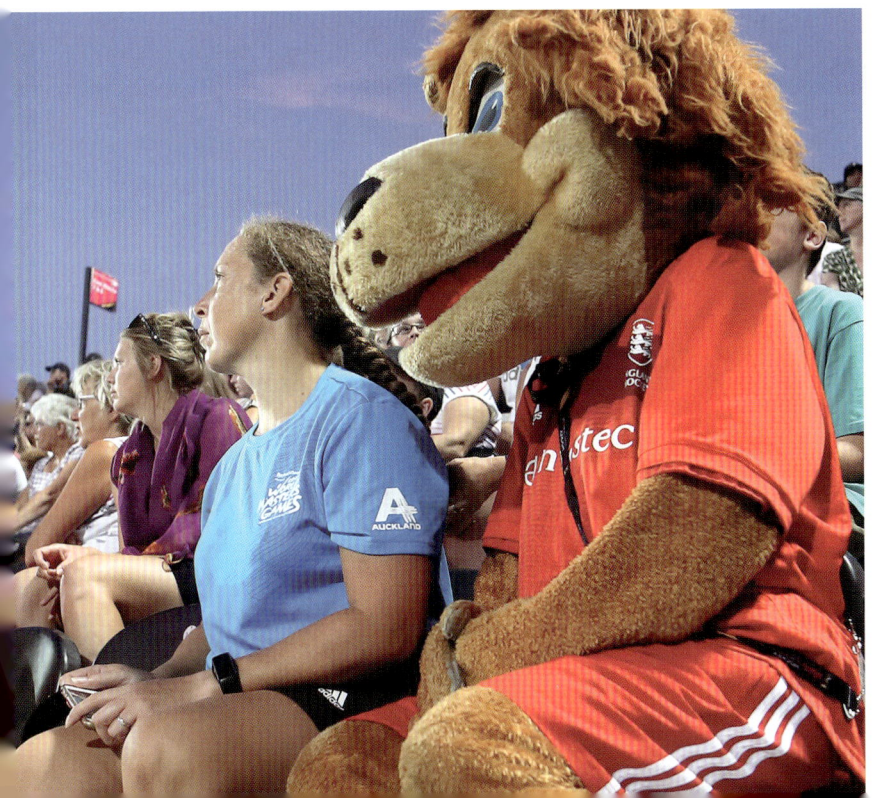

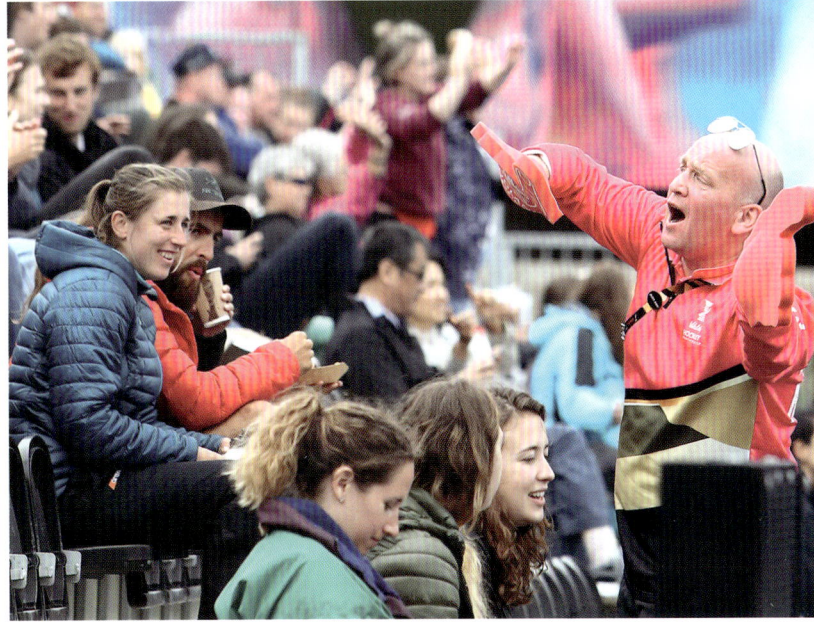

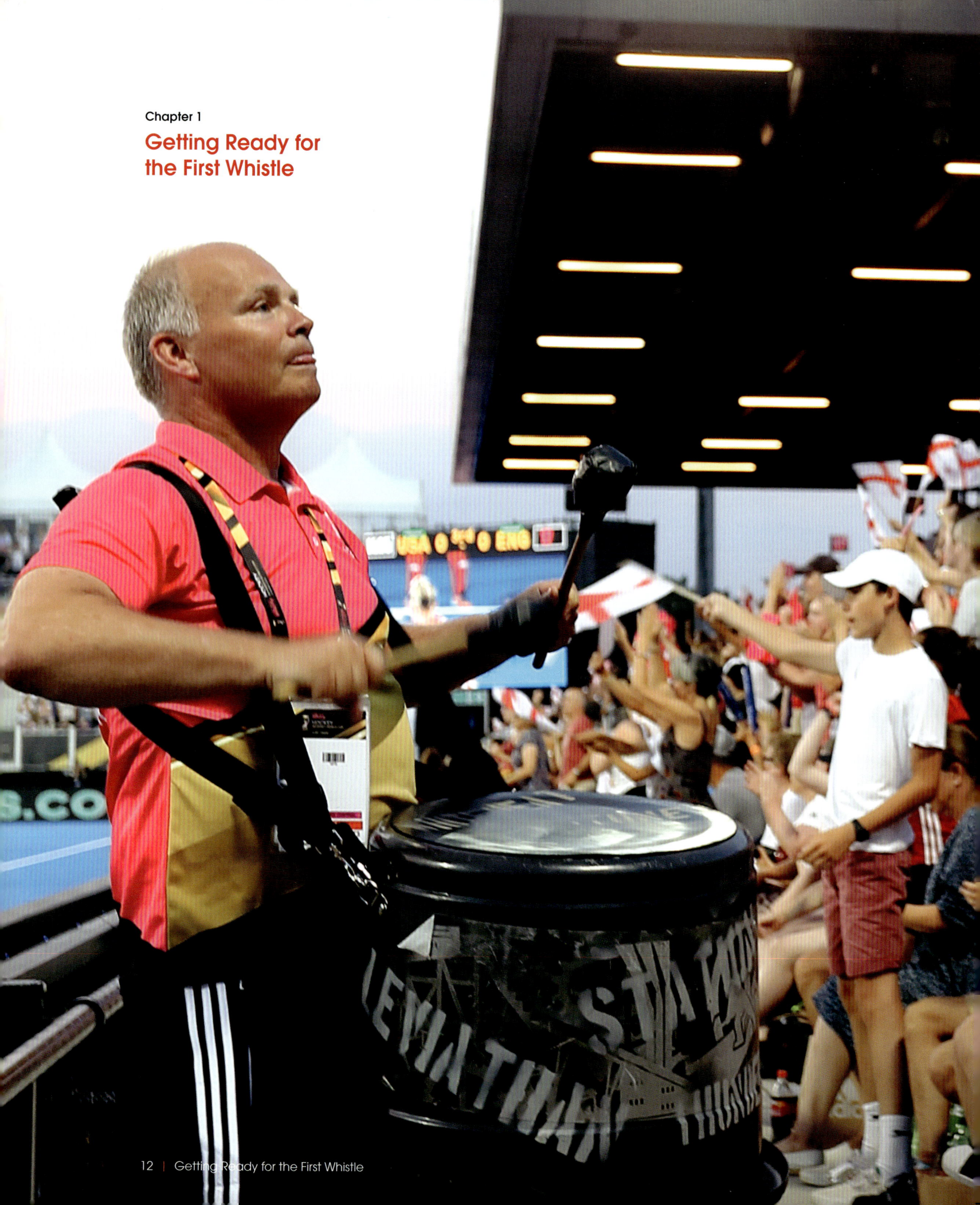

Getting Ready for the First Whistle

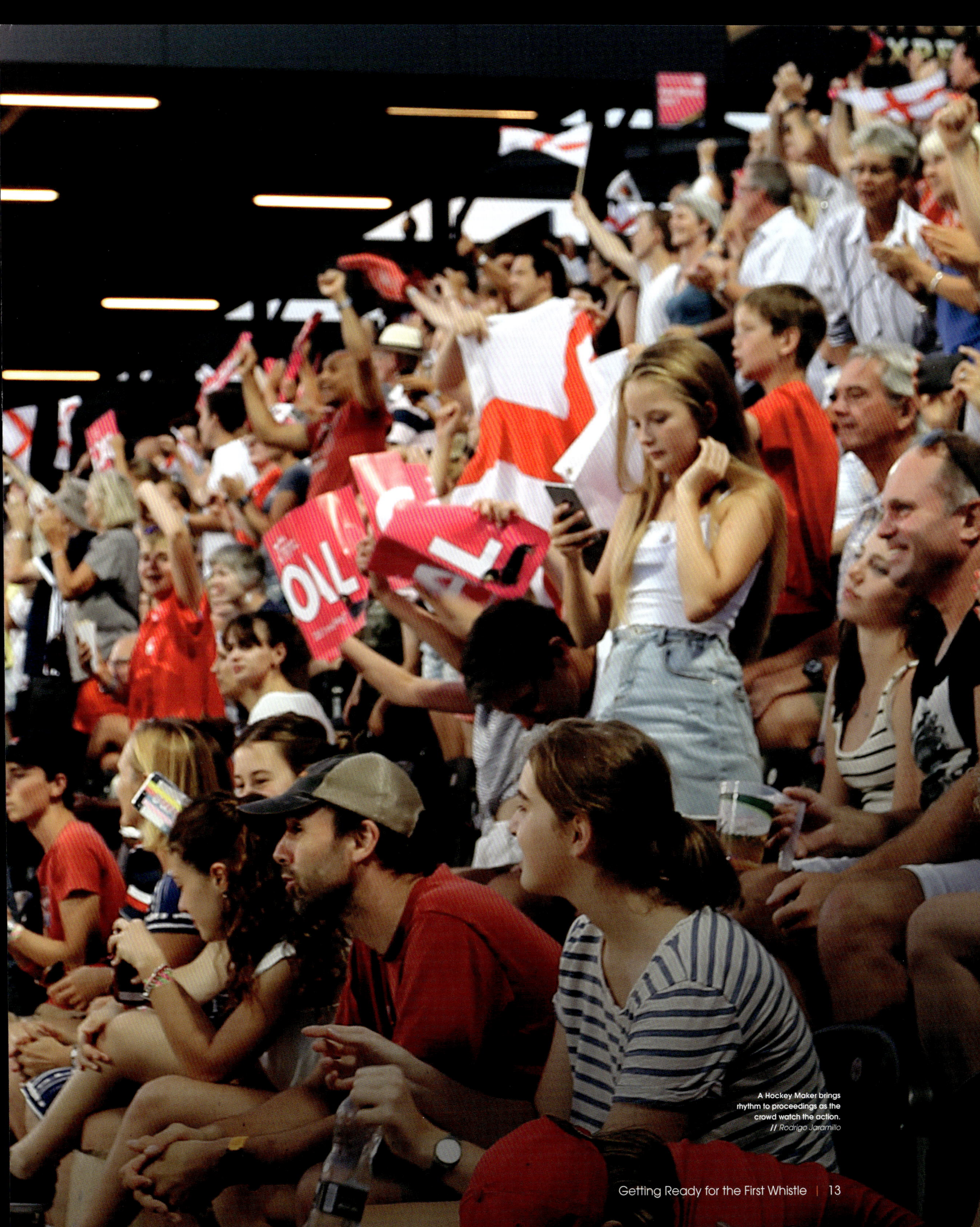

A Hockey Maker brings rhythm to proceedings as the crowd watch the action.
// *Rodrigo Jaramillo*

Chapter 1

Getting Ready for the First Whistle

'Every game is going to be like a final to us,' were the prophetic words of Ireland's head coach Graham Shaw as he prepared his assorted team of doctors, lawyers, physiotherapists and students for the biggest challenge of their lives, taking their place at the top table of hockey, the Vitality Hockey Women's World Cup London 2018.

Equally prescient was Spain's head coach Adrian Lock, as he warned: 'Prepare for a few surprises.'

At this crazy, anything-goes, prepare-for-the-unexpected, dramatic and tear-inducing World Cup, there was no such thing as a certainty. As World Cups go, this one had it all. High-ranked teams fell by the wayside, reputations were ignored and accepted practices turned on their heads as the form book was torn up in front of the huge crowds that flocked to the Lee Valley Hockey & Tennis Centre on a daily basis. Every day something happened that caused people to shake their heads in disbelief. It was that kind of event.

From the first sighting of the red, white and blue smoke emitted as the Red Arrows flew past to the heart-

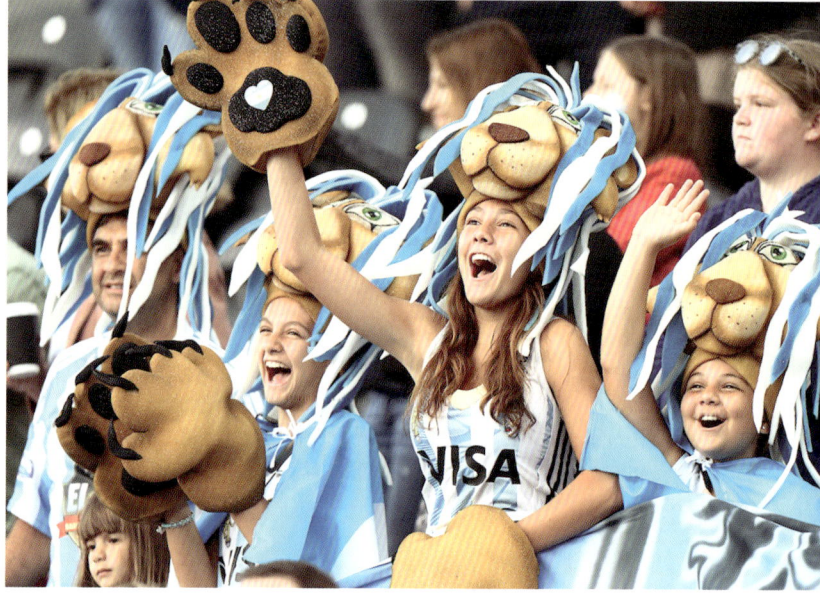

Las Leonas's loyal fans turned Lee Valley into a South American style fiesta. // *Rodrigo Jaramillo*

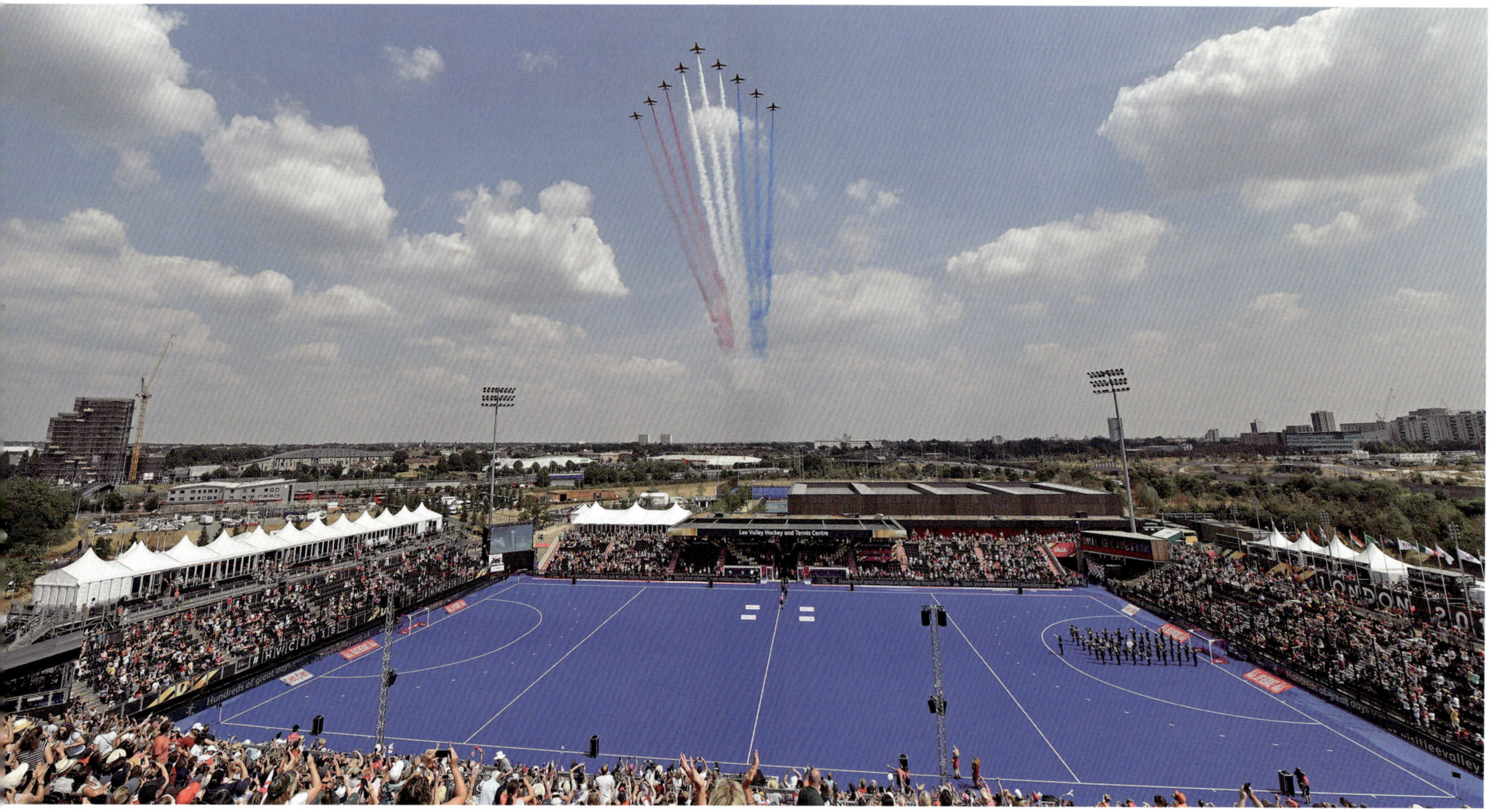

The Red Arrows, the display team of the Royal Air Force, were the highlight of a spectacular opening to the Vitality Hockey Women's World Cup. // *Ned Dawson / Planet Hockey*

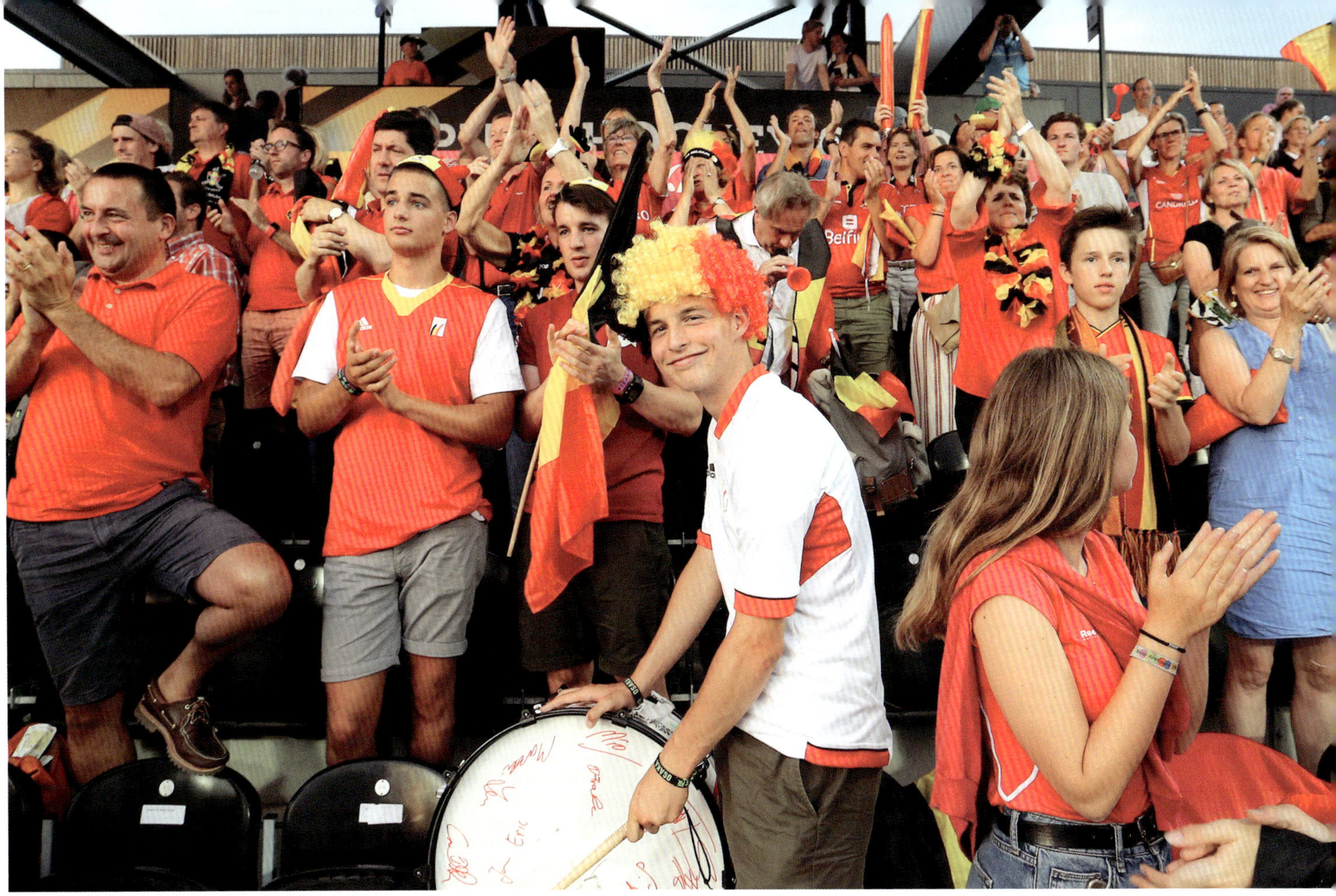

Fans of Belgium's Red Panthers, accompanied by their resident drummer, made themselves heard throughout. // *Rodrigo Jaramillo*

wrenching sight of World Cup hopefuls departing the competition earlier than expected; from the ever-ready smiles of the volunteer army of Hockey Makers to the swathes of blue and white-daubed Argentina fans who brought their own South American flavour to London's East End; from the mesmerising chanting of the Belgium fans, with their accompanying drum beat, to the never-faltering smiles of the Japanese team and their supporters. This was a major international sporting spectacle at its scintillating, dramatic, culturally-diverse best.

And yet, in the final analysis, calm and order was restored in the shape of the outstanding champions. If this event had been a firework display, the show's organisers would have been praised for adding all sorts of flair and surprises in the lead-up to the grand finale. But when it came to it, they couldn't change the final act – yes, they could add more colour, sparkle and noise but the centrepiece, the pièce de résistance will always be the biggest, boldest and best firework in the collection. And in this case it came in the shape of the reigning champions and undisputed world number-one side, the Netherlands. The national flags and colourful kits representing the 16 nations all added colour and vibrancy to this corner of London, yet somehow the orange shirts and orange flags always caught the eye. When the Oranje took to the pitch, there were guaranteed moments of pure hockey magic, all orchestrated by the lead magician on the sideline.

But this is not just an account of one outstanding team. It is a story with two very different themes running through it. Yes, on the one hand, it is the story of how one of the greatest female players of all time has evolved

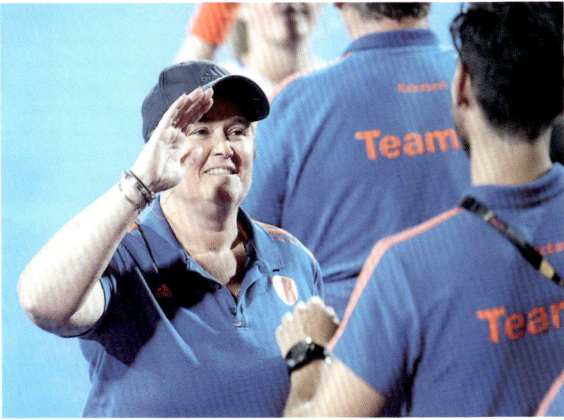

A double World Cup winner in her own right, Alyson Annan is now recognised as one of the world's top coaches. // *Frank Uijlenbroek*

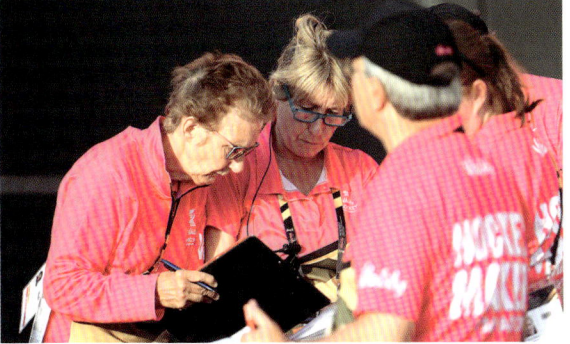

Vital to the whole event were the hard-working and professional army of volunteer Hockey Makers. // *Rodrigo Jaramillo*

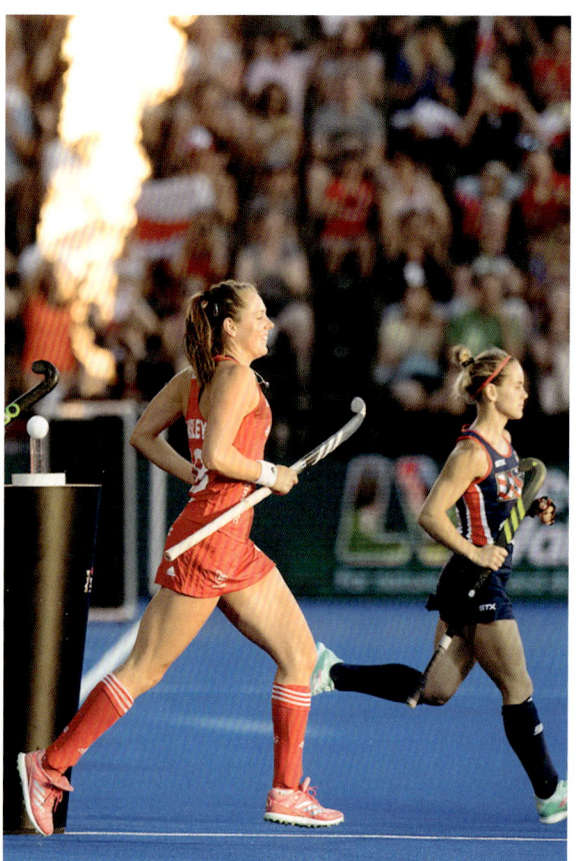

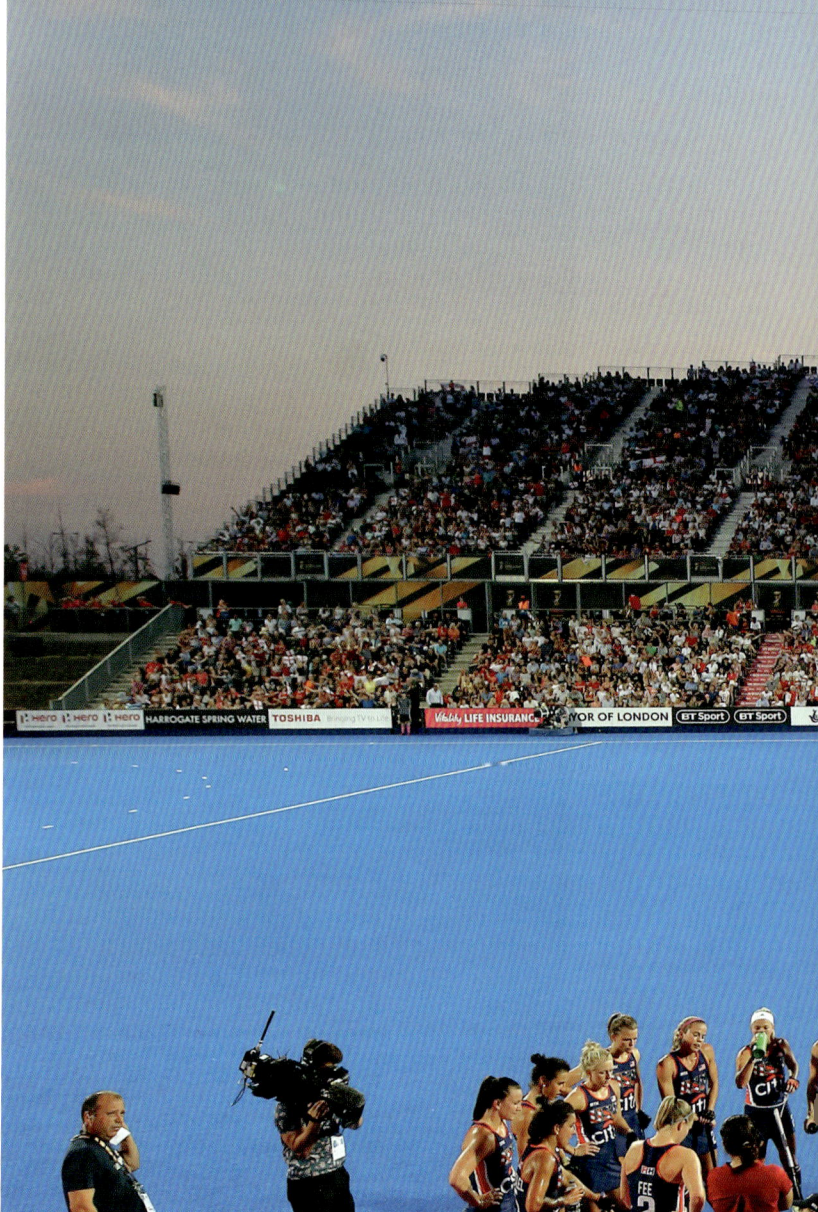

London's Burning. As if the hot temperatures weren't enough, players ran out on to the pitch through an avenue of flames. // *Frank Uijlenbroek*

into one of the best coaches in the world and how, over the course of 20 months, she harnessed a group of exceptionally talented individuals and blended them into one compelling, efficient and supreme team that was, quite simply, a cut above the rest. That is the one storyline that followed the script completely.

The second story is the rumbustious, rollicking tale of the 'others', which has all the elements of a darn good yarn. The most unlikely results, the most dramatic endings, the tears, the joy, the heartbreak and the ecstasy. In a nutshell, it is the reason we all love a great sporting spectacle.

The 14th edition of the women's hockey World Cup was the first time that the competition had been held in London and the host national association, England Hockey, was determined to make it an event to remember. Ever since the London 2012 Olympic Games, and the huge success of the temporary Riverbank Arena as a venue, England Hockey had been working tirelessly to establish a recognised home base on the London Olympic site. The Lee Valley Hockey & Tennis Centre – situated a few hundred metres away from the site of the Riverbank Arena – is the

world-class legacy facility that was created after the Olympics had left town and, over the past six years had played host to the men's and women's 2015 EuroHockey Championships, the men's and women's 2016 Champions Trophy events and the men's 2017 Hockey World League Semi-Finals. At each of these events, the host nation honed its presentation skills, trained more of its huge volunteer workforce and fine-tuned its catering, entertainments and side shows until they were absolutely ready to welcome hockey's premium championship.

In a wonderful nod to the past, the host nation established a large spectator zone, known as Fan Central, on the exact site on which the Riverbank Arena had stood. As well as all of the retail and food outlets, a giant screen ensured that hockey was being watched in the exact place where the Netherlands, Argentina and Great Britain had famously claimed the respective gold, silver and bronze medals in 2012.

The stadium itself, which usually has a capacity of 3,000, more than trebled in size to over 10,000. In the weeks leading up to the event, east Londoners watched as a new, towering addition to the London skyline took shape. To sit at

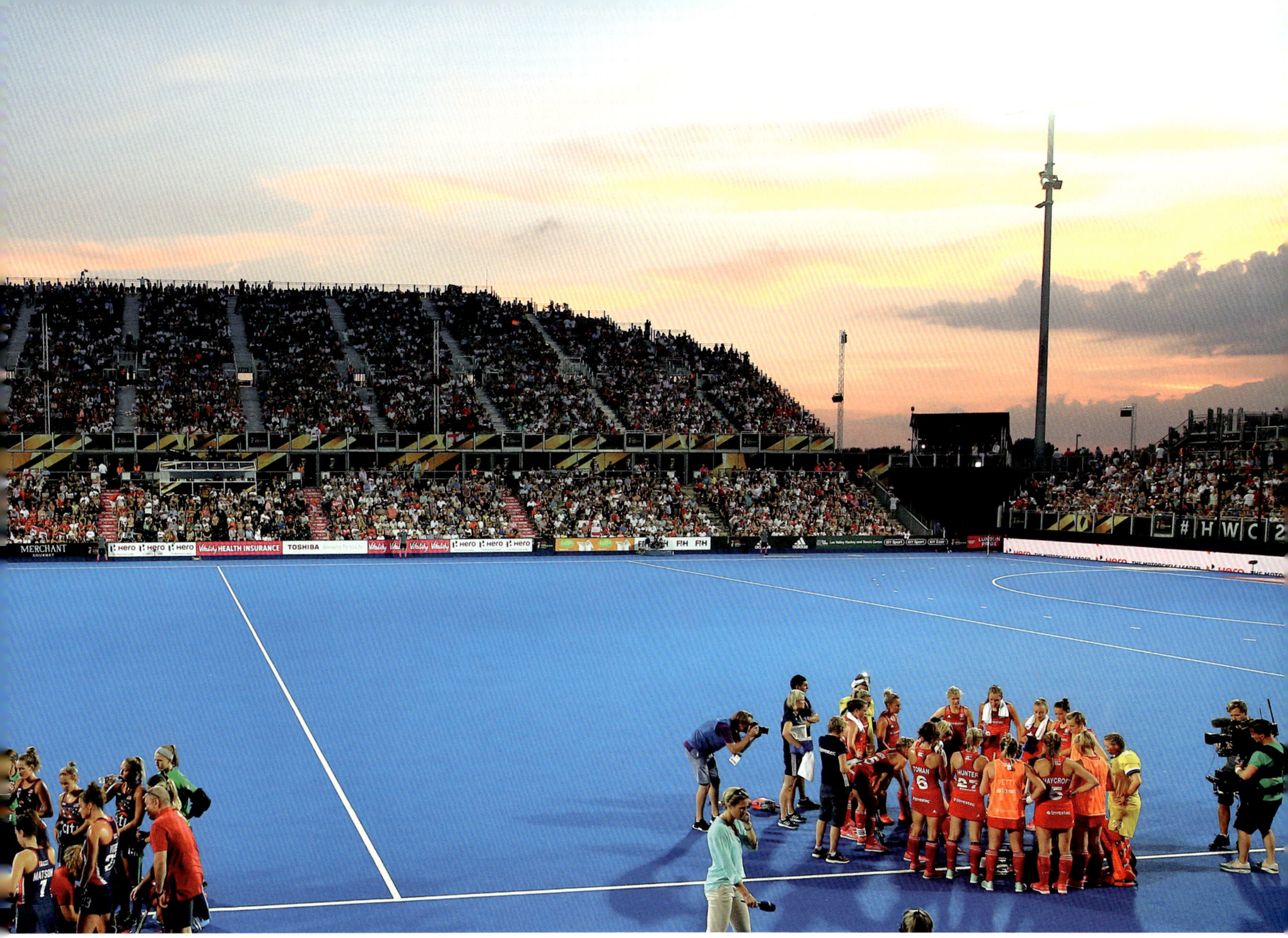

The Lee Valley Hockey & Tennis Centre has played host to a number of prestigious hockey events but the scale of the World Cup meant this was new territory. // *Rodrigo Jaramillo*

the very top of the colossal West Stand, gazing at the pitch below gave the sensation of staring vertically down on to the field of play itself. If you took a minute to look away from the action, the top levels of this behemoth of a sports stand offered spectacular views of London's iconic skyline. Local people, who had previously had no interest in the sport, began to take note. By the time the first match started, the buzz surrounding hockey and the World Cup in and around Stratford and the other east London boroughs was there for all to experience.

And this was by no means a London-centric event. More than 750 hockey clubs from across the UK were represented at the World Cup. From club members and officials attending formal meetings, training sessions and workshops to whole blocks of seats adorned with flags carrying the names of clubs, this was an event which galvanised the grass roots hockey spectators and a fair few people new to the game. England Hockey's legacy of promoting the sport across the UK was there for all to see.

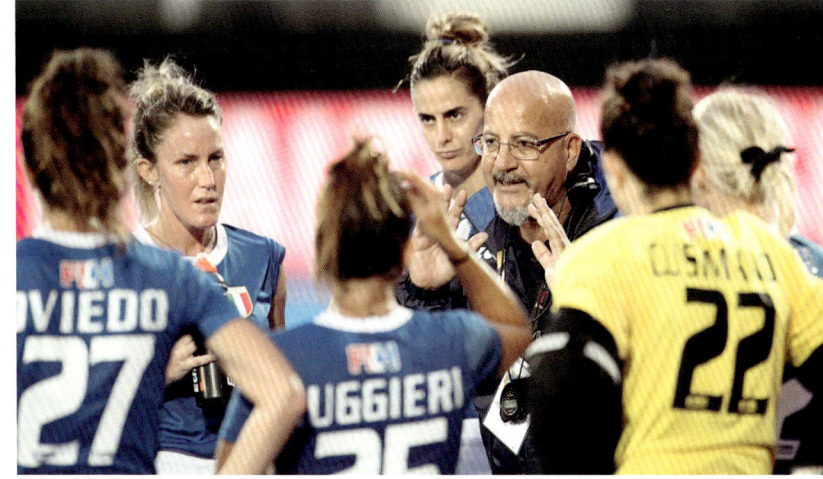

Travelling man: Roberto Carta had ensured Italy were prepared for World Cup action. // *Rodrigo Jaramillo*

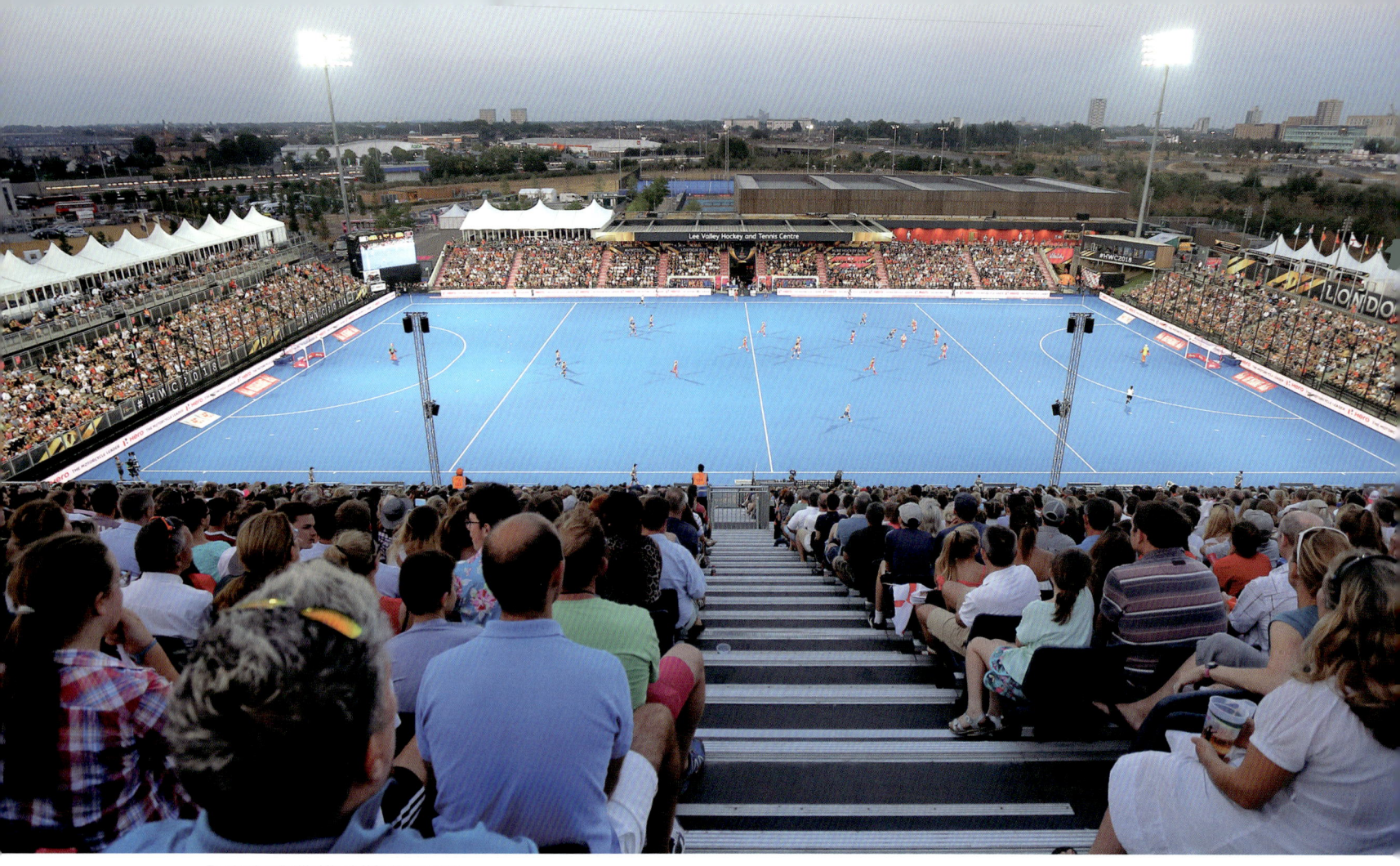

The view from the West Stand. // *Rodrigo Jaramillo*

There were 16 teams participating in the Vitality Hockey Women's World Cup, with the group stages consisting of four pools of four. These pools had been established by the sport's world governing body, the International Hockey Federation (FIH), based on each team's position in the FIH Hero World Rankings as of 6 November 2017. The first-placed team in each pool qualified for the quarter-finals. The second- and third-placed teams played cross-over matches to earn their places in the quarter-finals, meaning they played one, extra, do-or-die match to try to secure a berth in the next round. For the fourth-placed team in each pool, it was an early exit – just three games in the World Cup and then home. This was a brand-new format which left little room for error.

In preparation for the World Cup, most teams had travelled the globe in the previous months. Japan, with Australian-born head coach Anthony Farry, had been jamming in as much experience of playing in Europe as was possible in the final weeks before the action began. They arrived in the Netherlands on 23 June and then went on a whirlwind tour, including a Four Nations event in Breda which ran alongside the Men's Rabobank Hockey Champions Trophy 2018, test matches against Ireland and a Three Nations event against China and Belgium.

Likewise, the lowest-ranked team in London, the Azzurre of Italy, also went on their pre-World Cup travels. Preparations in the lead-up to the World Cup included a number of international matches – against Scotland, Russia,

The four pools, with FIH Hero World Rankings (WR) at the time of the competition:

Pool A	Pool B	Pool C	Pool D
Netherlands (WR:1)	England (WR:2)	Argentina (WR:3)	New Zealand (WR:4)
China (WR:8)	USA (WR:7)	Germany (WR:6)	Australia (WR:5)
Korea (WR:9)	India (WR:10)	Spain (WR:11)	Japan (WR:12)
Italy (WR:17)	Ireland (WR:16)	South Africa (WR:14)	Belgium (WR:15)

Ireland's Anna O'Flanagan would make a big name for herself in London.
// *Frank Uijlenbroek*

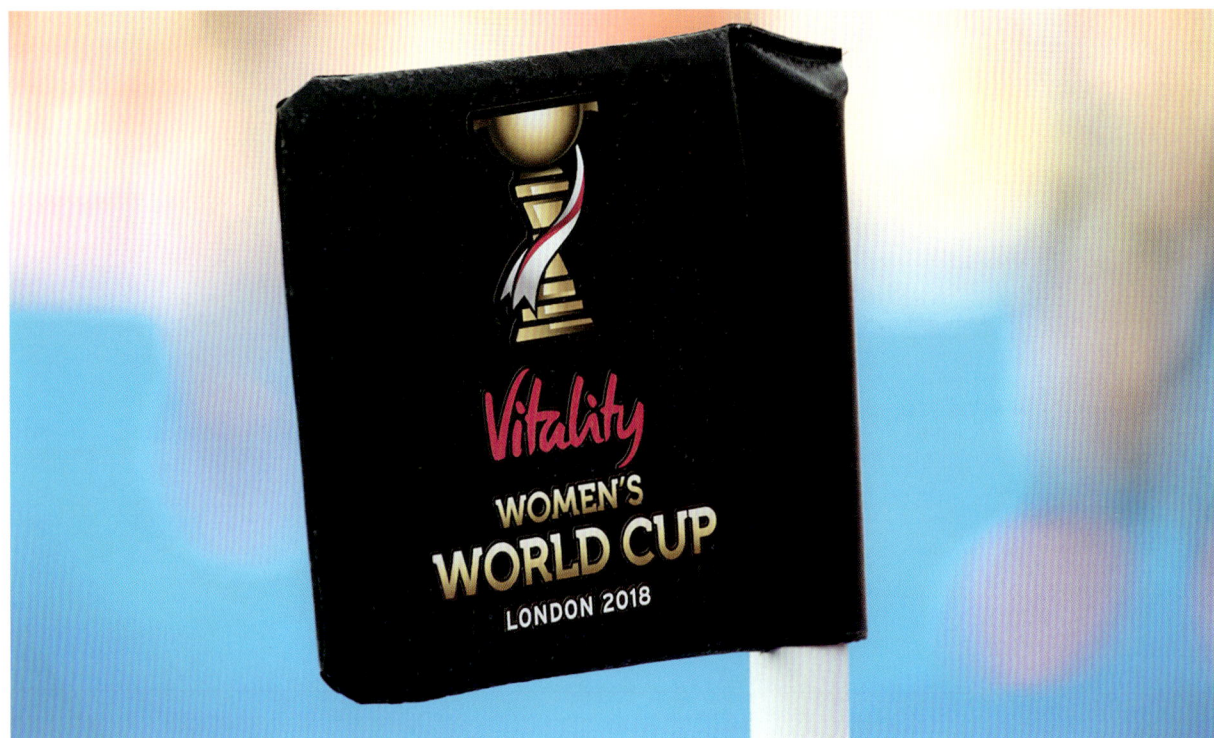

The stage is set. // *Frank Uijlenbroek*

France, Germany, Ireland and Argentina. Roberto Carta, Italy's vivacious head coach, explained why: 'International competition against these teams is vital. In the World Cup my team will be playing top ten-ranked sides that have much more high-level playing experience. Any opportunity to play against other nations and experience different styles of play is vital if Italy is to hold its own.'

A final practice match in London saw Carta's team play Japan. Again, practice against higher-ranked opponents with differing styles was vital if Italy were to do well in a pool containing China and Korea, two teams with similar playing characteristics to Japan's Cherry Blossoms. It was also a chance for the players to realise the enormity of the occasion. With some training sessions closed to the public, even an empty stadium, with its rows and rows of seats that reach up into the sky, was enough to set a player's heart racing and the adrenaline pumping.

One team that received an unexpected boost to their pre-World Cup preparations was Ireland. Until May 2018, the Green Army had had no additional funding, so the chance to travel to play practice matches was close to non-existent. A last minute sponsorship deal with finance automation software provider SoftCo meant the team could spend the last few weeks before London playing test matches and training together. Up to that point, Ireland had essentially been a team of 'amateurs', although only in the financially supported sense of that word. When it came to making sacrifices for their sport and giving everything to the 'shirt', the entire team were fully signed up professionals.

That said, Ireland's progress in recent years, including narrowly missing out on qualification for the Rio 2016 Olympic Games, had been in some way attributable to the fact that several senior players had gained experience playing abroad, with the likes of Chloe Watkins, Nikki Evans and Anna O'Flanagan all representing high-profile clubs in the hockey hotbeds of Germany and Netherlands.

With Hockey Ireland's resources limited in the extreme, the players plying their trade in Ireland were doing so as a hobby, rather than as a professional career. The training windows Graham Shaw had with his squad in the months following qualification for the World Cup were short. The benefit of having a core group of players living and playing abroad, fully immersed in hockey on a full-time basis, was a crucial factor in adding an extra layer of experience, in both mental and psychological terms.

'You've seen that with players who have gone abroad in the last few years, even the conditioning aspect of it, just being able to eat when you need to eat, recover when you need to recover and not having to worry about getting up to go to work at 7am in the morning,' said Shaw. For the rest of his squad, getting a balance between going to work and training for hockey meant the Irish players arrived in London knowing that they had already achieved a huge amount simply by being there. How much further could their journey take them?

It was the question that the 16 coaches and their respective playing squads were all asking themselves as the final preparations drew to a close. They would soon know the answers.

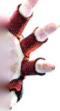

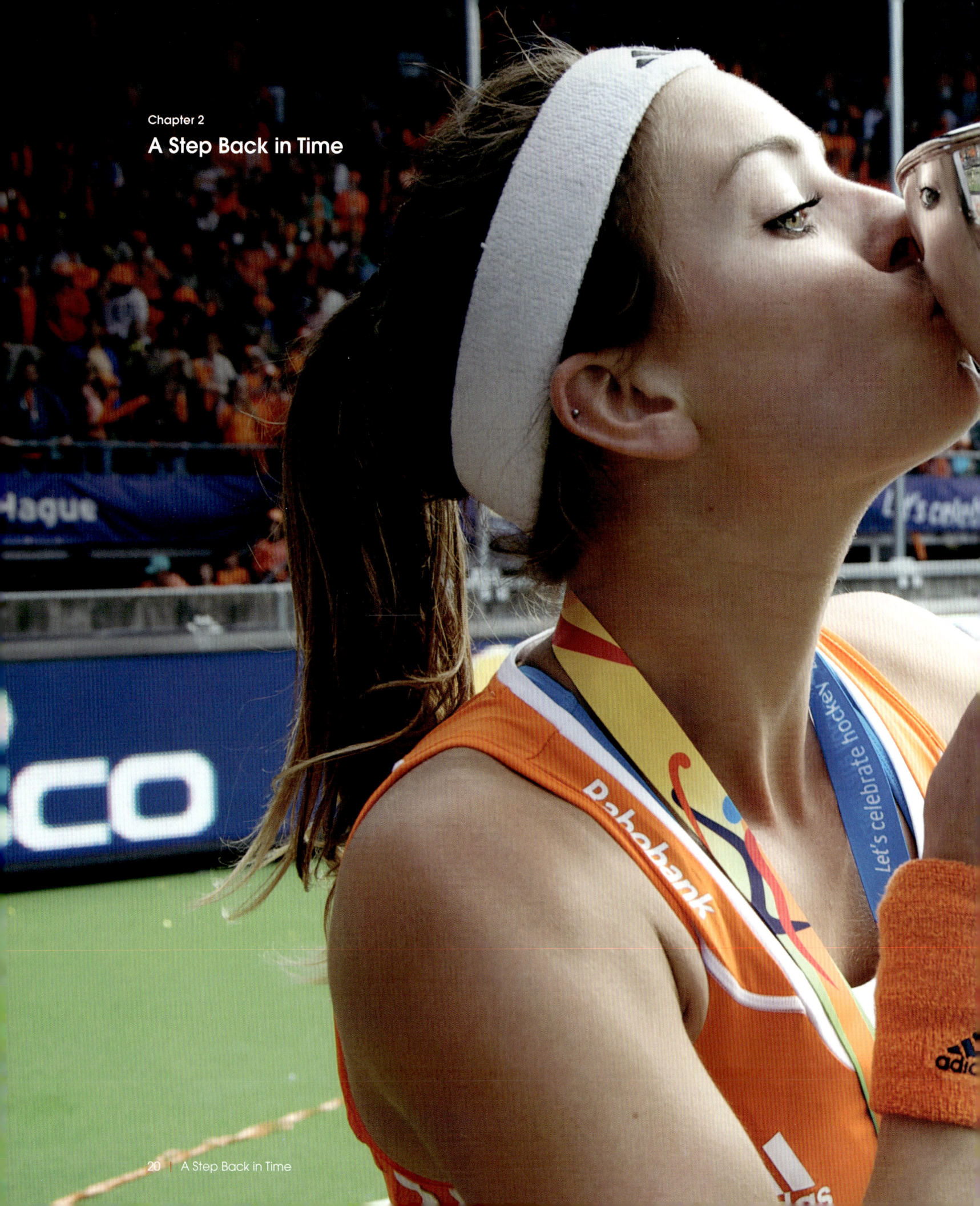

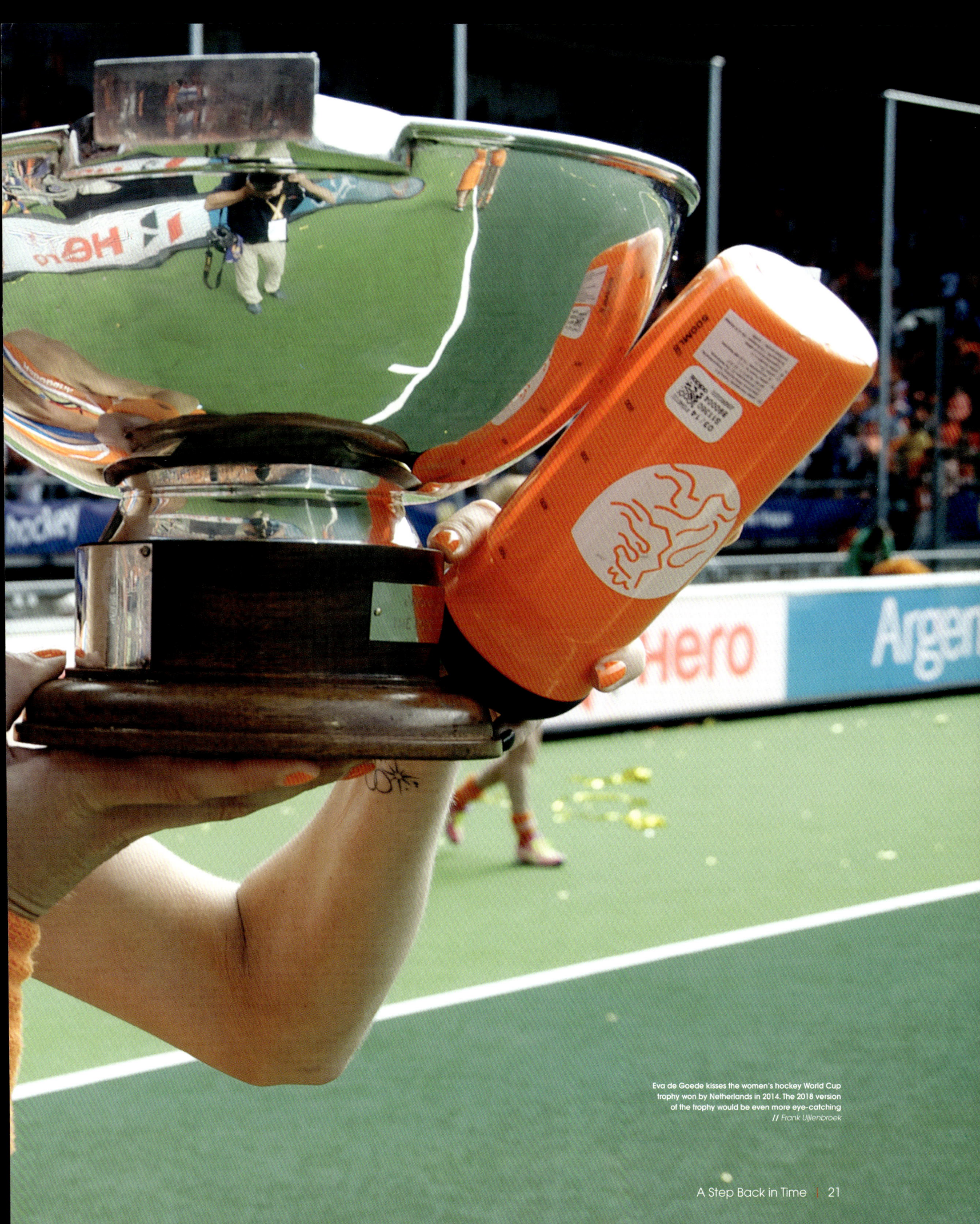

Eva de Goede kisses the women's hockey World Cup trophy won by Netherlands in 2014. The 2018 version of the trophy would be even more eye-catching
// Frank Uijlenbroek

Chapter 2

A Step Back in Time

The Vitality Hockey Women's World Cup 2018 has been heralded as the biggest hockey competition ever to take place in London. While that is undisputed, it is certainly not the first time a version of the women's hockey World Cup has been held in England. That honour goes to the International Federation of Women's Hockey Associations (IFWHA) competition, held in Folkestone, Kent in 1953 – the same year the present Queen Elizabeth II ascended the throne.

Prior to merging with the FIH in 1982, the IFWHA had been arranging global gatherings since 1933. The organisation was formed in 1927 and held its first conference in Geneva, Switzerland, in 1930. No competitions were held back then, purely exhibition matches. The first of these was staged in 1933 in Copenhagen; they were then held every three years until 1963 when the matches moved to a four-year cycle to prevent clashes with subsequent Olympic Games.

The 1953 IFWHA tournament was organised by the All England Women's Hockey Association but, under IFWHA rules, there could be no winning team. That 300 competitors representing 16 nations from around the world would travel from as far afield as New Zealand, India and South Africa to play in a friendly event defies belief these days, but does provide a good indication of the depth of passion and commitment that the players had towards the game.

The 'no winner' ruling was introduced and enforced to uphold the prevaling amateur status of the game. All IFWHA tournaments were strictly amateur; athletes competed purely for the love of the sport. What is more amazing is that this non-competitive model of play persisted until 1975, when the first IFWHA championship was played in Edinburgh, Scotland.

In a Pathé newsreel video released at the time, 300 athletes are shown marching on to the grass pitches behind their national flags. The commentator on the newsreel says many of the players had given up their jobs to take part in the event. The action itself was fast and furious, with the players wearing knee-length skirts, using sticks with long, hooked ends and shooting at a goalkeeper whose only extra safety equipment was a pair of old-style cricket pads. The use of protective helmets, gloves or chest pads of any kind was almost unheard of.

By 1975, the IFWHA tournament had grown so much that 22 teams were now taking part. These included many names familiar to today's audiences: the Netherlands, Australia, Argentina and New Zealand. Also among the participating nations were Denmark, Bermuda and Jamaica. The competition in Edinburgh was won by England who completed a 2-0 victory over Wales, with New Zealand claiming bronze by defeating the Netherlands on penalty strokes after the match finished with the scores locked at 1-1.

While the 1975 competition is not recognised by the FIH as an official Women's Hockey World Cup, it will always be remembered as an event of great significance. As well as being the first IFWHA event to promote competitive hockey, the introduction of a prize for the winner marked another very important debut: the quaich – a Scottish

IFWHA tournaments:

1933	Copenhagen, Denmark
1936	Philadelphia, USA
1939	Cancelled due to war (originally scheduled to be held in England)
1950	Johannesburg, South Africa
1953	Folkestone, England
1956	Sydney, Australia
1959	Amsterdam, Netherlands
1963	Maryland (moved to a four-year cycle to prevent clash with Olympic Games), USA
1967	Leverkusen-Cologne, West Germany
1971	Auckland, New Zealand
1975	Edinburgh (first trophy awarded), Scotland
1979	Vancouver, Canada
1983	Kuala Lumpur, Malaysia

friendship and drinking bowl initially sponsored by the Royal Bank of Scotland – would go on to take centre stage at official FIH events for years to come.

It was on the back of these successful and popular tournaments that the IFWHA and the men's International Hockey Federation (FIH) began to talk about a joint hockey federation. The 1980 Olympic Games in Moscow was the first step towards parity between the men's and women's hockey scenes and just two years later, in 1982, the current FIH was created as a result of the IFWHA merging with the men's Federation. The last IFWHA tournament was played in 1983 and, while there were earlier versions of the World Cup, men's and women's events started in 1986, with the men's and women's World Cups being held in the same year even if space and facilities didn't allow for them to be at the same venue.

There have only been two occasions when the events have been hosted together – Utrecht 1998 and The Hague 2014. The recent expansion of the World Cup to 16 teams will make future joint events unlikely, although not impossible.

Women's Hockey World Cup trophy gets an upgrade

Standing 50 centimetres tall and with a diameter of 31 centimetres at the top, the trophy raised by the winning captain following the final of the Vitality Hockey Women's World Cup London 2018 was a study in craftsmanship and tradition. It was also a trophy that nodded to history as it incorporated the original trophy that the winning captain, England's Anita White, lifted at the IFWHA Women's World Cup in Edinburgh in 1975. The original cup was donated by the Royal Bank of Scotland, and 1975 was the first time a team were declared winners and actually received a trophy.

The trophy was an ornate silver bowl – or quaich as it is known in Scotland – adorned with intricate engravings of thistles. It stood just 13 centimetres high.

The new trophy, presented on 5 August 2018 by HRH Sophie, Countess of Wessex and Dr Narinder Dhruv Batra, President of the FIH, to a jubilant Netherlands, was much taller and heavier than its previous incarnation. The additional 35 centimetres in height came from a beautifully decorated plinth and a heavily embellished silver column. The original silver bowl had been replaced with an identical one because its age was beginning to show and it would not have lasted another raucous celebration. The gold-plated handles, however, were the originals and had been attached to the new silver bowl, which sat proudly atop the plinth and column. The plinth itself was detachable because weight would have been a concern if the entire trophy was handed to the winning captain.

Matching the men's and women's World Cup trophies was a major driving force in the design of the new women's World Cup. Under the FIH's drive for gender equality and parity in all areas of the game, the new trophy had to be of equal size and stature to that of the men's prize.

Both trophies had intricate engravings on the column. For the women's trophy these carvings mirrored the thistle emblems that decorated the original. The neck of the trophy had a gold-plated pattern which added an extra layer of decoration.

The process, which was carried out by London-based goldsmiths and silversmiths Thomas Lyte, involved a silversmith spinning the silver on a lathe. An engraver worked on the decorative patterns on the plinth and column and a different engraver added the wording on the silver bowl.

Eva de Goede was lucky enough to get her hands on the World Cup trophy again in 2018, this time displaying the stunningly reworked version of the silverware.
// Frank Uijlenbroek

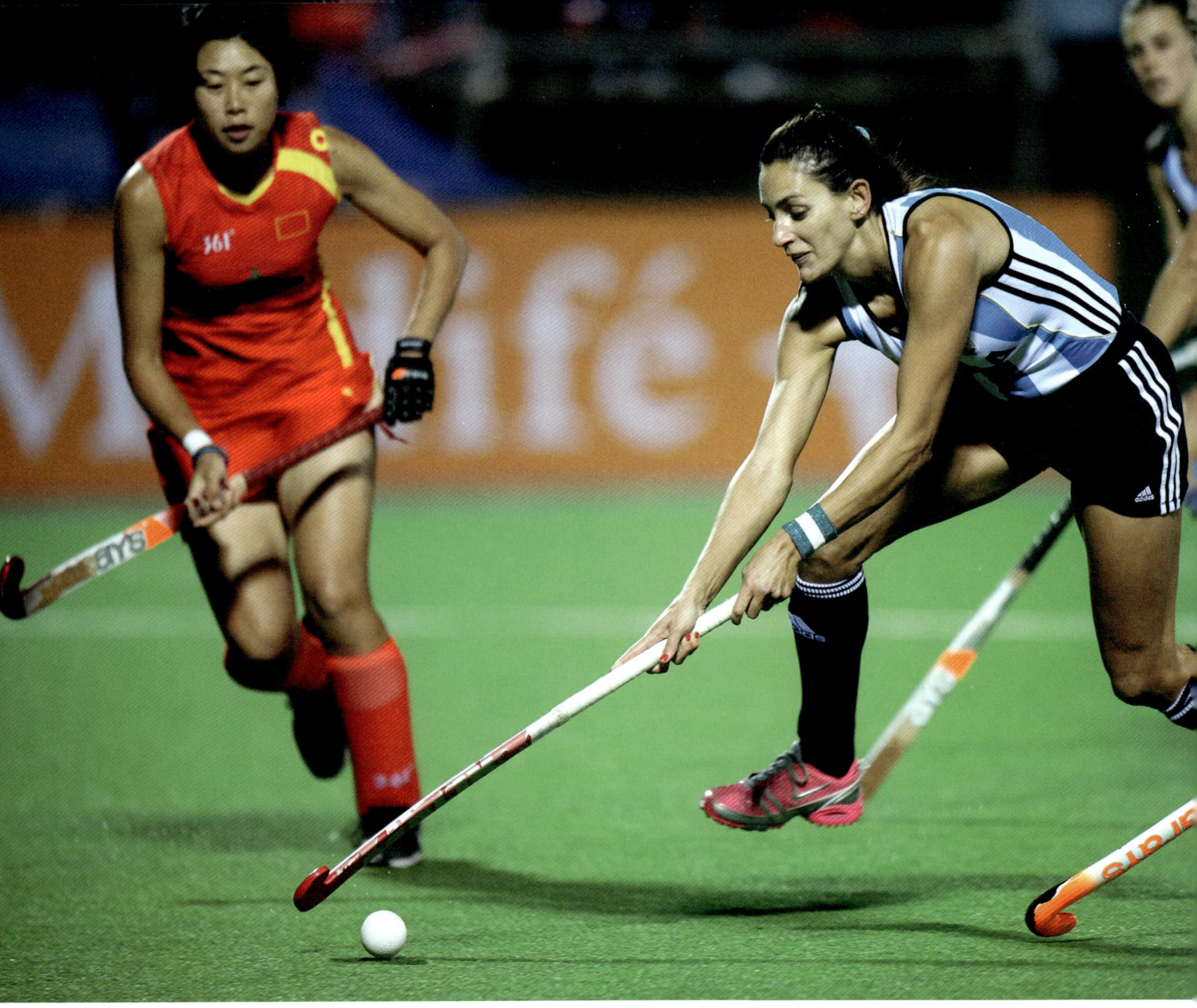

Rosario 2010 was, undisputedly, Luciana Aymar's World Cup. // *Frank Uijlenbroek*

1975 revisited

The spectacle that greeted the thousands of fans trooping into the Lee Valley Hockey & Tennis Centre, with the pyrotechnics, the on-pitch entertainment, the side stalls, the legions of Hockey Makers, was a million miles away from the earliest World Cup experiences.

Recorded for The Hockey Museum's Oral Histories project, England's Anita White recalled the 1975 World Cup which took place in Edinburgh, Scotland.

'England were not expected to do very well but sometimes a team just gets momentum and it starts going right and that was how it was for us,' says White.

'We had tough matches against New Zealand and Argentina and then in the final we played Wales. We won 2-0 and the team was really on song by then. We had

got into a rhythm and our confidence had built as we went through the tournament.'

'It was the most special occasion,' says England's Anne Lunt, who had joined the national team four years after giving birth to her daughter. 'I was proud to make my debut for the England team at a World Cup. My two best memories are walking out and singing the national anthem, and saving a certain goal off the line in our match against Argentina.'

Val Robinson played in five World Cups, including the 1975 tournament. 'You can't describe what it was like to walk out in front of all those supporters,' she says. 'It is obviously nothing like here [London 2018], but still you got the goose bumps, you had tears. In so many ways little has changed but in so many other ways, everything has.'

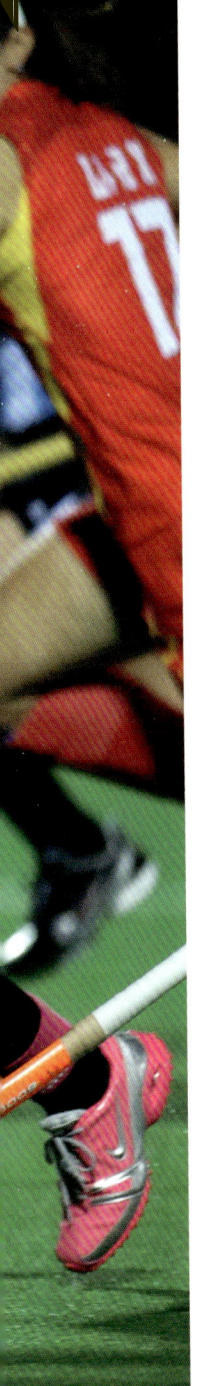

The Women's Hockey World Cup in recent times

If one thing has changed beyond all else, it is the creation of female hockey stars. As coverage has increased, so too has the profile of the players. Just ten years ago the sight of a fan wearing a replica shirt with a female hockey player's name on the back would have been astonishing. Now it is the norm.

Hockey has always had its heroes. Now, in the age of broadcasting rights, live streaming of games across the world and the proliferation of social media, the heroes have been given a stage. And there is no bigger stage on which to become a star than that of the World Cup.

Aymar lights up the World Cup

The 2010 World Cup in Rosario, Argentina, was all about one team and, in particular, one person – Luciana Aymar.

'It is not always necessary to have all the best players in one team to win,' said the superstar of Argentinian hockey, after her team lifted the World Cup in front of thousands of passionate fans of Las Leonas (The Lionesses), 'but when you put on the Argentina shirt, there is a heart, a legend and a mystique about playing for Las Leonas which means you want to win everything.'

Aymar's desire to play for 'the shirt' and to lift the trophy in front of her adoring fans led her to produce some moments of sheer magic throughout the course of the tournament. It also finally answered questions about whether she was a team player or a magician who worked alone.

'When Argentina had the World Cup in her home town of Rosario, Aymar was like a woman possessed,' said England's head coach Danny Kerry.

'She's always had a quality to open up the opposition with the ball but she worked collectively for the team throughout that World Cup. She brought a quality that most people felt that perhaps wasn't necessarily there.'

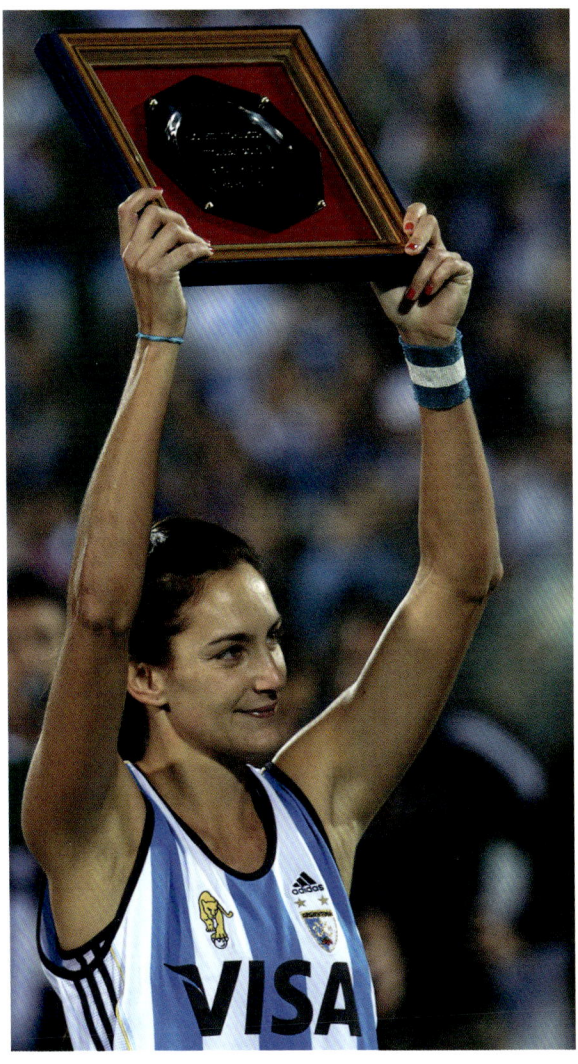

Aymar was named Best Player at the 2010 World Cup in Rosario, Argentina.
// Frank Uijlenbroek

It's not always necessary to have all the best players in one team to win... but when you put on the Argentina shirt, there is a heart, a legend and a mystique about playing for Las Leonas which means you want to win everything.

The event had it all: a carnival atmosphere, a vibrant and noisy crowd, wonderful Argentinian hospitality and the unique tingle of excitement that builds in the local area when the host nation is doing well.

Going into that event, Luciana Aymar had already won six of the eight FIH Player of the Year awards she would claim in a peerless career. She was absolutely at the height of her powers, dominating the world hockey scene. Constantly gliding over the turf, turning defenders inside out with her sublime stick skills: this was a genius at work and the golden girl of hockey could do no wrong.

In Argentina's opening game, Aymar scored a hat-trick against South Africa, thus setting out her intentions for all to see. Las Leonas then cruised to the top of their pool with further victories over Korea, Spain, China and England.

They beat Germany in a nerve-wracking 2-1 semi-final win, which left German defender Janne Müller-Wieland declaring the game 'one of the best World Cup experiences of my life'. Aymar scored the opening goal before Rosario Luchetti added a second. A strong fightback saw Germany push the Argentina defence to breaking point as Maike Stöckel brought the score back to 2-1, but to the home crowd's exuberance and delight, Argentina held on to set up an encounter with reigning champions the Netherlands, who edged past England in the other semi-final.

This match was a repeat of the 2010 Champions Trophy final that had taken place in Nottingham, England, which Argentina had won 4-2. But this was the World Cup and, as title holders, the Dutch were unlikely to willingly let go of the prize they had claimed at the 2006 event in Madrid, Spain.

For newcomer to the Dutch squad, Carlien Dirkse van den Heuvel, this was a baptism of fire: 'For me this was my first World Cup and I just felt like I was about to go through a whole new experience.'

Just how much of an experience it was, the midfielder admits, was something for which she was not prepared: 'I felt no problem about performing, the pressure was on the older players, like Janneke Schopman. For me, the unreal atmosphere in the stadium was where the pressure came.

'Leading into the game, our bus was late, nothing was going quite right. When we finally got on the bus, we drove through the streets of Rosario and normally people wave and cheer but not this time.'

The Netherlands team were given a police escort into the stadium and Dirkse van den Heuvel recalled one of the coaching staff turning to her and saying: 'It is crazy out there, just go out and enjoy it.'

'Well,' she said with a smile, 'I don't think enjoy is a word I would have used. That was just the craziest atmosphere ever. The crowd were jumping as one in the stands, and they

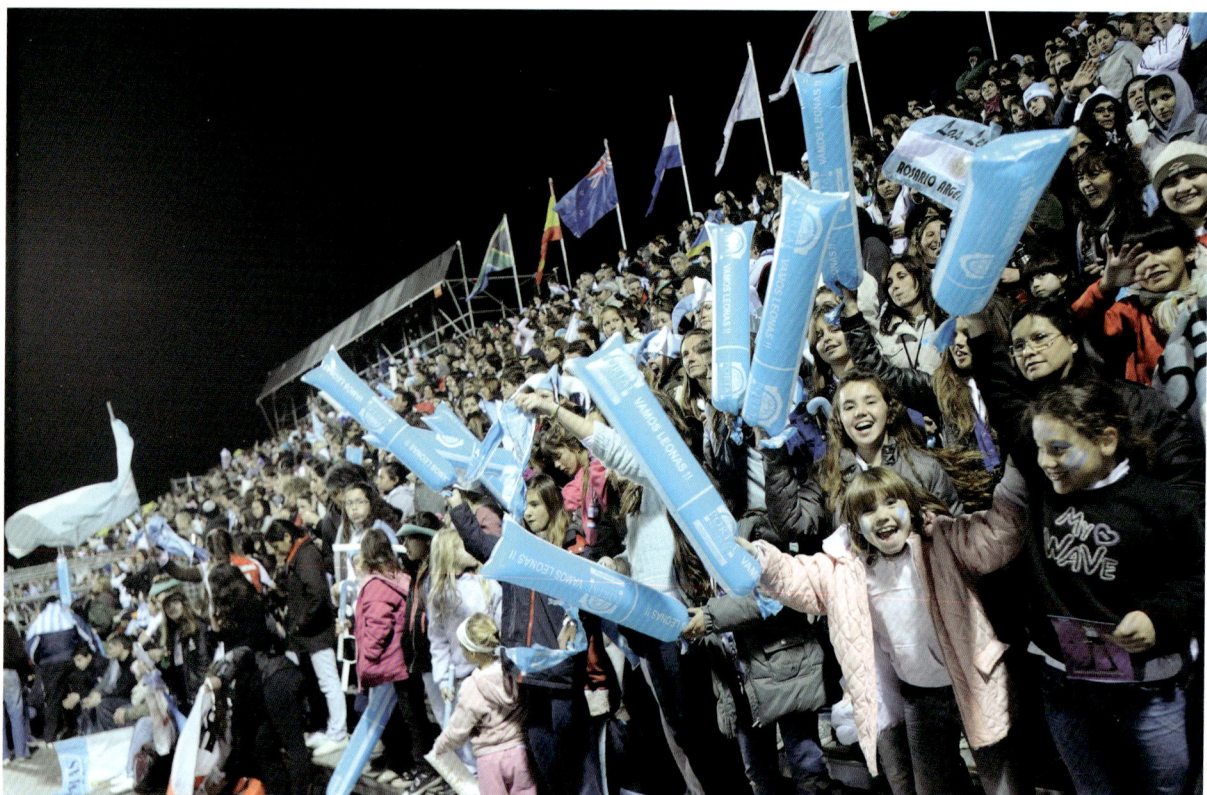

Argentina fans created a sensational atmosphere at the Women's Hockey World Cup 2010 in Rosario. // *Frank Uijlenbroek*

were crying through the national anthem…no one cries through the national anthem of Holland.

'We really were seen as the enemies that day. The Argentina players, they are always so loud with their music. It doesn't matter if they win or lose, they are still singing and dancing, and that is how the thousands of people in the stadium were as well. But Argentina were also the better team on the day.'

While the Netherlands were getting a villain's reception, for Aymar, this was a hero's homecoming. Playing her 300th international cap, what wouldn't she give to win gold to commemorate that landmark achievement?

Roared on by 12,000 expectant fans, it was Argentina who got off to the best start. Within three minutes Carla Rebecchi had opened the scoring after Aymar had drawn Dutch goalkeeper Joyce Sombroek off her goal line. It was an easy tap-in for Rebecchi and it sent the crowds wild with delight.

A penalty corner from Noel Barrionuevo extended the Argentina lead just before half-time but the Netherlands' own superstar, Maartje Paumen, fired home a penalty corner to halve the home side's lead. The win was sealed when Rebecchi scored her second. This time she volleyed the ball home after it bounced loose following a fierce shot from Soledad Garcia.

'We really wanted this title. The girls won all their matches playing with fight, passion and heart,' Argentina's head coach Carlos Retegui said on Argentinian television after the match. It was a point with which his captain, Aymar, agreed. 'This wasn't our best performance but we took our chances and defended with grit.'

Argentina became the third women's team to win an official FIH Women's World Cup as host nation, repeating a feat previously achieved by West Germany in 1976 and the Netherlands in 1986.

Hup hup Holland

And so to The Hague 2014, just the second World Cup event at which the men's and women's competitions were run simultaneously. In line with the FIH's drive to make the sport completely gender neutral, the matches received equal broadcast coverage whether they were men's or women's games, and the resources invested into both events were also equal in every way.

The Hague took its role as host to the Hockey World Cup extremely seriously and the streets around the stadium and in the heart of the city were bedecked in the national colour, orange. There were hockey events' all over the region, with beach hockey taking place at Scheveningen and the Masters' World Cup being held down the road at Rotterdam, alongside a disability hockey event.

At the venue itself, usually home to football club ADO Den Haag, the whole complex turned into a hockey mecca. The spectators' village was a place for hockey fans and their heroes to meet. The players passed through the village on their way to their buses, providing plenty of opportunity for players, their families and fans to mingle.

There were two pitches: the temporarily constructed Greenfields Stadium, which played host to some of the pool games in the opening rounds of the two events, and the main Kyocera Stadium. The capacity in the main stadium was 15,000 and, when it was full, the pitch and the stands became a cauldron. For many of the teams, crowds this size were a completely new experience and it was a daunting place to be.

South Africa players celebrate scoring in their shock triumph over England in 2014. // *Frank Uijlenbroek*

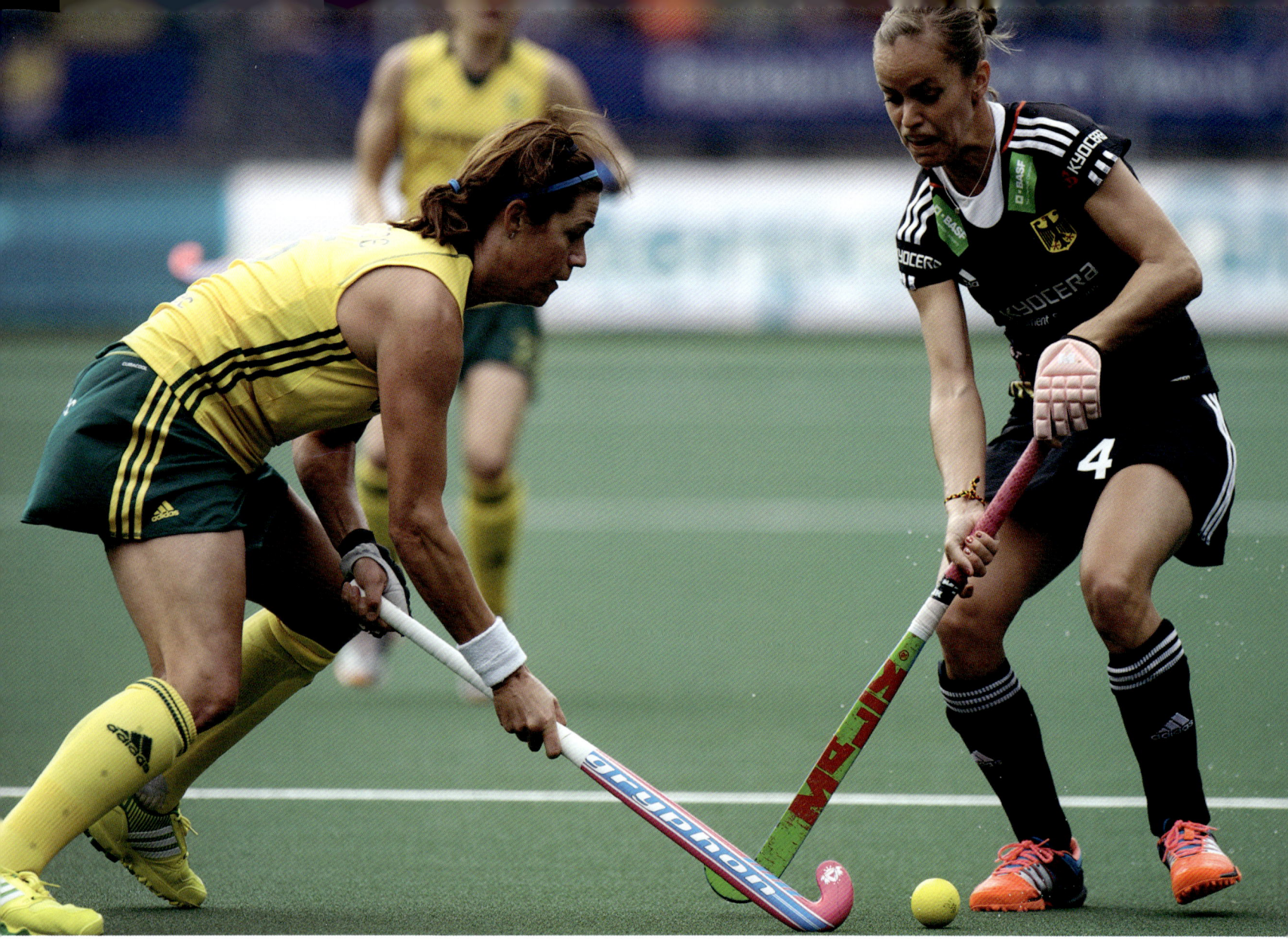

World record goalscorer Pietie Coetzee came back into the South Africa squad playing in defence. // *Frank Uijlenbroek*

Coetzee's dream return

As with all major events, there were side stories that added another level of intrigue. One such tale surrounded the South African hockey team.

The inclusion of 35-year-old Pietee Coetzee in the South Africa team came as a surprise to most of the hockey world. A gloriously talented goalscorer when she was at the height of her powers, Coetzee had been retired from the game for five years from 2005 until 2010 and, prior to this had not played an international match for months. When coach Giles Bonnet sent out his first team sheet, naming Coetzee in defence, it caused a ripple through the athletes' village.

There was a subtext: if Coetzee scored in the tournament, she would extend her own world record as the all-time leading goalscorer in women's international hockey. It was a record she had initially set in 2011, with the third of four goals she scored in a 5-5 draw with USA in the Champions Challenge in Dublin, which saw her overtake the 221 mark set by Russia's Natalya Krasnikova 20 years earlier. By the time she had stepped away for a second time, Coetzee had taken both her tally and the

world record to a staggering 285. Could this final return to the international scene see her also beat her own record? But playing at the back – she was brought in as a late replacement for Lenise Marais – and far from being at the peak of her powers? This was a big ask.

Coetzee's final match was the perfect ending to a glittering career. She scored her team's opener, leading them to a 2-0 win over Japan. This meant a ninth-place finish, two above their world ranking at the time, not to mention a new world record of 287. Whether that mark will ever be beaten, only time will tell.

Also creating their own side story were the team who had arrived in The Hague ranked 11th in the world. Team USA entered the tournament bringing with them their own style of fast, attacking hockey and a rumbustious, never-say-die attitude. The players from USA stormed to victories over England (2-1), China (5-0), Germany (4-1) and South Africa (4-2). They also drew with their Pan American rivals, Argentina (2-2). The quarter-final was approached with the same sense of adventure and suddenly USA went from underdogs to medal hopefuls.

Their incredible run came to an end in the cruellest of ways, a semi-final loss to Australia in a shoot-out. The score at the end of full-time was 2-2 but the Hockeyroos' Kellie White, Georgie Parker and Jodie Kenny all converted their shoot-out attempts with style and only Kelsey Kolojejchick was able to get past Rachael Lynch in the Australian goal. Despite that loss, the message to the international hockey world was clear – Argentina were no longer the only world-class hockey nation in the Pan American region.

One of the USA's pool-round opponents had been England. Led by head coach Jason Lee and with the experienced captain Kate Richardson-Walsh at the helm, England arrived in The Hague with their supporters expecting good things. Unfortunately, the team had experienced in-camp problems in the build-up and, while they were ranked number three in the world, the reality was that England were far from ready for the challenge of World Cup competition.

England's assistant coach at the time was Craig Keegan. 'It was evident before the World Cup that things weren't right within the group,' revealed Keegan in the book *The History Makers*. 'We had a trip to Germany a couple of months before and we had a number of team meetings during that week. Some issues arose that set alarm bells ringing. Some of those were leadership, or lack of it. Others were the result of interpersonal issues within the playing group. We didn't do enough about that before the World Cup…it was just left to fester.'

As loss followed loss, the England camp became an increasingly toxic place to be. The opening match defeat against USA was a shock result but losses against China and South Africa were even harder to swallow as these were both teams from whom Lee's side would have expected to take points. A 2-1 defeat to Argentina saw a slightly better performance from England but by then the damage had been done and a 3-1 loss to another team that was struggling – Germany – consigned the world number three team to playing an 11th/12th place play-off against Belgium, the lowest-ranked team in the event.

Georgie Twigg, who later went on to win gold at the Rio 2016 Olympic Games with a Great Britain squad containing numerous members of the team that competed in The Hague, said: 'Everyone just wanted to do something individually, it was just chaos. I remember being totally exhausted because we had no structure and it was just end-to-end. It was truly, truly awful.'

While these dramas were happening across the tournament, the host nation was sailing along towards the later stages of the event with consummate ease. If 2010 provided Aymar's stage, 2014 was to be the year of Maartje Paumen.

The opening match for the home nation set the tone – a 6-1 win over Japan. Kelly Jonker scored three and Paumen added two – a penalty stroke and a penalty corner. Belgium fell 4-0, with Paumen again among the scorers.

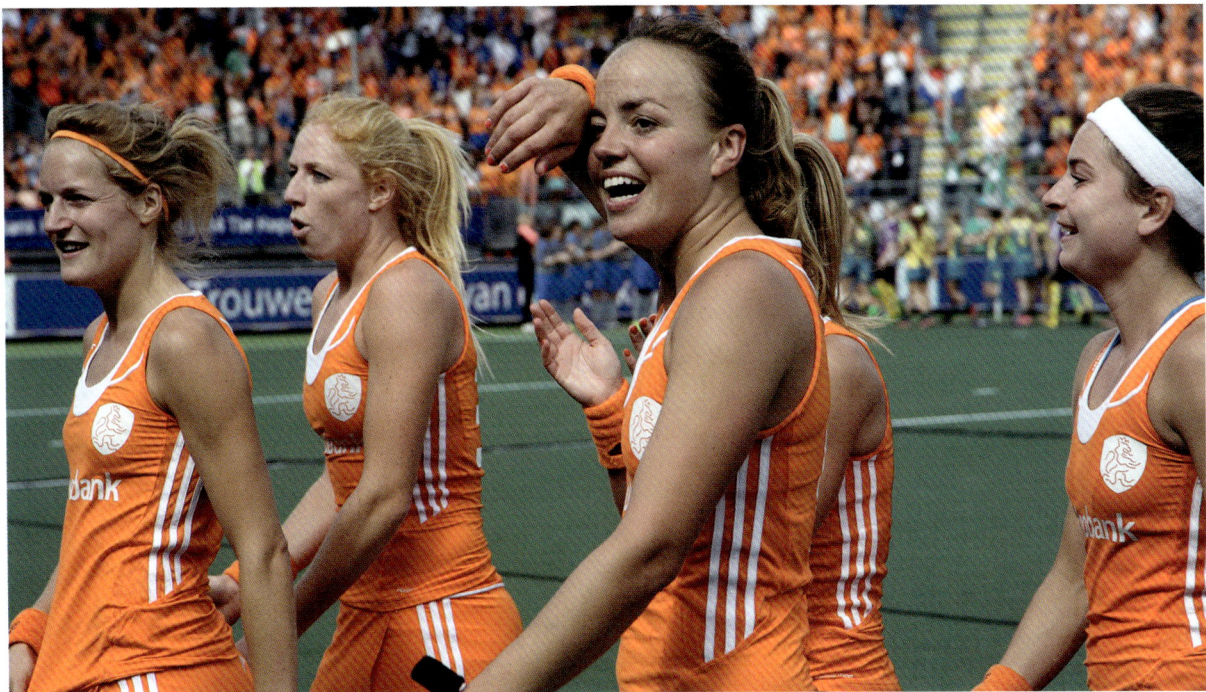

Maartje Paumen led the way as top goalscorer in the 2014 World Cup. // *Frank Uijlenbroek*

Paumen didn't get her name on the scoresheet as her team cruised to victories over New Zealand and Australia, but normal service resumed when she put two goals past Korea – a win that sealed the Oranje's place at the top of Pool A.

The Netherlands faced Argentina in the semi-finals – a rematch of the 2010 World Cup Final. This time it was Argentina facing a huge orange-clad crowd. And this time Luciana Aymar was well below par, with a hamstring heavily strapped and her movement restricted by injury and fatigue.

The Netherlands took the lead in the tenth minute through the teenage sensation Xan de Waard, before a penalty corner from Paumen and two goals from Kim Lammers saw off the threat from their old nemesis.

All that stood between the Dutch and their seventh World Cup was the gold and green of Australia. The Hockeyroos had enjoyed a fine tournament; their dual penalty corner specialists, Jodie Kenny and Anna Flanagan, had struck home on eight occasions – with Flanagan scoring six of those. Australia would undoubtedly present a threat but as the Netherlands strode out into the warm sunshine in front of a crowd of 15,000 mostly Dutch supporters, the outcome seemed inevitable.

Nine of the Netherlands' squad had been in Rosario four years earlier and suffered at the hands of a rampant home side and a large and vociferous home crowd. Now it was Australia's turn to feel the heat of a capacity crowd, mostly wearing orange.

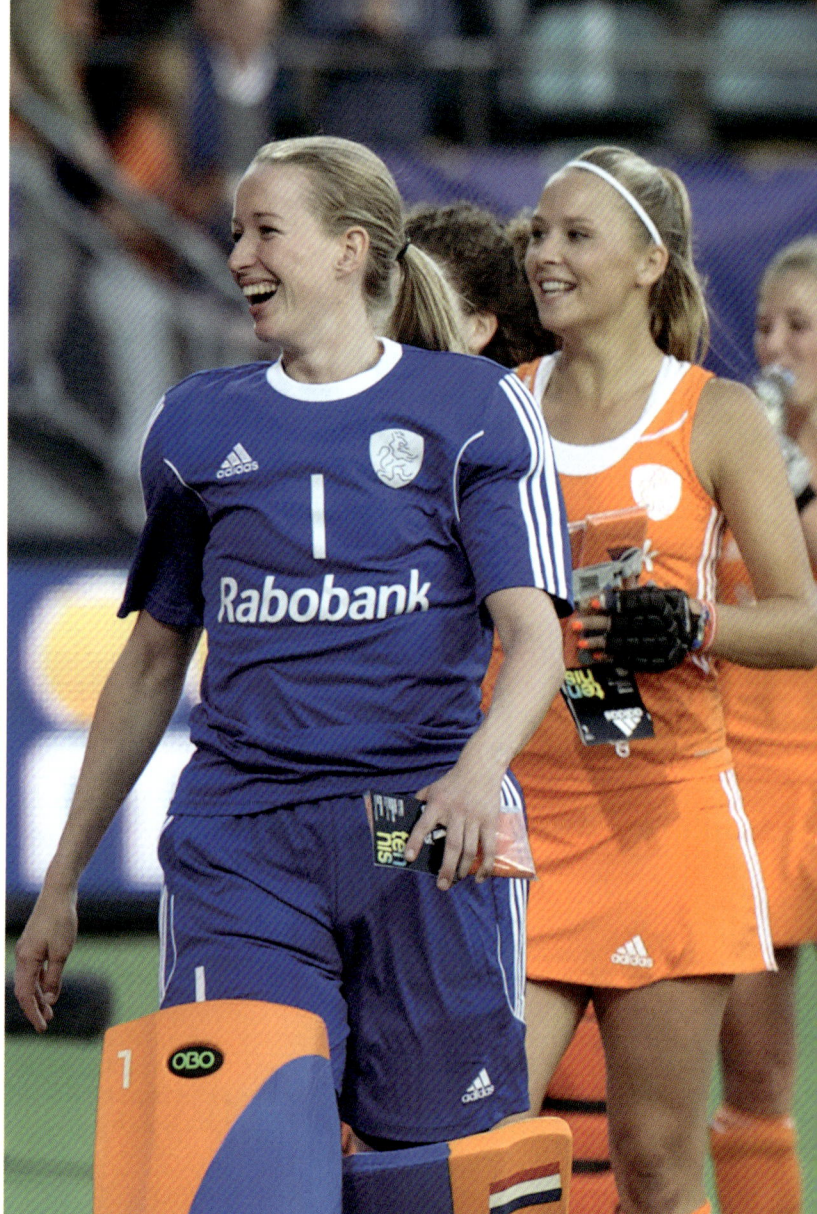
The all-conquering Dutch were close to perfection in The Hague. // *Frank Uijlenbroek*

She is a killer. If it is a pressure moment then Paumen is the person for the job.

Paumen opened the scoring in the 17th minute with a coolly taken penalty stroke to bring her own tally to seven and her team's record to an impressive 23 goals for and one against. On the day of her 200th cap and final game for the Netherlands, it was fitting that Kim Lammers should also score, her penalty corner goal effectively ending Australia's hopes of a first major gold medal since the Sydney 2000 Olympic Games. As the clock counted down the last ten seconds of the game, the Dutch players didn't even wait for the final whistle before they sprinted towards each other and hugged and danced with joy.

As the Oranje lifted the trophy to a cacophony of shouts and cheers, commentator and Olympian Sarah Thomas tried to articulate why the Dutch were so good. 'They get outcome after outcome in the circle and that is the difference. They play great passing hockey and they use each other and that sets them apart from every other team. They set the bar very, very high and then they always set out to meet those standards. They are the best in the world at the moment.'

'She is a killer,' was Kim Lammers' verdict on her captain and fellow goalscorer. 'If it is a pressure moment, then Paumen is the person for the job.'

With the memories of that campaign and stunning victory still sharp in the minds of many of the 2018 Netherlands squad, the question for coach Alyson Annan and her players was whether they could match the class of 2014?

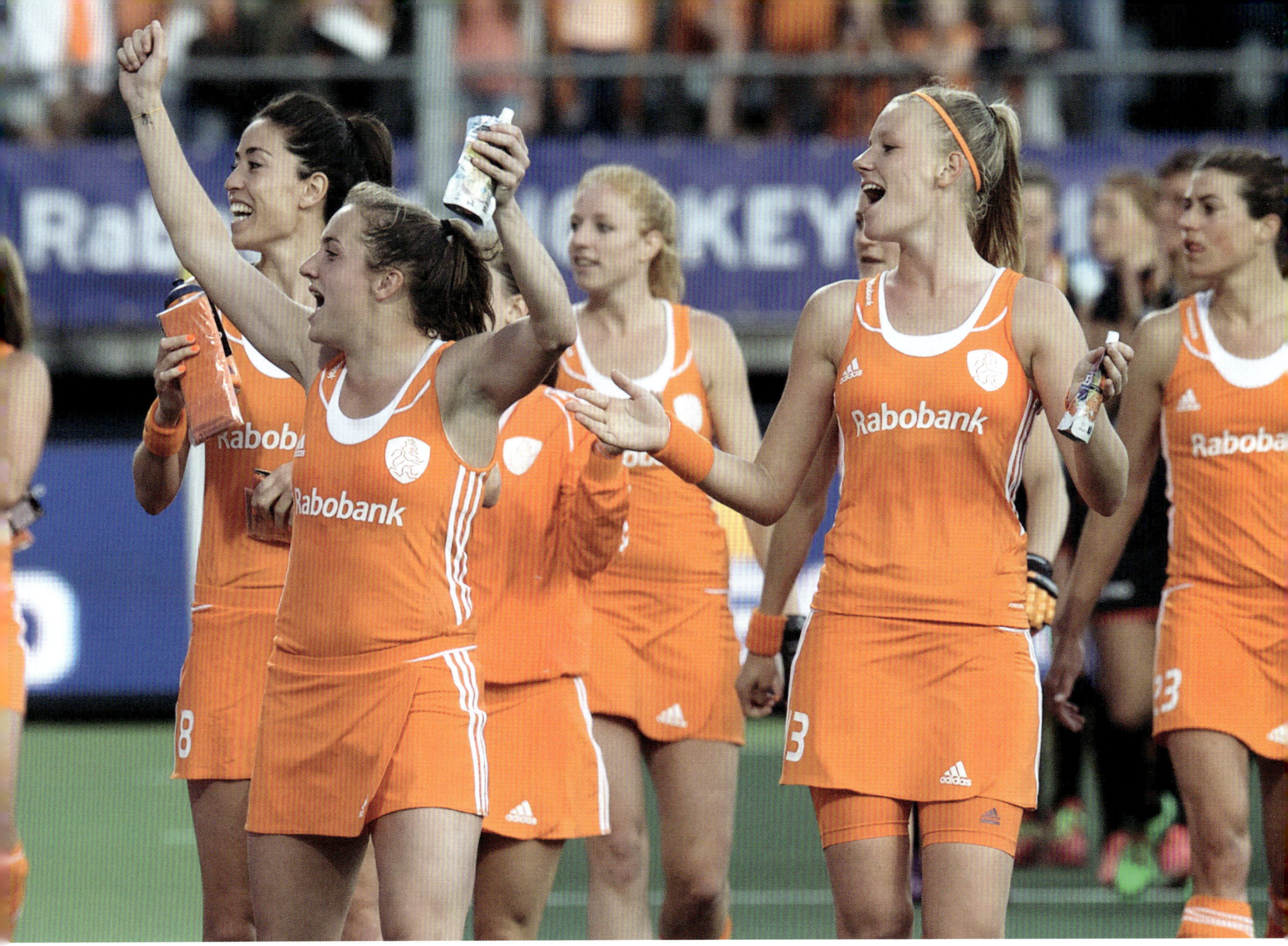

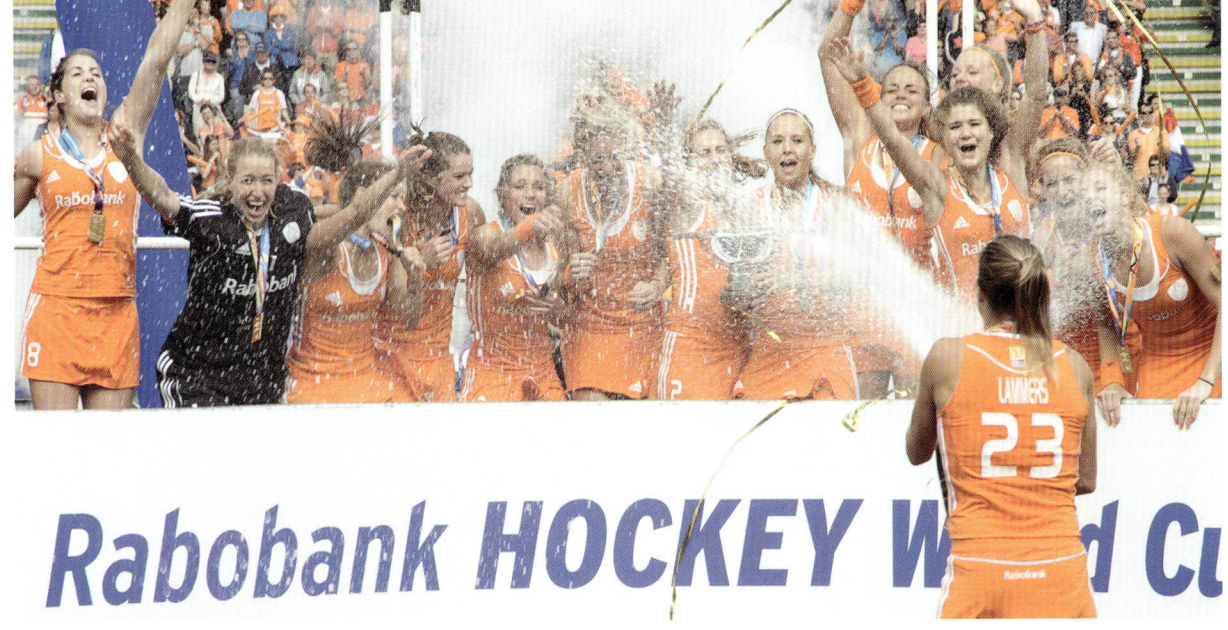

The Netherlands celebrate their 2014 title success in style. // *Frank Uijlenbroek*

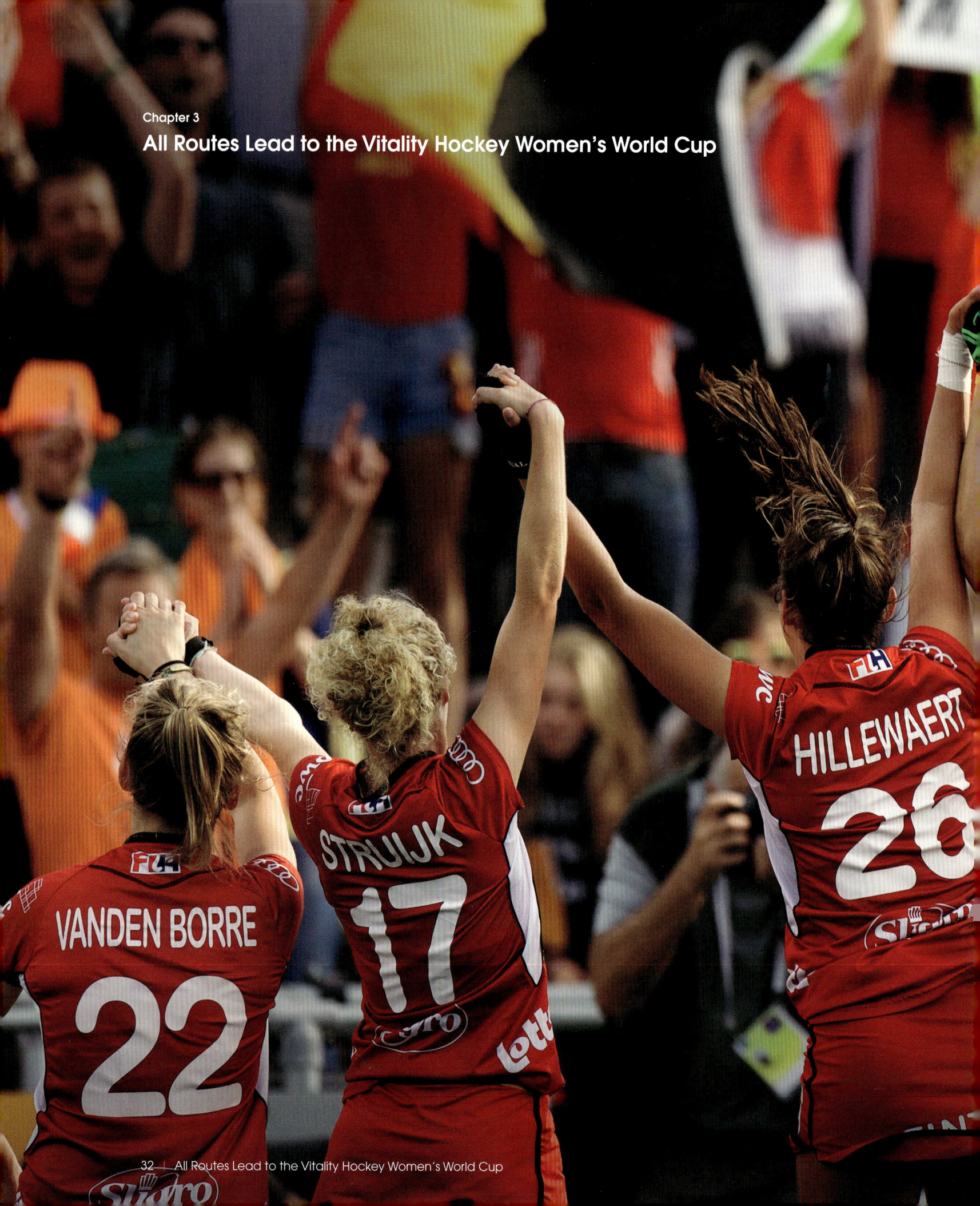

All Routes Lead to the Vitality Hockey Women's World Cup

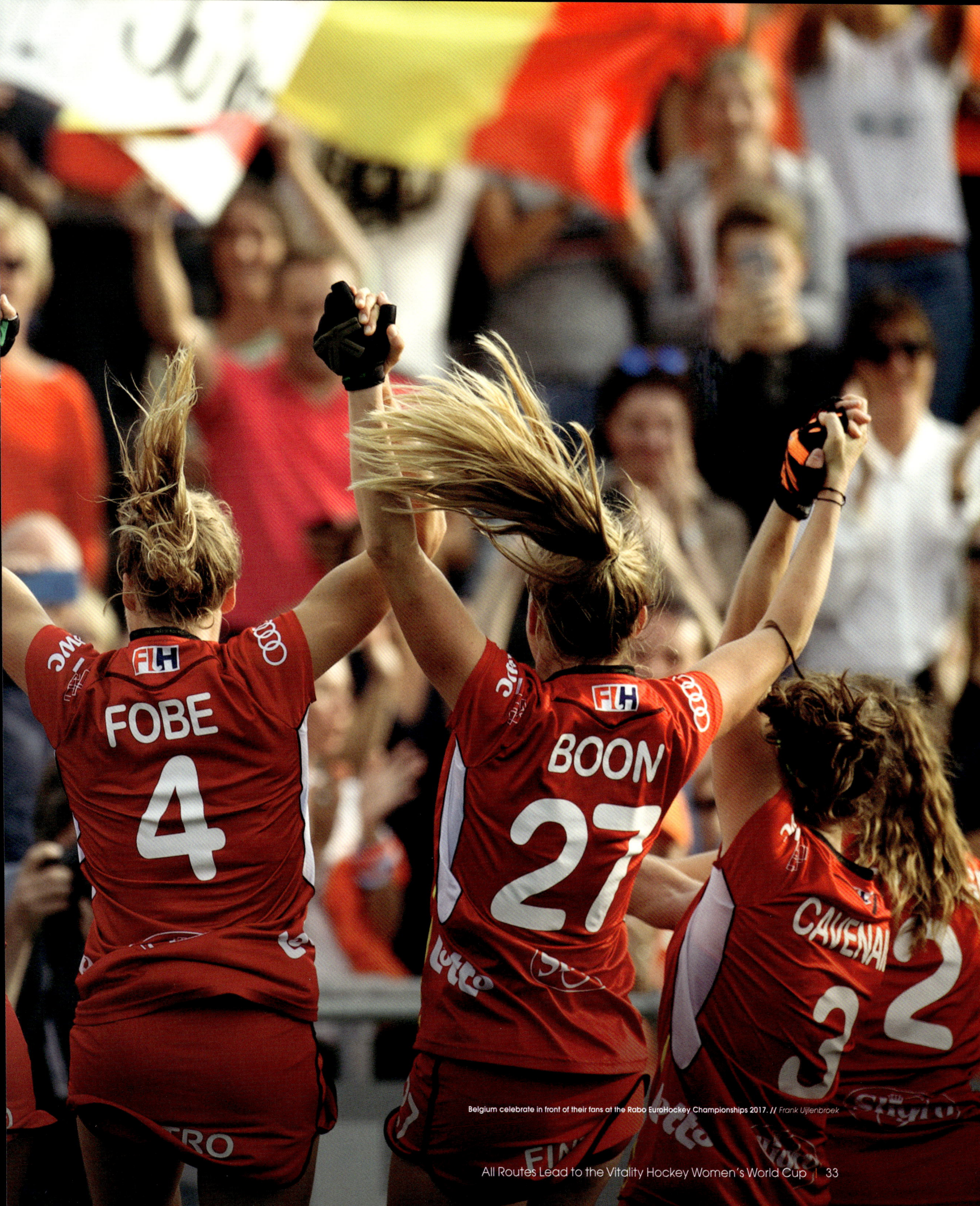

Belgium celebrate in front of their fans at the Rabo EuroHockey Championships 2017. // Frank Uijlenbroek

All Routes Lead to the Vitality Hockey Women's World Cup

Qualification for the Vitality Hockey Women's World Cup London 2018 was a two-year process, and nations had two means of earning their place at the top table of international hockey – via the Continental Championships or through the Hockey World League (HWL).

The qualification process through the Continental Championships' route was very straightforward. All five continents held their respective qualifying events in the two years preceding the World Cup. This meant that champions of Africa, Asia, Europe, Oceania and Pan America had all booked their places for the blue riband event and that their final positions in the Hockey World League were irrelevant.

The Hockey World League route was slightly more complex but provided a greater number of World Cup berths.

The league was introduced in 2012 and offered all nations, no matter what their position in the FIH Hero World Ranking, a chance to make it on to the biggest global stage. Comprising three rounds, the opening round was open to any nation with a world ranking below 20. As far as possible, these HWL Round One events were regional, so the 2017/18 season comprised Round One events in Peru, France, Ghana, Fiji and Singapore.

The top two teams, and, on occasion, the third-placed team, then went through to one of three Round Two events. Again, these were as localised as possible, but with the events being held in Canada, Spain and Malaysia some long-distance travel was required.

Thus it was that India found themselves travelling to Vancouver in Canada and both Italy and Ireland played their Round Two matches in Malaysia. For all three teams, the journey was worth the effort as they all qualified for the decisive Hockey World League Semi-Final.

It was at the Hockey World League Semi-Final events that things really begin to heat up. A top-five finish at the competitions in Brussels and Johannesburg was enough to guarantee World Cup qualification. However, with some teams already qualified through their continental championships and more to follow at the continental competitions ahead, some teams that finished further down the standings in the Hockey World League Semi-Final competitions found themselves, albeit after a long and nervy wait, with a ticket to the World Cup safely in their hands.

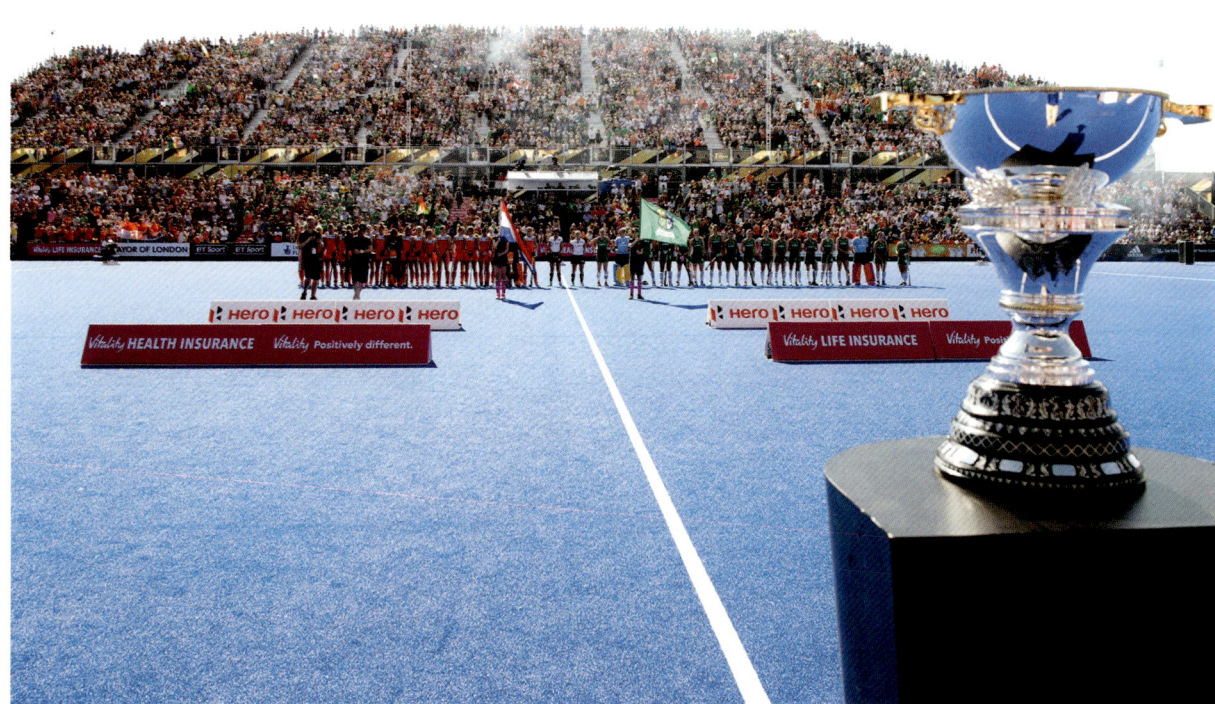

The Netherlands and Ireland line up for the final of the Vitality Hockey Women's World Cup. // *Frank Uijlenbroek*

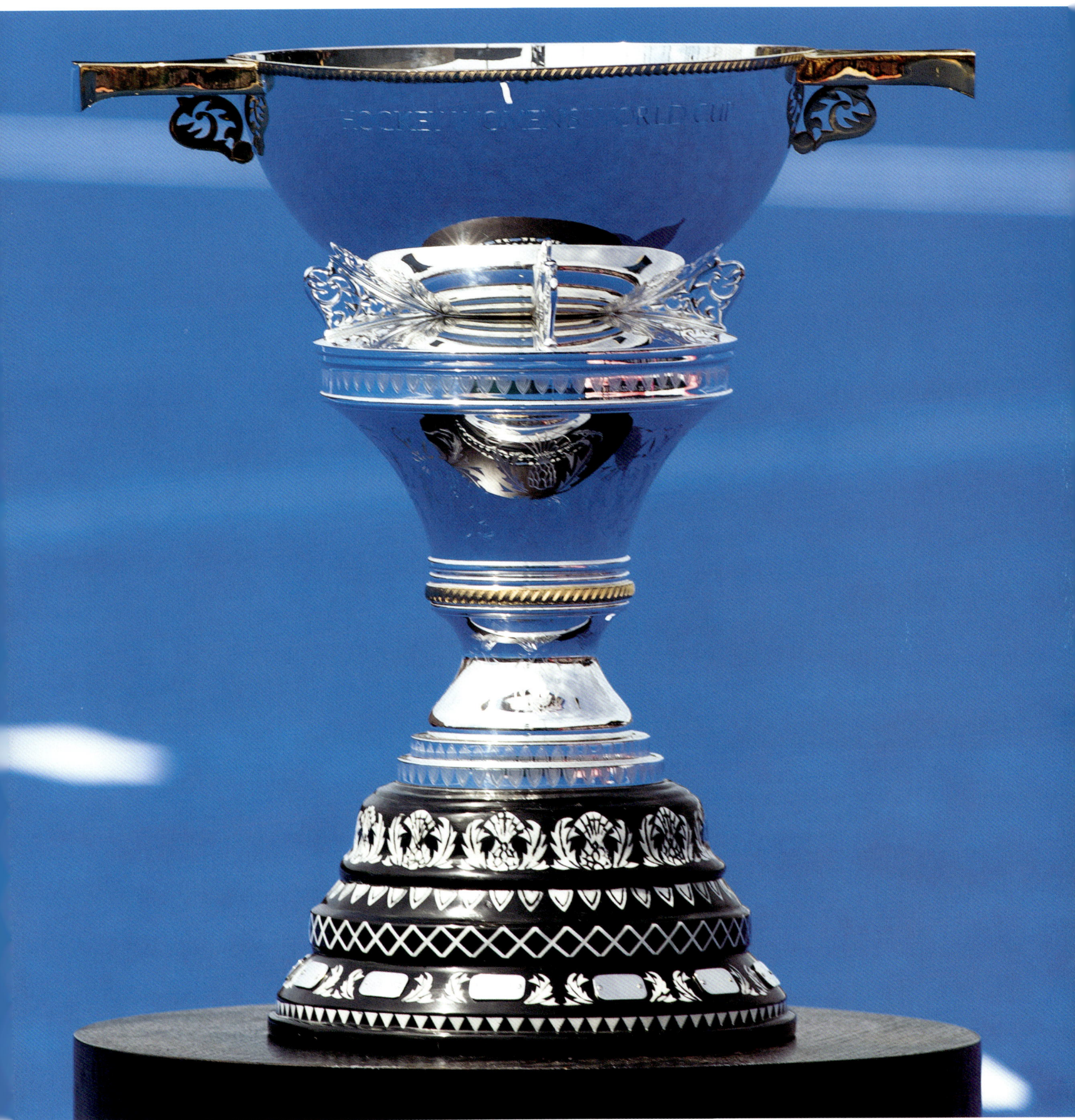

The newly redesigned trophy on display. // *Koen Suyk*

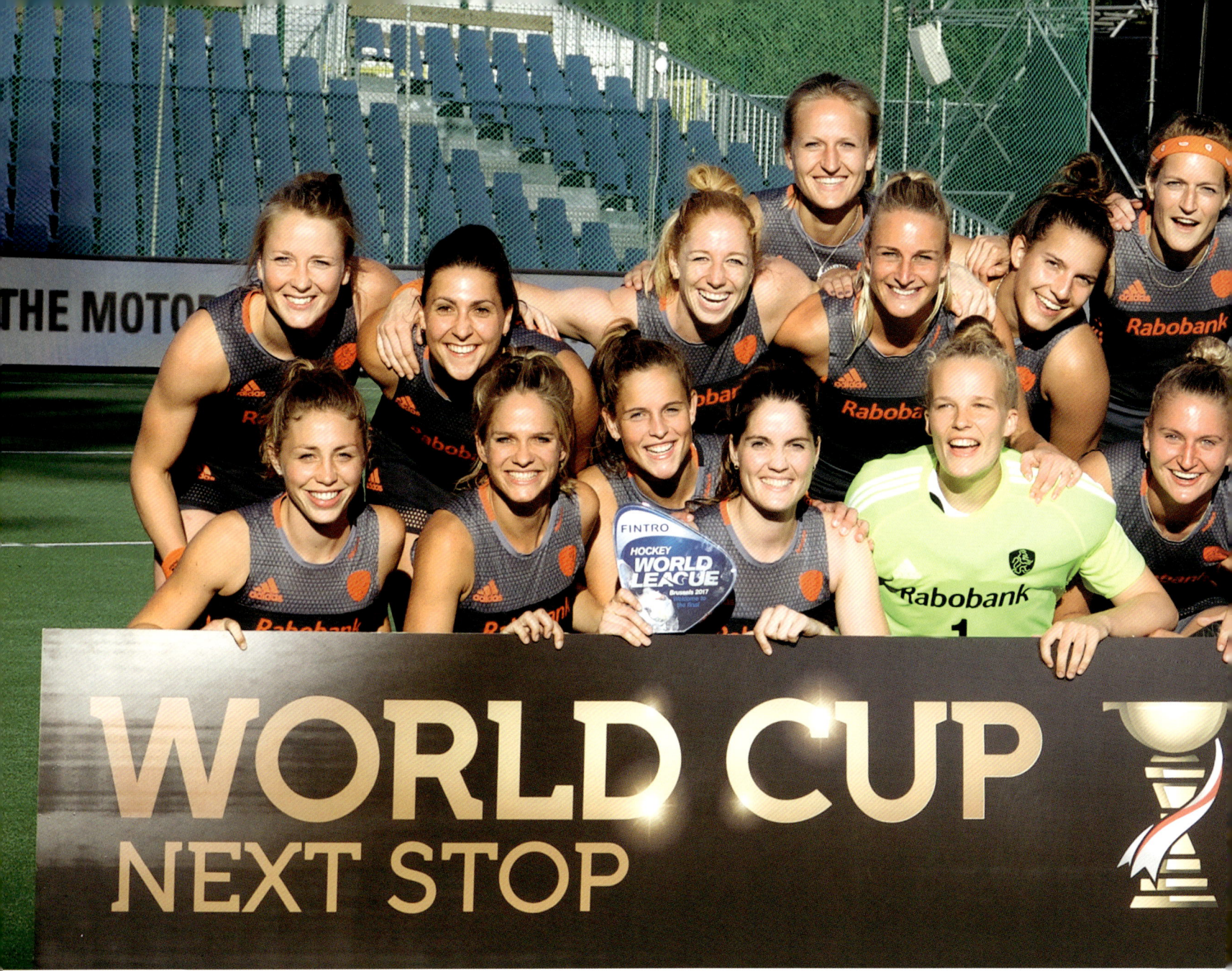

The Netherlands booked their World Cup ticket at the Fintro Hockey World League Semi-Final 2017 in Brussels, Belgium. // *Frank Uijlenbroek*

World Number One – The Netherlands

The Netherlands, the World Cup reigning champions and number one-ranked team in the world, hit a rich vein of form coming into 2017. A number of retirements following the Rio 2016 Olympic Games left head coach Alyson Annan – the former Australia international, FIH Player of the Year in 1998 and 2000, and double World Cup and Olympic gold medallist – with a pathway cleared to instil more of her own ideas and practices.

'I only had a very short time with the squad leading up to Rio,' said Annan as she reflected back. 'I still think we should have won the gold [at the Rio Olympic Games], because we played well, but it wasn't to be.'

The next year, however, Annan's squad became invincible.

At the Hockey World League Semi-Final in Brussels, Belgium they scored 24 goals and conceded just one, meaning they swept to victory and clinched qualification for the World Cup.

The semi-final of the event, against the Black Sticks of New Zealand, was the only stumbling block. The match finished with the score locked at 1-1, sending the contest into a nerve-wracking shoot-out. New Zealand thought they had won the shoot-out but a smart video review by the Dutch saw the Black Sticks' potentially match-winning goal from Olivia Merry disallowed meaning the scores remained level. Margot van Geffen took advantage of the reprieve to put the Netherlands ahead and New Zealand's Grace O'Hanlon was devastated to see her shot saved by Anne Veenendaal to give the Netherlands the win.

At the EuroHockey Championships, played on home soil in Amstelveen a few weeks later, it was much of the same. Netherlands won all their pool matches and then beat England 1-0 in the semi-final to set up an encounter with Belgium. Goals from Carlien Dirkse van den Heuvel, Kelly Jonker and Ireen van den Assem were enough to end the Red Panthers' challenge, meaning that the Netherlands had qualified for the World Cup twice over.

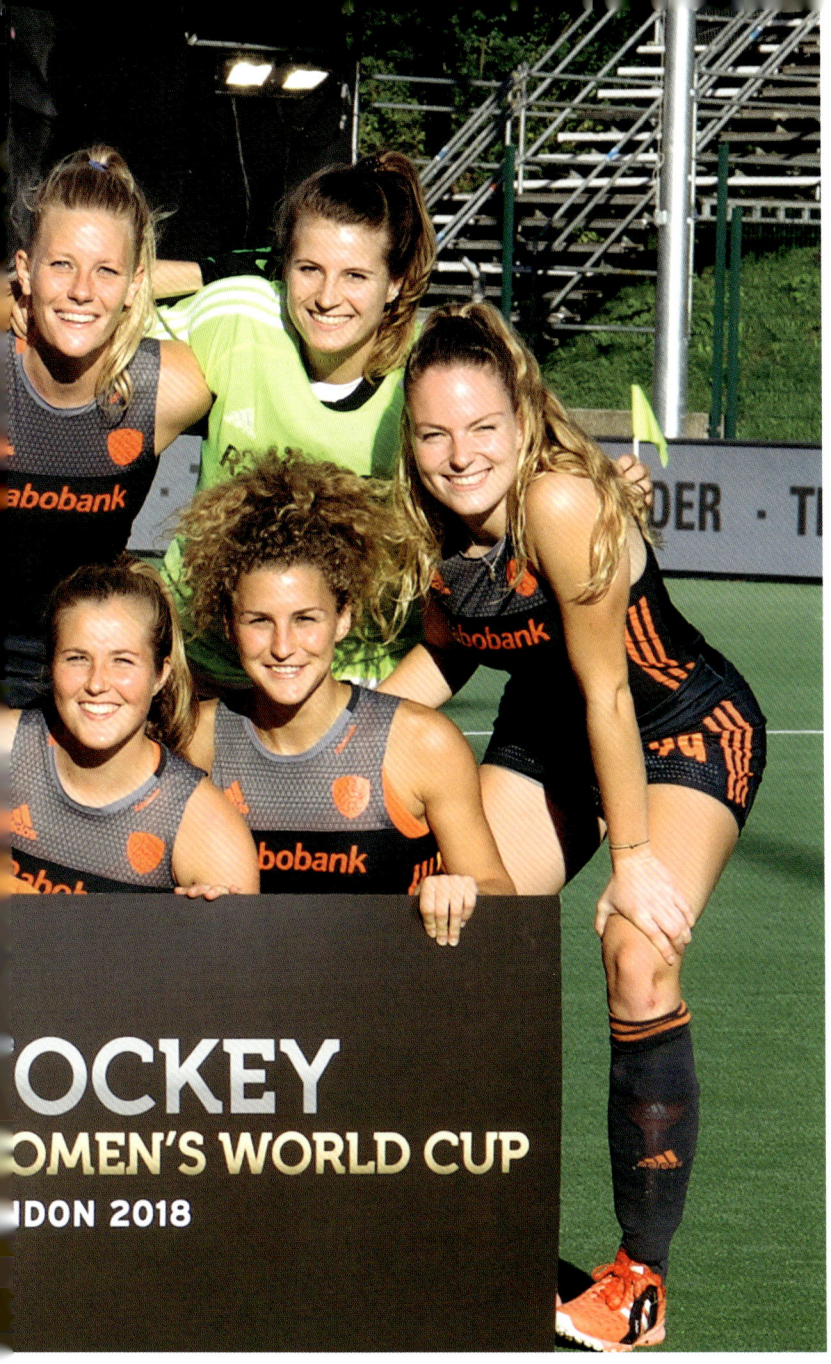

'It is a really exciting group and we have really gelled well. We went to the USA at the start of 2018 to play a four match series but it was really cool because we had a lot of time to bond and get to know each other. For example, we went to San Francisco and spent one morning doing team-work and the rest of our time there just doing our own thing. That balance between training, playing and relaxing helps enormously.'

A key factor in the rebuilding process is the coach. Alyson Annan admits that she sometimes finds it difficult to communicate but like all the best coaches she recognised what needed to change and the result has been a much more relaxed head coach and a far better, two-way communication between coach and players.

'Alyson has definitely changed,' said Van Geffen before the EuroHockey Championships. 'We had a feedback session with her. She is calmer than she was before Rio. But I can imagine the stress she was under. Before Rio she was with us for just nine months. That is a really short period. Now we have got to know each other more and know how to communicate with each other and that is a big difference.'

Speaking before the Hockey World League Semi-Final, experienced midfielder Carlien Dirkse van den Heuvel gave some insight into the team's attitude.

'We love to play hockey, it is as simple as that. And we love to win. When losing a match no longer matters, then it is time to stop playing.'

Dirkse van den Heuvel – 31 at the time of the Vitality Hockey Women's World Cup London 2018 – was one of the few 'older' players to continue playing after three previous World Cup cycles. She explained that Annan had given her a new sense of purpose and adventure within the squad and she was relishing the chance to keep going 'hopefully to Tokyo 2020'.

Another relative elder of the squad was Margot van Geffen. 'A whole rebuilding process started after Rio,' said the 28-year-old defender-turned-midfielder. 'There were lots of players who all quit playing; a lot of them had been leaders so a new group had to be formed.

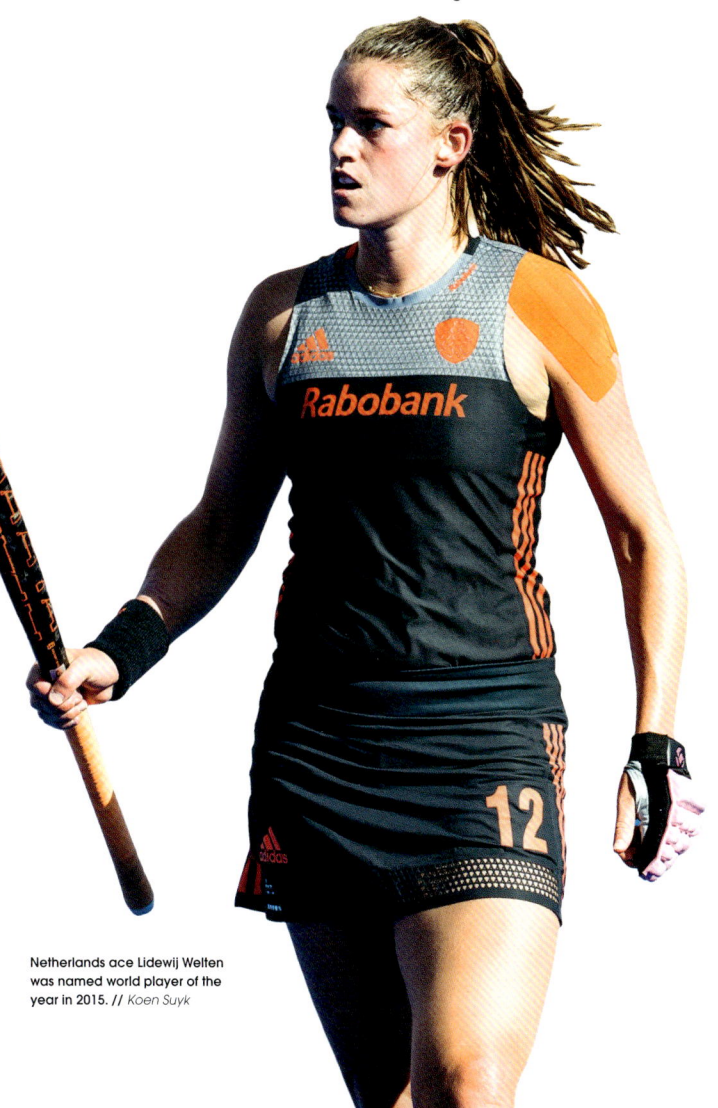

Netherlands ace Lidewij Welten was named world player of the year in 2015. // Koen Suyk

World Number Two – England

As hosts, England were able to be very relaxed in their World Cup build-up as they had a place booked from the moment London was named host city. Head coach Danny Kerry could not have been more pleased as it meant he could take experimental squads to both the European Championships and the Hockey World League Semi-Finals. After a number of high-profile retirements in the aftermath of the Rio Olympics, this was a luxury for Kerry.

'I want to use every opportunity to put my players under pressure so they really learn how to think and make decisions for themselves,' said the England tactician. 'This could mean asking the coach driver to deliberately get lost on the way to the ground so the players have reduced warm-up time or an interruption to their usual preparations.'

Kerry was also keen to give his new players as much experience as possible. Over a 12-month period, England played numerous test matches so that even the newest squad members had a high number of caps next to their names. For Kerry, the psychological power of not being seen as a newcomer was vast.

'When you see some of the opposition with hundreds of caps next to their name, it shouldn't affect the player's self-confidence but it does.'

When Great Britain claimed the gold medal at the Rio 2016 Olympic Games, one of the areas that Kerry said he wanted to improve upon with his squad was the integration of the staff and squad members. In the past, there had been a palpable 'them and us' divide between the players and the coaching team. Always one to look for improvements in all areas of the squad's preparations, this was one of the challenges that Kerry set his England team.

'Without a doubt it is better. And that is due in particular to the terrific leadership of Alex Danson,' said the head coach. 'I know we can never be as one, particularly at tournament times, but we are as close to being a unified squad of players and staff as it is possible to be.'

England's first major event of 2017 was the Hockey World League Semi-Final in Johannesburg, South Africa. Although the team didn't need to qualify via this route for the World Cup, the top four-placed teams also qualified to compete in the showcase end-of-year event – the Hockey World League Final in Auckland.

For England, qualification for this event would give yet another opportunity for the players to gain even more top-class competition. In the event, losses to Japan and USA left England playing for third place against Argentina – a match they won 5-2, thereby securing their ticket to Auckland for the 2017 Hockey World League Final.

The one thing that England captain Alex Danson and her team did not expect was to play much of the competition in South Africa with their coach lying in hospital after suffering a serious heart problem.

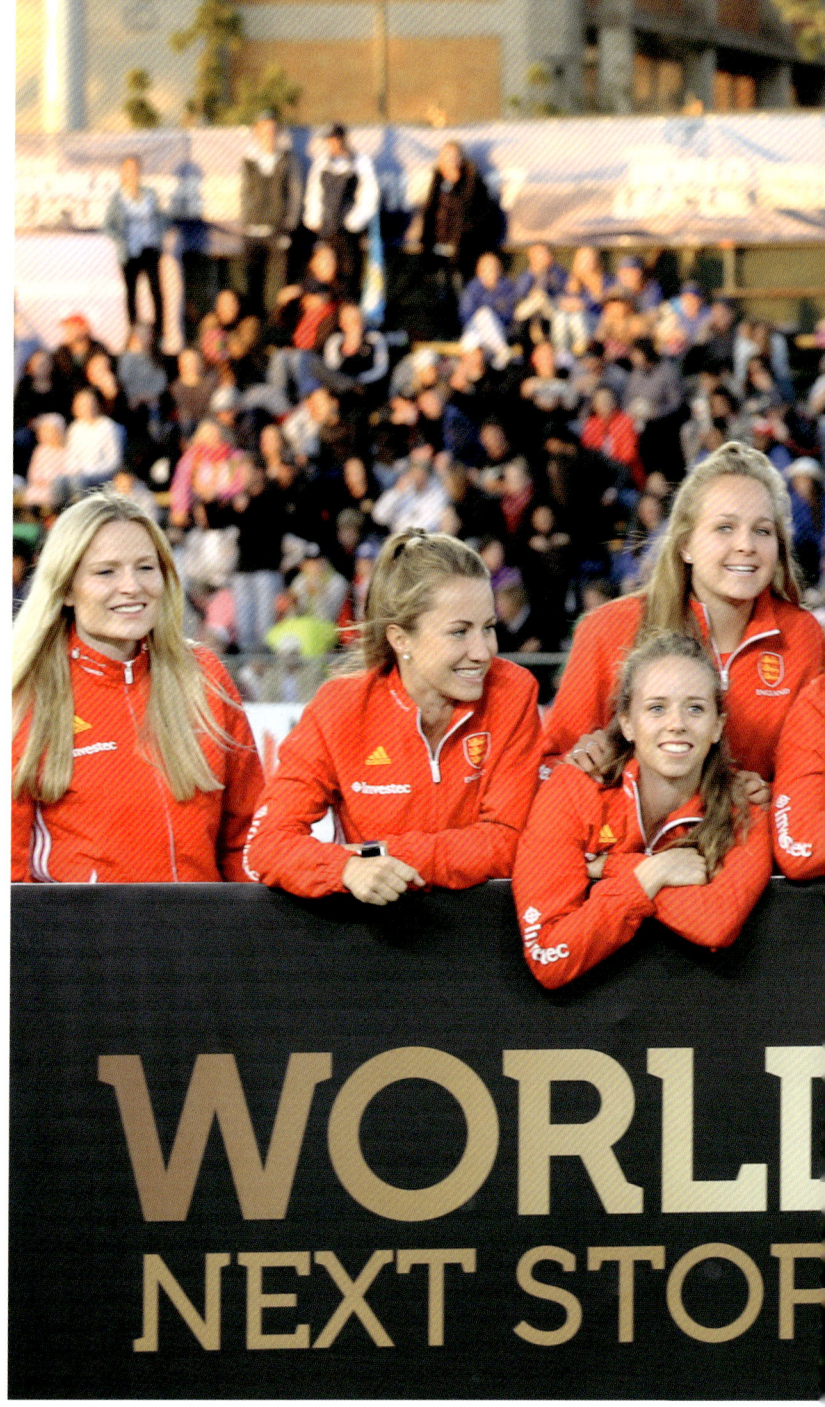

England, pictured at the Hockey World League Semi-Final 2017 in Johannesburg, South Africa. // *Rodrigo Jaramillo*

In an interview with the *Hockey Paper*, Kerry said that he was lucky to still be alive. The head coach had been in his room in a hotel in Johannesburg when he felt pain in his chest and arms. Initially he thought he would sleep it off but he was forced to go to hospital by the team doctor, Cath Lester.

After arrival in hospital, Kerry required two separate blood tests before the heart attack was confirmed, while a separate angiogram diagnosed a blocked artery as the cause.

It took three days in intensive care before his condition stabilised and he was then offered the option to return to the UK for surgery or to have the procedure in South Africa.

'Initially I wanted to go back home to be with my family, but I was advised that it was better not to delay,' said Kerry, whose wife was flown out to be with him before the operation.

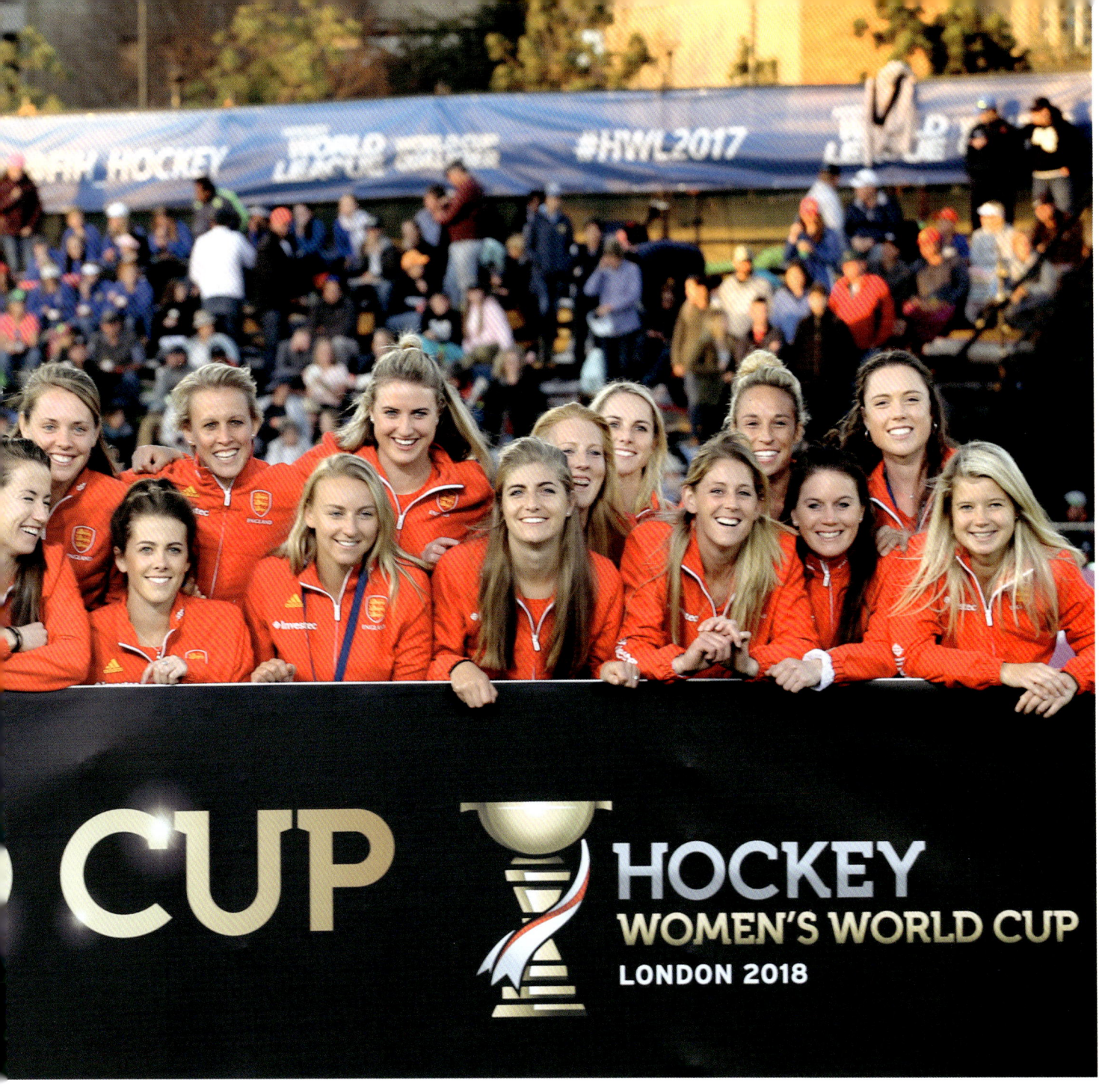

He did manage a video call to his children – who were four and six at the time – back in the UK, but said, 'trying to make it a positive environment for them,' was one of the hardest moments of his life.

'It was really tough because you're putting on a very brave face for them and trying to smile and laugh when you're not feeling like it so much,' he said.

Five days after being admitted to hospital Kerry was fitted with three metal stents in his heart, but from the moment he awoke he began impressing the doctors who were astounded by his rapid recovery. He then spent two weeks under observation in the Johannesburg hospital before flying home under strict medical supervision.

This frightening incident left Kerry contemplating his future, but after a month's break from work, he returned to the fold determined to press on with his ambitious plans for England and Great Britain.

While Kerry had been taking time off, England had been busy contesting the 2017 EuroHockey Nations. They had taken the title in 2015 after an exhilarating final against the Netherlands but this was not to be their tournament, although they did claim another medal at a major championship when they defeated Germany 2-0 to win bronze. As an added bonus, defender Hollie Webb – who became Hollie Pearne-Webb soon afterwards following marriage – was named player of the tournament.

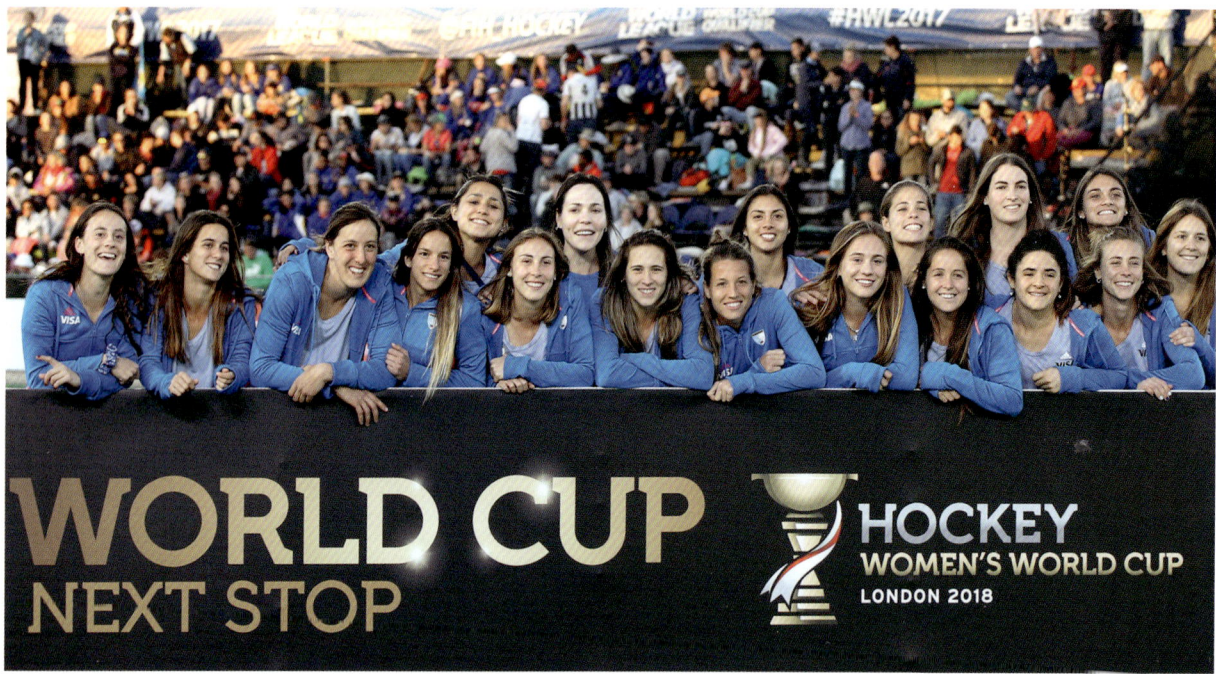

Argentina finished fourth at the Hockey World League Semi-Final 2017 in Johannesburg, South Africa. // *Rodrigo Jaramillo*

World Number Three – Argentina

Argentina went through a rocky period by their standards between 2016 and 2018. A seventh-place finish at the Rio 2016 Olympic Games was a painful experience and one that was made even tougher when long-serving stalwart Carla Rebecchi announced her retirement.

Las Leonas continued to be off their usual pace at the Hockey World League Semi-Final in Johannesburg. They began well, winning all their pool games, including a 4-0 win over Pan American rivals USA and a 2-0 win over China. In the semi-finals, however, they fell to a 2-1 defeat at the hands of Germany and then lost the bronze medal match to England by a 5-2 margin. Despite that, a fourth-place finish meant that World Cup qualification was confirmed and a place at the Hockey World League Final was also secured.

Winning ways resumed shortly after they returned from Johannesburg when Argentina won the Pan American Cup handsomely, a victory that will have tasted particularly sweet as continental rivals USA could only muster a third-place finish.

At the Hockey World League Final in Auckland, Las Leonas started their campaign very much as they did at the Semi-Final competition in Johannesburg. Three pool games meant three straight wins. Their opponents in the competition quarter-finals were the home team New Zealand, who, by contrast, had endured a shocking tournament up until that point. New Zealand weathered an Argentina attacking storm after Delfina Merino had burst into the circle in just the second minute of play to put Argentina ahead.

Just when it looked as though it was going to be a rout, the game turned into an enthralling contest of attack and counter-attack. When New Zealand equalised and then moved ahead, the fight gradually drained from Las Leonas and they were uncharacteristically subdued as New Zealand clung on to their one goal advantage.

Captain and current highest-capped player in the squad, Delfina Merino, the 2017 FIH Player of the Year, explained what it was like to be part of the Leonas squad. 'Being a Leona in Argentina is not just wearing your shirt and being a good player, it is about different values and different ways of living. The things you do or don't do. We have to show our values consistently through our behaviour. It is not simply a case of saying: "you should do this, or you should do that"; we must show the way as well.

'We have to feel things intrinsically. If we do not feel it inside, it is difficult to live the Leonas way. It is a challenge for us though. We have been in the squad a long time and the generation coming through has changed a lot.

'For me, when I joined the Leonas, there were a lot of players who had been there for a while. We just entered as a couple of young players and quickly learnt how to be a Leona. Now there are a lot of younger players, bringing their own values – but I like that, I really like their energy.

'I have never felt like I am done with all this. I have never had that feeling but of course sometimes when I do get really tired, I can be sitting in a lecture at university and I feel my eyes closing because I am so tired and I think, "Oh my god, what am I doing", but those are rare lapses. When I have them all the time, then I will know it is time to stop.

'I look back at the end of each season and I ask myself: "Was it worth it?" and every season I think: "Oh yes, that was worth it."'

As they made their final preparations for the World Cup campaign, many of the hockey pundits began to look to Argentina and their fast maturing squad as the team that might go all the way and win their third gold medal to add to the titles claimed at the 2002 Perth and 2010 Rosario events.

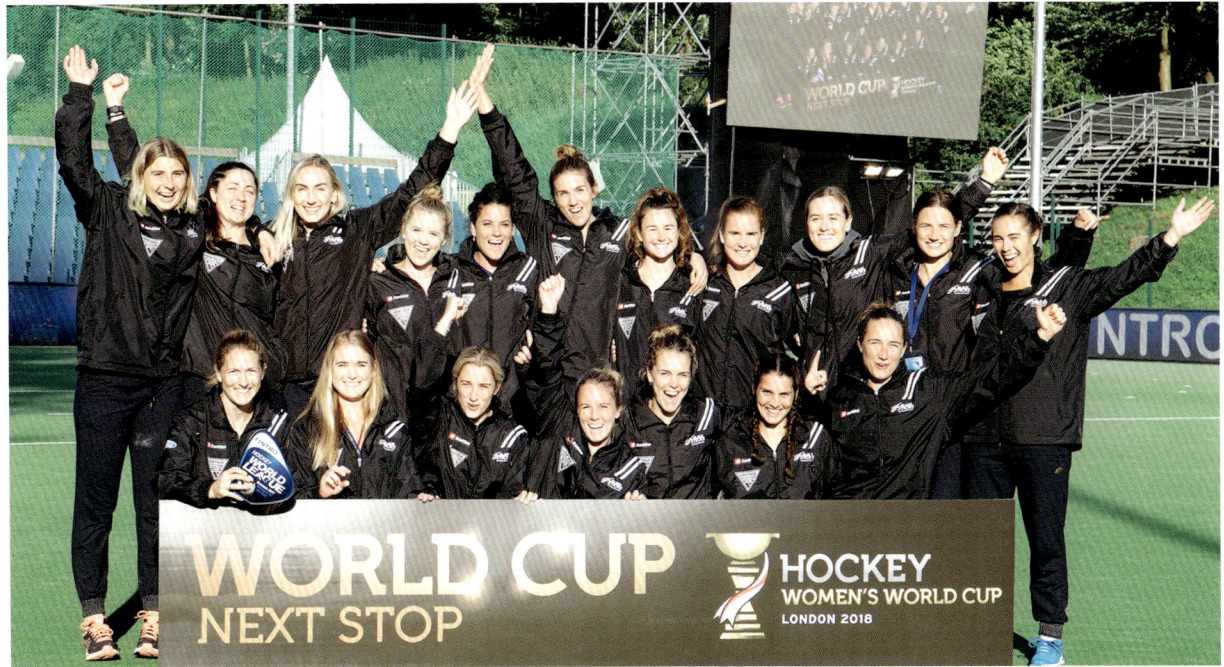

New Zealand finished third at the Fintro Hockey World League Semi-Final 2017 in Brussels, Belgium. // *Frank Uijlenbroek*

World Number Four – New Zealand

The entire team erupted as Ella Gunson fired home the fifth shoot-out goal as New Zealand sought to pull off a notable victory over the Netherlands in the Hockey World League Semi-Finals.

Elation turned to dismay as the Netherlands called for an umpire review and the goal was disallowed as a result. The Netherlands went on to win the shoot-out and, in beating China, they also won the entire competition.

New Zealand regrouped to beat Korea by a solitary goal, thus winning a bronze medal and securing their qualification for the 2018 World Cup, but this defeat really hurt.

The team had enjoyed a good tournament, beating every other team except Belgium on their way to the semi-final round. They had taken special delight in defeating Oceania rivals Australia by a workmanlike 2-0 scoreline and head coach Mark Hager was pleased with his side's progress to that point.

Their performance in the pool matches at the Hockey World League Final, in front of a home crowd in Auckland, gave the head coach far less joy.

A 4-0 drubbing at the hands of the Dutch kicked things off. This was followed by a 2-1 loss to lower-ranked Korea and a 3-1 beating by the USA.

The Black Sticks were at the bottom of their pool, meaning they would face Argentina in the quarter-finals. This was a daunting prospect as Argentina were unbeaten at that point and were playing some sublime hockey.

Things didn't start well as Argentina took the lead within two minutes. The Black Sticks regrouped and, with captain Stacey Michelsen driving the team forwards, they staged a remarkable comeback. The final 2-1 scoreline didn't do justice to a game that was energetic, aggressive and absorbing.

The final saw New Zealand face the Netherlands, a team who were fast becoming their nemesis. And the Dutch were in an invincible mood. The Black Sticks held out until the 24th minute but then Kelly Jonker, Maria Verschoor and Laurien Leurink all found their way past the New Zealand defence to consign the home team to a 3-0 defeat and the silver medal.

The Commonwealth Games was the Black Sticks' last major event in preparation for the Vitality Hockey Women's World Cup and they completed that tournament with a stylish performance, beating England in the semi-finals in a shoot-out before demolishing Australia in a 4-1 rout to claim the gold medal for the first time in their history.

Stacey Michelsen driving the team forward.
// *Frank Uijlenbroek*

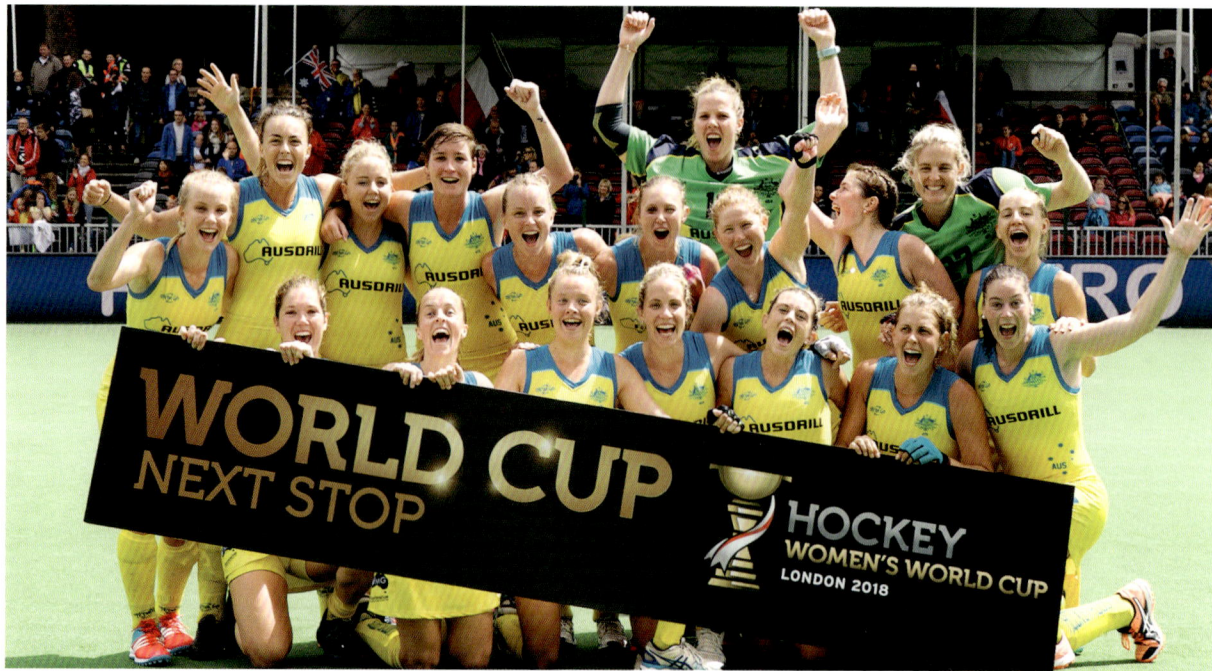

A fifth-place finish at the Fintro Hockey World League Semi-Final 2017 in Brussels, Belgium earned Australia a World Cup ticket. // *Frank Uijlenbroek*

World Number Five – Australia

Australia arrived at the Hockey World League Semi-Final in Brussels full of hope and with a new-look squad. A chastening fifth-place finish certainly gave head coach Paul Gaudoin plenty to think about. Poor performances against Oceania rivals New Zealand and China were the team's undoing and the Hockeyroos found themselves unable to qualify for the Hockey World League Final, instead facing a battle with Italy to qualify for the World Cup. In the event, they took the all-important fifth spot but not before a few nervous moments on the part of Gaudoin and his team.

A few months later Australia bounced back to win the Oceania Cup, beating New Zealand twice in the process. A 2-1 win in the round robin stages was followed by a 2-0 victory in the final. Jane Claxton and Kristina Bates were the scorers who helped Australia re-establish themselves at the top of the continental's pecking order.

The Gold Coast 2018 Commonwealth Games was Australia's chance to get some top-quality opposition in front of a loud home crowd. Things went smoothly as the host nation won all bar one of their pool matches. A 1-1 draw with New Zealand was the only glitch.

The semi-finals saw them beat fellow World Cup contenders India by a solitary goal and then they faced none other than their nearest neighbours New Zealand in the final.

The recent history between the two teams made for compelling reading. New Zealand had knocked the Hockeyroos out of the Rio Olympic Games and finished ahead of them in the Hockey World League Semi-Final. The Black Sticks had also jumped above Australia in the FIH Hero World Rankings.

And this was to be yet another time Australia were thwarted by New Zealand. The 4-1 loss was as tough as it could get for the team and once again Gaudoin was back to the drawing board trying to rediscover Australia's winning formula.

The head coach did not hold back as he assessed his team's performance at the Gold Coast Commonwealth Games. 'It was pleasing to make the final but our performance was disappointing. I think credit to New Zealand, who played a very good game and came to play. We need to learn from that.

'We need to recognise when you get an opportunity, you've got to take it. We've got to be more ruthless in terms of when we play big matches. That's important for us. I'd rather this be now than the World Cup but at the same time, when you play in a final, it's an opportunity to get that feeling and the pressure that goes with that. We didn't get the result we wanted. We didn't deserve to get the result we wanted on our performance on that day. We want to make sure we're learning, building and improving every time we get an opportunity to represent Australia.'

But Australia is a nation that is used to producing winners and with goal-scorers such as Kathryn Slattery, Madison Ratcliffe, Georgina Morgan and Emily Smith in the side, the Hockeyroos knew they had both the time and the talent to rebuild before London 2018. There was also the prospect of the return of Jodie Kenny after the birth of her son Harrison. If the towering penalty corner specialist was fit in time for London, the Hockeyroos would have another potent weapon in their armoury.

Australia's history at the World Cup was a bright one. They had been at every World Cup since 1981 and in that time they had twice been crowned champions – in 1994 and 1998. They also had three silver medals and a bronze. With Kenny back, the team gelling under their charismatic coach and an innate ability to back themselves in the big tournaments, this had all the makings of being a good year for the Hockeyroos.

World Number Six – Germany

Two gold medals and a total of six medals from World Cup appearances as first West Germany and then Germany had made Die Danas the fourth most successful team in women's World Cup history. That glorious past had not been evident in recent years, however. While Germany's early performances were a string of first- to- fourth-place finishes, the team had managed only seventh, two eighth places and a fourth place since 2002.

However, Germany were a team that had been making steady and planned progress over the previous few years and an Indoor World Cup gold medal won in February 2018 was a real boost to the squad. Many of the World Cup contenders were part of the indoor team and were looking to 'do the double'.

The team sealed their place in the Vitality Hockey Women's World Cup London 2018 when they won all their pool matches and then beat South Africa to reach the final four of the Hockey World League Semi-Final in Johannesburg. This was followed by a stunningly composed display in their semi-final to beat Argentina – a performance that showed just what the squad were capable of. They then lost in the final to USA, a match that saw the two sides locked at 1-1 when the final whistle blew. Unusually for Germany, it was the shoot-out where they came undone. If there is one team that can match the Germans for coolness under pressure, it is USA. The USA team live by their 'no fear' motto and, after teenager Erin Matson put the ball away to make it 3-2, the German team were forced to accept the silver medal.

The Hockey World League Final in Auckland gave former Belgium international Xavier Reckinger, Germany's new head coach, a chance to see his team perform under big-match pressure. Although the team started well enough with wins over England and China, they then fell by the wayside, suffering defeat in the pool to Argentina before losing another shoot-out, this time to Korea. This put Die Danas in the losing quarter-finalists' match, again facing Argentina. A loss and a sixth-place finish was not the year-end that Germany or Reckinger wanted.

However, Reckinger had been appointed on the same morning that the squad list had to be announced for the Hockey World League Final. A bright and innovative coach, with a rich pool of talent to select from, Reckinger knew it was a race against time to get the squad to where he wanted. But, equally, this was a challenge he was happy to accept.

'I am lucky in that I worked with the squad for the Rio cycle,' said Reckinger. 'So I know them well. I am only planning on tweaking the processes that Jami [Jamilon Mülders, the previous head coach of Germany] has put in place and building on his foundations. There may be more changes after the World Cup, that I will assess later, but I think we have a very good balance between the experienced players and the exciting new players.'

Confidence was re-established in February when Germany hosted the men's and women's Indoor World Cup. It was a spectacular event, with thousands of spectators filing through the doors of the Max-Schmeling-Halle every day. Germany's women's team were supreme and many of that squad were given the chance to do the double.

'This was a debate for me,' said Reckinger. 'On the one hand, letting the players go for the Indoor World Cup ate into my preparation time, and we don't have a lot of that anyway. On the other hand, here is a chance for the players to experience World Cup hockey, with an intense atmosphere and a large crowd. These are experiences that the players can learn from. And they have also learnt how to be winners on an international stage. That is all valuable. I think, on balance, it is worth losing that preparation time with them. We will see.'

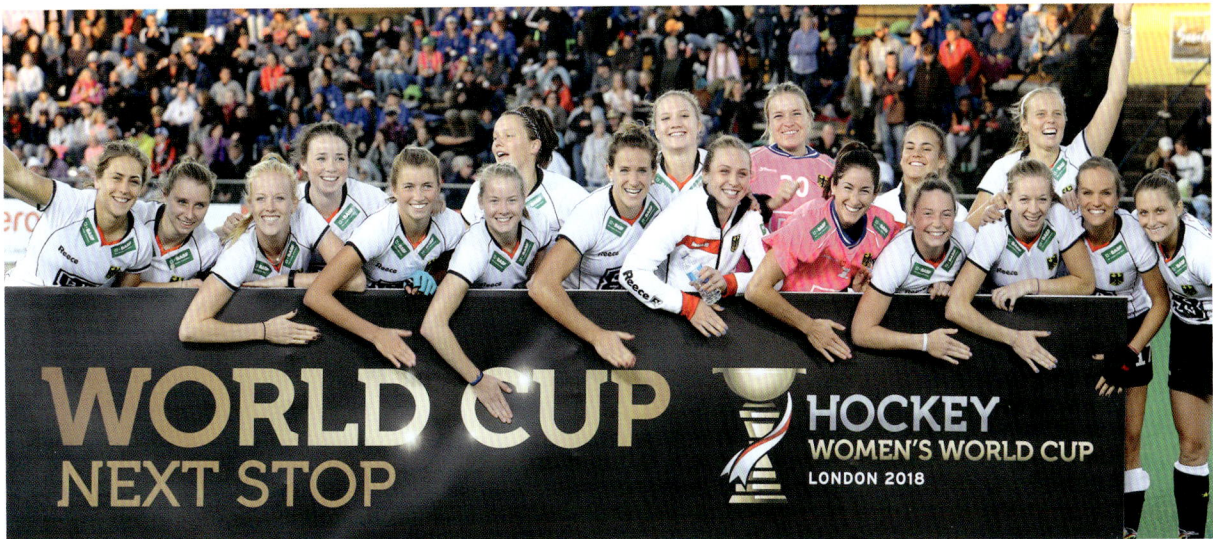

Germany finished second at the Hockey World League Semi-Final 2017 in Johannesburg, South Africa. // *Rodrigo Jaramillo*

World Number Seven – USA

There is always a palpable air of excitement when USA take to the field. At the 2014 Hockey World Cup the world saw what they were capable of. Head coach at the time Craig Parnham had taken a group of extremely dedicated athletes, whose work rate was second to none, and had given them an extra layer of nous and tactical ingenuity. The team that went to The Hague were ranked 11th and finished fourth.

Under Janneke Schopman, who replaced Parnham in 2015, the side grew in tactical awareness. The canny Dutch-woman knew what it took to win and suddenly her team appeared more grown up, their 'do-or-die' attitude tempered with some European logic. In Melissa Gonzalez, Schopman had found a perfect leader. The hard grafting defender never stopped running and would, if needs be, drag her team across the line. She was backed up by the cool-headed and razor-sharp Michelle Vitesse. The team were also full of exuberant talent, with exceptional teenage attacker Erin Matson a prime example.

The USA success story just kept rolling on. After a pretty average London 2012 Olympic Games, everything changed. A move to the headquarters of women's hockey at Spooky Nook, Pennsylvania was the catalyst. The appointment of Parnham was inspired and in 2014, when USA won the Champions Challenge in Glasgow, the journey began for real.

Glasgow earned them the reputation as the team that just never gave up. This was true of both the semi-final and the final of the HWL Semi-Finals in Johannesburg. First USA came from 1-0 down against England with just three minutes remaining and then they won the subsequent shoot-out. In the final, they were 1-0 down to Germany and, with two minutes remaining, they took the match to a shoot-out – and won.

London 2018 was USA's ninth appearance at a World Cup and they arrived at the event full of optimism, after a series of good performances in which they had beaten higher-ranked opposition in major competitions. In 2016, they won bronze at the Champions Trophy and finished a strong Olympic campaign in fifth place. They also won gold at the Pan American Games in 2011 and 2015. Under Schopman, the team had developed the strategy to match the work ethic.

World Number Eight – China

China's first appearance at a World Cup came in 1990 when they finished sixth. The highest finish for the Asian team was in 2002, when they broke the hearts of the host nation, Australia, and took the bronze medal.

China had been at every World Cup since but the team's record was not great. In The Hague in 2014, it was another sixth-place finish when they lost 4-0 to New Zealand. Many of the 2014 team had become senior members of the squad and, in Brussels at the Hockey World League Semi-Final, China looked to be in a good state. They began slowly, as was their habit at major events, but they were strong from the quarter-finals onwards and took the game to the Netherlands in the final, losing 2-0 but joyfully securing their place at the World Cup.

It is always uncertain which team China are going to bring to each tournament. Head coach Jamilon Mülders, who took charge of the China national team in October 2017, suggested that the squad that had earned the right to play in London was not necessarily the squad that would be seen at the World Cup. While several stronger players would be returning to the squad after recovering from injuries, the same number would be rested for the forthcoming Asian Games, which were scheduled for the middle of August 2018. 'The China Hockey Federation place a lot of importance on the Asian Games,' explained the German coach, who was learning to speak Chinese but carried out most of his coaching with the help of a translator. 'For me, that might make things difficult but my priorities for this year are clear. We will see what happens.'

USA earned their World Cup ticket with a stylish first-place finish at the Hockey World League Semi-Final 2017 in Johannesburg, South Africa // *Rodrigo Jaramillo*

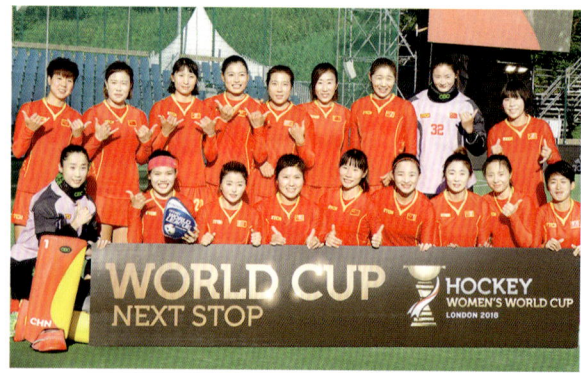

China sealed their spot in London with a second-place finish at the Fintro Hockey World League Semi-Final 2017 in Brussels, Belgium. // *Frank Uijlenbroek*

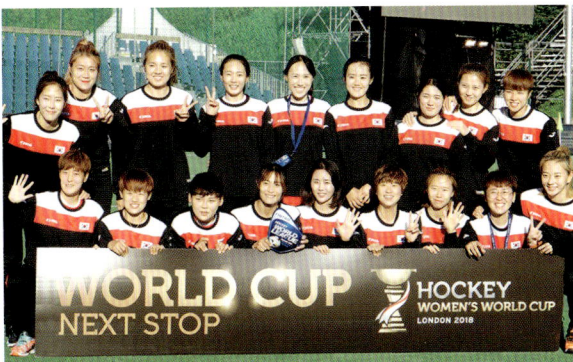

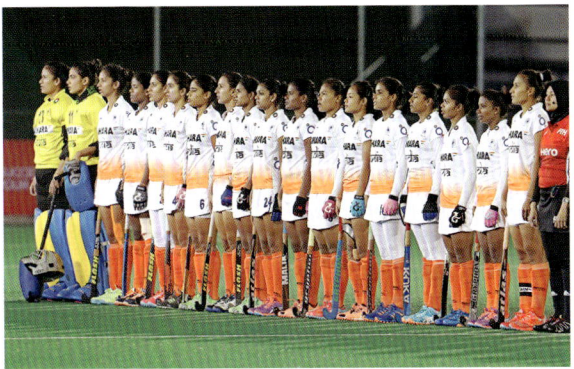

A fourth-place finish in Belgium at the Fintro Hockey World League Semi-Final 2017 was enough to secure Korea a world cup place. // *Frank Uijlenbroek*

India's victory at the 2017 Asia Cup was enough to earn them a place at the Vitality Hockey Women's World Cup in London. // *Rodrigo Jaramillo*

World Number Nine – Korea

Korea had been to the past eight World Cup competitions, although their performances, with the exception of a bronze medal in 1990, were mediocre. Two fifth-place finishes, two sixth places, a seventh and a ninth indicated that Korea were a team lacking the final polish that could turn a consistent team into a championship-winning team.

The Korea performance in Brussels at the Hockey World League Semi-Final confirmed this analysis. Korea were good enough to reach the semi-finals, and hence qualify for the World Cup, but they couldn't match China for tactical nous or New Zealand for physicality. They also lost 9-0 to a rampant Netherlands earlier in the tournament. That said, in Cheon Seul Ki and Cheon Eunbi, Korea boasted excellent goalscorers and their defence was disciplined and hard-working.

World Number Ten – India

India women's hockey team had been making steady progress in the previous few years, moving up the FIH Hero World Rankings as well as making the cut for the major events. They qualified for the 2016 Olympic Games on the back of a strong Hockey World League campaign in 2015 and they earned their place in London after a convincing win over their Asia rivals China in the Asia Cup.

The coaching team had been through some upheaval with head coach Sjoerd Marijne moving to the men's national team and being replaced by Harendra Singh. After India men returned from the Gold Coast 2018 Commonwealth Games without a medal, Marijne found himself back in charge of the women's team and Singh was moved to take charge of the men's side.

Lalremsiami is the youngest player in our team. I remember how, when I was 15, I played in my first World Cup and it was just so exciting. She brings an extra energy that we feed off.

Going into London, Korea were also able to call on the services of one of their most enduring goalscorers, Park Mi Hyun, a player who instilled grit into her side whenever she took to the field. At 32, Park Mi Hyun was rested as much as she was played, but when she did come on to the pitch, things happened.

Coach Huh Sang Young would need other players to replicate some of Park Mi Hyun's physical strength and tactical intelligence if Korea were to find a way for his skilful but tactically naive side to outmanoeuvre the opposition. At the end of the Hockey World League Semi-Final, team captain Kim Jongeun said: 'Every time we play a European side, we learn a little more.'

Sjoerd Marijne had a way of connecting with his players and, as his team attempted to achieve their highest ever finish at a World Cup – they made the semi-finals in 1974 and since then had finished no higher than ninth – the mantra going around the Eve's camp was that this was a team who wanted to write their own history and change how women's hockey was seen in India.

Certainly they brought to London all the flair and style that the hockey-loving nation is famous for, plus the work ethic and structure that has developed as a result of their experiences in the Hockey World League and at the Rio 2016 Olympic Games. In Rani, Savita, Vandana Katariya and Navjot Kaur, they had masses of experience – and, while they clearly loved working for Harendra Singh, in Sjoerd Marijne, they had a head coach who was giving his team a winning mentality.

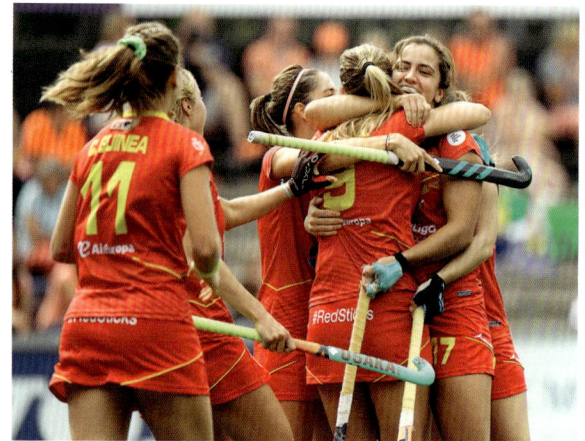

Spain finished seventh at the Fintro Hockey World League Semi-Final, which was enough to secure World Cup qualification place. // *Frank Uijlenbroek*

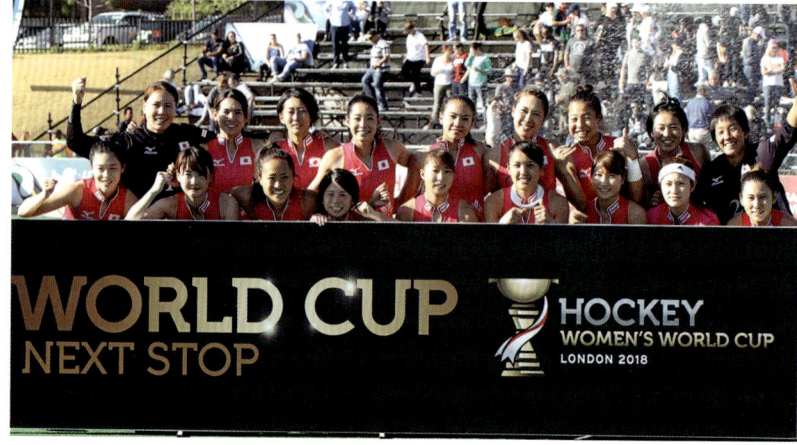

A sixth-place spot at the Hockey World League Semi-Final in Johannesburg, South Africa won Japan's Cherry Blossoms the chance to compete at the Vitality Hockey Women's World Cup. // *Rodrigo Jaramillo*

World number 11 – Spain

Spain women were the 13th team to qualify for the Vitality Hockey Women's World Cup in London. This was the Spanish women's 11th foray into World Cup competition. Their fourth-place finish in Madrid in 2006 was their highest finishing place to date.

Spain did not qualify for the 2014 World Cup but the team revived under English coach Adrian Lock, with a fifth-place finish at the Rio 2016 Olympic Games and a convincing first place at Hockey World League Round Two in Valencia.

Qualification this time around came after they recorded a seventh-place finish at the Hockey World League Semi-Finals in Brussels. They held their nerve to beat the host nation Belgium in a shoot-out and, in doing so, increased their chances of qualifying for the World Cup.

The Netherlands won the EuroHockey Championships, which were Europe's continental qualifier and, because the Dutch had already qualified as winners of the Hockey World League in Brussels, a qualification spot was left clear for the Red Sticks, who were the next highest-ranked finishers at both Hockey World League Semi-Final events (Johannesburg and Brussels).

Since then Lock and his team had been continuing to develop a team culture that suited the players. Hard work, taking responsibility and being accountable for their own processes and outcomes and an energetic and innovative style of play now characterise the team – Spain might have entered the event as underdogs, but as Lock said with a smile, 'you can expect some surprises at this World Cup'.

Julia Pons of Spain.
// *Frank Uijlenbroek*

World Number 12 – Japan

Thanks to host nation England finishing in the top five in Johannesburg at the HWL Semi-Final, the sixth-place finisher at the event also qualified for the 2018 World Cup. So, despite losing to a lower-ranked South Africa (WR:14) in the fifth/sixth play-off, Japan (WR:12) would be making their eighth appearance at the World Cup. The Cherry Blossoms' 1-0 win in Johannesburg over England (WR: 2) and 2-0 victory against Asian rivals India (WR:10) was a sign that coach Anthony Farry was getting his team to a place where they could compete with the top teams.

Japan first contested a World Cup in 1978, when they finished a creditable sixth. Since then, their highest position was fifth in Madrid in 2006. With Tokyo 2020 just around the corner, Japan's national team were looking for a good performance in London as a precursor to a successful performance in front of home crowds just two years later.

One of the biggest challenges facing the Cherry Blossoms was their ability to perform on the big stage. If the largely home-supporting crowds of London 2012 and Rio 2016 were replicated in Tokyo 2020, then coach Anthony Farry was determined his players would be ready to benefit from it. While Japan's prospects of winning a medal in London at this World Cup were slim, Farry was playing the longer game.

'We have a few athletes that have played in either a World Cup or at the Olympic Games so the experienced athletes can share their feelings with the less experienced ones,' said the Australian. 'However, one of the greatest things to see is the excitement and energy of athletes that comes from seeing and experiencing something for the first time.

'You can simulate and talk about scenarios all you like, but until you are faced with the reality of the situation it's hard to pinpoint exactly how they will react. We'll be keeping our focus on what we can control, our processes and really looking to have fun and enjoy the atmosphere.'

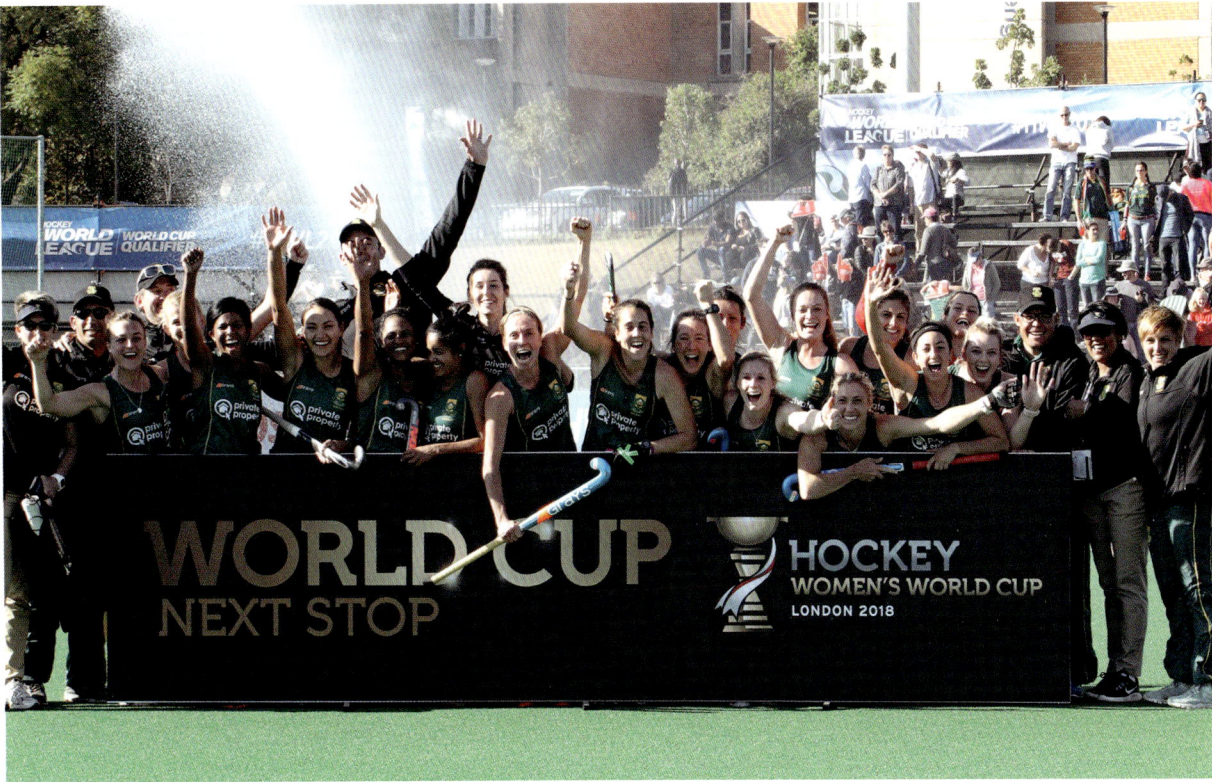

South Africa finished fifth in front of a home crowd at the 2017 Hockey World League Semi-Final, securing a World Cup place in the process. // *Rodrigo Jaramillo*

World Number 14 – South Africa

South Africa booked their place in the World Cup thanks to a strong finish to the HWL Semi-Finals on home turf in Johannesburg. Having missed out on the 2016 Olympic Games, this team were determined to ensure they would be on the plane to London to contest their sixth World Cup. The African nation had been present at every edition since South Africa was allowed on to the international stage following the end of apartheid.

The best finish by South Africa to date was their first appearance in 1998 when they took seventh place. In The Hague in 2014, they finished ninth, after beating two higher-ranked teams (England and Japan). Having spent one Olympic cycle away from top international competition, South Africa were keen to prove their credentials and move back up the rankings from 14th place.

South Africa's place at the World Cup was confirmed when they won the African Championships, but as captain Nicolene Terblanche pointed out, the continental championships are not a true testing ground. South Africa's nearest competitor in terms of rankings was Ghana, who had a world ranking of 29. Coach Sheldon Rostron said the best preparation his players had was a series of regular matches against the junior men's national teams. While their preparations for the event may not have matched those of the nations who were able to play test matches across the globe, there was little doubt that South Africa's performance would, as usual, be full of heart and endeavour.

World Number 15 – Belgium

The last team of the 16 to qualify for the Vitality Hockey Women's World Cup, Belgium's Red Panthers, were certainly worthy of their place at the event, following a terrific few months of ever-improving performances.

At the 2014 Rabobank Hockey World Cup in The Hague, Belgium finished in last position, beaten by England in a shoot-out in the 11/12 play-off. Since then a new coaching structure and a new head coach, plus the backing of the Royal Belgian Hockey Association, had transformed hockey for the women's national team.

A silver medal at the Rabobank EuroHockey Championships in 2017, where they lost to the Netherlands, was Belgium's first medal at a major competition since 1978, when they won a bronze at the World Cup in Madrid. But the Red Panthers were already beginning to show their bite as they put in some good performances in the Hockey World League Semi-Final on home turf in Brussels in 2017.

At that event, Belgium opened their account with a 9-0 win over Malaysia and then, buoyed by the confidence of that result, they beat high-ranked New Zealand 1-0. Over the remainder of that tournament the team recorded two more drawn matches but lost the subsequent shoot-outs to Korea and Spain – again both teams who were higher ranked.

Those shoot-out losses and the subsequent nervous wait to see if they had qualified for the World Cup proved to be character building and by the time the EuroHockey Championships came around, Belgium were determined to show that they were no flash-in-the-pan side.

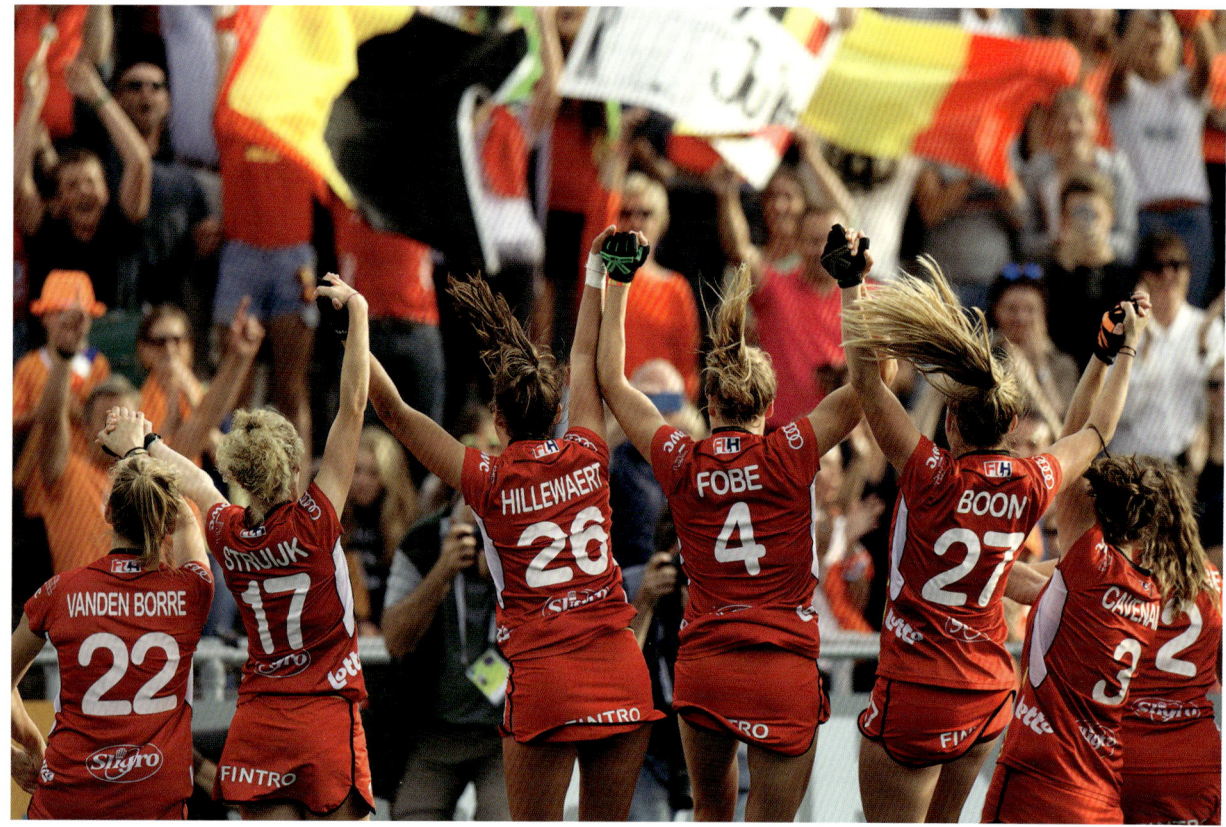

Belgium finished eighth at the Fintro Hockey World League Semi-Final, a position that secured the Red Panthers a berth at the Vitality Hockey Women's World Cup. // *Frank Uijlenbroek*

Head coach Niels Thijssen, who took over the role in 2017, had had time to work with his charges and the first thing to be implemented was a tough physical fitness regime. At the beginning of his tenure as head coach, Thijssen said the team would never be able to compete at the top level in terms of skills and tactics until each player could keep going for the duration of the game.

With the physical fitness covered, their mental capacity to bounce back from disappointment much improved and a talented group of players within the squad, Belgium were heading to London with high hopes of a good showing.

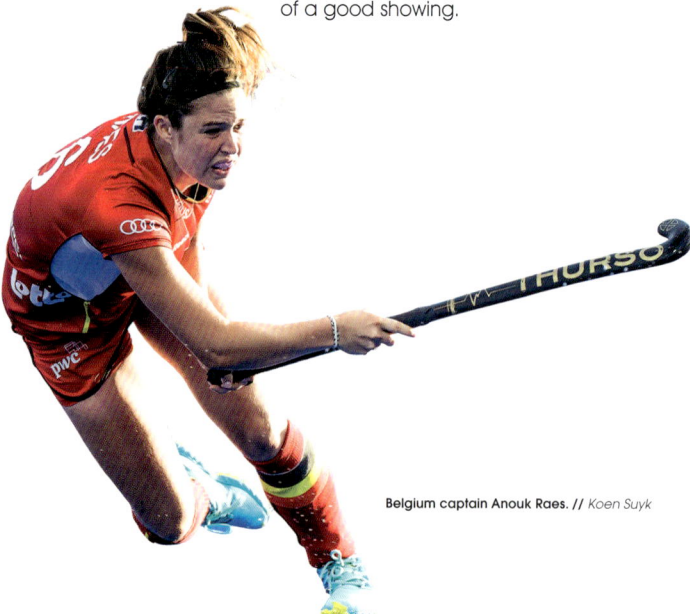

Belgium captain Anouk Raes. // *Koen Suyk*

World Number 16 – Ireland

Ireland women were making their first World Cup appearance since 2002, having been assured of a ticket to London on the back of a strong Hockey World League campaign and results going their way in the continental championships. The Green Army performed well at the Hockey World League Semi-Final in Johannesburg, claiming seventh place thanks to a battling 2-1 win over India in their final match which left them on the verge of World Cup qualification. Their Vitality Hockey Women's World Cup spot was confirmed a few months later when Australia and New Zealand – two teams that had already achieved qualification for London – reached the final of the Oceania Cup continental championship, opening the door for Ireland who were next in line.

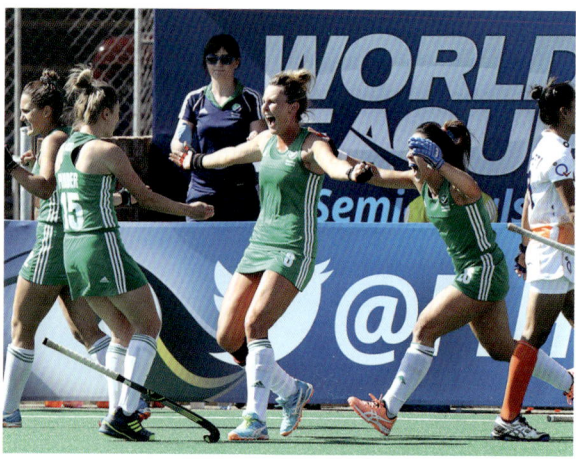

A seventh place finish at the Hockey World League Semi-Final in Johannesburg, South Africa sent Ireland to their first World Cup since 2002. // *Frank Uijlenbroek*

After a 16-year absence, Ireland were looking forward to competing in their fourth World Cup following appearances at the Amsterdam 1986, Dublin 1994 and Perth 2002 events. Their best finishing position came on home soil at Dublin 1994, where they finished in 11th place. The team, coached by former Ireland men's international Graham Shaw, had more than enough talent to outstrip their previous best performance. With more than 250 international appearances to her name, the influential Shirley McCay commanded respect both on and off the field, while quicksilver attacker Anna O'Flanagan had earned a reputation as a feared goalscorer who could turn a game in the blink of an eye.

With just weeks to go, the Ireland team finally got a sponsor, which allowed them to play a series of training matches before the competition. Until then, the team had been virtually unfunded and training had had to fit around work and study.

World Number 17 – Italy

Italy women qualified for the Vitality Hockey Women's World Cup 2018 by virtue of a sixth-place finish at the Hockey World League Semi-Finals in Brussels. This was be Italy's first appearance at the event since 1976, when they finished tenth.

Qualification for the event was a remarkable achievement for the Italians, who were ranked 17th in the world and arrived at the Hockey World League Semi-Final as outsiders for qualification. Two draws with Korea and China, who were ranked several places higher, and a win over Scotland were enough to propel Italy into a finishing position that would give them a good opportunity of qualifying for the World Cup. Of all the teams making the journey to London, Italy were one of the shining examples of the opportunities offered by the Hockey World League for a lower-ranked team to improve and progress.

Preparations in the lead-up to the World Cup included international matches against Scotland, Russia, France, Germany, Ireland and Argentina. For head coach Roberto Carta, playing higher-ranked teams was a vital part of his team's preparations.

'The preparation matches were so important because they were very tough,' said Carta. 'We made lots of mistakes but the important thing was that we learnt from those mistakes. Every match can be seen as a victory whether you win or lose, so long as you have learnt from it. For me, making a mistake means finding a solution to ensure the same error is never made again.'

In an event situation, this approach works well. It means a team can improve as the tournament progresses, ironing out problems and finding solutions along the way. 'There is no such thing as perfection and every team can be beaten,' was Carta's defiant reply when asked how his side would fare against the Netherlands in their final Pool A match.

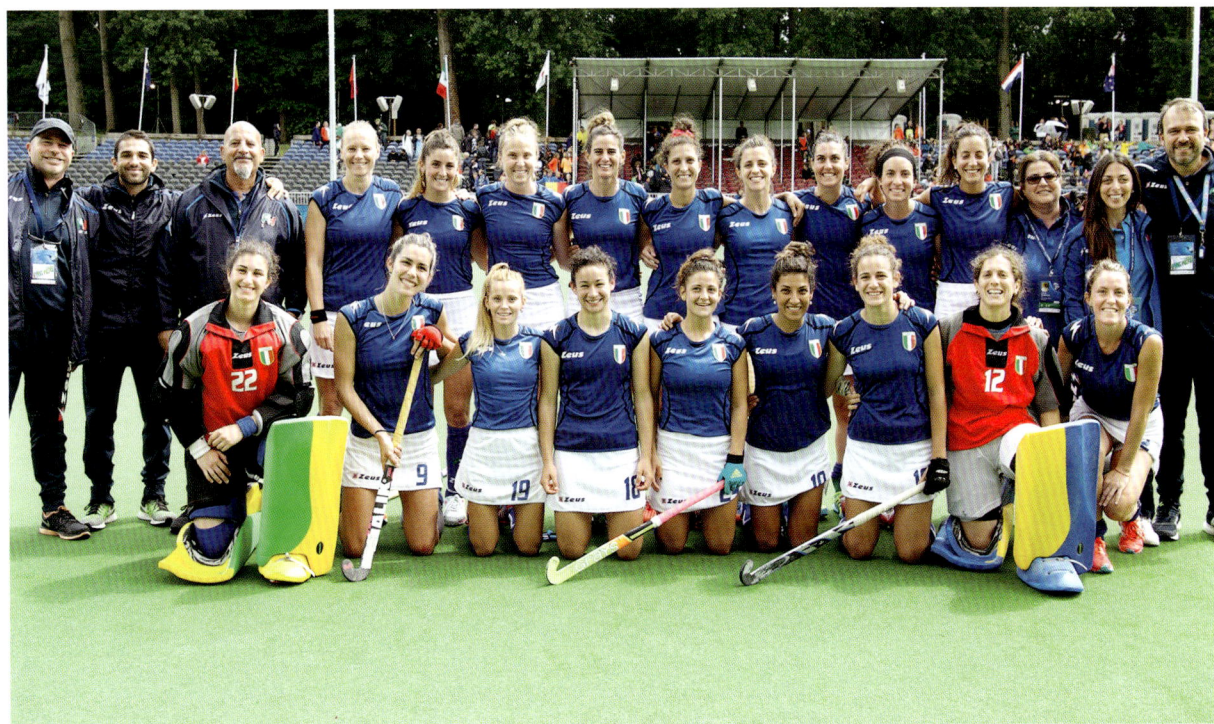

Italy finished in sixth place in Brussels at the Fintro Hockey World League Semi-Final, a performance that earned them World Cup qualification. // *Rodrigo Jaramillo*

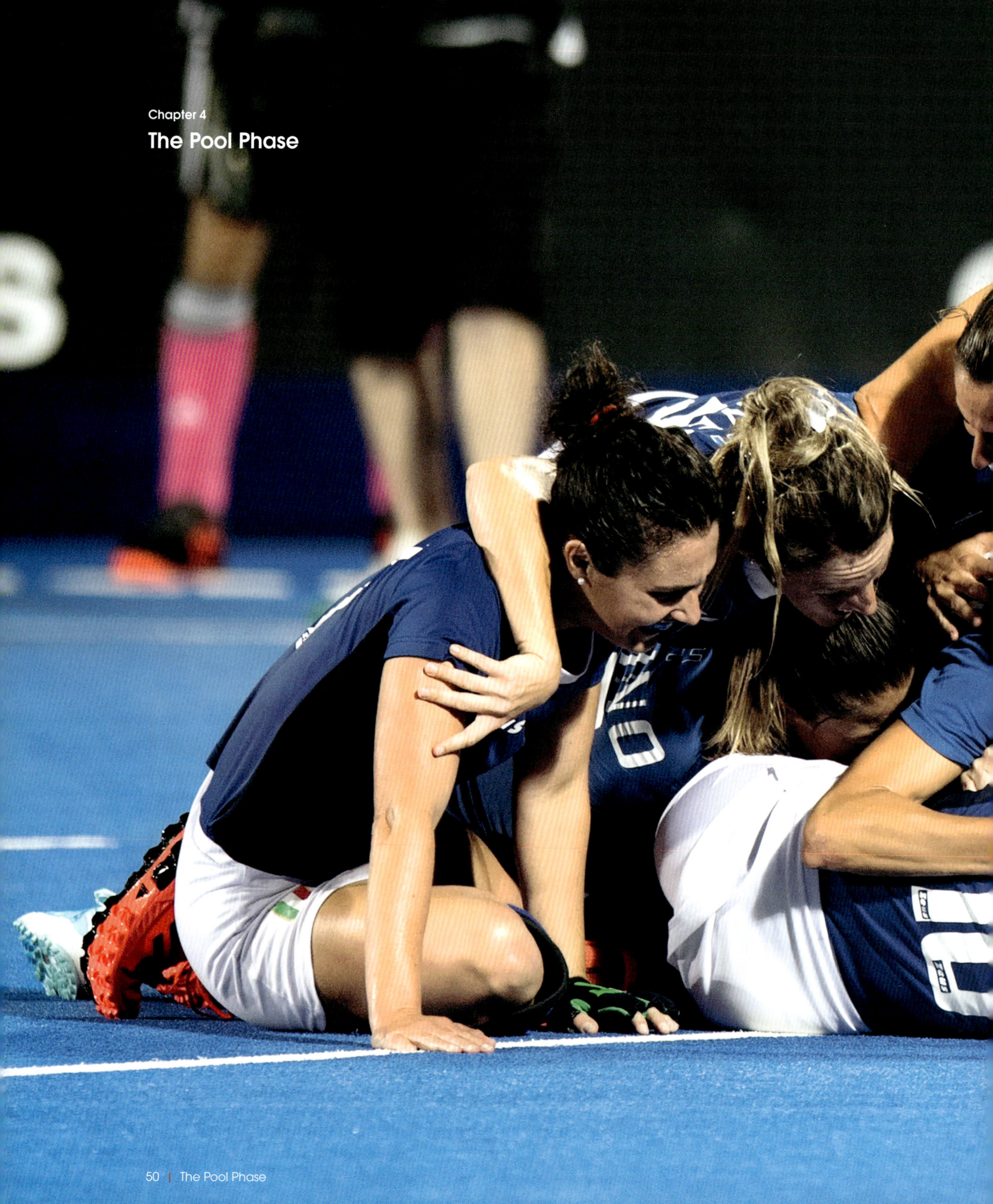

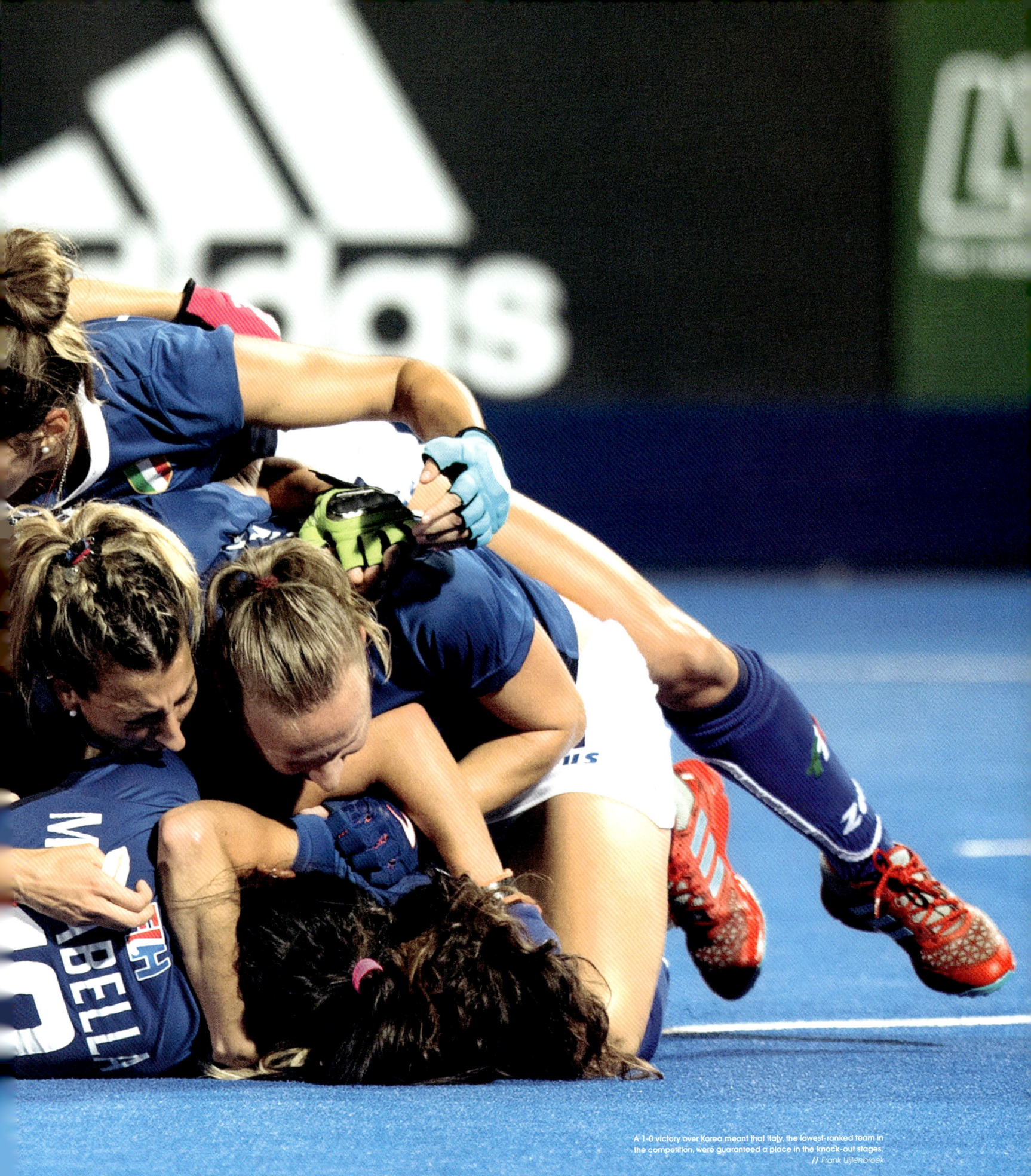

A 1-0 victory over Korea meant that Italy, the lowest-ranked team in the competition, were guaranteed a place in the knock-out stages.
// Frank Uijlenbroek

Chapter 4

The Pool Phase

Day 1 – Saturday 21 July 2018

Germany and Ireland excel as World Cup bursts into life

Four and a half years after the International Hockey Federation (FIH) revealed that England's bid to host the Hockey Women's World Cup 2018 had been successful, the opening day of the competition had finally arrived. At the time of the announcement back in November 2013, then FIH President Leandro Negre described England's proposal as being 'truly extraordinary', with praise quickly given by the sports minister of the British Government, Helen Grant, who stated that the country would 'deliver a truly outstanding tournament on the Olympic Park', and that the event would 'take the women's game to new heights'.

The hopes and expectations voiced by hockey's world governing body and the British Government ensured that the host nation was under no illusions about the requirement to put on a truly spectacular show. It was hardly surprising, considering the still-fresh memories of the sell-out crowds that flocked to the Riverbank Arena on an almost daily basis to watch the spellbinding hockey competitions at the London 2012 Olympic Games. The arrival of an event as iconic as the women's hockey World Cup on the Olympic Park – this time at the Lee Valley Hockey & Tennis Centre, the Olympic legacy facility built a few hundred metres from the site of the temporary Riverbank Arena – was a mouth-watering prospect for everyone connected to the sport.

The pressure of needing to at least match the staggering success that hockey enjoyed at the London 2012 Olympic Games intensified further in 2014 when the Netherlands set a new benchmark in terms of how to deliver a hockey World Cup. The joint men's and women's Rabobank Hockey World Cup 2014 was an epic showcase for the sport, with the Dutch organisers temporarily converting the 15,000-capacity Kyocera Stadium – home of football team ADO Den Haag – into one of the world's finest hockey arenas. With hundreds of thousands of fans witnessing the action over the duration of the 16-day competition, many were left wondering how London's Olympic Park – defeated by The Hague in the bidding process for the 2014 hockey World Cups – could possibly follow such a glorious celebration of the sport.

However, the pressure to deliver was nothing new to the city of London, which had faced a similar problem in the lead-up to the Olympic Games of 2012 following the jaw-dropping spectacle emphatically delivered by China at Beijing 2008. The secret to London's success in 2012 was never about trying to better what had been achieved in Beijing, it was simply a belief in their ability to do it differently and 'inspire a generation' of future sports stars. It was an approach that the Organising Committee of the Vitality Hockey Women's World Cup London 2018 would also adopt, and the results were there for all to see on the wonderful first day of the competition.

Thanks largely to the warmest of welcomes by the smiling faces of the Hockey Makers, England Hockey's vast army of experienced volunteers so named because they 'make the hockey happen', the fans who arrived at the main transport hub in nearby Stratford immediately knew that this was no ordinary hockey event. The spectators journeyed through the wonderful Queen Elizabeth Olympic Park along the Vitality Mile, soaking up the atmosphere as they made their way past numerous iconic London 2012 stadia still very much in use. They were heading to the site of a stadium long gone but definitely not forgotten.

The Riverbank Arena was the epicentre of Olympic hockey in 2012 but, following the conclusion of the Games, the area was redeveloped into parkland as part of the ongoing Olympic legacy for the city. It was a venue where moments of Olympic history were created, the stage where both the Netherlands, women and the men of Germany successfully defended the titles they had won in Beijing four years earlier. Despite those wonderful memories, it seemed unlikely that the hockey family would ever return en masse to the exact spot where those Olympic medals were won. Or so we thought.

The construction of a colossal stand at the Lee Valley Hockey and Tennis Centre certainly solved the significant problem of how the arena would cope with the huge demand for tickets to the showpiece event, but created a new problem for the fan village, which had previously been located where the temporary new terracing had been erected. The solution proved to be fitting for the occasion, with Fan Central being

Germany's Charlotte Stapenhorst shows supreme skill in her team's World Cup opener against Pool C opponents South Africa. // Rodrigo Jaramillo

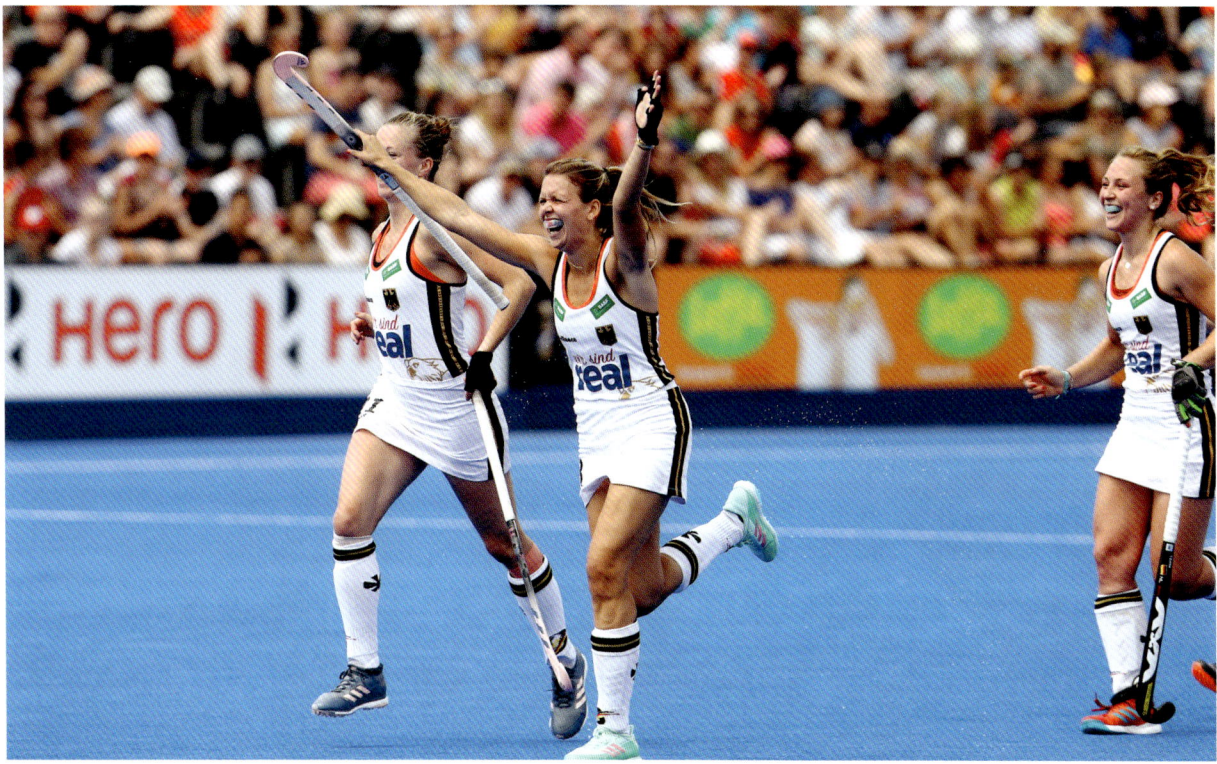

Anne Schröder shows her delight as Germany make an impressive start to their World Cup campaign. // *Rodrigo Jaramillo*

positioned on the exact spot where the Riverbank Arena once stood, creating a tangible connection to the memories of London 2012.

Being open to ticket holders and non-ticket holders alike, Fan Central would become the go-to destination for hockey fans from every competing nation. With a big screen, live music, numerous places to eat, drink and shop, an on-site display from The Hockey Museum as well as regular signing sessions from the World Cup athletes themselves – a hugely popular attraction throughout the event – it served to raise excitement levels even further on the road to Lee Valley. The anticipation reached even greater heights on the Walk of Stars, with the names and achievements of some of

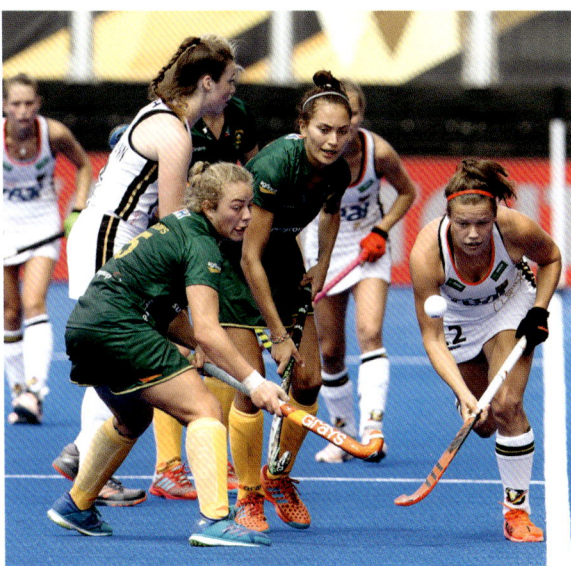

More fine work from Germany live-wire Charlotte Stapenhorst, moving down the left past South Africa's Simone Gouws. // *Rodrigo Jaramillo*

the greatest female hockey players of all time strategically placed on the pathway that guided fans to the venue.

For those lucky enough to be present on the opening day of World Cup action at the Lee Valley Hockey & Tennis Centre, it was a day that they would never forget. A sell-out 10,500 crowd packed into the stadium to witness two sensational matches in the opening session, not to mention a fly-past by the Red Arrows, the world-famous aerobatics display team, who thrilled the fans by decorating the sky with their familiar red, white and blue smoke trails. The hosts had left no stone unturned in their efforts to ensure that this event would not go unnoticed. The time had come for the teams to shine, and shine they did.

The opening match of the first session saw Germany, the world champions of 1976 and 1981 (as West Germany) take on African continental champions South Africa in Pool C, with the European giants completing a thoroughly deserved 3-1 victory. The result gave an early indication that the team coached by former Belgium men's international Xavier Reckinger were in form and very much ready to make a serious challenge for the title – although in a pool also containing the always-dangerous Argentina and unpredictable Spain, Germany knew that they could take nothing for granted.

Die Danas – who started the competition at sixth in the FIH Hero World Rankings, eight places higher than 14th-ranked South Africa – were very much the better side in the opening period, controlling possession and creating chances to force some good early saves from South Africa goalkeeper Phumelela Mbande. The inevitable opening goal of both the match and the 2018 edition of the women's hockey World Cup came a minute before the quarter-time break, with 22-year-old Viktoria Huse – who had only made

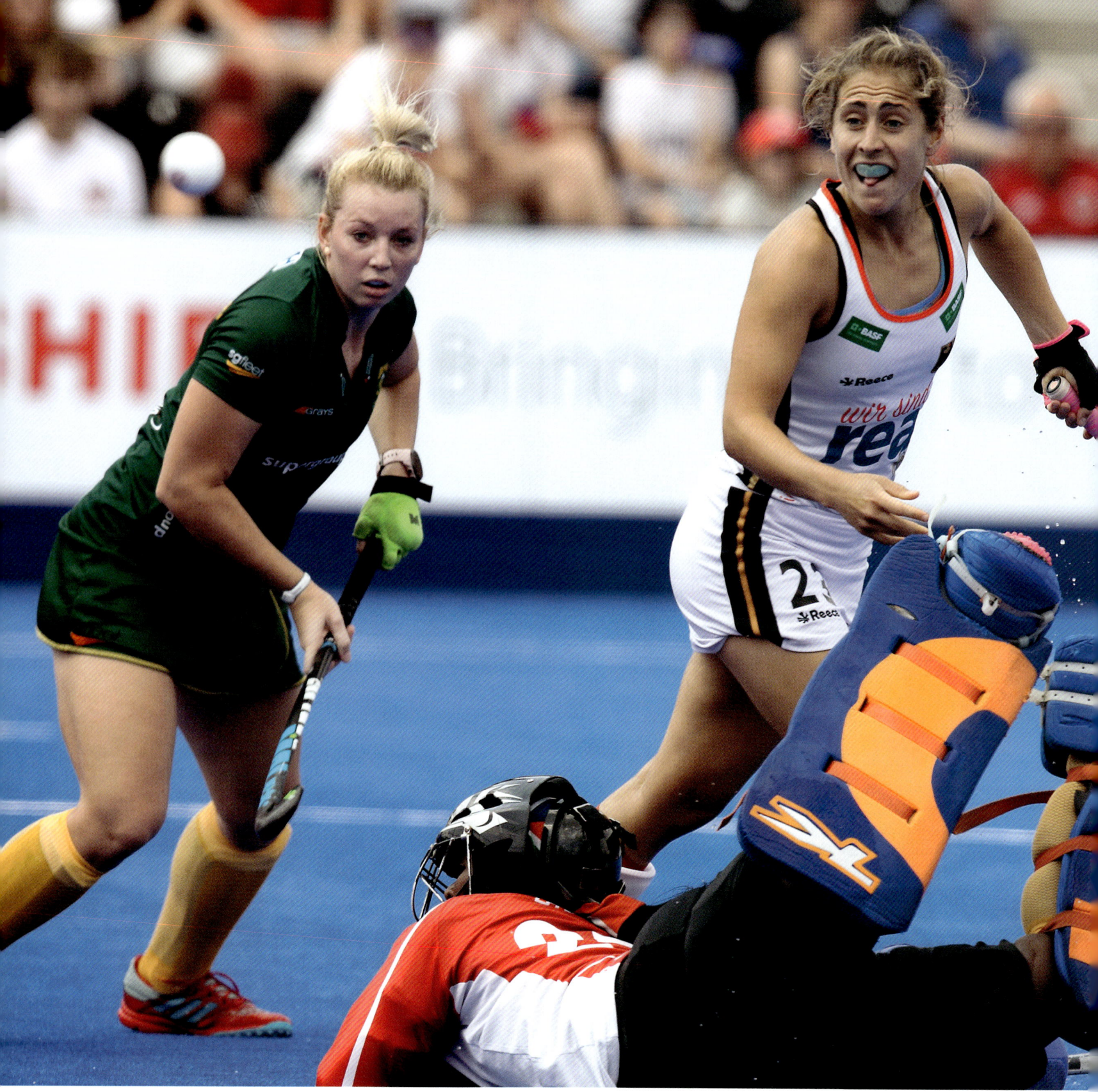

Germany's Marie Mävers scoops the ball over onrushing South Africa goalkeeper Phumelela Mbande. // *Rodrigo Jaramillo*

her senior international debut just over a year earlier – deceiving Mbande with a smart turn before slotting into an open goal.

Germany extended their advantage two minutes into the third quarter when the breathtakingly brilliant Charlotte Stapenhorst fired home from close range before South Africa,

who certainly grew in confidence as the game progressed, hit back thanks to a deflected penalty corner slap-shot from Lisa-Marie Deetlefs. It would prove to be only a consolation, however, with Huse claiming her second of the match with a 54th-minute penalty stroke to ensure that all three points went to Germany.

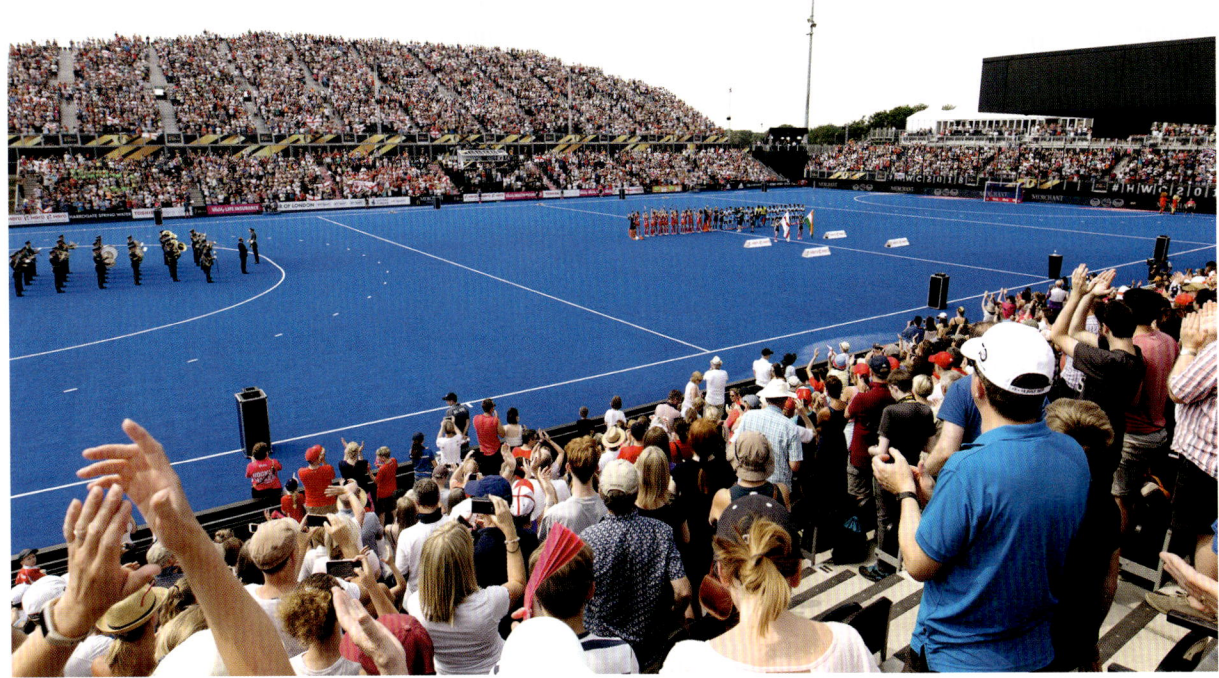

A massive crowd flocked to witness the host nation in action. // *Rodrigo Jaramillo*

Reacting to media questions about her team's impressive display in their opening fixture, Viktoria Huse certainly did not attempt to downplay Germany's ambitions in London. 'We are here to win, for sure,' said Huse. 'We have a good team and we all know each other very well. There is a great atmosphere in our camp.'

With only the pool winner being guaranteed a berth in the quarter-finals – the second and third-placed teams faced an additional knock-out match to qualify, while the nation that finished bottom would be eliminated – the importance of getting points on the board early was known to all 16 nations competing in London. The 10,500 fans in the stadium witnessing second-ranked England's Pool B clash with India (WR:10) were well aware of this fact and did their best to create a cacophony of noise throughout the anthems and into the early stages of the first half.

England thrilled the home fans by winning, although they failed to convert a penalty corner

England goalkeeper Maddie Hinch voices her frustrations.
// *Rodrigo Jaramillo*

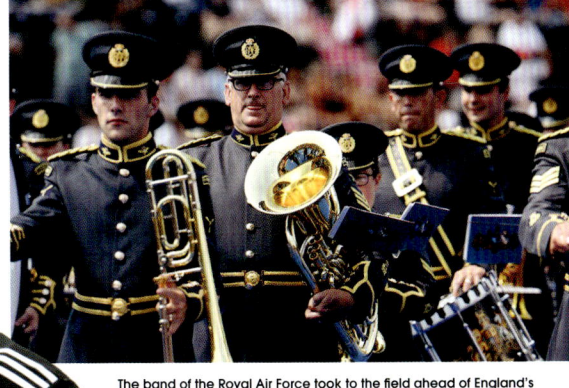

The band of the Royal Air Force took to the field ahead of England's opening World Cup match against India. // *Rodrigo Jaramillo*

in the opening seconds, but India – who were beaten 6-0 by England when the teams met in the bronze medal match at the Gold Coast 2018 Commonwealth Games – were far from overawed by either the occasion or the feverish passion of the partisan crowd. It was 'The Eves' rather than England who were the first team to have a shot in anger, with England goalkeeper Maddie Hinch comfortably kicking clear a strike from Navjot Kaur, a moment that triggered a change in mood from the England supporters, who suddenly realised that their team were in for a stern test.

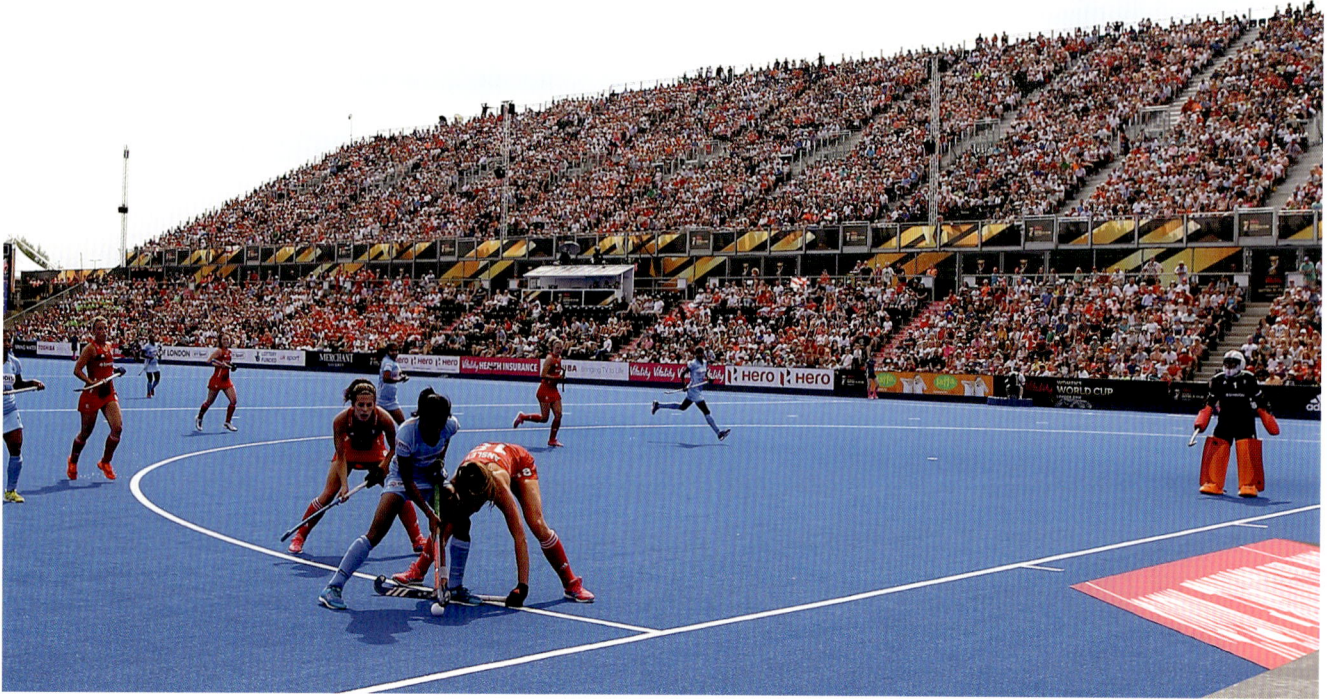

India on the attack as the fans witness the action from the huge West Stand. // *Rodrigo Jaramillo*

England were unusually wasteful in front of goal, something that they were left to rue in the 25th minute when Neha Goyal deflected home from close range to put India 1-0 up at half-time and give England head coach Danny Kerry plenty to think about.

The hosts spent most of the third quarter camped in Indian territory. Alex Danson and Lily Owsley both grew in stature as the game progressed, with their trademark attacking runs eliciting huge roars of approval from the fans. Owsley was particularly influential in the final quarter, and, when Kerry decided to replace Hinch with an attacking player with ten minutes remaining, the breakthrough that England had been searching for finally came. The excellent Owsley was the scorer of the equaliser, forcing home from close range six minutes from time after India failed to deal with a penalty corner, ensuring that the match finished with the honours even at 1-1.

Speaking after the game, Kerry said: 'I think as we are competitive people we can become fixated with the result and we are probably disappointed with it, but focusing on the level of performance, particularly in that second half, we absolutely dominated and I can't ask for more. The atmosphere was amazing, you could really feel the crowd getting behind us in that second half.'

The points dropped by England and India gave Pool B rivals USA (WR:7) and Ireland (WR:16) the opportunity to capitalise when they met in the opening match of the

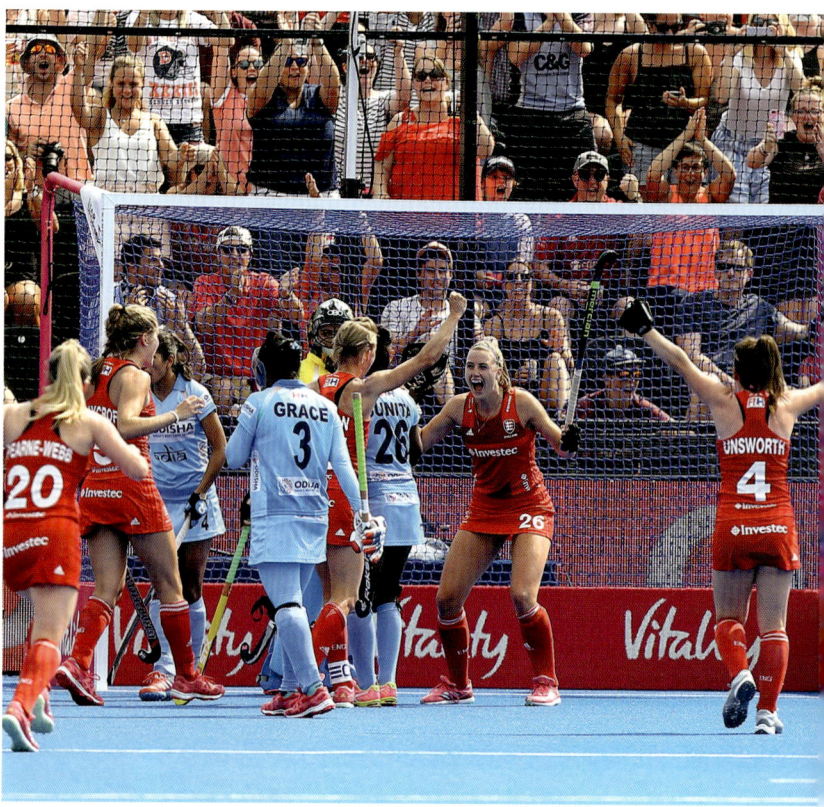

England's players rush to congratulate Lily Owsley on scoring the equaliser. // *Rodrigo Jaramillo*

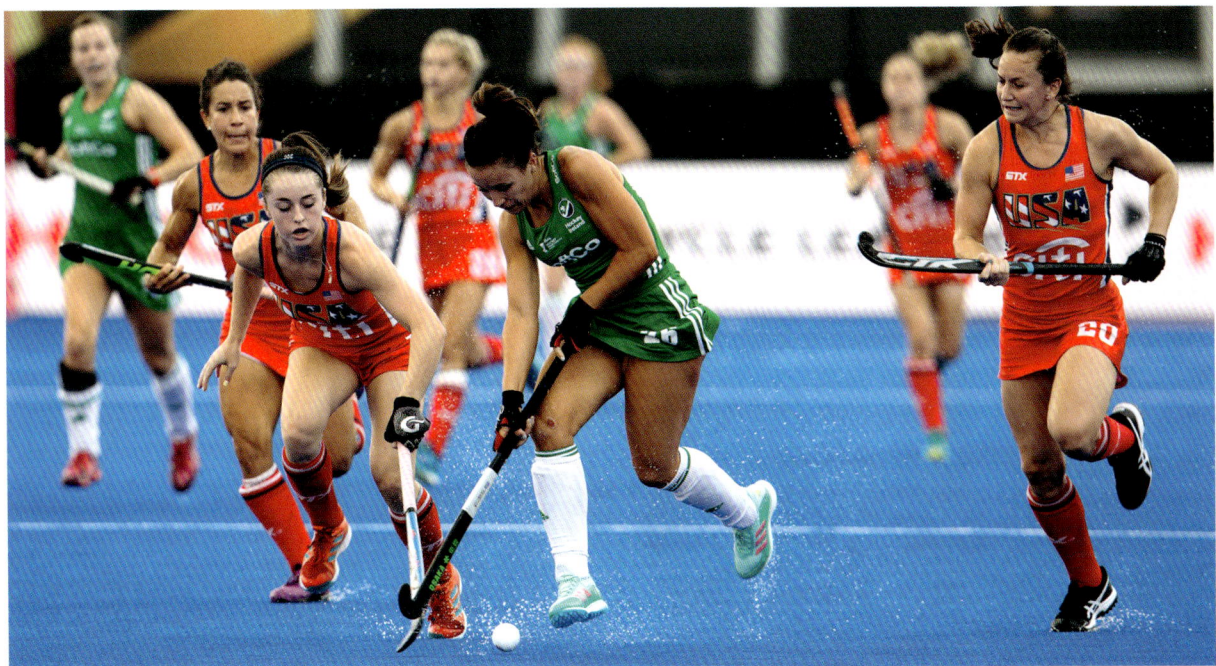

USA's teenage star Erin Matson (left) tries to stop Anna O'Flanagan on another Irish break forward. // *Rodrigo Jaramillo*

second session. It was unquestionably the best match of an extraordinary first day, with the second lowest-ranked team in the competition outplaying the nation that had finished fourth at the Rabobank Hockey World Cup 2014.

The Green Army – playing their first World Cup match for 16 years – were outstanding in the opening quarter, taking a 1-0 lead after just five minutes when Deirdre Duke produced a calm and collected finish after finding herself one-on-one with USA shot-stopper Jackie Briggs. That advantage was doubled thanks to a fierce penalty corner strike from Shirley McCay, but an ingenious penalty corner routine from the Americans, finished off by Margaux Paolino, made the score 2-1 at the end of the first quarter.

USA were very much in the ascendency in the second quarter, but they could not find a way past Ireland's outstanding goalkeeper Ayeisha McFerran, who was named Vitality Player of the Match. While McFerran was in sparkling form, her goal also led a charmed life when another high class USA penalty corner routine hit the crossbar ahead of half-time.

The killer blow arrived six minutes after half-time and again it was Duke who was the scorer, finishing off a rapid counter-attack with a close-range shot that rattled the pads of USA goalkeeper Briggs before bouncing over the goal line, and giving the team coached by former Ireland men's international Graham Shaw a stunning 3-1 victory that saw them finish the day as the surprise leaders of Pool B.

'We just decided to go out and enjoy it,' said delighted Ireland forward Anna O'Flanagan after the match. 'We had a certain amount of confidence that we could win this game, we had done a lot of homework on USA and we stuck to our plan. And you saw it out there, everyone was giving 100 per cent. The midfield and forwards were chasing back and defending, everyone was putting bodies on the line.'

A superb opening day of the competition was rounded off in style when 2014 World Cup finalists Australia (WR:5) got Pool D underway against Japan (WR:12). The balance of play between the Hockeyroos and the Cherry Blossoms was far closer than many would have predicted, with the first quarter finishing with the scores locked at 0-0 before Australia made the first mark on the scoreboard in the first minute of the second period. Rosie Malone was the scorer, expertly guiding a penalty corner past Japan's keeper Megumi Kageyama and into the roof of the net.

Seconds later, Kageyama was forced to spring into action again to deny an Australia team aiming to take total control, with the shot-stopper racing out to thwart Brooke Peris who was clear on goal. However, she could do little to stop Emily Hurtz, who touched home

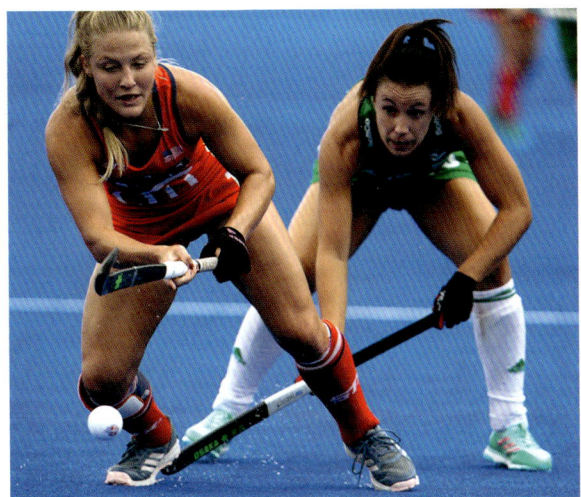

Ashley Hoffman of USA under pressure from Ireland's Anna O'Flanagan. // *Rodrigo Jaramillo*

Anna O'Flanagan on the charge for Ireland. // *Rodrigo Jaramillo*

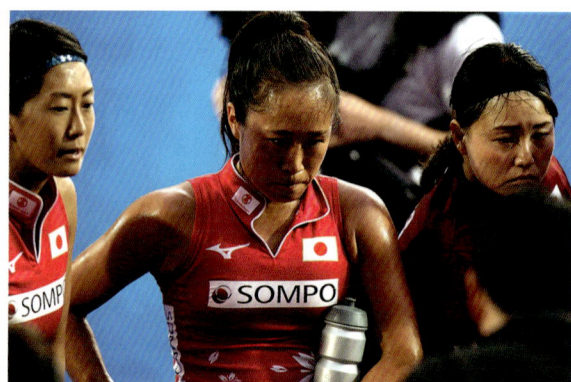

Shihori Oikawa and her Japan team-mates listen to coaching instructions ahead of the final quarter. // *Rodrigo Jaramillo*

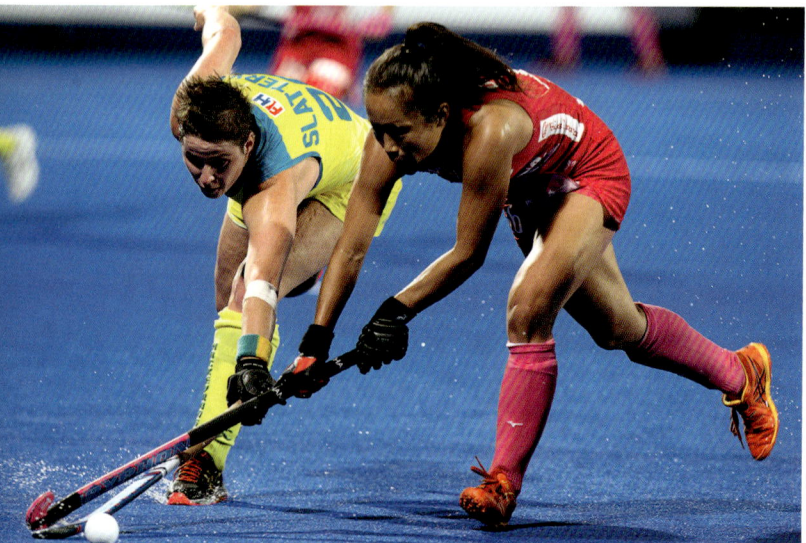

Australia's Kathryn Slattery and Shihori Oikawa of Japan battle for possession. // *Rodrigo Jaramillo*

Australia's second goal at the end of a wonderful sequence of passes through the midfield.

Things continued in much the same vein in the third quarter, with Japan demonstrating plenty of promise but Australia showing a ruthless streak in front of goal that helped them to a 3-0 lead, with ever-reliable penalty corner expert Jodie Kenny opening her World Cup by flicking gloriously into the top corner.

Despite trailing by three goals, Japan gave a terrific showing in the latter stages of the game with Motomi Kawamura reducing the deficit with a powerful effort past Australia's Rachael Lynch to spark hopes of a comeback. Lynch was called into action numerous times before Japan struck again through Akiko Kato's scrambled finish, but with barely enough time left on the clock to restart the match, the goal came too late to deny Australia the victory.

Speaking after the game, Jodie Kenny said she was pleased with how her team had started their campaign but admitted that there were things to learn and improvements to be made. 'It was nice to get a win for our first World Cup game, starting the campaign with a bang, but there is lots to learn from that game,' said Kenny, who scored her 109th international goal in what was her 202nd appearance for the Hockeyroos. 'We came out firing but then we gave them too many opportunities in that second half and they managed to get two back. We had to ride it out as Japan threw everything that they had at us. Yes, we managed to give away those two goals but it could have been worse had it not been for some good defending.'

The opening day of the Vitality Hockey Women's World Cup London 2018 had truly been a magnificent occasion from start to finish, both on and off the field. With a further 15 days of match-play featuring the greatest hockey teams in the world, the fans knew that this was just the beginning.

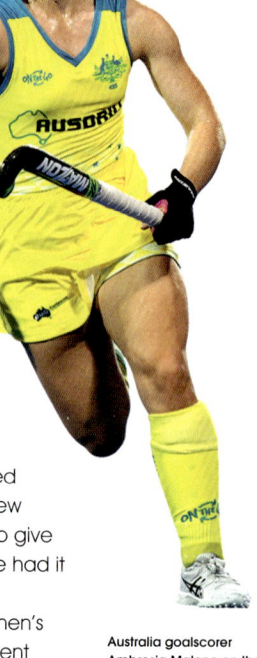

Australia goalscorer Ambrosia Malone on the charge against Japan. // *Rodrigo Jaramillo*

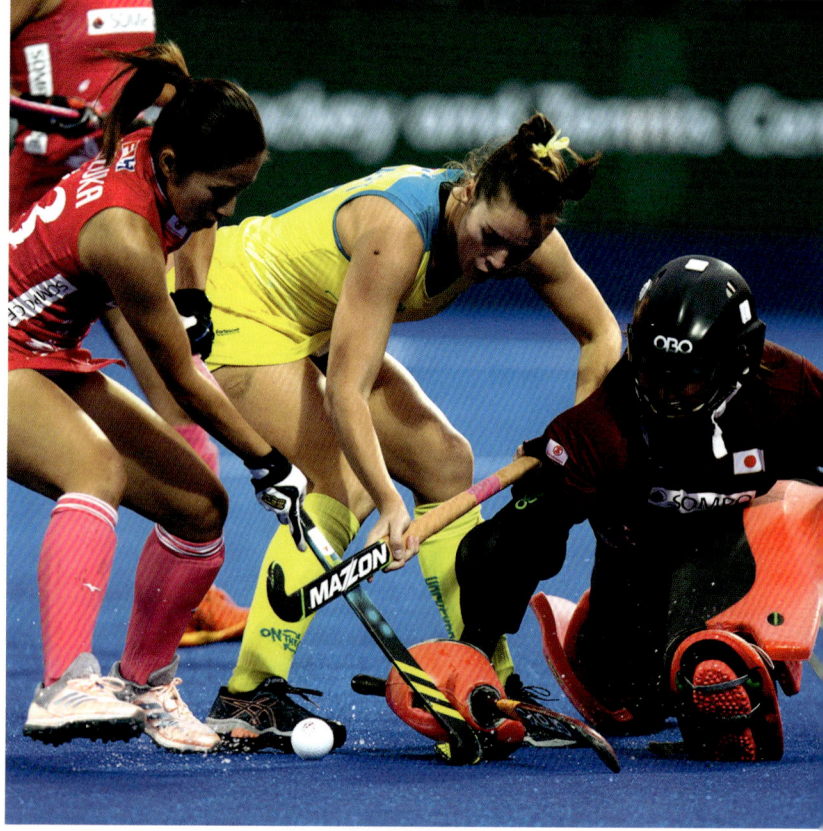

Goalkeeper Megumi Kageyama and Miki Kozuka do their best to deny Australia's Grace Stewart. // *Rodrigo Jaramillo*

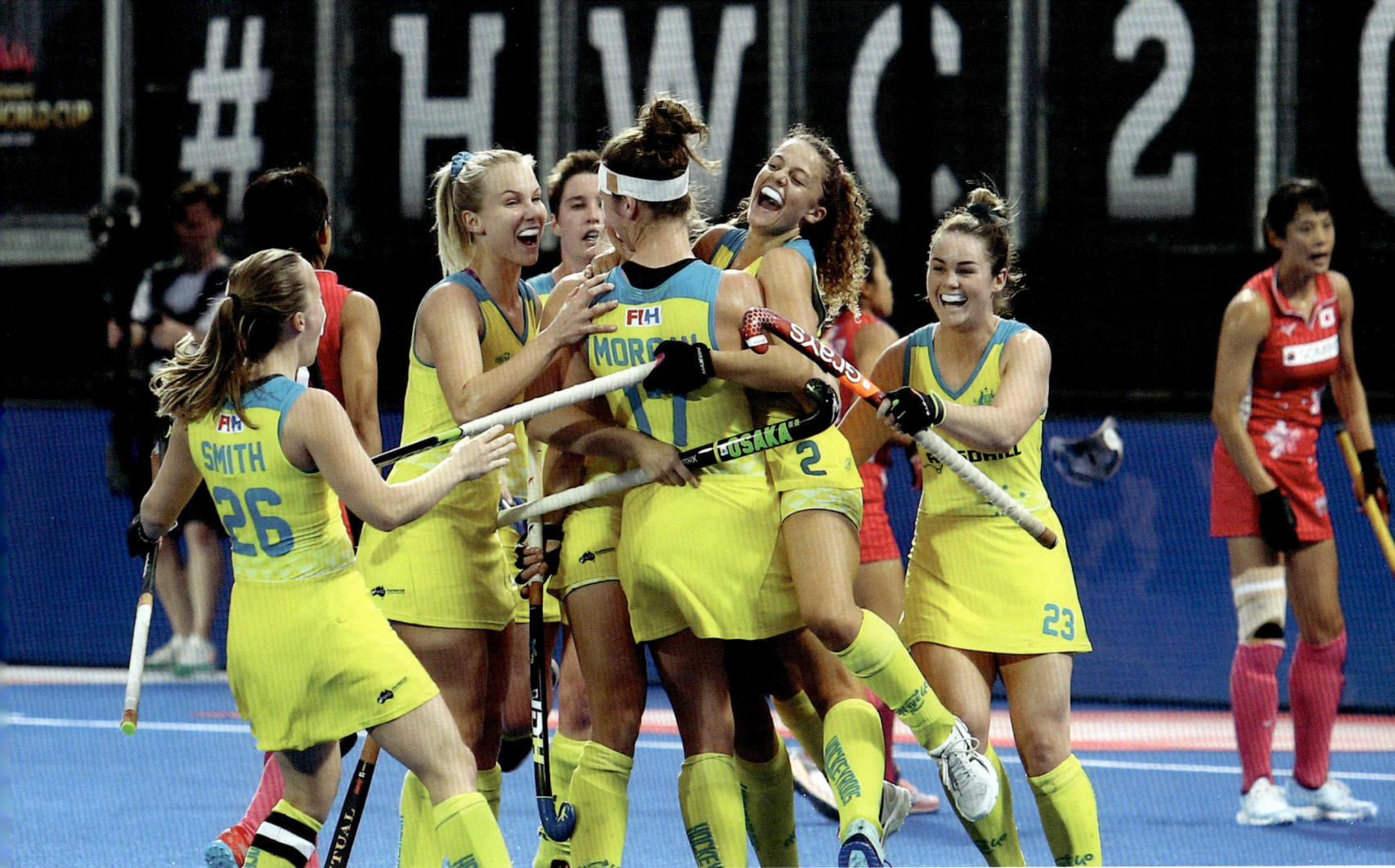

Australia players celebrate their opening goal, scored by Ambrosia Malone (#2). // *Rodrigo Jaramillo*

Results – Day 1 – Saturday 21 July 2018

Session 1

Pool C

Germany   **3-1**   **South Africa**
Viktoria Huse 14m FG, 54m PS   Lisa-Marie Deetlefs 40m PC
Charlotte Stapenhorst 32m FG

Vitality Player of the Match: Viktoria Huse (GER)

Pool B

England   **1-1**   **India**
Lily Owsley 54m PC   Neha Goyal 25m FG

Vitality Player of the Match: Alex Danson (ENG)

Session 2

Pool B

USA   **1-3**   **Ireland**
Margaux Paolino 15 PC   Dierdre Duke 5m FG, 41m FG
Shirley McCay 12m PC

Vitality Player of the Match: Ayeisha McFerran (IRL-GK)

Pool D

Australia   **3-2**   **Japan**
Ambrosia Malone 17m PC   Motomi Kawamura 36m FG
Emily Hurtz 22m FG   Akiko Kato 60m FG
Jodie Kenny 35m PC

Vitality Player of the Match: Jodie Kenny (AUS)

Pool Standings – End of Day 1

Pool A – No matches played

Pool B

Pos	Team	Pld	W	D	L	GF	GA	GD	Pts
1	Ireland	1	1	0	0	3	1	2	3
2	England	1	0	1	0	1	1	0	1
3	India	1	0	1	0	1	1	0	1
4	USA	1	0	0	1	1	3	-2	0

Pool C

Pos	Team	Pld	W	D	L	GF	GA	GD	Pts
1	Germany	1	1	0	0	3	1	2	3
2	Argentina	0	0	0	0	0	0	0	0
3	Spain	0	0	0	0	0	0	0	0
4	South Africa	1	0	0	1	1	3	-2	0

Pool D

Pos	Team	Pld	W	D	L	GF	GA	GD	Pts
1	Australia	1	1	0	0	3	2	1	3
2	Belgium	0	0	0	0	0	0	0	0
3	New Zealand	0	0	0	0	0	0	0	0
4	Japan	1	0	0	1	2	3	-1	0

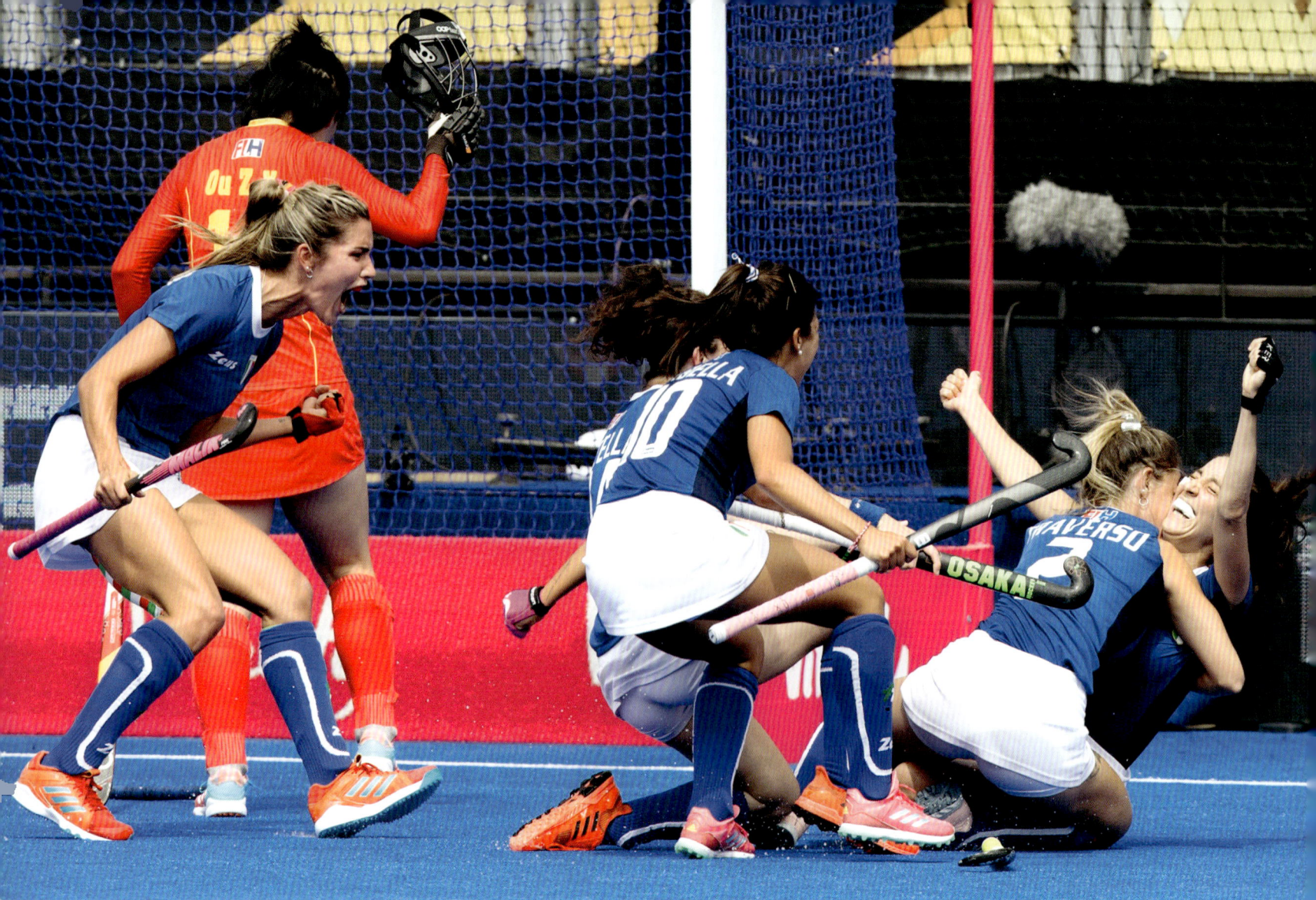

Sheer delight for Italy as Lara Oviedo puts her side ahead against their higher-ranked opponents. // *Rodrigo Jaramillo*

Day 2 – Sunday 22 July 2018

Azzurre rewrite history while Argentina announce their arrival

History was made on the second day of the competition when Italy, who at 17th in the FIH Hero World Rankings were the lowest-ranked team in the competition, recorded their first ever win at a World Cup. Italy last featured in an official FIH World Cup in 1976, but the way they took to the top tier of world hockey in their opening game against eighth-ranked China was nothing short of brilliant. The Azzurre started the match with an intensity and purpose that took both the spectators and the opposition by surprise.

The match swiftly settled into a classic encounter between two very different styles of play. China impressed in the opening moments of the match with their expansive game, creating space as they moved the ball from side to side, using every piece of the turf. The giants of Asian hockey were confident with long passes and they frequently made forays up the pitch in both the left- and right-hand channels. The problem for Jamilon Mülders' team was that

this was exactly where Italy wanted them to go. A packed and energetic Italian midfield were happy to see the Chinese team take the ball wide, leaving them free to reign supreme in the middle of the pitch. As the game ticked along, the blue shirts began to impose a press that moved higher and higher up the field, putting increasing pressure on the China defence.

'We were told prior to the match to go out and play attacking hockey in the China half of the game,' said Italy's Jasbeer Singh. 'We just grew in confidence as the match went on. This is our first World Cup for 42 years and we have worked hard to get it right both from a fitness and skills side, but also tactically.'

For Singh this was a particularly sweet moment as her mother, Gianna Singh, had been part of the Italian squad that competed in the 1976 World Cup.

China were alerted to the danger posed by their opponents when Giuliana Ruggerieri was able to shoot at will after a sequence of passes picked a hole in the Chinese defence and left the striker free. Her shot buzzed harmlessly wide of the goal but the spectators began to sense a ranking upset might be on the cards.

The goal, when it came, was a piece of magic from Valentina Braconi. She latched on to a blocked shot and slammed the ball past Ye Jiao in the China goal.

For Mülders, one problem was the fact that the China Hockey Association had made it clear that the Asian Games, which were beginning in the middle of August, was a priority for the team. For this reason, Mülders' squad was missing some key personnel. While the German coach understood the importance of the Asian Games and the subsequent prize of qualification for the Tokyo 2020 Olympic Games, it was galling to know that he only had access to a below-strength team.

'Of course it hurts,' said Mülders, as he reflected on his team's performance. 'No coach wants to come to a competition knowing that he does not have all the players he would choose. But I cannot stand and protest this to people. I must get on with it and use it as a further learning process for these players. We are here, we will do our best, we will learn a little more about our players and they will learn more about us as coaches and then we will go back to China and prepare for the Asian Games.'

Just as the Italian forwards were playing their part in pressurising the China defence, so their defence was standing firm in the face of any attack. Chiara Tiddi was

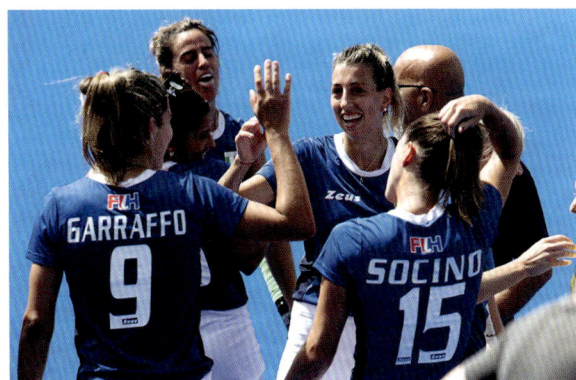

Italy's players congratulate themselves on a hard-earned victory. // Rodrigo Jaramillo

marshalling her defensive unit with her usual focus and calm and, if the ball did get through, the China strikers found Italy's goalkeeper Martina Chirico in magnificent form. At one point she pulled off an amazing double save, diving first to her right and then bouncing up to dive to her left and deny China the equaliser.

The second half started in much the same vein. China played with composure when they had the ball and there were some pitch-splitting passes from left to right and back again, but when it came to direct activity towards goal,

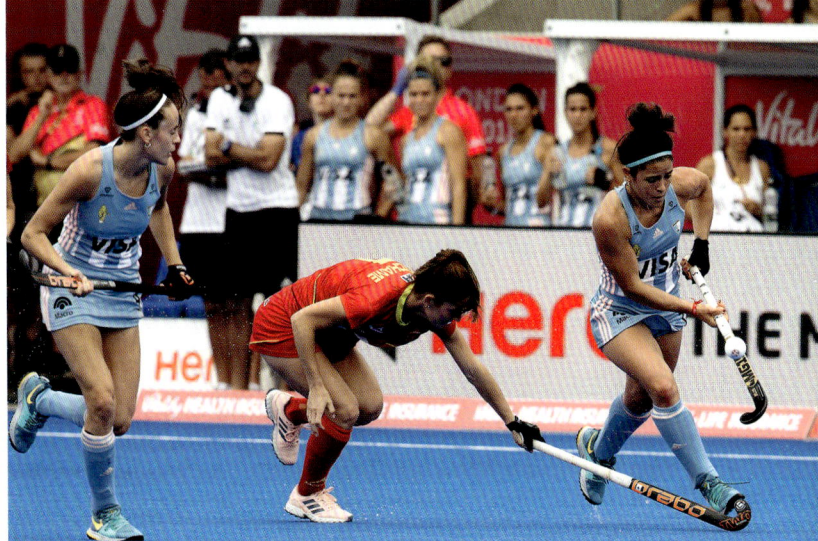

Argentina's Maria Granatto puts her magical skills to good use to evade the challenge of Carlota Petchame of Spain. // Rodrigo Jaramillo

it was the Italians who seized the initiative. The second goal for Italy came when Lara Oviedo slid in to deflect a penalty corner strike. The well-rehearsed move left the Chinese defence wrong-footed.

China started to get their own creative moves going as the third quarter counted down. Guo Qiu picked up the ball and weaved her way through the Italian defence before releasing Zhong Jiaqi. Jiaqi's shot struck the side of the goal but the signs were there that China were responding. As an Italian player was sent from the pitch for two minutes, following a rule infringement, Mülders took the brave decision to go for broke in an attempt to close the gap in the scoreline. He placed the keeper for the last two minutes of the quarter so that, with the Italians a player down, the Asian team had a two-player pitch advantage. Of course, the manoeuvre also meant China were fragile if Italy were able to gain possession of the ball and mount an attack.

To Mülders' dismay the plan backfired as the experienced Italian side stole possession in midfield and released Ruggieri who made no mistake as she shot home into the empty goal.

China's chance to capitalise came with eight minutes left on the clock as Maria Garraffo was given a yellow card. The level of naivety of the China players was revealed as it was actually Italy who took the initiative, keeping possession deep in Chinese territory as the suspension counted down. As Mülders and his players trudged from the pitch, the Italians celebrated as if they had won a cup final.

An upset looked to be on the cards when Spain took an early lead against the 2014 World Cup bronze medallists Argentina. Against the run of play, Spain broke from the

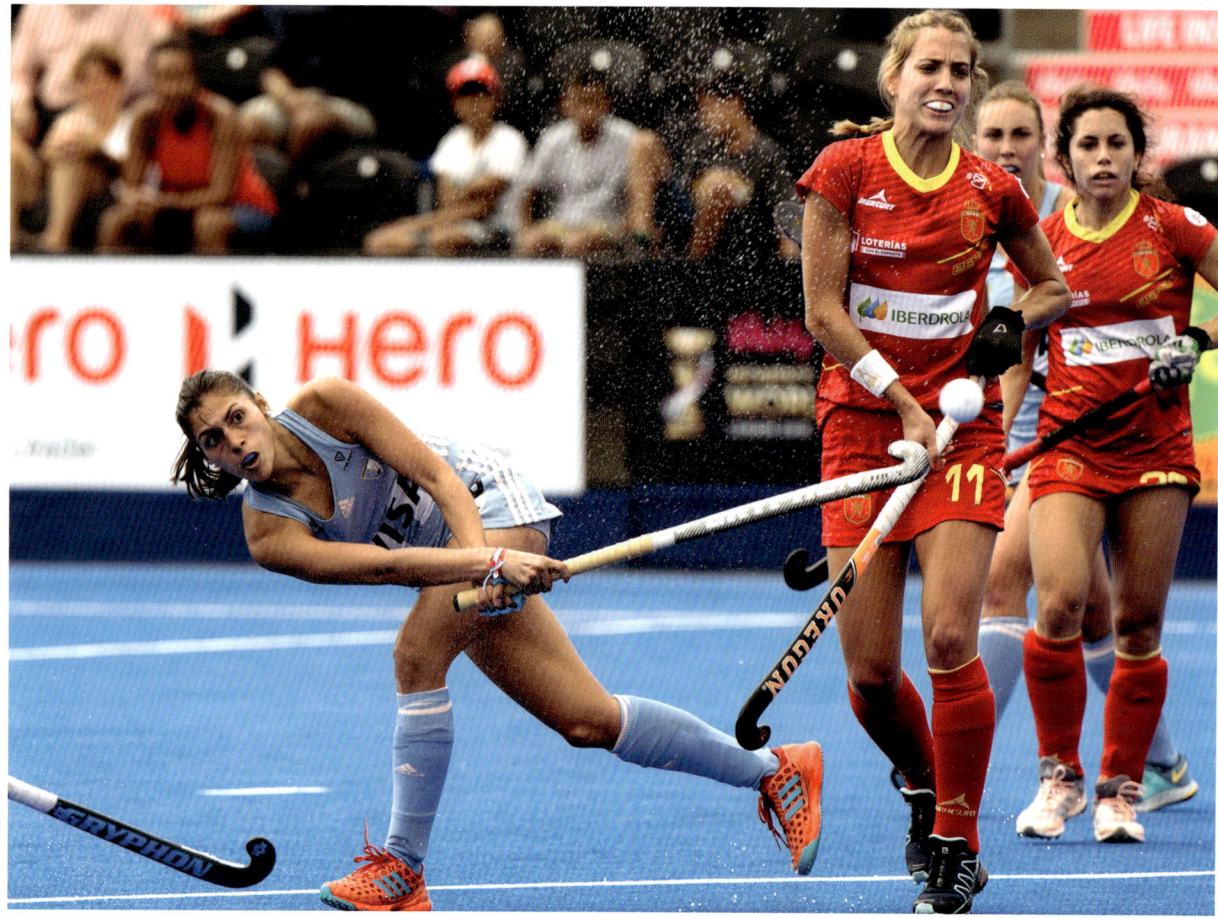

What a strike! Argentina's Maria Ortiz finds the top corner to put Las Leonas into a 2-1 lead. // *Rodrigo Jaramillo*

midfield and created an attack that was fast and, importantly, unexpected. As numerous Spanish players jabbed and poked at the ball as it bounced around the Argentina circle, goalkeeper Belen Succi finally got a foot to it. The ball flew in the air and Carola Salvatella was on hand to bat the ball past Succi. For a few minutes there was an eerie hush among the Argentina fans in the hockey arena.

Argentina's response, however, was swift, as, five minutes later, penalty corner specialist Noel Barrionuevo swept in a shot for Julieta Jankunas to deflect past Maria Ruiz in the Spanish goal.

If the equaliser was timely, the next Leonas goal was nothing short of sensational. Maria Ortiz picked up the ball on the left-hand side of the Spanish circle and unleashed a blistering shot that was perfectly placed into the top right corner of the net. Six games in and the spectators might have witnessed the goal of the tournament.

The third goal was a reflection of Argentinian tenacity when they are at their attacking best. The move began with captain Delfina Merino, who played the ball forwards into the circle. An initial shot from Maria Granatto was blocked by Ruiz but Merino had continued her run and slipped the rebound to Agustina Albertarrio who had an empty goal to fill.

Spain huddled and attempted to regroup but this was Las Leonas at their consummate best. Merino ran the ball into

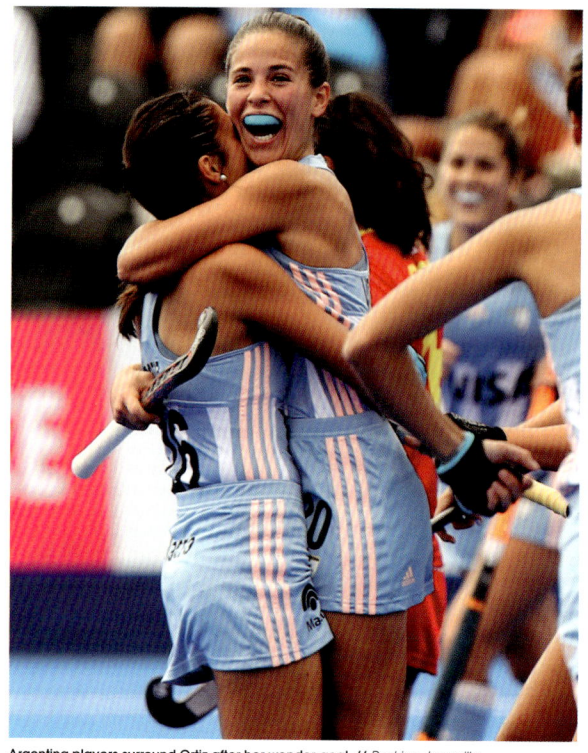

Argentina players surround Ortiz after her wonder-goal. // *Rodrigo Jaramillo*

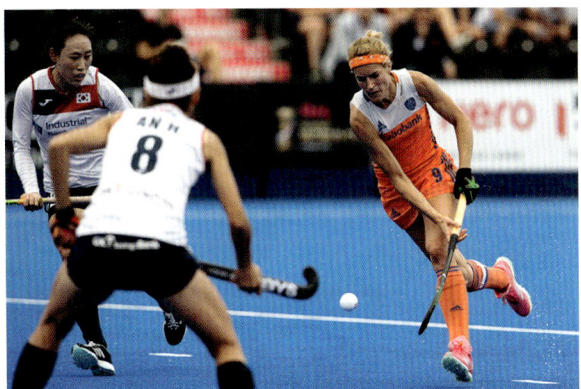

Netherlands captain Carlien Dirkse van den Heuvel on the attack against Korea.
// *Rodrigo Jaramillo*

the circle and her pass to Ortiz was perfect. The striker hit the ball first time and squeezed it through the gap between post and keeper to take the score to 4-1 going into half-time.

It was captain Merino herself who benefitted from the next attack. A goalmouth scramble saw the ball partially covered by Ruiz and, as the keeper desperately tried to clear, Merino prodded the ball over the line.

The final quarter saw Argentina hit their super six as Noel Barrionuevo stepped up to fire home a penalty stroke after an infringement in the circle. With the game effectively wrapped up, Argentina let their concentration slip momentarily and Spain were able to force a penalty corner. An innovative routine allowed Beatriz Perez to sweep the ball home and restore some pride for the Red Sticks.

For Spain's English-born head coach Adrian Lock this was an outcome that was both expected and, in some ways, welcome. 'We always knew this would be tough,' he said. 'It is not a game we had any illusions about. Argentina are number three in the world and we haven't played them for ten years. In so many ways it was a good game to play first because now we can reflect on today, learn from the things that didn't work and be ready for the other two pool games. We competed today; it was just a few mistakes that let us down.'

If Argentina were responsible for the most impressive goal of the day, then the reigning world champions scored the fastest. The opening goal in the Netherlands versus Korea game came within 20 seconds of the start – the second speediest goal in the history of the women's hockey World Cup. The fastest goal had also involved Korea – Kim Jong Eun's goal against England 14 seconds into the game in the Rosario World Cup of 2010. And,

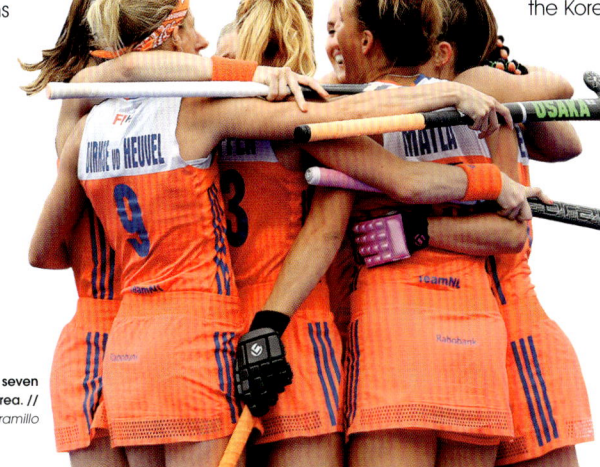

Netherlands celebrating one of the seven goals that they scored against Korea. //
Rodrigo Jaramillo

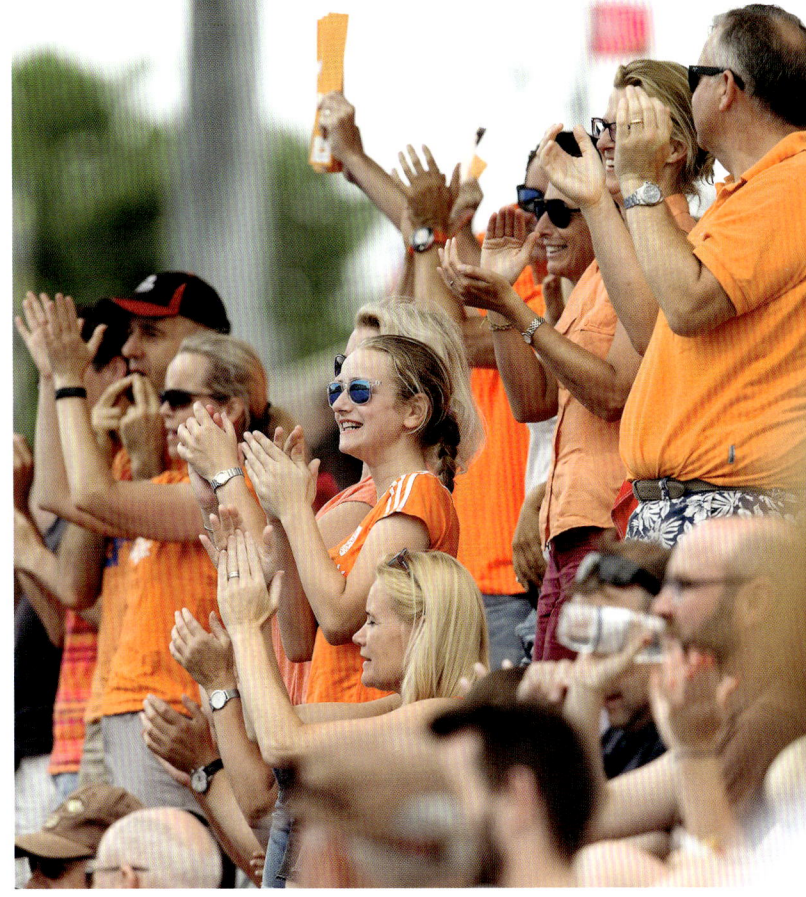

Dutch fans show their support after witnessing a comfortable victory for their side. // *Rodrigo Jaramillo*

as the Netherlands' goals rattled in over the course of the first half, the game had all the makings of a record-breaking women's hockey World Cup win too – an accolade held by West Germany who beat Nigeria 10-1 in 1978.

The opener was scored by Frederique Matla, who was able to capitalise on some neat interchanges between her team-mates to slot the ball past Bae Sora in the Korea goal. The Korean players looked at each other in astonishment as the Dutch celebrated and jogged back for the restart.

The same speed and fluidity was in evidence just three minutes later as Lidewij Welten found her way through the Korea defence to open her World Cup account. For the Dutch midfielder, this was a third World Cup but just her second World Cup goal. It was clear that this one was every bit as enjoyable as her first, a goal against Japan in the Netherlands' 5-2 win in Rosario 2010. Goals followed in quick succession, with Kitty van Male scoring twice, Matla adding her second and Laurien Leurink and Kelly Jonker all scoring before half-time. The Korea goalkeeper was substituted after the fourth goal went in, but this was the Dutch team in unstoppable form and Bae's replacement, Hwang Hyeon, was also unable to stem the flow of goals.

It said something about the Netherlands' approach to this game that they were back on the pitch after the half-time break long before the match was due to restart. There was an air about the world number one side of wanting to get the job done.

Despite the Netherlands' eagerness to get going in the second half, the third quarter was a quieter affair, as Korea adjusted to the pace and ferocity of the attack and marshalled their defence. The Netherlands were still creating chances but these were either hit wide, struck the post or were blocked on route to goal.

The final quarter was much the same. The Netherlands held possession and created chances but the high tempo and urgent nature of their earlier attack had dissipated. This was a case of job done for the reigning champions and there was clearly plenty left in reserve.

Speaking after the game, Frederique Matla explained that the coaching instructions at half-time had been to push for more penalty corners. In the opening half

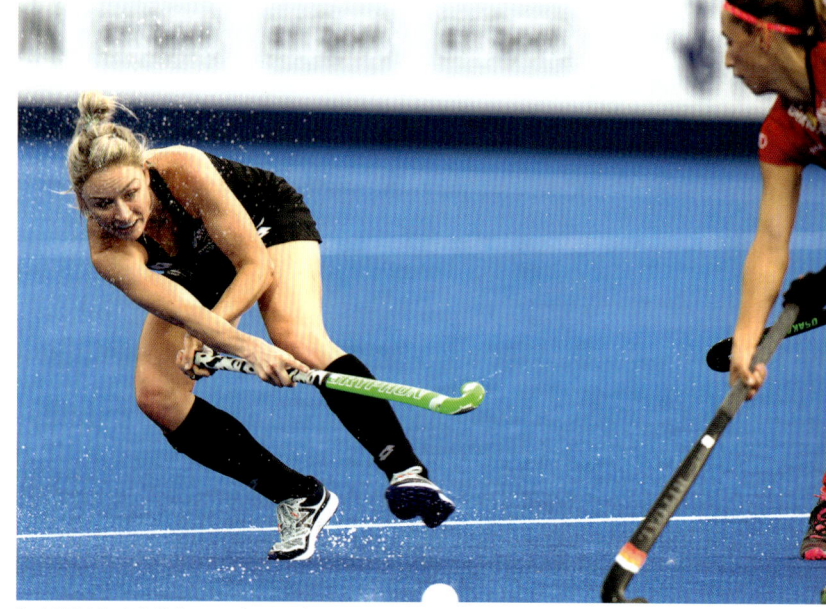
Black Sticks' star Anita McLaren sends a pass forward. // *Rodrigo Jaramillo*

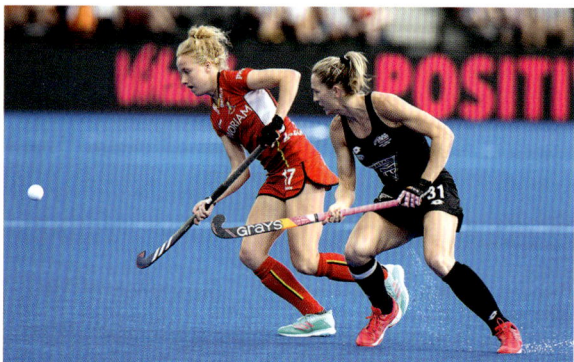
Belgium's Michelle Struijk keeps control despite the attentions of brilliant Black Sticks' captain Stacey Michelsen. // *Rodrigo Jaramillo*

all seven goals had come from open play and head coach Alyson Annan wanted her penalty corner team to get some practice. Matla added that the target before the game had been to score at least one goal in each quarter – the question was whether the coach would be delighted with an over-achievement in the first half, or disappointed with underachievement in the second half. Annan gave nothing away: 'There are still lots of improvements to be made,' was all she would say in post-match interviews.

In the final match of the day, New Zealand's Black Sticks faced the challenge of Belgium's Red Panthers. The Gold Coast 2018 Commonwealth Games champions came to the World Cup on a wave of confidence and with a world ranking of four, but Belgium's ranking of 13 belied a squad who had made huge progress under head coach Niels Thijssen.

Both teams created plenty of chances in the opening exchanges but it was actually the lower-ranked team that put early pressure on the Black Sticks' goal. However, against the run of play, it was New Zealand who got the breakthrough, with Kelsey Smith scoring from a penalty corner.

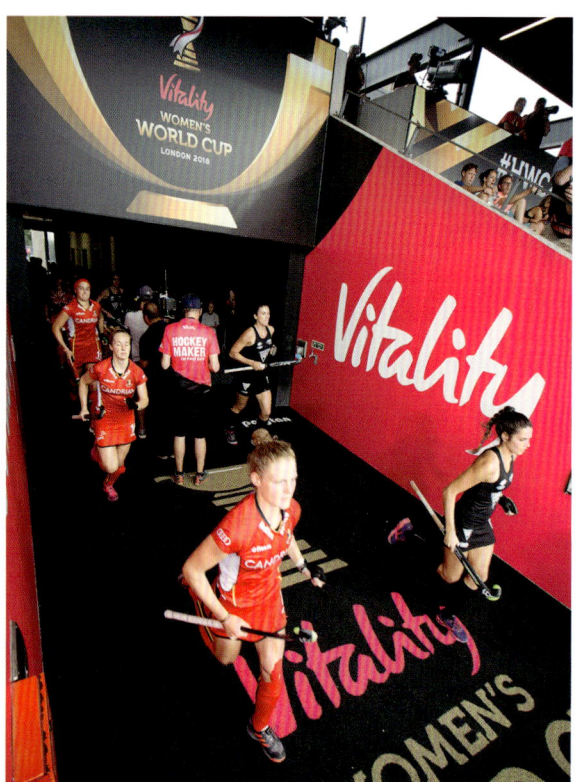
Belgium (red) and New Zealand (black) take to the field for the final match of the opening weekend. // *Rodrigo Jaramillo*

The Belgium of old might have been downhearted but Thijssen had injected new belief into the squad and they were straight back at the Black Sticks' defence; a ball that bobbled around the circle was finally slammed home by Louise Versavel to equal the scores.

The Red Panthers went one better a few minutes later as an imaginative cross from the left side of the field found Jill Boon unmarked in the circle. The striker had no hesitation in shooting home to give her side the lead.

The half-time break proved more advantageous to the New Zealand team as they came out firing on all cylinders. Just two minutes into the half Shiloh Gloyn levelled the score from a penalty corner and seconds later Olivia Merry put her side ahead as she strode into the Red Panthers' circle and struck home.

For a few minutes this knocked the Belgium team back but the 2017 EuroHockey Championships silver medallists were made of sterner stuff and so the game went back and forth as two hard-working teams strove to get a result. The game was finely poised as it entered the final quarter, with Belgium creating much pressure but always looking susceptible to an attack from the supremely fit New Zealand side.

Boon had the chance to equalise when she was again found in space in the circle – her clever movement a constant thorn in the Black Sticks' side – but her shot flew viciously wide.

The three points went to New Zealand, but Belgium's performance suddenly made Pool D a very interesting place to be.

Results – Day 2 – Sunday 22 July 2018

Session 1

Pool A

China	0-3	Italy
		Valentina Braconi 17m FG
		Lara Oviedo 32m PC
		Giuliana Ruggieri 45m FG

Vitality Player of the Match: Lara Oviedo (ITA)

Pool C

Argentina	6-2	Spain
Julieta Jankunas 8m PC		Carola Salvatella 3m FG
Maria Ortiz 15m FG, 28m FG		Beatriz Perez 49m PC
Agustina Albertarrio 22m FG		
Delfina Merino 31m FG		
Noel Barrionuevo 48m PS		

Vitality Player of the Match: Julieta Jankunas (ARG)

Session 2

Pool A

Netherlands	7-0	Korea
Frederique Matla 1m FG, 11m FG		
Lidewij Welten 4m FG		
Kitty van Male 9m FG, 23m FG		
Kelly Jonker 14m FG		
Laurien Leurink 17m FG		

Vitality Player of the Match: Xan de Waard (NED)

Pool D

New Zealand	4-2	Belgium
Kelsey Smith 24m PC		Louise Versavel 28m FG
Shiloh Gloyn 32m PC		Jill Boon 30m FG
Olivia Merry 32m FC, 54m PS		

Vitality Player of the Match: Olivia Merry (NZL)

Pool Standings – End of Day 2

Pool A

Pos	Team	Pld	W	D	L	GF	GA	GD	Pts
1	Netherlands	1	1	0	0	7	0	7	3
2	Italy	1	1	0	0	3	0	3	3
3	China	1	0	0	1	0	3	-3	0
4	Korea	1	0	0	1	0	7	-7	0

Pool B – No matches played

Pool C

Pos	Team	Pld	W	D	L	GF	GA	GD	Pts
1	Argentina	1	1	0	0	6	2	4	3
2	Germany	1	1	0	0	3	1	2	3
3	South Africa	1	0	0	1	1	3	-2	0
4	Spain	1	0	0	1	2	6	-4	0

Pool D

Pos	Team	Pld	W	D	L	GF	GA	GD	Pts
1	New Zealand	1	1	0	0	4	2	2	3
2	Australia	1	1	0	0	3	2	1	3
3	Japan	1	0	0	1	2	3	-1	0
4	Belgium	1	0	0	1	2	4	-2	0

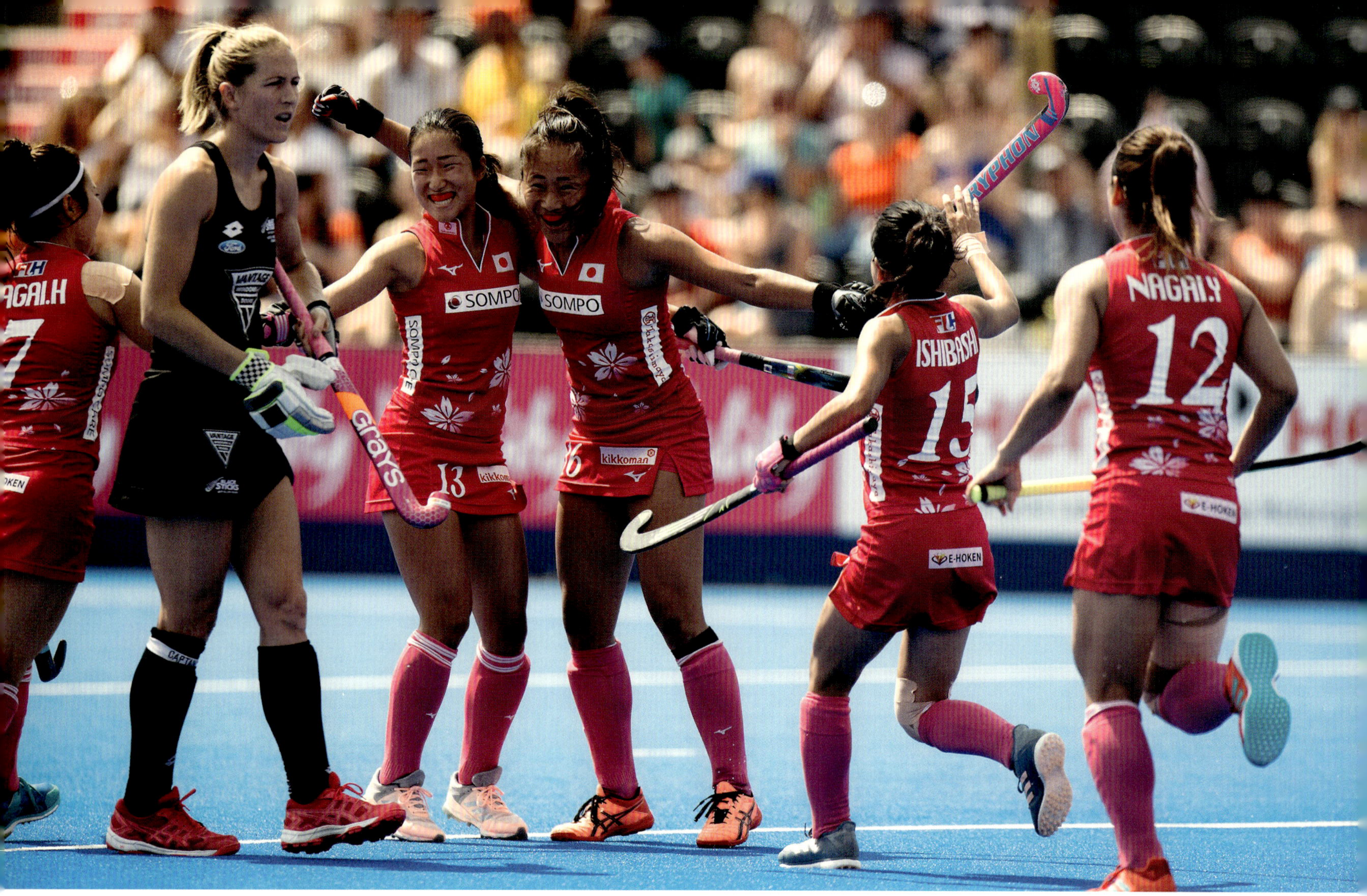

Shihori Oikawa (centre, #16) celebrates scoring the opening goal for the Cherry Blossoms. // *Frank Uijlenbroek*

Day 3 – Tuesday 24 July 2018

Japan blossom against New Zealand and Belgium benefit from 'Turnover Thursday'

Pool D was blown wide open on the third day of competition as yet another high-ranked team fell to a tactically astute opponent. New Zealand, who had enjoyed a rich vein of form in the months prior to the Vitality Hockey Women's World Cup London 2018 would have been confident going into their second game, but the Cherry Blossoms were a team on the way up.

The day's opening match was played in extreme heat as temperatures in London rocketed to the mid-thirties; the temperature on the pitch was several degrees higher.

Adding to New Zealand's confidence was the fact that they had played and beaten Japan in a number of recent test matches. But this was a World Cup and nothing was a certainty.

While New Zealand had secured three points after a tough game with Belgium, Japan had been on the wrong side of a 3-2 loss to Australia. In that game, Japan had started slowly and turned a potentially clear-cut loss into a much closer affair, with two quick goals in the final minutes of the game.

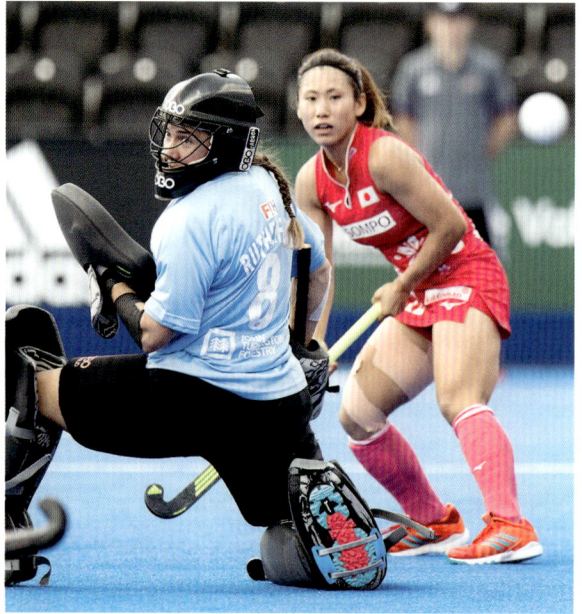

New Zealand goalkeeper Sally Rutherford looks back as a Japanese attack goes just wide of the target. // *Frank Uijlenbroek*

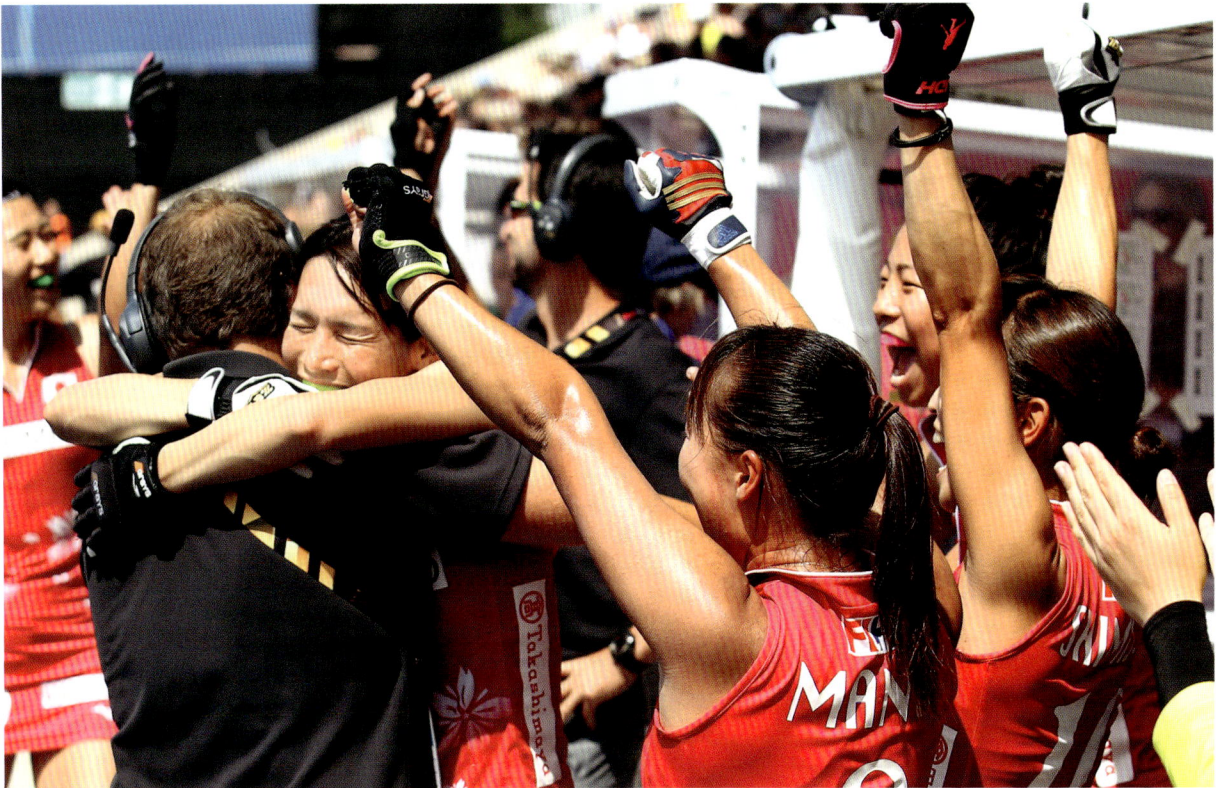

Japanese joy as the team claim a shock victory over New Zealand's Black Sticks. // *Rodrigo Jaramillo*

So the two questions ahead of the game were, whether New Zealand had recovered from their exertions and whether Japan would pick up the momentum they had developed over the course of their opening match.

The first half was an open affair, with New Zealand playing their usual expansive and fast-running style of play and Japan looking for innovative passes that got their strikers in behind the Black Sticks' defence.

It was Japan who created the majority of chances in the half. The first of these came when Yu Asai found Motomi Kawamura in front of goal and unmarked. The striker deflected the ball fractionally wide of Sally Rutherford in the New Zealand goal. Three penalty corners for the Cherry Blossoms also failed to provide a breakthrough but it was clear that Japan were paying no heed to the large disparity between the teams in the FIH Hero World Rankings.

As temperatures rose, so the players' fatigue levels began to show. Passes from both teams were going astray and on several occasions a good run ended in no outcome purely because players were running out of energy.

After the break, it was Japan who demonstrated that they were adapting to the hot conditions best. A well-disciplined high press put the Black Sticks under huge pressure and Japan were eventually rewarded with a fourth penalty corner. Shihori Oikwawa was on hand to slam the ball past Rutherford from the top of the circle.

New Zealand came back hard seeking an equaliser but Japan were able to step up and break down the play. A quick break left Minami Shimizu with a one-on-one with the keeper and the nifty midfielder was able to dance around the sliding tackle and slot home to double the Cherry Blossoms' lead.

However, New Zealand were not a team to give up and, with nine minutes left, Mark Hager's side won a penalty stroke after a foul tackle prevented a certain goal. Anita McLaren made no mistake as she struck the ball into the bottom right-hand corner, and the Gold Coast 2018 Commonwealth Games gold medallists were back in the game.

With five minutes left Japan were reduced to ten players and a penalty corner was awarded to New Zealand. The large contingent of Black Sticks' fans held their breath but the shot flew harmlessly wide.

At the start of the event, Japan's Australian-born coach Anthony Farry had spoken of his team's need to learn from every match. The way the Cherry Blossoms coped against a New Zealand team that oozed caps and experience suggested that his team were taking him at his word.

'We learnt a lot from our previous game against Australia,' said Japan's Yui Ishibashi, as she reflected on her team's performance. 'We planned to operate a high press and then try to work around the New Zealand defence.'

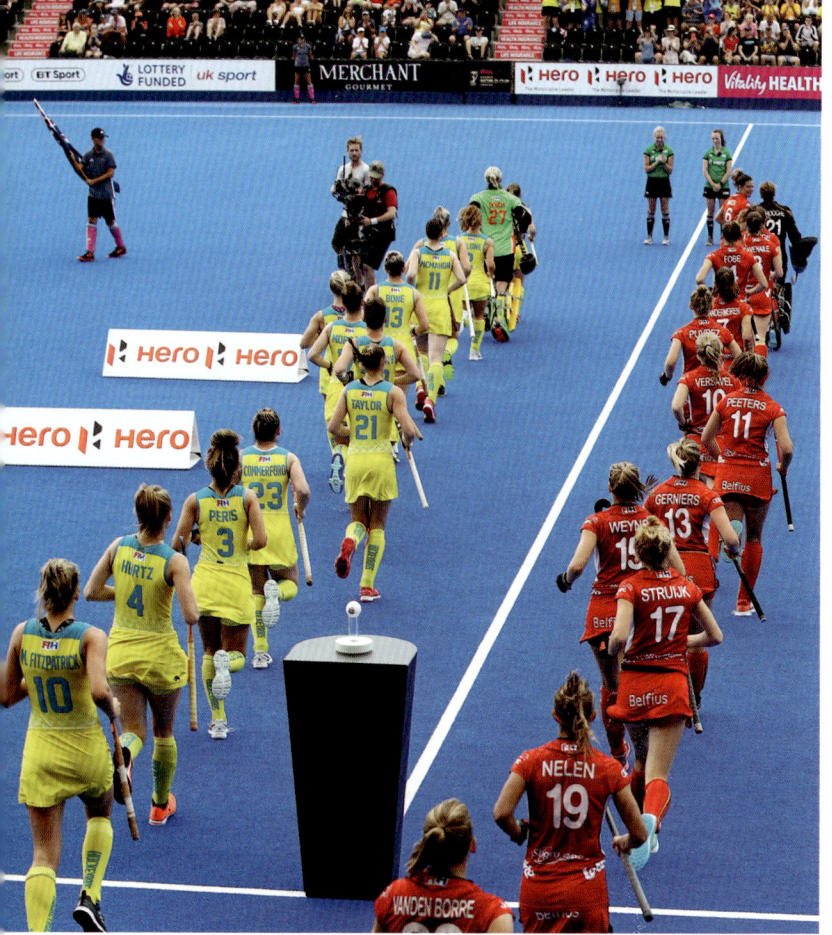

Australia and Belgium take to the field for the second Pool D meeting of the day.
// Rodrigo Jaramillo

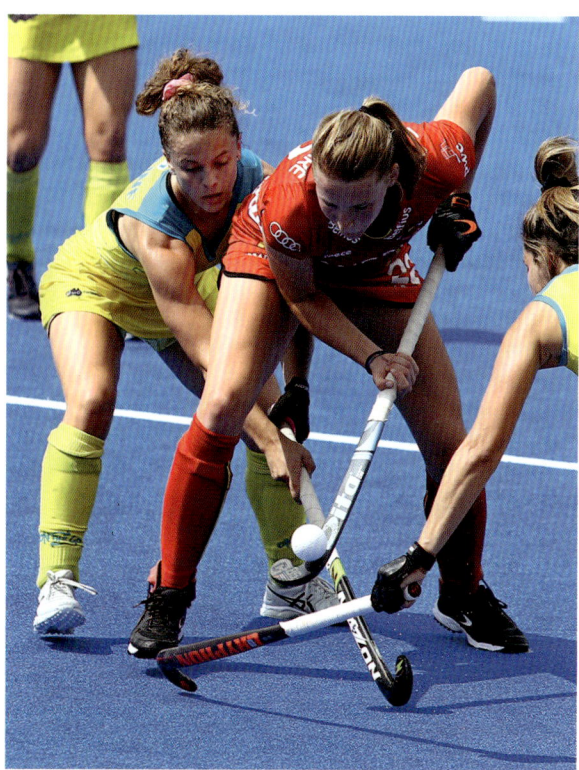

Belgium's Stephanie Vanden Borre lifts the ball over two Australian sticks.
// Rodrigo Jaramillo

The second game of the day saw another Oceania team in action as Australia faced Belgium. The Hockeyroos hit the ground running and for the first quarter it looked as if the 2014 silver medallists were going to rack up a number of goals. The Belgium of a few months earlier may well have succumbed to the pressure but the Red Panthers had toughened up under head coach Niels Thijssen and, with Aisling D'Hooghe in great form in goal, the Hockeyroos could find no way through.

As the second quarter counted down, however, the Red Panthers began to find their feet and possession evened out. Stephanie Vanden Borre showed a sublime piece of skill to take the ball out of her own defence and release Anne-Sophie Weyns, but the Australia defence looked rock solid as they took their turn at defending.

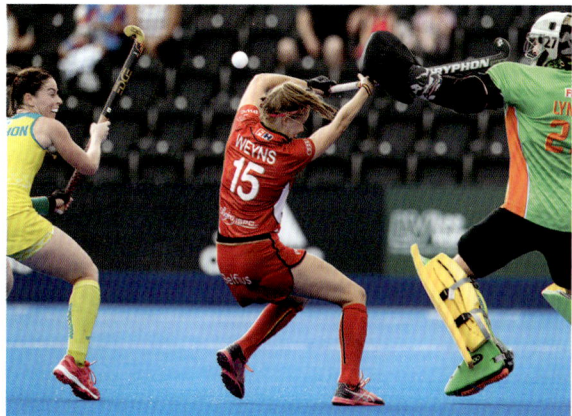

Australia goalkeeper Rachael Lynch makes a crucial block to deny Belgium's Anne-Sophie Weyns. // Rodrigo Jaramillo

The second half saw Belgium grow in confidence as the Australia threat failed to produce a goal. Australia were using their strength and speed to spread the ball around but Belgium were soaking up the pressure and then looking to make quick breaks through the centre of the field. The tactic nearly worked as Alix Gerniers wriggled between two Australia players to release Weyns. Her shot was stopped by Rachael Lynch, who then showed her class in recovering and saving the follow-up attempt.

Still Australia kept knocking on the door. Jodie Kenny lined up for a trademark penalty corner but the Belgium defence held firm.

The Red Panthers created their own chances, with Stephane Vanden Borre and Michelle Struijk, particularly, causing problems for the Australia defence. Lynch was called into action when Louise Versavel had the ball on the edge of the circle. The keeper was quickly off her line to eliminate the danger.

After the game Lynch said: 'We knew it would be a hard game and we had to be "on" every minute of the game. We had some good patches, where we did some really good things and we got lots of opportunities, but then they did too.'

Stephanie Vanden Borre explained the change in the Belgium team: 'Two years ago we really started to increase our physical preparation. We are the best state of fitness we can be. We have just been training, training, training. We really have played under fatigue, which has really helped us to improve our thinking and decision making. We have a training session called "Turnover Thursday", where we train under duress.'

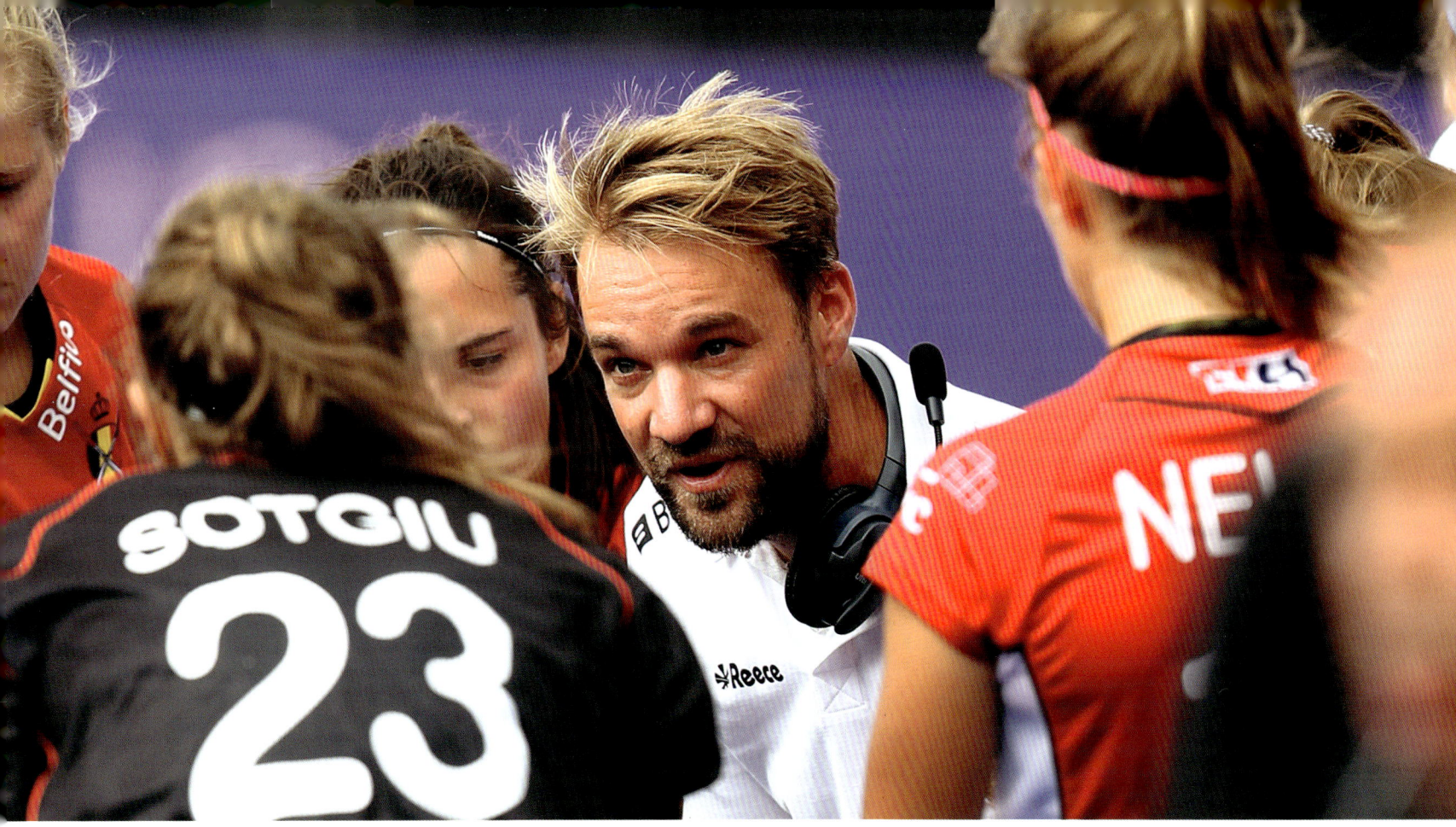

Belgium head coach Niels Thijssen issues his instructions. // *Rodrigo Jaramillo*

The current Belgium team had been on an upward trajectory over the past four years. The Red Panthers finished 12th out of 12 teams at the 2014 Rabobank World Cup in The Hague. Then, they were comprehensively outplayed but in 2018, with silver from the 2017 Rabobank EuroHockey Championships under their belt, they were a team that oozed new-found belief.

'In the past we lost a lot of games because we were not fit or not fit enough, but we have worked hard in the past few years and now we are really, really fit,' said striker Jill Boon. 'We have made huge steps forwards,' she continued. 'We play with a huge amount of passion and we really celebrate every goal now.

'The fact that we are fitter and can do extra metres, that is what our coach Niels Thijssen has been telling us. If you want to compete with those teams you have to make those extra metres to make yourself free and give yourself space. We also have very creative and hard-working midfielders who can find us when we make leading runs.'

Results – Day 3 – Tuesday 24 July 2018

Pool D

Japan	2-1	New Zealand
Shihori Okawa 35m PC		Anita McLaren 52m PS
Minami Shimizu 48m FG		

Vitality Player of the Match: Minami Shimizu (JPN)

Australia	0-0	Belgium

Vitality Player of the Match: Barbara Nelen (BEL)

Pool Standings – End of Day 3

Pool D

Pos	Team	Pld	W	D	L	GF	GA	GD	Pts
1	Australia	2	1	0	0	3	2	1	4
2	New Zealand	2	1	1	1	5	4	1	3
3	Japan	2	1	1	1	4	4	0	3
4	Belgium	2	0	1	1	2	4	-2	1

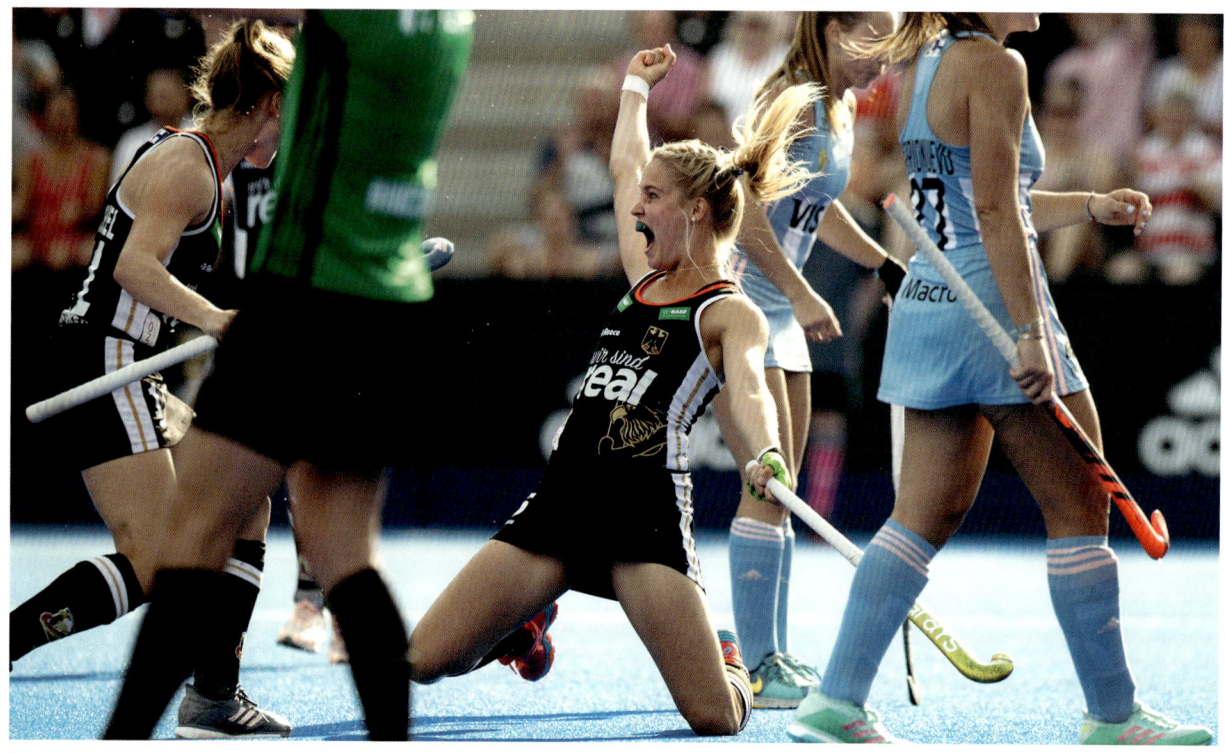

Hannah Gablac opened the scoring for Germany with an early strike. // *Frank Uijlenbroek*

Day 4 – Wednesday 25 July 2018

Germany light up the World Cup with consummate display

Fireworks and flame throwers – if the 2018 summer wasn't hot enough, then things at the Vitality Hockey Women's World Cup went into inferno mode on the fourth day of action. This was the first day that England Hockey's organising committee had needed to consider how to get 10,500 supporters into the stadium on a working day, and the furrowed brows of the event management team the day before told its own story.

'It actually couldn't have gone better,' a relieved Sally Munday, chief executive officer of England Hockey, later reported. 'The team talked through some scenarios and solutions and it worked like clockwork. The crucial thing was to get people to leave Fan Central in plenty of time before the start of the match so we were very clear with our communications. The messaging from the Hockey Makers and over the speakers at Fan Central was straight to the point: "You must

leave at this time, otherwise you will miss the start of the first game." The curve of movement from Fan Central to the Arena had to be perfect.'

The planning and preparation worked. By the time the first match of the session was underway most of the four stands were filled and the Lee Valley Hockey & Tennis Centre was rocking.

First up was a sizzling encounter between two teams who had both tasted World Cup success. Germany's last win in 1981 (playing as West Germany) took place before any of the current players were born, but some of Argentina's players still remembered the incredible night on which they had won the World Cup in Rosario in 2010 and they were eager for more of the same.

While the largely English crowd were here to cheer on their team in the second game of the evening, they could not fail to be dazzled by the quality of the preceding match, in which Germany put in a performance that would send ripples

Charlotte Stapenhorst scored twice as Germany's Die Danas claimed a fine 3-2 victory over Argentina. // *Frank Uijlenbroek*

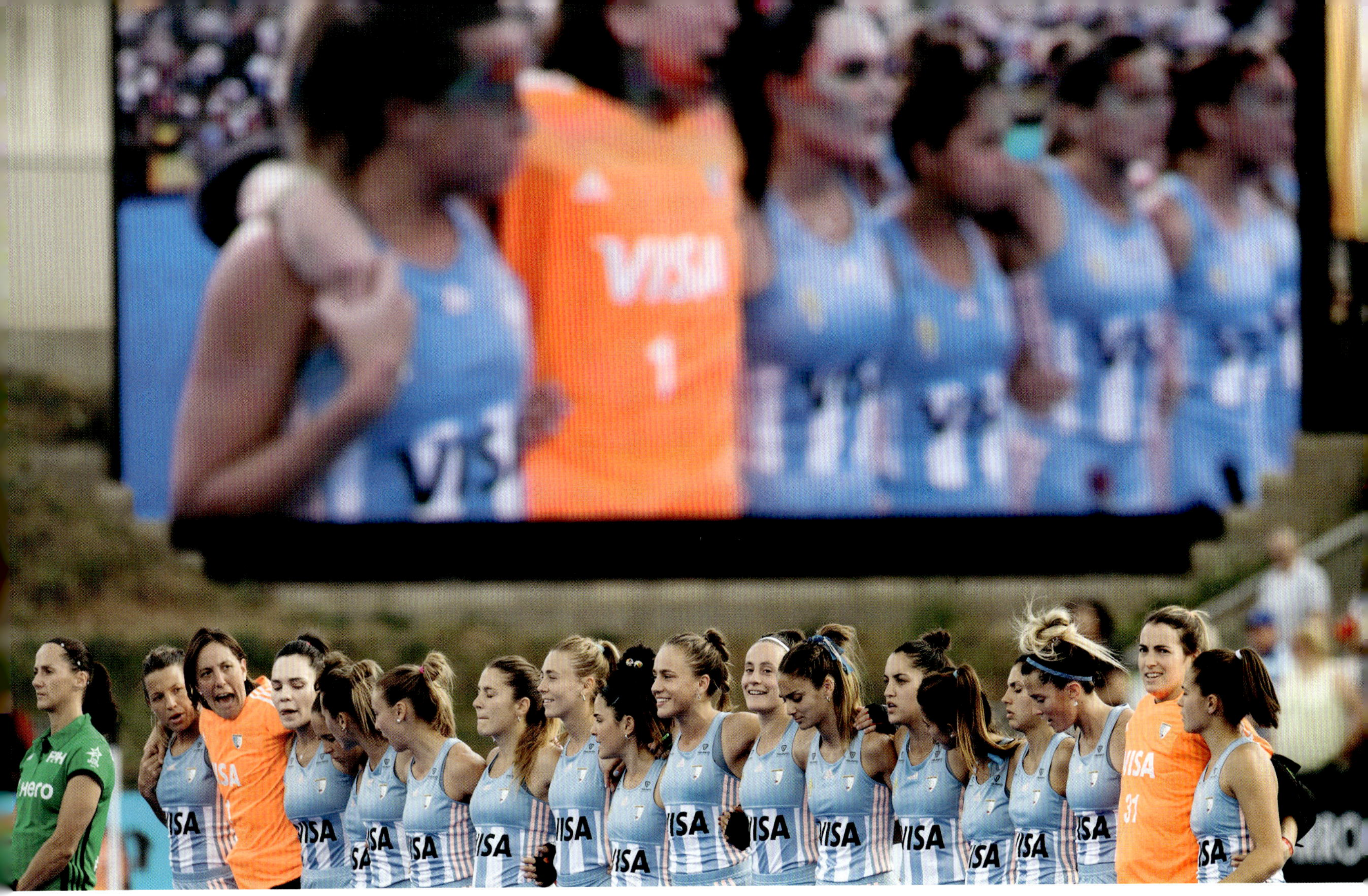

Argentina players await the national anthems ahead of their Pool C clash with Germany. // *Frank Uijlenbroek*

through the watching coaches in the stands. 'Germany were very, very special tonight,' was former German head coach Jamilon Mülders' reaction as he watched the team he had taken to bronze at the Rio 2016 Olympic Games play a mature and stylish game. '[Head coach] Reckinger and [assistant coach] Keller have implemented new things which have made them better and revitalised them. It is lovely to see.'

The teams had both got a win under their belts already. Argentina had briefly gone behind Spain but had

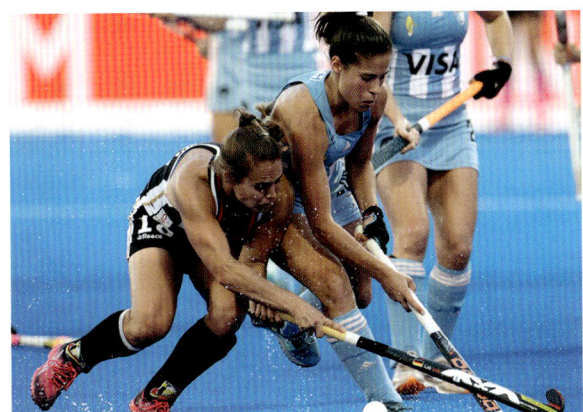

Germany's Lisa Altenburg (in black) puts in a strong challenge on Lucina von der Heyde of Argentina. // *Frank Uijlenbroek*

bounced back in devastating style to win 6-2, while Germany had put in a strong display to beat South Africa 4-1. The performances in the opening matches suggested that both teams were peaking at the right time, and the players looked in confident mood as they belted out their national anthems and enjoyed the display of flames that accompanied their entrance on to the field.

Despite the Argentina team's reputation for starting quickly, it was Germany who took the lead in the fifth minute when Hannah Gablac slotted home for her first goal of the World Cup. The forward received the ball with her back to goal, twirled and slotted home past Belen Succi in the Argentina goal.

Far from sitting back on that lead, for the next few minutes it was all Germany as they attacked and won a series of penalty corners. Coach Xavier Reckinger was impassive as each opportunity failed to produce a second goal, but the team and the people on the bench were unable to hide their dismay when Argentina, having soaked up the pressure, shot down the other end of the pitch and won a penalty corner. Florencia Habif was the scorer, and her delight was evident as she leapt into the arms of her captain Delfina Merino and pumped her fist towards the Argentine contingent in the crowd.

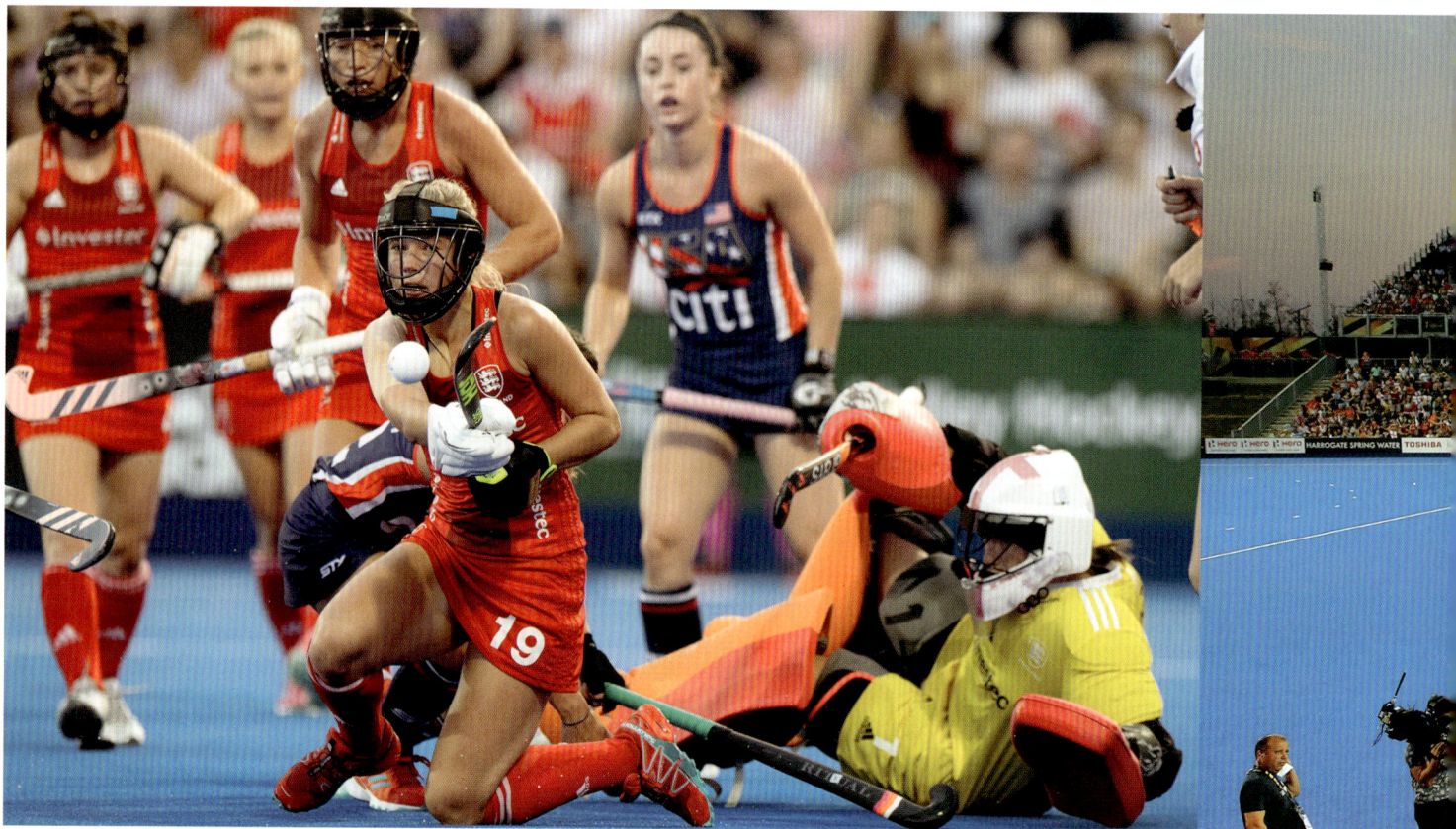

England's Sophie Bray (#19) clears the ball away to safety. // *Frank Uijlenbroek*

Despite conceding, Die Danas were far from deterred and needed just four minutes to re-establish their lead. Charlotte Stapenhorst was on hand to slap home the ball after some tricky stick skills from one of the newer team members, Elisa Gräve. The 21-year-old showed great composure to hold possession as she manoeuvred past the Argentina sticks. The ball was mid-air when Stapenhorst stepped in and dispatched with clinical precision past goalkeeper Belen Succi.

Germany's third and Stapenhorst's second was a belter from the in-form striker. First, she took the ball wide into the right-hand side of the Argentina circle. Then, ignoring the Argentina defender who was desperately trying to force her wide, Stapenhorst unleashed a shot that flew into Succi's goal at head height and with unstoppable force.

The scoreline might have read 3-1 but this was a far from one-sided encounter. Argentina nearly pulled one back as Noel Barrionuevo sent a shot past Julia Ciupka's goal but the speed of the German counter was astounding and the 2014 World Cup bronze medallists came perilously close to conceding a fourth goal. The ebb-and-flow nature of the game meant that no sooner had Argentina withstood that attack than they were creating their own chances. Maria Ortiz, who had scored a wonder-goal the previous match, was in the perfect position to reduce the deficit to one goal as she slipped the ball past Ciupka.

If Ciupka was annoyed at letting that goal in, she more than redeemed herself with the point-blank range save she made at the start of the second half. The ball was struck with ferocity by Julieta Jankunas but Ciupka reacted quickly to palm the ball to safety.

The second half saw no further goals but the quality of competition was more than enough to keep everyone on the edge of their seats. Both Ciupka and Succi were in constant action and the speed of counter-attack – by Maria Granatto and Delfina Merino for Argentina and Stapenhorst and Altenburg for Germany – was relentless.

With five minutes left, Las Leonas really hit Germany hard but the experienced German team knew how to see out a game and Argentina were unable to get the equaliser. Ciupka was called on to make further reaction saves but, when Argentina's captain Merino was sent from the field for two minutes, Argentina knew the game was slipping from their grasp. Marshalled by their captain Janne Müller-Wieland, Germany held on for the three points and a tight hold on the top of the pool. Former Argentina star and World Cup winner Mercedes Margalot summed up the problem: 'In two years' time the team will be at their peak but there is too much inexperience at the moment.'

'I think that was a great game of hockey tonight,' was German captain Janne Müller-Wieland's verdict on the game. 'It was so exciting to play in front of that

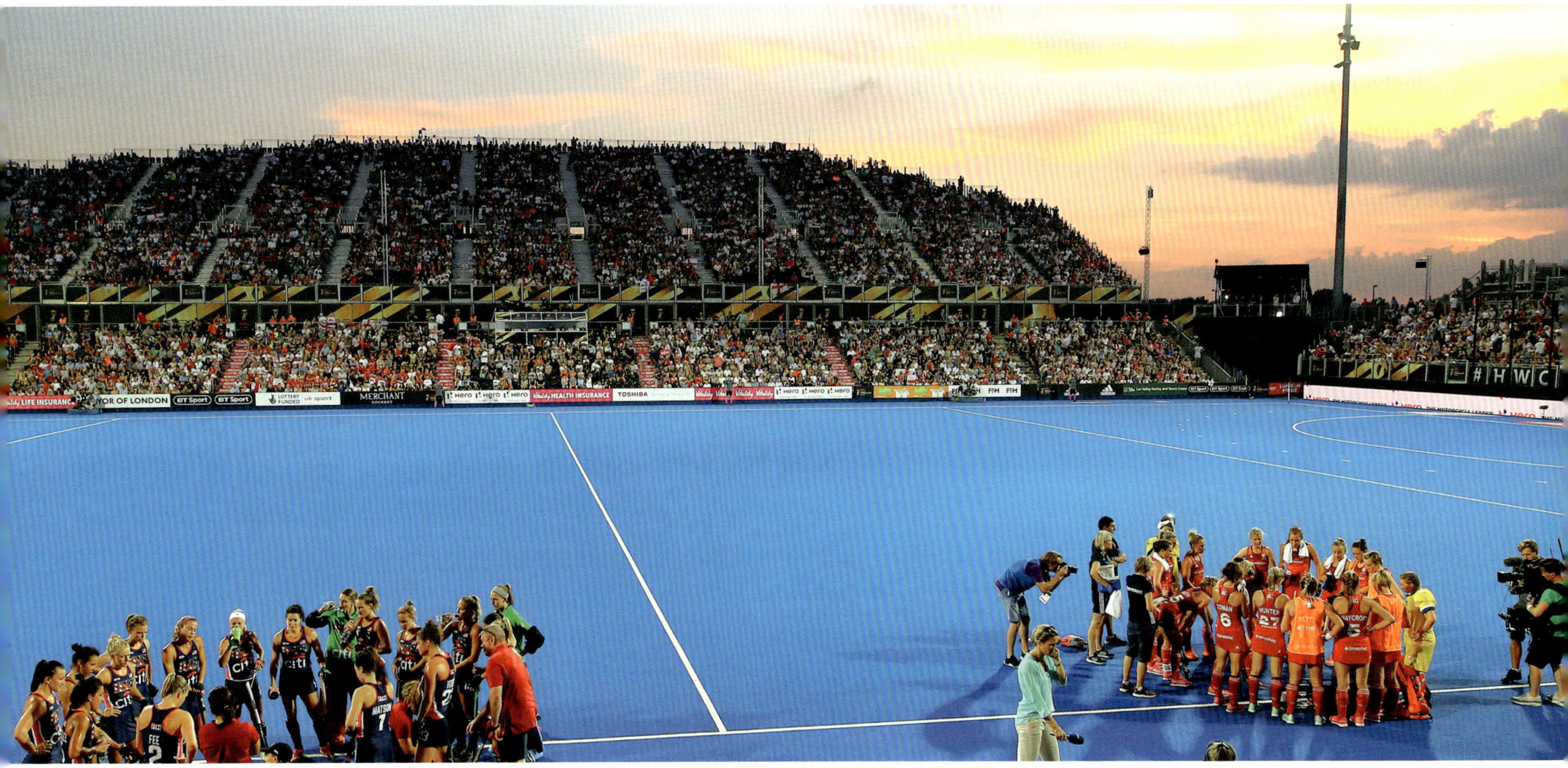

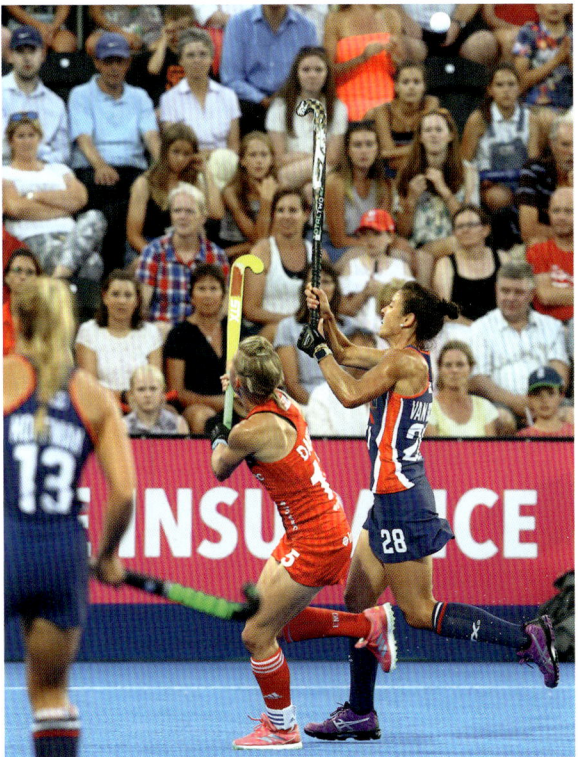

The setting sun turns the sky orange above a packed Lee Valley Hockey & Tennis Centre. // *Rodrigo Jaramillo*

England captain Alex Danson (in red) and USA's Caitlin van Sickle
chase after an overhead pass. // *Rodrigo Jaramillo*

crowd and I think the British really appreciate a good
sporting spectacle.

'We were lucky to take an early lead but Argentina
are a world class team so we knew they would come back
and it would be really close. For the final minutes of that
game it was all about defending. I think in Britain they refer to
it as the German way of playing.

'We wanted to control the game and we had several
phases in the second half where we said: "Let them run at
us." But we have several very good young players in midfield
and on the forward line and sometimes they just want to
go. The senior players sometimes have to tell them to calm
it down, pass backwards and conserve their energy a little.
I understand their excitement, the atmosphere here is like a
cup final every match and many of our players were in Berlin
for the Indoor Hockey World Cup – I think we would all like
that feeling again.'

A capacity crowd, mostly sporting red and waving
the flag of St George, combined with the knowledge that
a win was crucial, was enough to set nerves jangling for
England as they took to the field against USA. There was
visible tension in the faces of the squad as they lined up for
the national anthem. Alex Danson was able to muster a smile
as the crowd and players acknowledged her 200th cap for
England – a tally that catapulted her into a rarefied trio –
along with Jane Smith and Kate Richardson-Walsh – who had

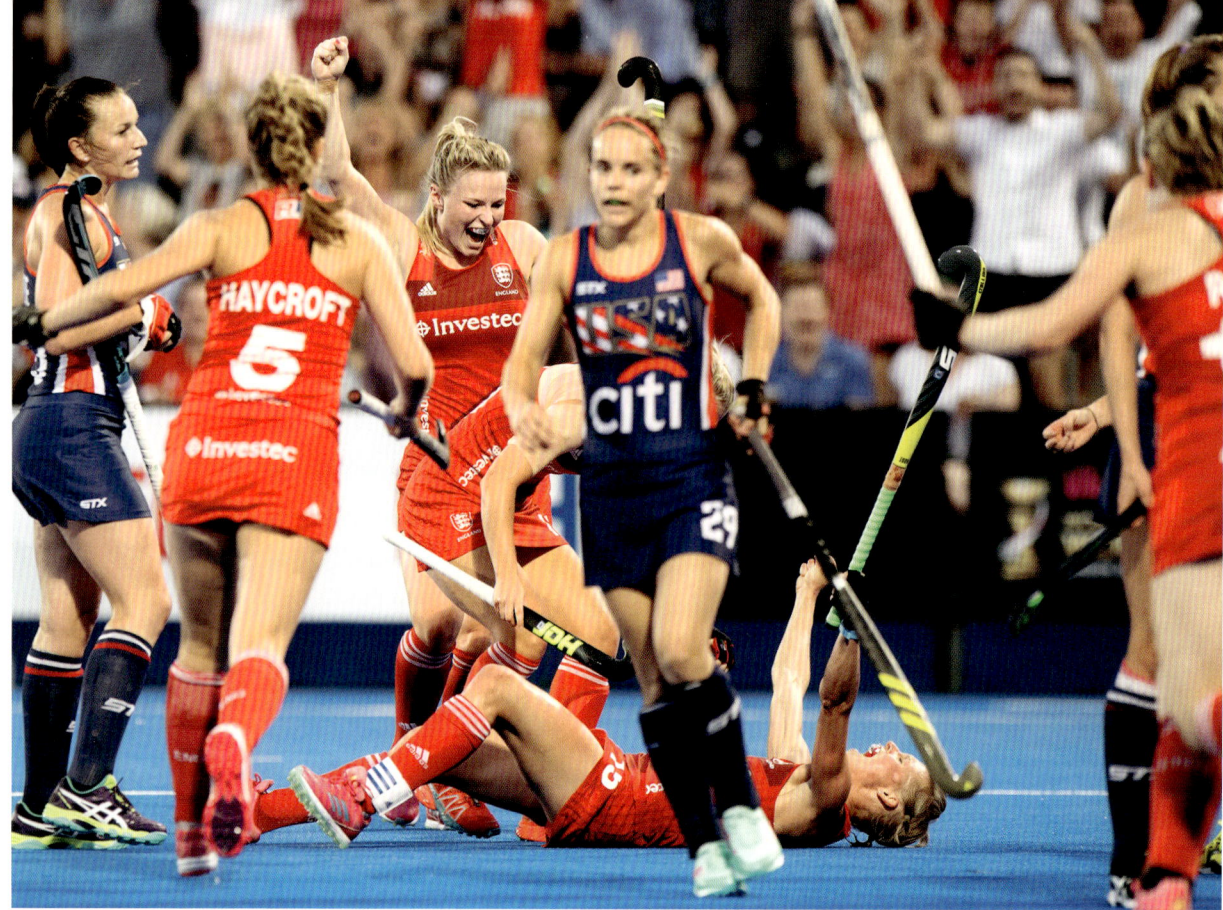

Alex Danson (on the ground) scored a wonderful individual goal to put England ahead. // *Frank Uijlenbroek*

represented England 200 times. The figure did not include appearances made for Great Britain.

For USA this was also a match from which they needed a result. They had succumbed to a surprise ambush by Ireland in their first match, losing 3-1 to a team ranked nine places beneath them. The team had put on a brave face but it was obvious that there was concern in the USA camp that they could be looking at a shock early exit from the tournament. If England had looked nervy as they stood shoulder to shoulder during their national anthem, then USA had tension etched all over their faces.

It was thus unsurprising that the opening half was a cagey affair with both sides probing for breaks in their opponent's defence but staunch work by both defensive units meant the teams entered the half-time break at 0-0, with only two shots troubling Maddie Hinch in the England goal and five shots putting her counterpart Jackie Briggs under pressure. This did not mean that there was any lack of action. England's Hannah Martin used her speed to create space but missed her shot. USA star Michelle Vitesse sparked an attack that saw Hinch pull off a tremendous save in the England goal and then Briggs was called on to make a save as Susannah Townsend's shot sent the ball high in the air and off the crossbar. Briggs was quickest to the ball and thwarted the incoming England attackers.

Possibly the moment of the World Cup, from a host-nation perspective, took place in the 34th minute when Alex Danson weaved her way through the USA defence and slotted the ball home to give England the lead. The goal was trademark Danson, her footwork and balance was spot-on as she dodged the tackles before unleashing her world-famous backhand shot past Briggs. The roar of the crowd was ear splitting and, for a few

minutes, England looked in the ascendency. But USA were not a team to ever give up and, in the shape of Erin Matson, they had a striker with the fearlessness of youth. Five minutes after Danson had sent the crowd into raptures, Matson sent a deadly hush round the ground. The 18-year-old picked the ball up on the wide left and drove towards the circle. Her position seemed innocuous but the shot that rasped off her reverse stick left Hinch stranded and the scores even.

'It was a move we practise a lot in training back at Spooky Nook,' said Matson later, referring to the team's training facility in Manheim, Pennsylvania. 'It was a perfectly weighted ball from Gonz [Melissa Gonzalez]; I was able to take it in my stride. Without that great pass I wouldn't have scored. She held the ball and fed it at the perfect moment. I was a bit taken aback when the entire stadium went silent though. We were all cheering on the pitch but the stands were silent except for little pockets of USA support.'

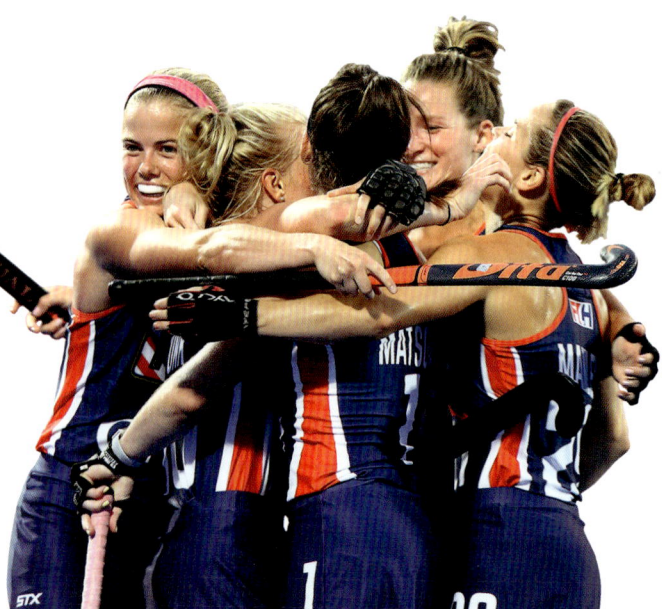

USA celebrate Matson's wonder-goal.
// *Rodrigo Jaramillo*

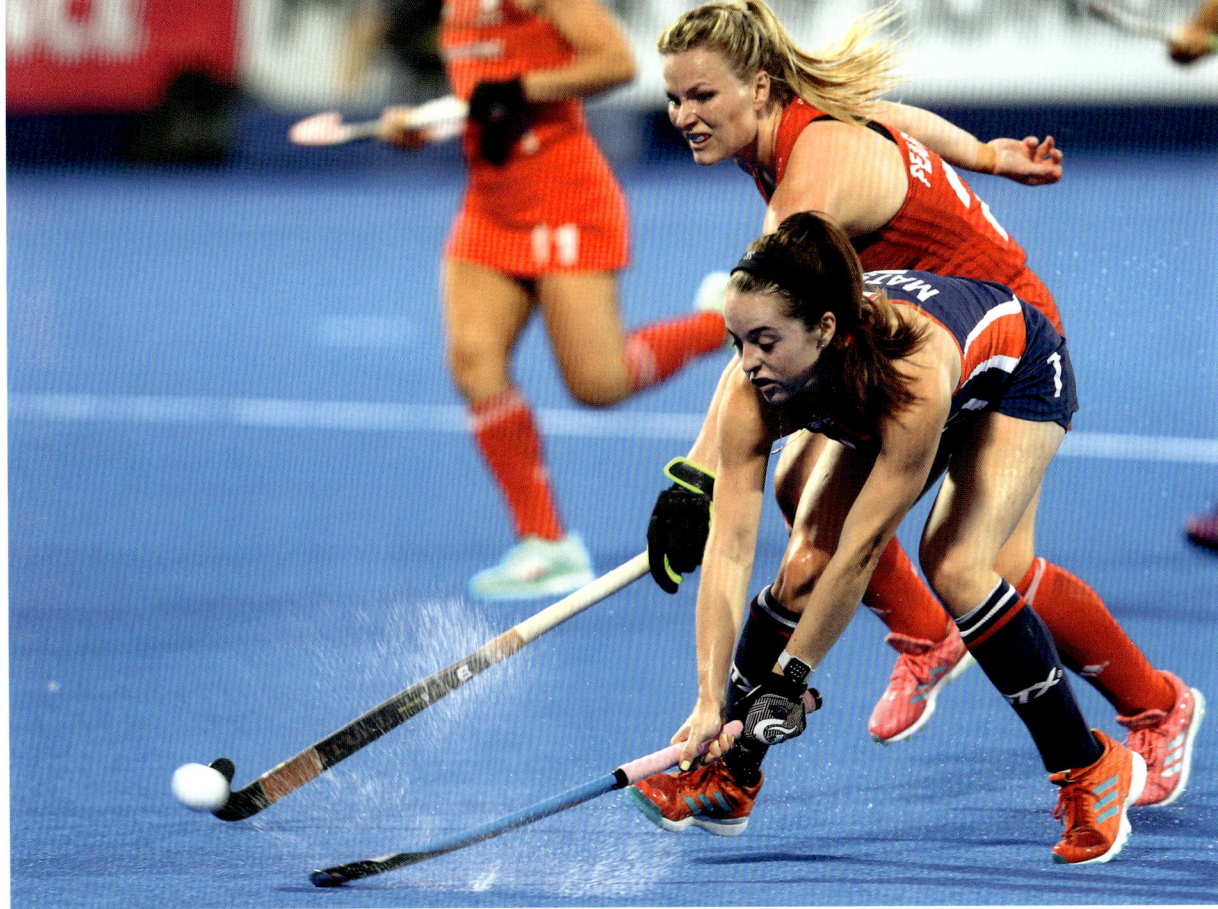

Erin Matson scored a brilliant equaliser against the hosts to ensure that USA claimed a share of the points. // *Rodrigo Jaramillo*

As the game counted down, the tempo rose in both camps and the work rate of the athletes reached even higher levels. Sophie Bray was in a race to the ball with Briggs, an encounter which left the England player in a heap. There was no quarter given by either team as they both searched for the elusive breakthrough. A tremendous save by Hinch in the closing seconds of the game was met with a sigh of relief from most of the 10,500 onlookers and as the teams trooped off the pitch it was clear both sets of players could not have given more.

'That was tough,' was England defender Laura Unsworth's reaction as she reflected on the game. 'I think we limited USA to just a few chances, in fact I only really remember the shot that led to the goal. That was a case of two very fit teams going at each other. I guess that will always result in a tight game.'

England's coach Danny Kerry agreed with Unsworth's assessment: 'I think the USA had the better of the first quarter but after that I think we shaded it. I can't ask any more of the girls tonight – they gave everything. If we play like we did today against Ireland, we'll be in with a shout.'

The result made for better reading for England as it meant they went into their final pool game knowing a draw would be enough to send them through to the quarter-finals. For USA, nothing less than a win over their next opponents would do.

Results – Day 4 – Wednesday 25 July 2018

Pool C

Germany   **3-2**   **Argentina**
Hannah Gablac 6m FG   Florencia Habif 16m PC
Charlotte Stapenhorst 20m FG, 25m FG   Maria Ortiz 30m FG

Vitality Player of the Match: Charlotte Stapenhorst (GER)

Pool C

USA   **1-1**   **England**
Erin Matson 39m FG   Alex Danson 34m FG

Vitality Player of the Match: Alex Danson (ENG)

Pool Standings – End of Day 4

Pool B

Pos	Team	Pld	W	D	L	GF	GA	GD	Pts
1	Ireland	1	1	0	0	3	1	2	3
2	England	2	0	2	0	2	2	0	2
3	India	1	0	1	0	1	1	0	1
4	USA	2	0	1	1	2	4	-2	1

Pool C

Pos	Team	Pld	W	D	L	GF	GA	GD	Pts
1	Germany	2	2	0	0	6	3	3	6
2	Argentina	2	1	0	1	8	5	3	3
3	South Africa	1	0	0	1	1	3	-2	0
4	Spain	1	0	0	1	2	6	-4	0

Day 5 – Thursday 26 July 2018

Ireland's call answered as Green Army continue to amaze

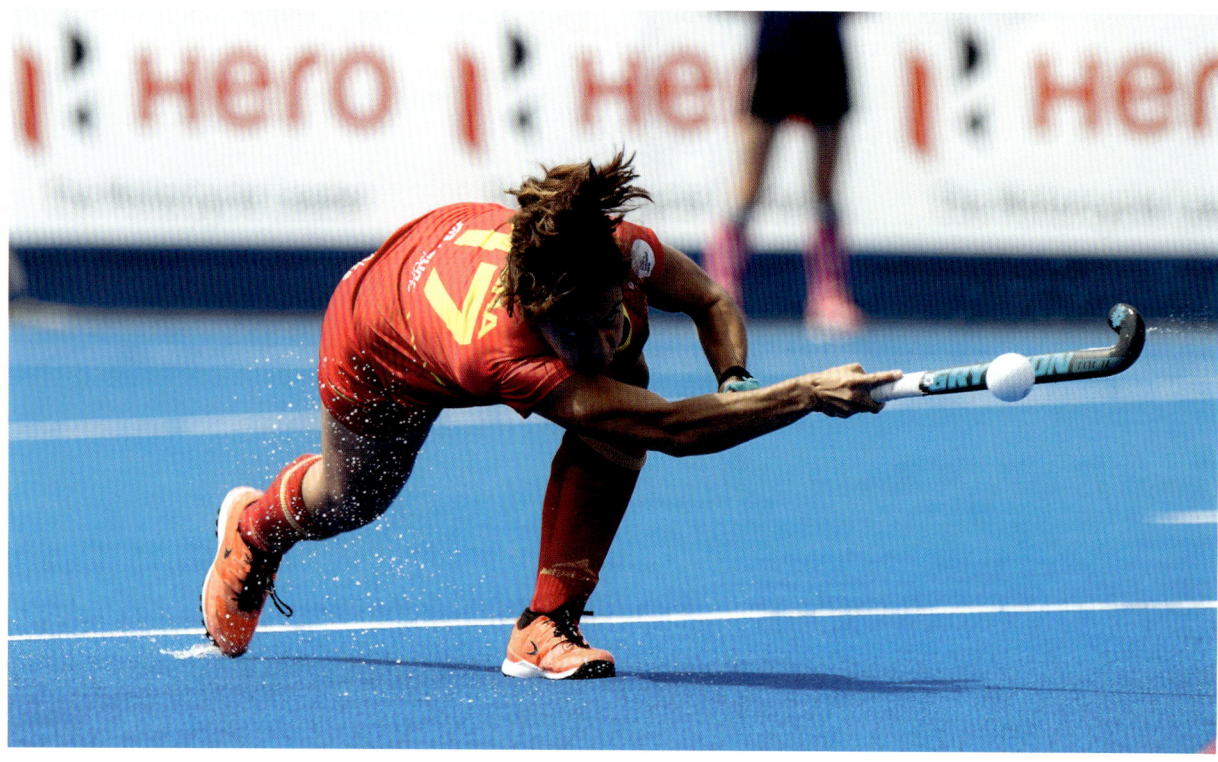

Lola Riera scored two superb penalty corners for the Red Sticks against South Africa. // *Frank Uijlenbroek*

Thursday 26 July was yet another hot and humid day at the Lee Valley Hockey & Tennis Centre, something which had been an unexpected feature throughout the early stages of the showpiece event in London. An early-afternoon session ensured that both of the day's matches would be played while the sun was at its hottest, with Pool C rivals Spain and African continental champions South Africa being the first teams to take to the field in the mid-day game.

After both teams had suffered defeat in their opening matches – Spain losing to Argentina, with South Africa going down to Germany – there was an urgent need to get points on the board in the hope of keeping their competition alive. A win for either team would have been a huge step towards a place in the cross-over play-offs, although with Germany now on six points, the chances of winning the pool to claim a direct ticket to the quarter-finals looked slim. While a second- or third-place finish in the pool would mean needing to win an additional play-off match to reach

the quarter-finals, it was infinitely better than the guaranteed elimination that would come from finishing fourth.

The Red Sticks of Spain were unquestionably the better team in the first two quarters and an utterly dominant performance in the opening period established a commanding 2-0 advantage. Lola Riera netted with an unstoppable penalty corner drag-flick that sailed into the top right corner via the crossbar, a stunning strike with which to open the scoring. That lead was doubled when attacking midfielder Berta Bonastre tapped in one of the easiest goals she will ever score on the international stage, finishing off a wonderful passing move that tore open the South Africa defence to make the score 2-0 after just ten minutes. With South Africa head coach Sheldon

South Africa's Nicole Walraven (in white) under pressure from Alicia Magaz of Spain in their Pool C meeting. // *Frank Uijlenbroek*

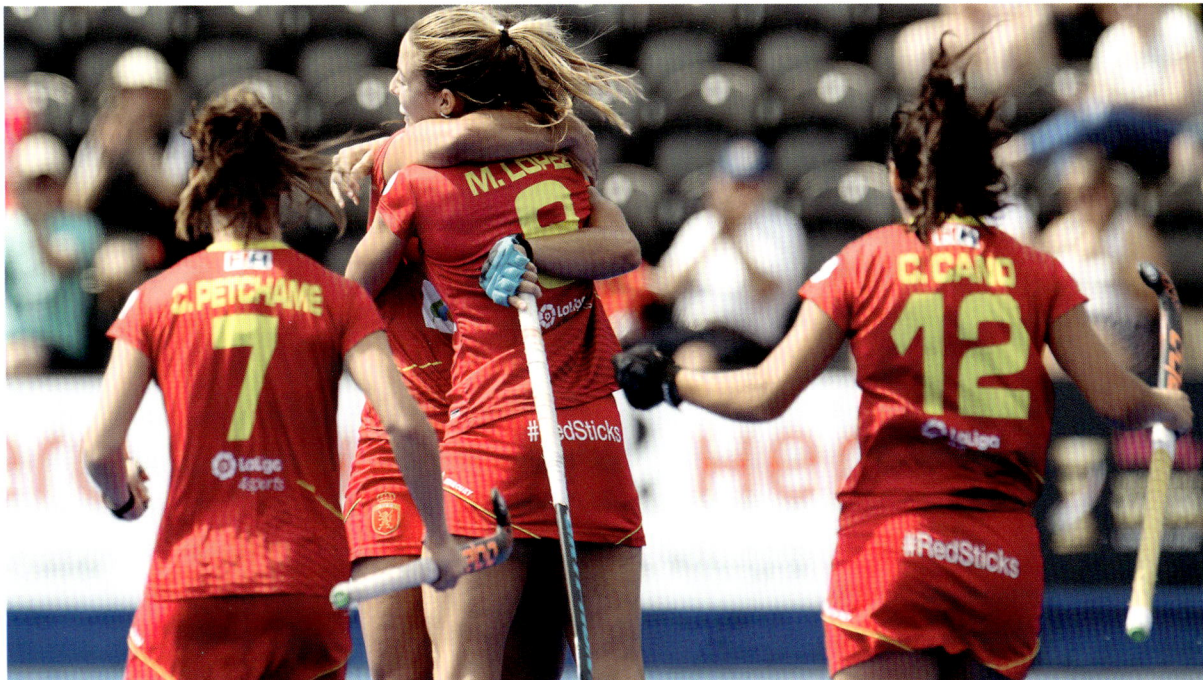

Maria Lopez hugs goalscorer Lola Riera moments after a stunning penalty corner effort opened the match scoring. // *Frank Uijlenbroek*

Rostron well aware that defeat to Spain would leave his team requiring victory against third-ranked Argentina in their final Pool C fixture, the champions of Africa started the third quarter with a new sense of purpose and looked completely reinvigorated. Their determination to take the game to their opponents was rewarded when defender Kara-Lee Botes scored from a penalty corner, showing a cool head to find the target after the initial effort was blocked by Spanish defender Xantal Gine. South Africa had given themselves a lifeline, but the spark of a comeback was quickly extinguished when the rampant Spaniards hit three goals without reply to effectively end the contest before the fourth period had even begun.

Carlota Petchame was the star of the quarter, scoring two goals of differing styles but both superb in quality to give Spain a three-goal cushion over their opponents. Petchame followed up a thunderous backhand effort with a wonderful piece of skill, wrong-footing South Africa goalkeeper Marlise van der Tonder before casually rolling the ball under the shot-stopper's body into the unguarded net. Carola Salvatella made it 5-1 following a defensive mistake from South Africa, all but guaranteeing victory for the Red Sticks.

Riding the crest of a wave of confidence, Spain were at the top of their game from start to finish in the fourth quarter, creating chance after chance and bringing the very best out of Van der Tonder, who was forced into making a

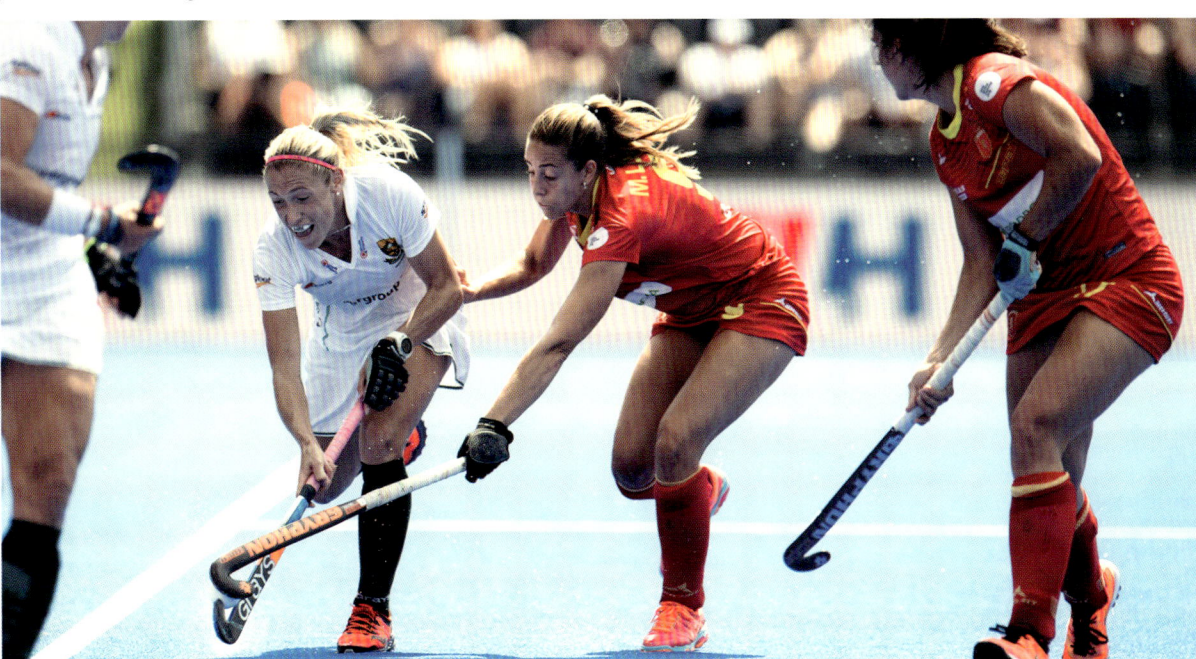

Shelley Jones of South Africa is challenged by Spain's Maria Lopez. // *Frank Uijlenbroek*

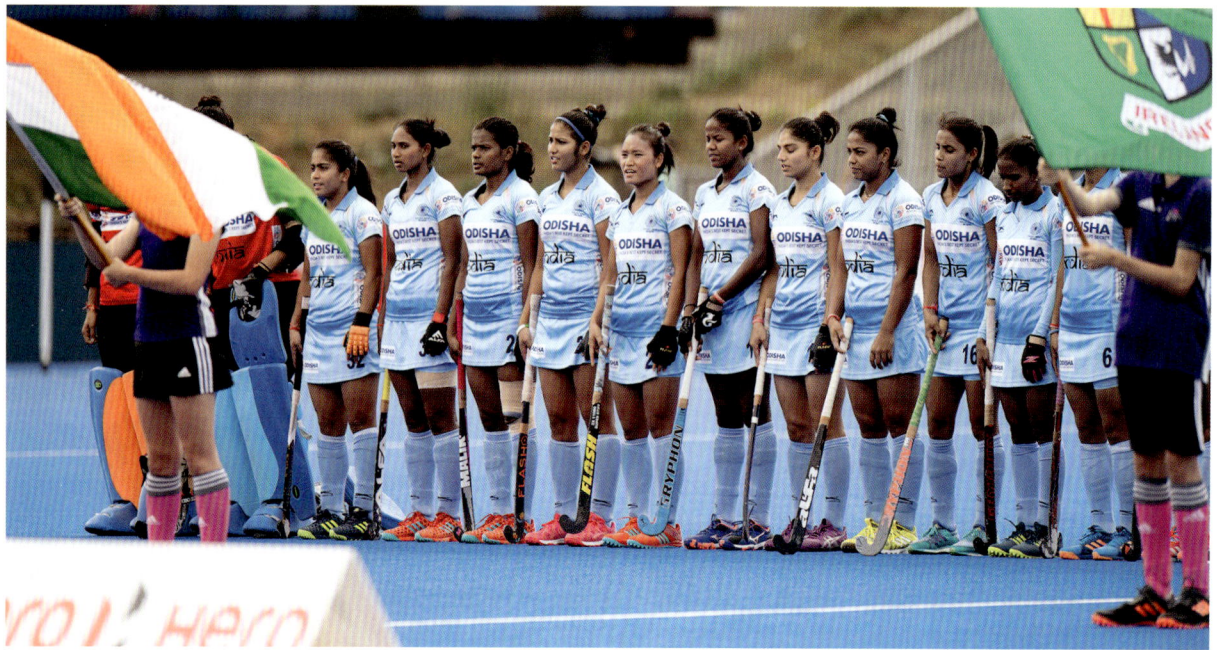

India (in blue) faced Ireland (green, right) in what would be a pivotal Pool B encounter. // *Frank Uijlenbroek*

string of brilliant saves. The South Africa goalkeeper could do little about the goals she did concede, as Spain produced penalty corner routines that were as good as anything seen in the previous 12 matches played at the Vitality Hockey Women's World Cup London 2018. Lola Riera struck again with another sensational penalty corner flick into the roof of the South African goal. Bonastre joined Reira and Petchame as players with a two-goal haul from the contest with another set-piece to complete a comprehensive 7-1 victory.

'We have spent a long time working on penalty corners and for a while, now, they haven't come as good in tournaments as we would have liked them to,' said Spain head coach Adrian Lock in the post-match interviews. He was clearly delighted that his team's World Cup challenge was now up and running. 'At Rio [Olympic Games] they weren't great, with the execution letting us down. But today the result of a couple of years of weekly work came together.'

The quality of the performance – Spain's best-ever result at a World Cup, eclipsing the previous record of 5-1 against Nigeria at the Madrid 1978 event – sent a clear message to all other nations that this was a team that had enough firepower to hurt any team competing in London. The result also provided a welcome boost to their confidence levels ahead of their final Pool C match against another team full of self-belief, table-toppers Germany, in a potentially fascinating encounter on Saturday 28 July.

'We know them well as a lot of our players play in Germany', continued Lock. 'We will focus on our game. They have outstanding players so we are conscious about what they can do, but we will focus on us.'

After watching his team record a sensational 3-1 victory over higher-ranked USA on the opening day of the competition, Ireland head coach Graham Shaw was all smiles ahead of the Green Army's Pool B meeting with India. It was

hardly surprising, especially after England's 1-1 draw with the Americans the previous day had meant that the second lowest-ranked team in the entire competition were just one win away from topping the pool and reaching the Vitality Hockey Women's World Cup quarter-finals, something which would guarantee Ireland a top-eight finish at a women's hockey World Cup for the first time in their history. Shaw knew that beating two higher-ranked teams in successive matches was not going to be easy, but the nature of the USA triumph had left the Irish girls feeling as if they could, both metaphorically and figuratively, take on the world.

Suggestions that the sizzling playing conditions would favour India proved unfounded as Ireland put on an excellent display of counter-attacking hockey in the opening period, nullifying India's danger players while also looking extremely threatening going forward. Ireland's lightening start to the contest was rewarded when exceptional forward Anna O'Flanagan sent a brilliant penalty corner deflection high into the roof of the Indian net. It was an absolutely unstoppable strike from O'Flanagan, whose crucial touch on the initial slap-shot from Shirley McCay gave India goalkeeper Savita no chance of saving.

India were far from outplayed in the opening two quarters, creating numerous chances, but were unable to find a way past Ayeisha McFerran, the 22-year-old goalkeeper who was rapidly establishing herself as one of the stand-out players of the competition. Gurjit Kaur came close to levelling the scores five minutes ahead of half-time, beating McFerran with a low penalty corner drag-flick that was heading to the bottom-right corner of the goal before defender Hannah Matthews got her stick in the way to guide the effort around the post.

India certainly had the better of the third quarter and won a trio of penalty corners, but, despite their best efforts,

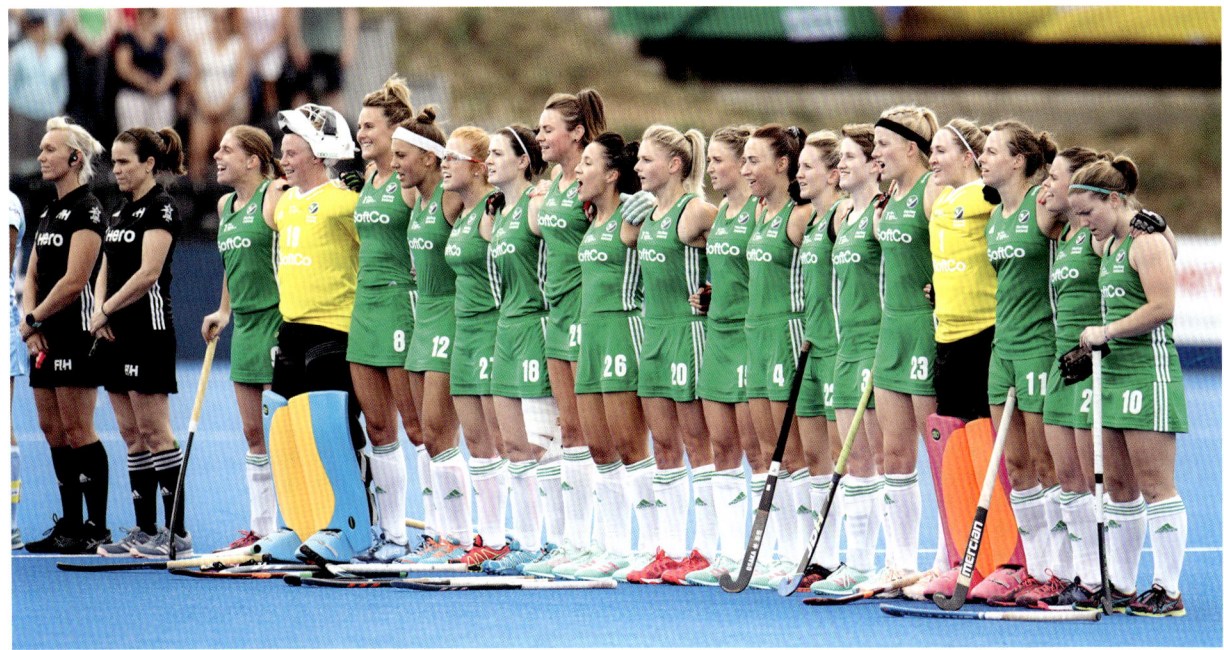

The Green Army sing Ireland's Call ahead of their meeting with India. // *Frank Uijlenbroek*

the Asian continental champions were continually thwarted by an Ireland defence that was playing with structure, discipline and a level of composure that, considering the importance of the match, almost defied logic.

Nicola Evans missed a glorious opportunity to seal Ireland's place in the competition quarter-finals when she failed to connect with a terrific pass across the face of Savita's goal, before India went for broke and replaced their goalkeeper with an outfield player in search of an

equaliser. It was a gamble that almost paid off when the ball fell to India's inspirational captain Rani in the dying stages of the contest. Unfortunately for Rani, her tame shot was confidently kicked away by McFerran before the sound of the hooter signalled the end of the match and triggered scenes of joyous celebrations from the Irish players, coaching staff and fans. Graham Shaw was overcome with emotion at the significance of Ireland's incredible, improbable achievement. Ireland had won Pool B with a game to spare,

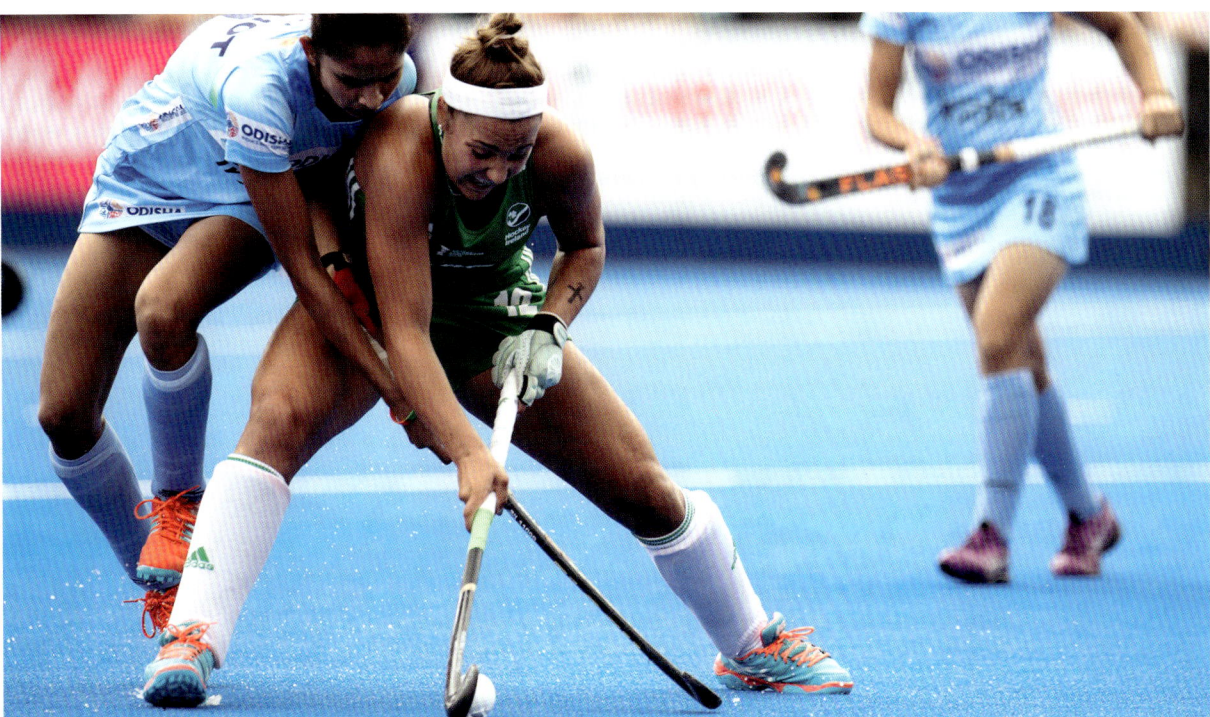

Elena Tice – who is also an Ireland cricket international – protects the ball from India's Navjot Kaur. // *Frank Uijlenbroek*

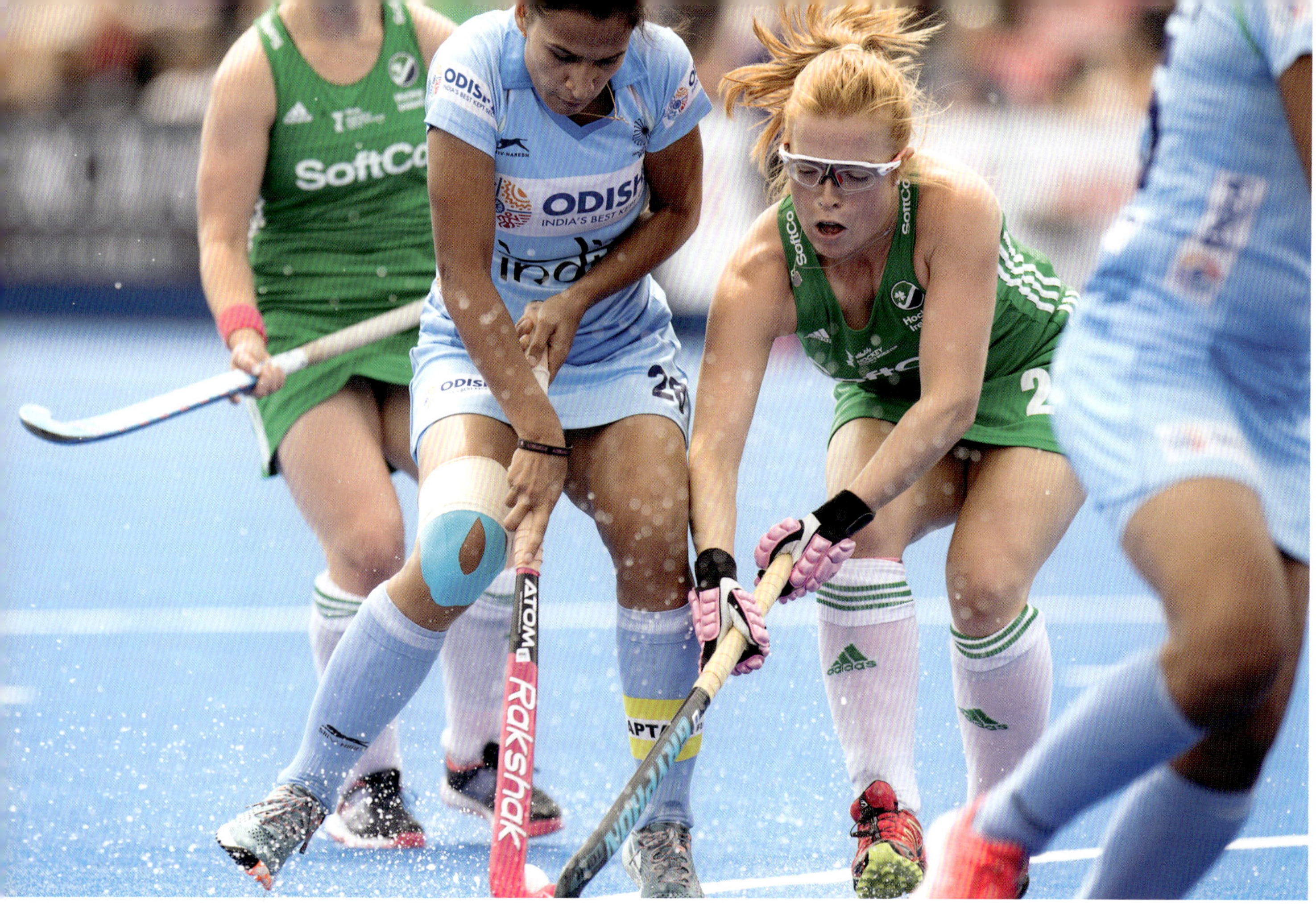

India captain Rani shows quick hands to evade the challenge from Ireland's Zoe Wilson. // *Frank Uijlenbroek*

becoming the first nation to qualify for the quarter-finals of the Vitality Hockey Women's World Cup London 2018.

'Ah, it's just brilliant,' said a delighted Nicola Daly, a player rendered almost speechless by the Green Army's sensational achievement before gathering enough composure to assess the match. 'It was really hot out there and I think both teams struggled but we had a game plan and stuck to it as far as we could. We don't fear anyone. We are ranked 16 and we have no pressure. The crowd brings so much energy, it was a great turnout again today and I expect we will have a great turnout when we play England on Sunday.'

News of Ireland's ground-breaking achievements in London gained a huge amount of media coverage back home. Celebratory images adorned the back pages of virtually every major national newspaper in the country, with *The Times*, The *Irish Times* and The *Irish Examiner* all splashing this wonderful Irish sporting success story on their front pages. For renowned hockey writer Stephen Findlater, this was something unprecedented in his time covering the sport.

'The coverage suddenly went off the charts, something totally unknown in my 12 or so years covering the game for national newspapers in Ireland,' said Findlater. 'For the first two games, there were only three or four Irish journalists in London. By the end, it was overflow section time in the press box as RTE [the national broadcaster] had five people of their own. The weird thing is how much of a surprise it all was to the editors. I freelance and had touted my wares to loads of outlets, knowing that only one other print journalist

had booked in for the tournament. Most were indifferent, many didn't even respond. You get used to things like this in the past. Suddenly the phone was hopping; even Al Jazeera in Qatar wanted a piece of the story, putting the clip in a kind of weird, worldwide slot straight after a Russian military rock festival which probably gives a decent idea of how surreal it all was.'

For Ireland, the opportunity to play home favourites England in front of a sell-out crowd on Sunday 29 July was one that they would relish. The Green Army had nothing to lose, which was not something that could be said for an England team who could still be eliminated if results did not go their way. It was a similar situation for India, who,

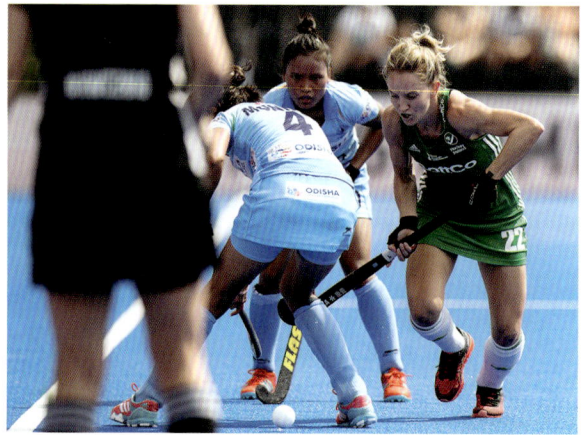

India's Monika cannot stop Ireland's Nicola Daly from making progress upfield.
// *Frank Uijlenbroek*

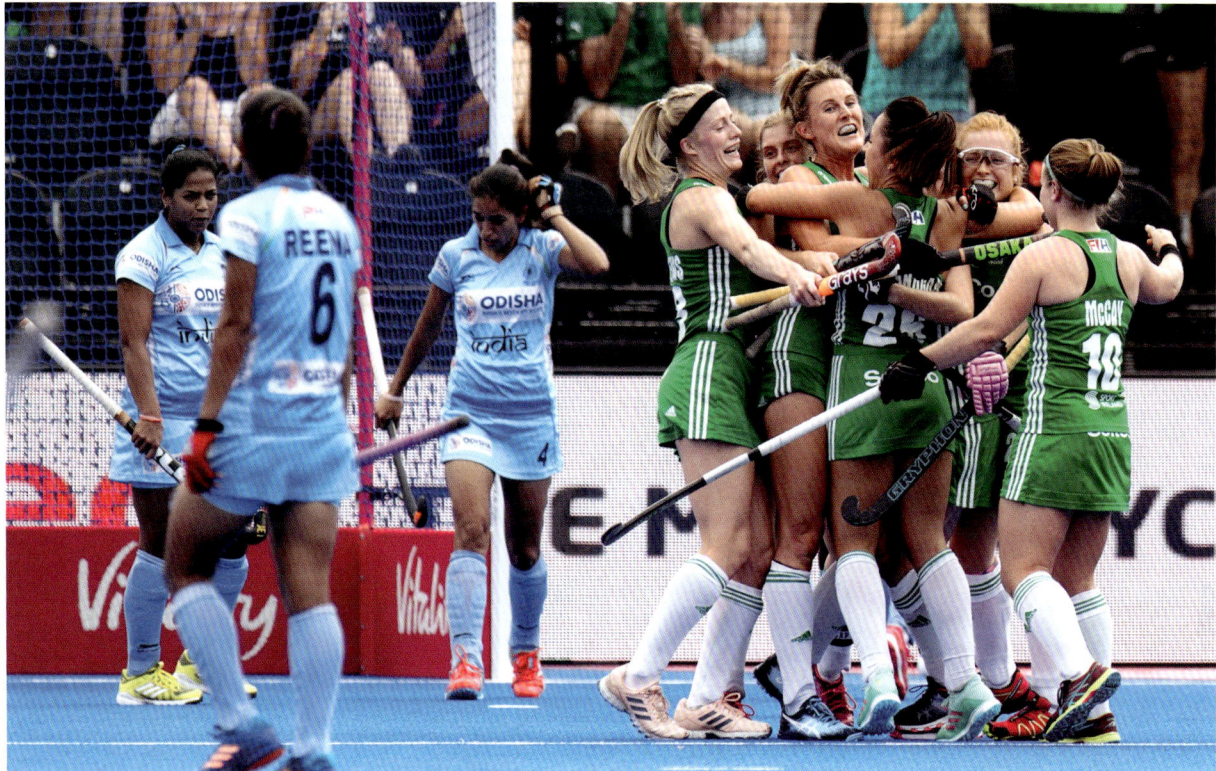
Ireland celebrate following Anna O'Flanagan's unstoppable penalty corner goal. // *Frank Uijlenbroek*

with one point from their two games, now needed at least a draw to stay ahead of USA, their final pool opponents, on goal difference. Reflecting both on his team's defeat to Ireland while also looking ahead to that crucial clash with the Americans, also scheduled for Sunday 29 July, India head coach Sjoerd Marijne was firmly of the belief that there was plenty to be positive about.

'I think if we look at possession and shots, then we had the lion's share, but in these matches, if you don't put your chances away then you won't get the outcome you perhaps deserve,' said the Dutchman. 'I am happy with the way we played, we just need to make sure we get an outcome when we face the USA.'

Results – Day 5 – Thursday 26 July 2018

Pool C

Spain	**7-1**	**South Africa**
Lola Riera 2m PC, 48m PC		Kara-Lee Botes 35m PC
Berta Bonastre 10m FG, 55m PC		
Carlota Petchame 37m FG, 42m FG		
Carola Salvatella 45m FG		

Vitality Player of the Match: Carlota Petchame (ESP)

Pool B

India	**0-1**	**Ireland**
		Anna O'Flanagan 13m PC

Vitality Player of the Match: Shirley McCay (IRL)

Pool Standings – End of Day 5

Pool B

Pos	Team	Pld	W	D	L	GF	GA	GD	Pts
1	Ireland	2	2	0	0	4	1	3	6
2	England	2	0	2	0	2	2	0	2
3	India	2	0	1	1	1	1	-1	1
4	USA	2	0	1	1	2	4	-2	1

Pool C

Pos	Team	Pld	W	D	L	GF	GA	GD	Pts
1	Germany	2	2	0	0	6	3	3	6
2	Argentina	2	1	0	1	8	5	3	3
3	South Africa	2	1	0	1	9	7	2	3
4	Spain	2	0	0	2	2	10	-8	0

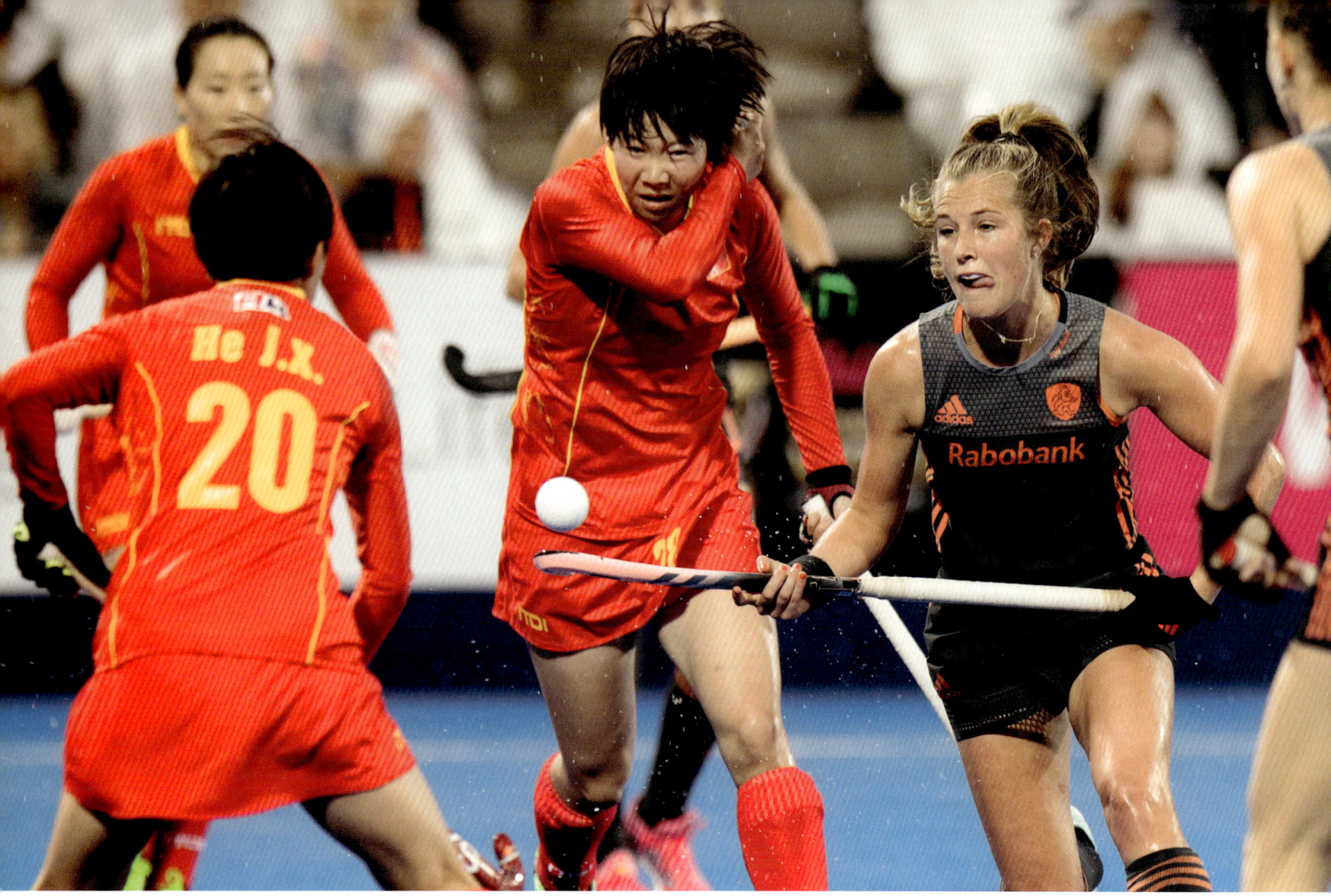

Xan de Waard controls the ball mid-air. // *Frank Uijlenbroek*

Day 6 – Friday 27 July 2018

Netherlands continue to cruise while Italy steal the headlines

The heat that had been suffocating London for the previous two months finally boiled over on Day 6, leaving the organisers anxiously scanning the horizon for signs of thunder and lightning.

When the rain came it was intense and the Lee Valley Hockey & Tennis Centre was soon awash as the heavens opened. Rain jackets and black plastic bags were in abundance as the spectators stoically took their seats and prepared for the evening's hockey action.

Thunder and a deluge of rain may have marked the start of the sixth day of competition at the Vitality Hockey Women's World Cup but it was a lightning strike from Italy that provided the highlight of the day. The lowest-ranked team at the tournament soaked up 59 minutes of Korea pressure and then struck with a counter that sealed their second win of the tournament and a guaranteed place in the cross-over round.

Prior to the Italian smash and grab win, the Netherlands had been putting on the style once again as they took to the field against China. The Dutch had already

taken the lead through a Caia van Maasakker penalty-corner goal when the London skyline turned dark and then the rain, thunder and lightning arrived. Eight minutes into the game both teams were withdrawn from the pitch until the lightning, and the threat to safety it posed, had passed by.

When the teams came back out, after an eight-minute break, they had six minutes to get warmed up and refocus their minds. Despite the impromptu break, the Netherlands continued as if nothing untoward had occurred.

One of the concerns for head coach Alyson Annan after the Netherlands' 7-0 win over Korea in their opening match, was that her team had not had a chance to practise penalty corners. All seven goals in that match had come from open play, with the Dutch only winning four penalty corners during the match. As defender turned midfielder Margot van Geffen pointed out, the Netherlands' aim was to always get an outcome – whether that be a goal or a penalty corner. In the opening match they had just been too good at scoring.

A veteran of two previous World Cups and three Olympic Games, Lidewij Welten was a player who understood the importance of attending to every detail, and she answered her coach's demand. In the seventh minute, she brilliantly weaved her way through the China defence and neatly placed the ball on a foot to win a corner. As Caia van Maasakker strode up to take her position at the top of the circle, there really was only one outcome.

The 1-0 lead was extended when Kelly Jonker scored her second goal of the tournament; the speedy and agile attacker left the defenders chasing shadows as she darted goalwards. Laurien Leurink joined the party when she made it 3-0. Her goal resulted from a quick counter-attack which started with the Netherlands' goalkeeper Annie Veenendaal. The keeper pulled off a great save and her clearance found Eva de Goede who in turn found Leurink. Her finish was as high in quality as Veenendaal's save.

China came out for the second half with a renewed sense of urgency and a quick attack earned them their only penalty corner of the game. This was dealt with by the Dutch defence and business resumed as Welten scored two goals, including one which was knocked into the goal by a Chinese defender.

The knowledgeable crowd in the Lee Valley Hockey & Tennis Centre were impressed with this virtuoso performance, but the biggest cheer went up when China scored their first

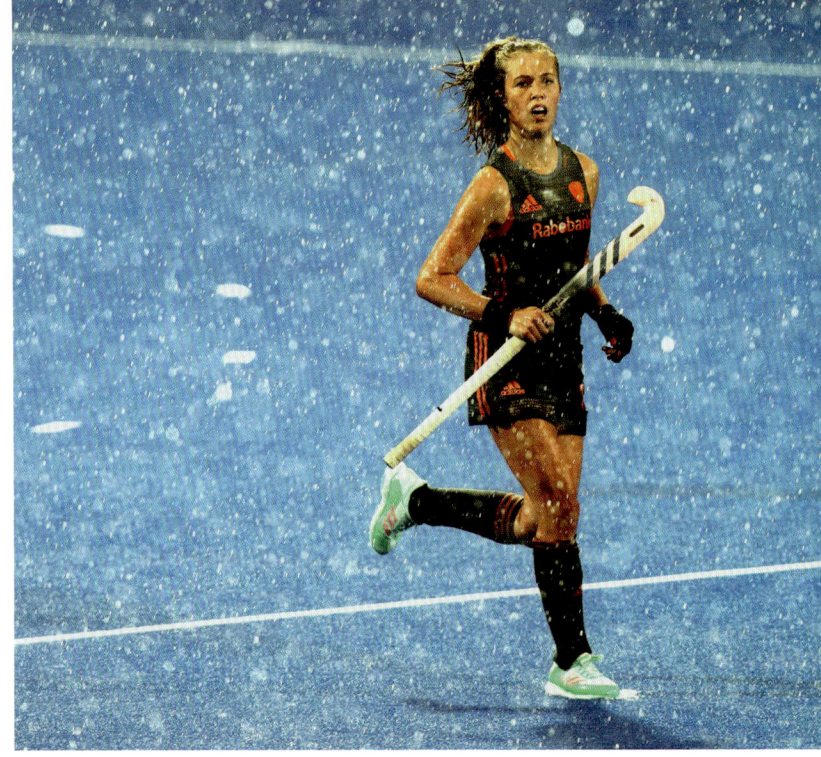

Dutch ace Xan de Waard remains unaffected by the playing conditions during the Netherlands' Pool A encounter against China. // *Rodrigo Jaramillo*

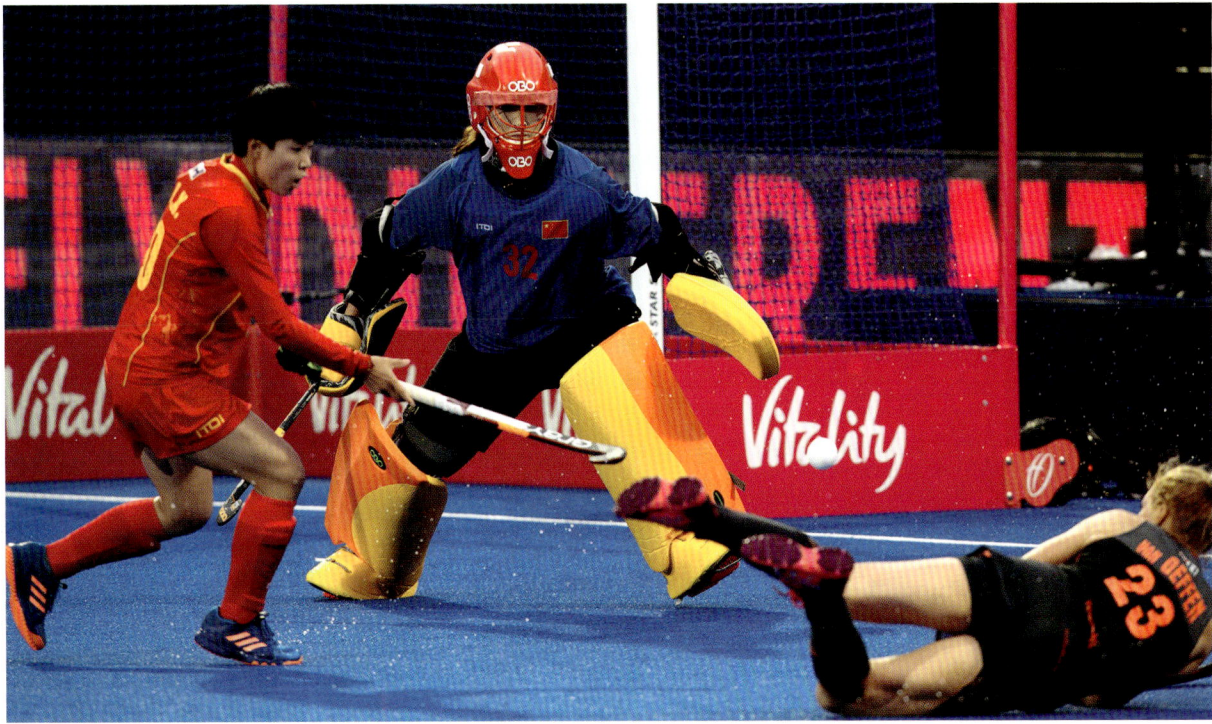

A diving Margot van Geffen gives China's defence plenty to think about. // *Rodrigo Jaramillo*

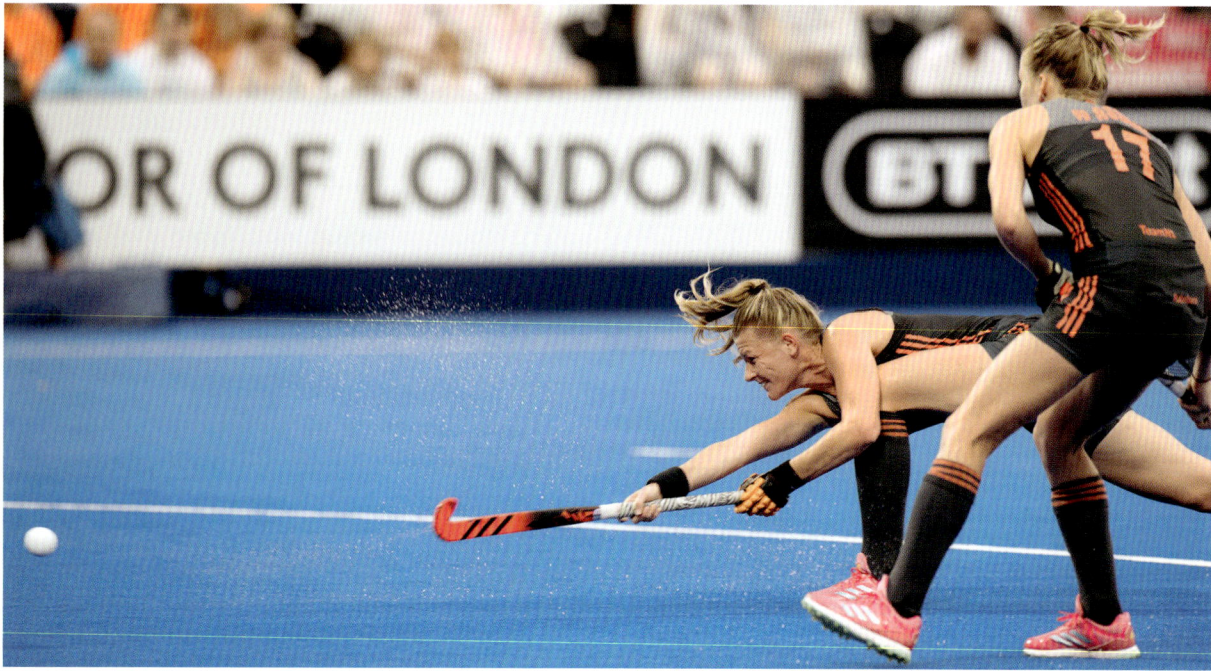

Caia van Maasakker was the scorer of the first Dutch goal against China, netting with a 13th-minute penalty corner. // *Frank Uijlenbroek*

goal of the tournament. Yong Jing picked up the ball from a wayward Dutch pass and drove into the circle. Her reverse stick shot was wickedly fierce and flew past Veenendaal into the top corner. Her celebrations, and those of her team, were worthy of a cup final.

Order was restored as Kitty van Male added her name to the score-sheet and the Dutch were able to celebrate another job well done.

For head coach Alyson Annan and her team the challenge was how to keep the team on track, with the number of rest days between matches. Due to the nature of the tournament and the fact that there were 16 teams and four pools, the Dutch schedule included three rest days between their first and second match. Margot van Geffen revealed that the Dutch had resorted to a very British way of relaxing between games. 'We needed to get away from the venue for a while, so we went to Bisham Abbey [England Hockey's headquarters] and had some training sessions there,' said van Geffen. 'Then we had a boat trip on the Thames and played an old English game called Croquet and had High Tea, with scones and cream.'

'The croquet turned into a contest between the "youngsters" and the "oldies",' added team-mate Eva de Goede. 'Of course the oldies won; we always do.'

This small insight provided yet another clue to the Netherlands' approach to the sport. For the team in orange, it was all about having the right balance of competition and fun. While an impromptu game

of croquet might seem an inconsequential activity, for team spirit it was invaluable. It is a point that De Goede emphasised: 'We have a great team and we enjoy playing together. It is important that we have a good mix of older and younger players. We make sure the structure is there and that everyone knows their place within it. Our strength as a squad is that we trust ourselves and play the way we want to play. We score a lot of team goals, involving many people in the build-up, and that is very good. Most importantly, we are having fun.'

While the Netherlands' win over the China team was both serene in nature and par for the course, the next match was anything but.

The Netherlands ended their second game of the World Cup with maximum points and a goal difference of +13. // *Rodrigo Jaramillo*

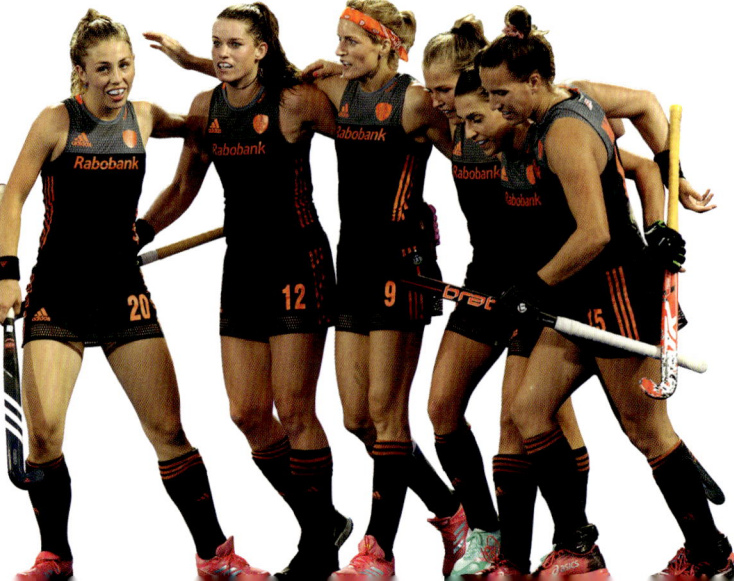

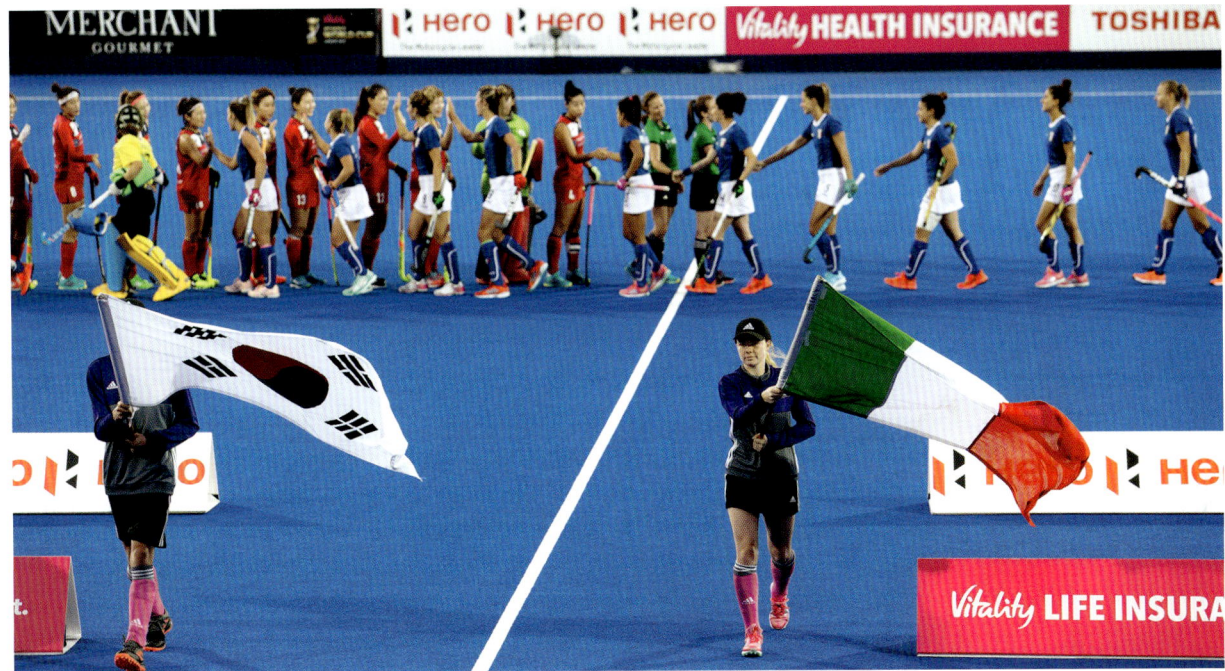
The teams and officials shake hands ahead of Korea's Pool A meeting with Italy. // *Rodrigo Jaramillo*

Korea had been battered by the Netherlands in their opening pool match and, while head coach Huh Sang Young had been pragmatic about the loss, conceding that the Dutch were the best team in the world, he was certainly looking for three points against the lowest-ranked team in London.

The three-day break had repaired the Korea team's confidence and they took to the field with clear attacking intent. Time and again, the red shirts of Korea poured forward with the ball, trying to create the space needed to launch an attack on the Italian goal.

Unfortunately for the higher-ranked team, they found the Italian midfield and defence in defiant mood. Marshalled by captain Chiara Tiddi, the Azzurre formed their own fortress ahead of their circle and much of the game was played out between the two circles. When Korea did break through, they found a tiny but indomitable barrier in their path. Martina Chirico may have been one of the smallest goalkeepers competing in the World Cup, but she was also one of the most athletic. Time and again, her incredible reactions and reading of the game meant that the Korea attack was foiled at every turn.

Italy themselves were no slouches when it came to attacking and, in the form of Lara Oviedo, they had a forward who could turn most defensive units inside out. For much of the first half, however, Italy's forays into the Korea half of the pitch were more a case of relieving pressure than attacking the goal with any intent.

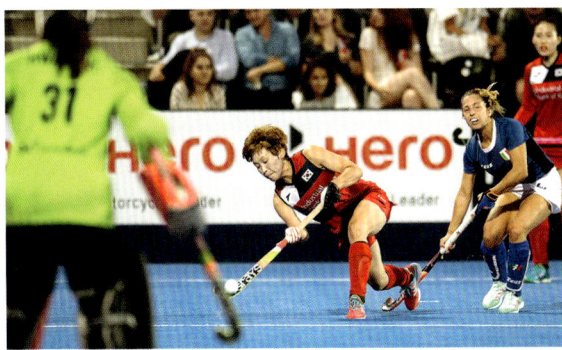
Action from the early stages as Korea (in red) faced Italy (blue). // *Frank Uijlenbroek*

The second half saw Italy begin to play their attacking game a little more. When Korea's Lee Yurim was sent from the pitch with a green card, Italy's coach Roberto Carta sensed a moment to strike. He exhorted his players to attack and his experienced defenders answered the call. Forty-year-old Agata Wybieralska made some age-defying runs up the right side of the pitch while Tiddi made lung-busting charges through the middle, much to the delight of the large Italian contingent in the stands. Korea survived that storm and began to exert their own pressure, winning three penalty corners in quick succession. Cheon Seul Ki fired a vicious shot at the goal on the second of these, but Chirico continued to impress as she saved that attempt and then continued to control the circle, positioning

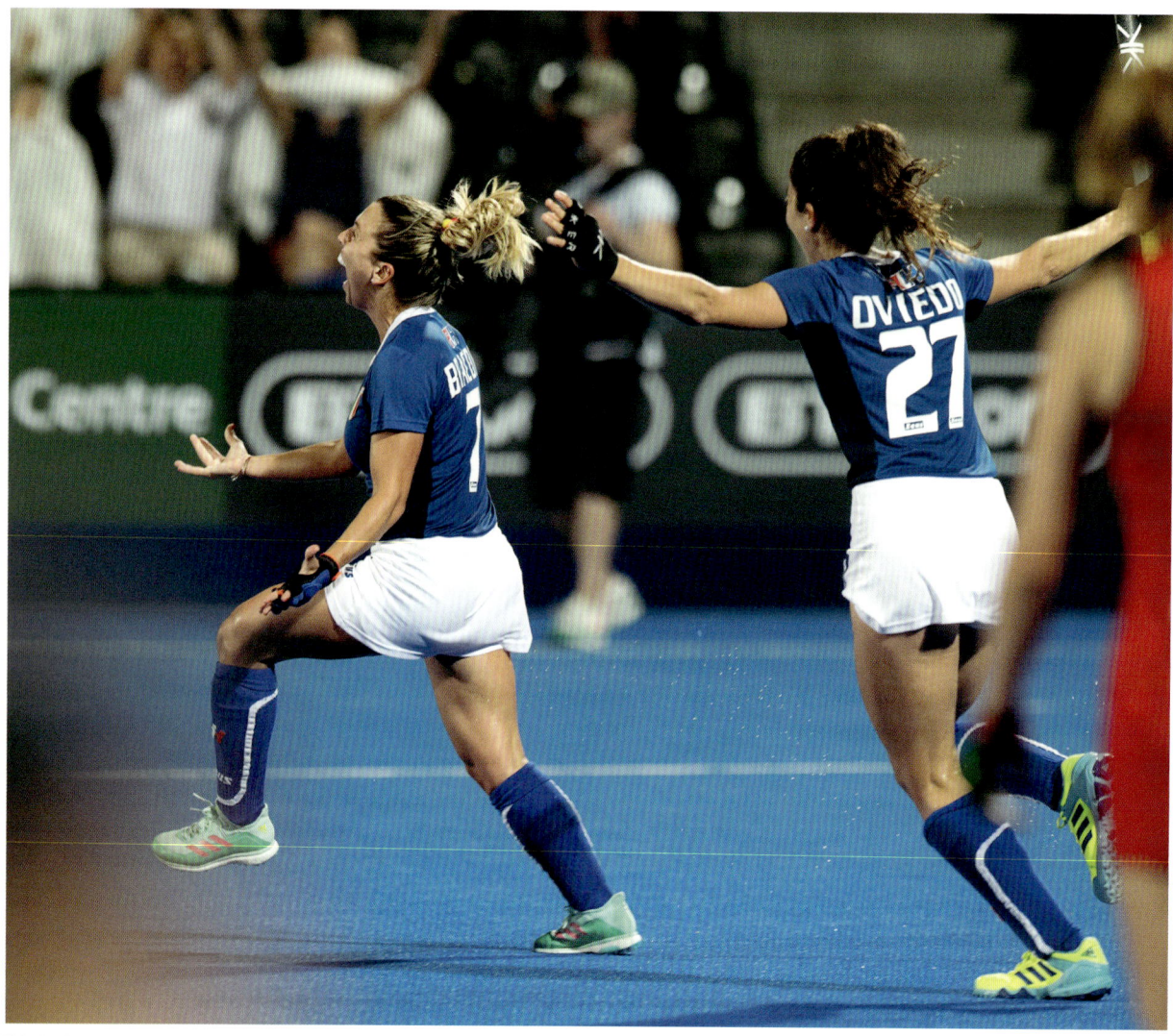

Valentina Braconi gave Italy a dramatic victory thanks to a winning strike that arrived with just seconds of the contest remaining. // *Frank Uijlenbroek*

her defenders and clearing any ball that managed to get through the blue line.

With just three minutes left, Korea's Cho Hyein had the perfect opportunity to put her side ahead when she received the ball from star forward Park Mi Hyun in front of the Italy goal. Her first touch let her down and the momentary halt to play gave the Italian defence time to regroup.

As the clock counted down, everyone watching the match would have been forgiven for assuming a draw. With 10 seconds on the clock Oviedo collected the ball in the Korea circle after yet another pitch-splitting pass from Tiddi. Her shot rebounded into a crowded area in front of the goal and, as the clock read two seconds remaining, Valentina Braconi slotted the ball home, giving her team two wins from two games and, more importantly, a guaranteed place

in the cross-over play-off matches to ensure that they would not be eliminated from the pool phase.

For Italy this was their own piece of history, a point that Italian midfielder, Eugenia Bianchi made as she spoke after the game. 'For us, every one of these games is our own cup final. We came into this event as the lowest-ranked team but we came with no fear and our confidence is growing. 'Now we are through to the next stage and we have a chance to make more history.'

Italy's Valentina Braconi would play a vital role in the outcome of her team's meeting with Korea. // *Frank Uijlenbroek*

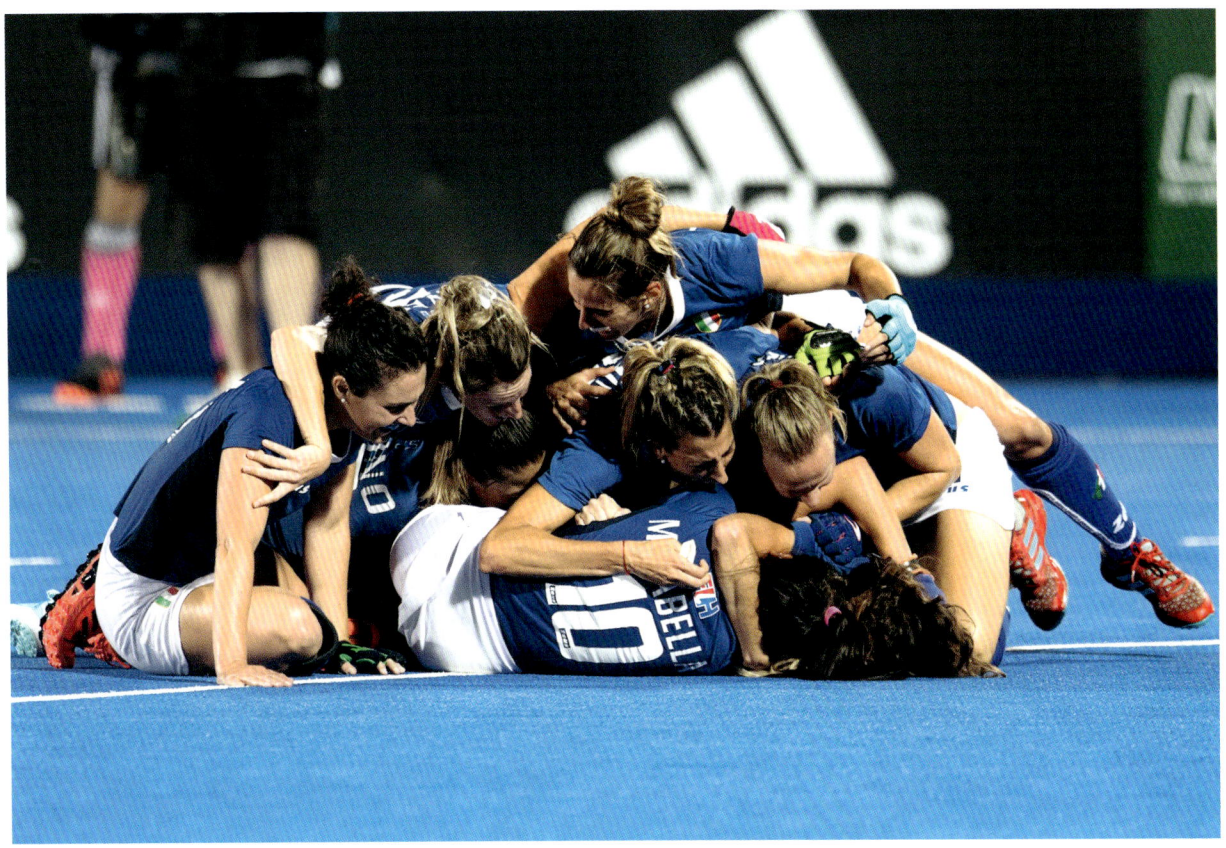

A 1-0 victory over Korea meant that Italy, the lowest-ranked team in the competition, were guaranteed a place in the knock-out stages. // *Frank Uijlenbroek*

Results – Day 6 – Friday 27 July 2018

Pool A

China	**1-7**	**Netherlands**
Yong Jing 57m FG		Caia van Maasakker 13m PC
		Kelly Jonker 15m FG
		Laurien Leurink 24m FG
		Lidewij Welten 30m FG, 37m FG
		Kitty van Male 56m FG
		Xan de Waard 59m FG

Vitality Player of the Match: Laurien Leurink (NED)

Korea	**0-1**	**Italy**
		Valentina Braconi 60m FG

Vitality Player of the Match: Martina Chirico (GK - ITA)

Pool Standings – End of Day 6

Pool A

Pos	Team	Pld	W	D	L	GF	GA	GD	Pts
1	Netherlands	2	2	0	0	14	1	13	6
2	Italy	2	2	0	0	4	0	4	6
3	Korea	2	0	0	2	0	8	-8	0
4	China	2	0	0	2	1	10	-9	0

Day 7 – Saturday 28 July 2018

Die Danas and Hockeyroos do the business while Argentina falter

Going into the last round of pool matches, it was quite remarkable that the only guaranteed quarter-finalist remained the second lowest-ranked team, Ireland. So tight were the pools that all 16 teams still had a chance to qualify for the knock-out stages, even if some teams' chances were more remote than others.

The talk around the stadium was all about Ireland, Italy, Belgium and Japan, teams that were playing free-flowing, fearless and innovative hockey and who were challenging the perceived world order. As the pundits explored all options it was becoming clear that for one of the lower-ranked teams, a semi-final place was not out of the question.

There are some things that don't change too much over time, however, and it was little surprise to see Germany making serene progress through the pool matches. Although

Die Danas had endured a torrid time at the 2014 World Cup in The Hague, this edition saw them right back on track. In their opening game they had made short work of South Africa, winning 4-1. It had been more of a surprise when they had dispatched Argentina 3-2 in a thrilling game. Now they were facing European rivals, the up-and-coming Spanish.

As the match got underway, it was Spaniards who made the brightest start. The Red Sticks won a penalty corner early on and, with their recent success in the set-piece, Germany were right to line up with apprehension. Julia Ciupka in the German goal and her well-trained defence had done their homework, however, and the resulting shot from Begoña Garcia was cleared to safety.

Germany quickly created their own opportunity when Lena Micheel burst through with her devastating speed and flair. The result was a penalty corner which was worked

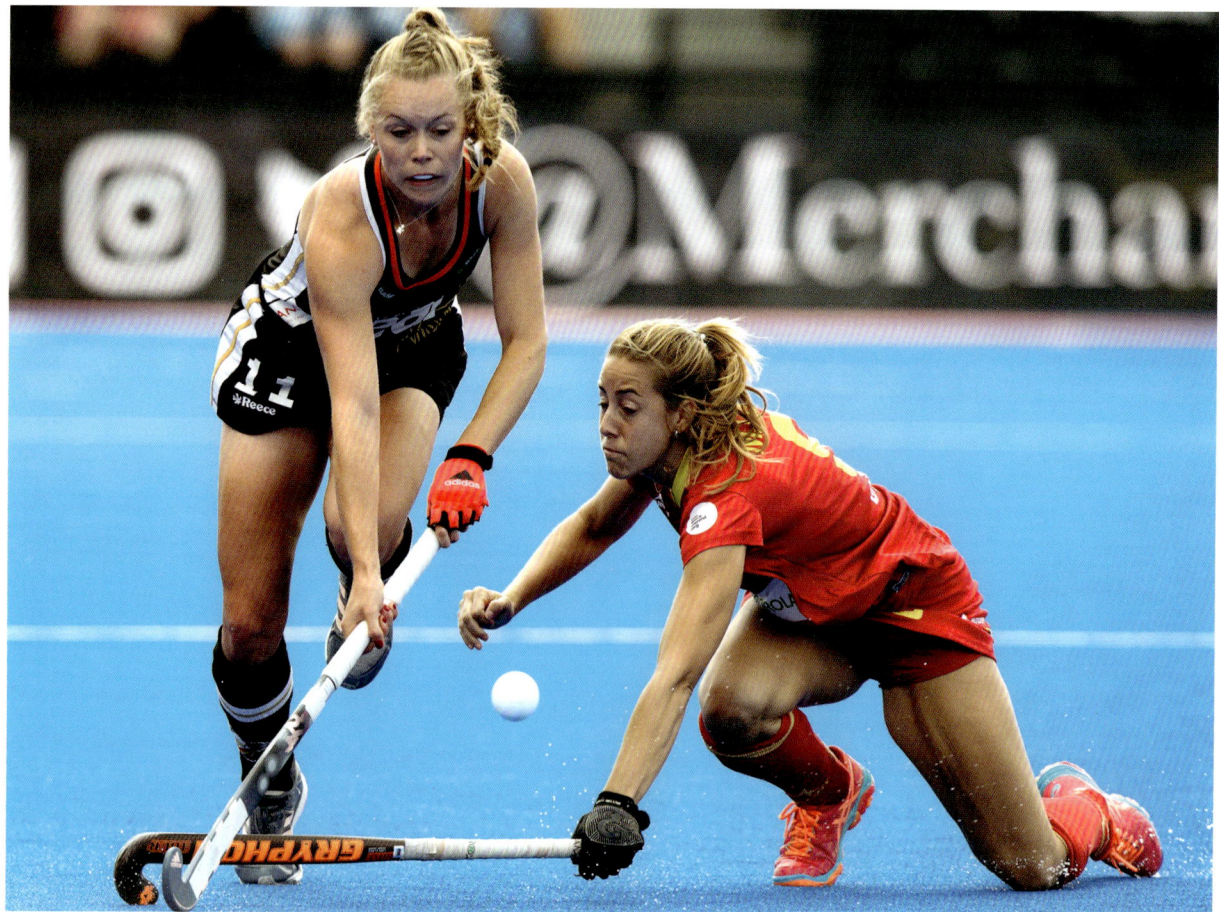

Germany's Lena Micheel accelerates down the right, skipping past Spain's Maria Lopez. // *Rodrigo Jaramillo*

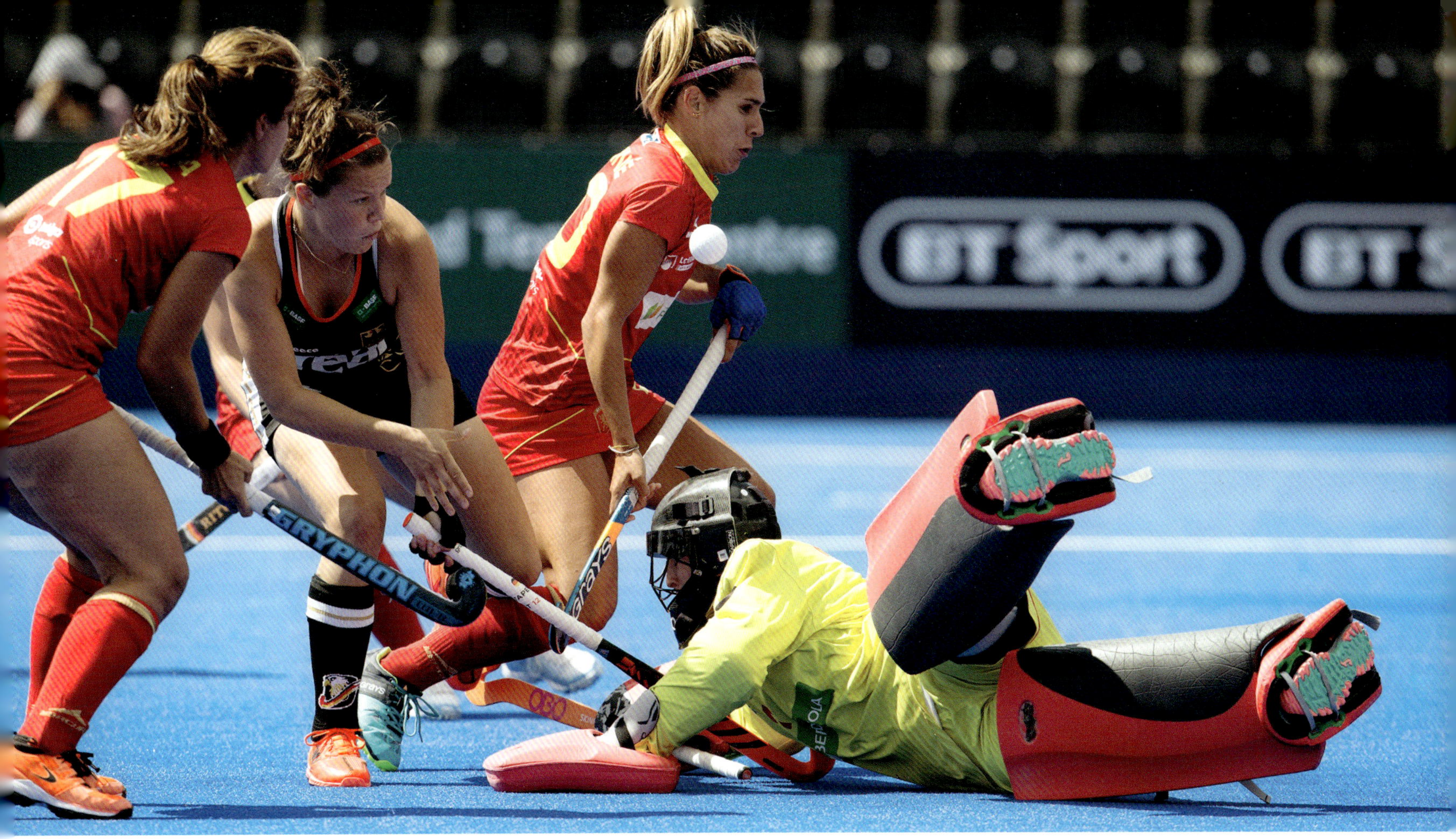

Germany star Charlotte Stapenhorst causes chaos in the Spanish circle, with goalkeeper Maria Ruiz called into action. // *Rodrigo Jaramillo*

beautifully. Anne Schröder injected the ball and the switch back to her from the top of the circle caught Spain totally unawares. Schröder lifted the ball high over Maria Ruiz in Spain's goal and Germany were on their way.

Schröder was one of three players who had been in The Hague for the 2014 World Cup. The scars of that tournament had mended over time but her fellow survivor Franzisca Hauke said, with a little shudder, that going into such a tournament unprepared had been a horrible experience. Head coach Xavier Reckinger's approach since taking control of the squad in October 2017 had been to give the fast and skilful Schröder and Hauke more freedom to run at the opposition, and the tactic was paying dividends.

'We don't have one or two star players, we are a team who works hard for each other,' said Hauke. 'Since 2014 we have had a lot of changes. Germany was always known as the hardest nation when it comes to defending but now we are playing a really attacking game as well. We want to shoot more goals, it is not enough to just defend our goal. We are also much more fit than we were four years ago, and that is key. And the freedom Xavier has given to us, to play different positions, well that uses our strengths and works really well.'

In the second quarter, Spain again came out the faster and started to play creative hockey in an attempt to get behind the German midfield. Germany reacted to the challenge by strengthening their presence in midfield and cutting out Spain's route to goal. Selin Oruz, Viktoria Huse and the third survivor of the World Cup in The Hague, Janne Müller-Wieland, were central to stemming the Spanish flow.

The German defences, however, were caught off-guard by a fantastic piece of skill. As the end of the quarter neared, a mazy run by Begoña Garcia earned Spain their second penalty corner of the match. The ball was played in and bounced high in the air. Quickest to react was Xantal Gine, who plucked the ball from the air and angled it into the goal. This was the cause of a great celebration by the Red Sticks and, subsequently, there was a bounce in the team's step and a confidence in their demeanour that had been missing in the first quarter.

One of the pleasures of watching the Spanish side play at this tournament was the energy and speed with which the Red Sticks attacked. Instigator of many of these moves was captain Georgina Oliva. This match was no different as

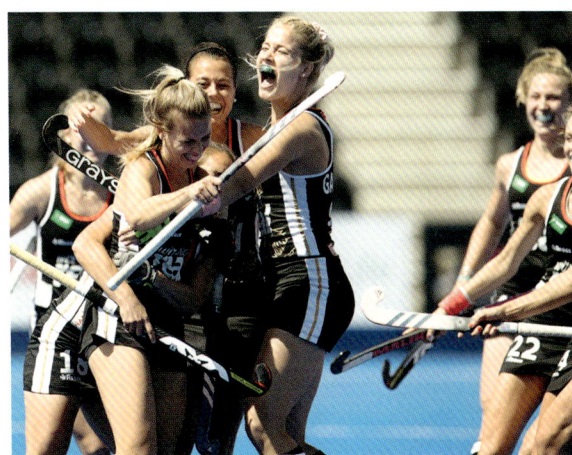

Anne Schröder (second from left) is congratulated for scoring Germany's opening goal.
// *Frank Uijlenbroek*

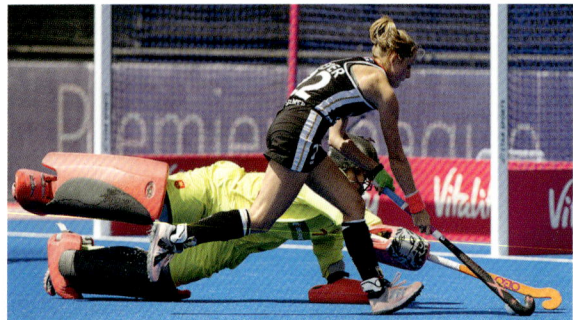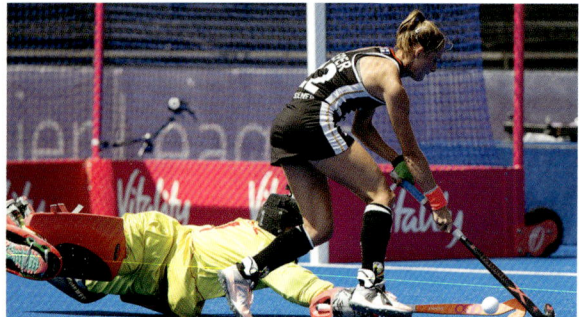

Spain shot-stopper Maria Ruiz pulls off a superb save to deny Germany's Cecile Pieper, although it did not stop Die Danas from topping Pool C with their third successive victory. // *Rodrigo Jaramillo*

the hugely energetic Spanish midfielder burst through to win Spain's third penalty corner. But Germany were not a team to make the same mistake twice and their defence was alive to the threat of the Spanish penalty corner variations and the slipped pass was cut out.

A quick German counter led to Germany's own penalty corner opportunity. The shot was high and dangerous but Ruiz rose to the challenge and gloved the ball away. Still Germany pushed and just seconds later restored their lead when Oruz was on hand to push the ball home after Hannah Gablac had taken the ball around the back of the Spanish defence.

The lead was increased further when Viktoria Huse's penalty corner flew emphatically towards the goal.

Marie Mävers showed her poacher's instinct in front of goal as she got the lightest of touches to score her first goal of the tournament.

Germany nearly made it four as the ever-dangerous Lisa Altenburg ran the ball from her own circle. Her wicked cross eluded everyone, including team-mate Gablac who was just centimetres from the ball as it whizzed past everyone.

Spain's Berta Bonastre was pragmatic as she spoke after the game. 'We were definitely competitive out there today but we made some little mistakes and they were the difference between us and Germany. It was the same with our match against Argentina. It was not a 6-2 game, but we made mistakes which were punished.

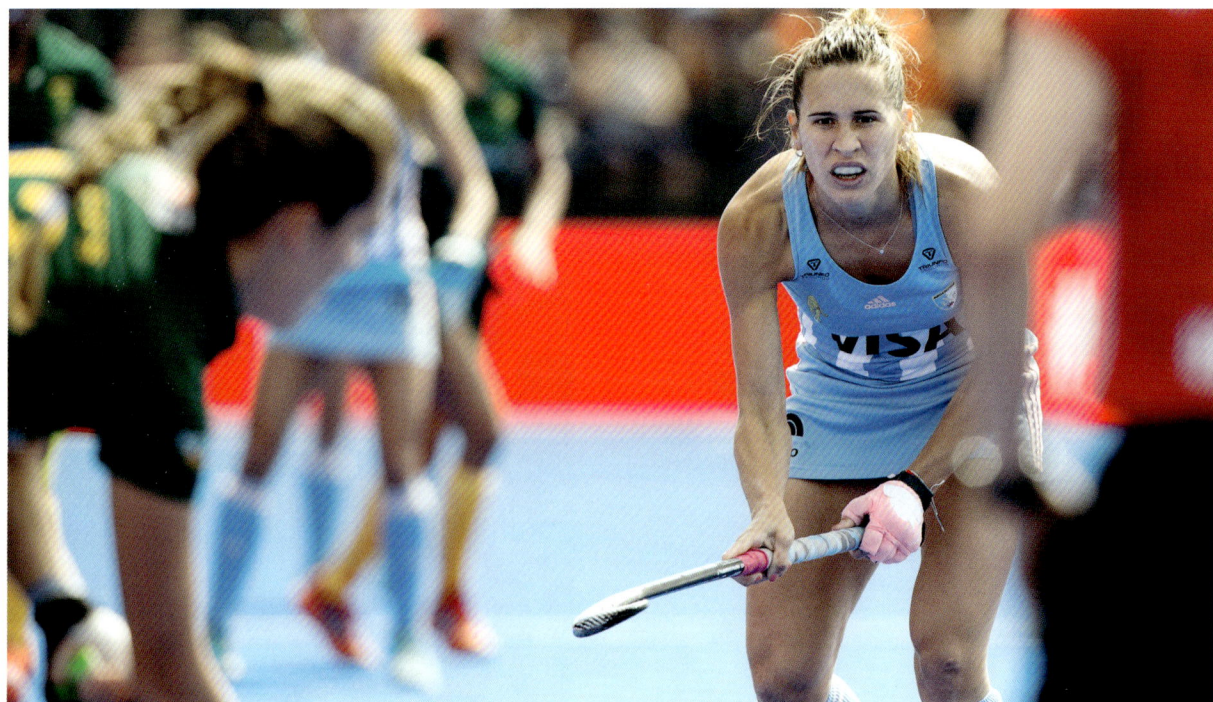

Argentina were in for a tough ride in their final Pool C match against South Africa. // *Rodrigo Jaramillo*

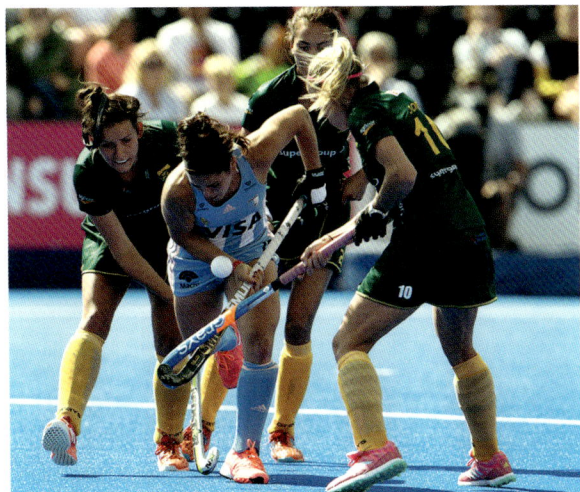

A trio of South Africa players do their best to stop the ever-dangerous Maria Granatto of Argentina. // *Rodrigo Jaramillo*

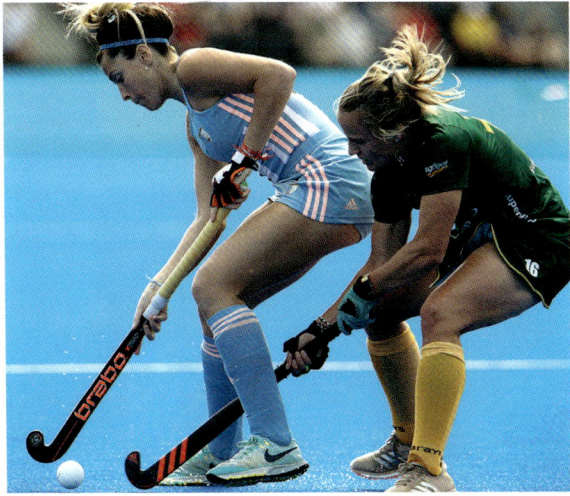

Argentina's Agustina Albertarrio under pressure from Erin Hunter of South Africa. // *Rodrigo Jaramillo*

'It is frustrating because we are there, we are competing, we get penalty corners. We win or lose games in the circle and it didn't go for us today,' she added.

Adrian Lock, Spain's head coach, was also taking the longer view on the match. For him, the challenge was not just to perform at this World Cup but to make Spain's presence at major events a regular occurrence. 'In the past with Spain there has not really been a long-term outlook, it has all been a bit short-term. The changing culture we have looked to implement since we have been in charge will allow us to change physically, to change mentally and will last within the team way beyond me and the current players.

'I think a change in culture is the most important thing a team can develop,' he added. 'Everything else becomes

a consequence of that – fitness, skills and tactical awareness. It is long-lasting. It's changing but very slowly.'

South Africa lined up for their final Pool C match against Argentina knowing that only a win would give them any hope of progressing into the next round. Even then, it had to be a win with a goal margin of at least eight. The last time South Africa had taken a point from Argentina was in the 2006 World Cup in Madrid, when they drew 2-2. Even the indefatigable Shelley Jones knew it was an all but impossible task: 'Yes, we will go out and leave nothing out there. We all know the importance of winning our last game and the psychological impact that can have.'

For Argentina, Germany's earlier success over Spain meant Las Leonas could not top their pool and so even

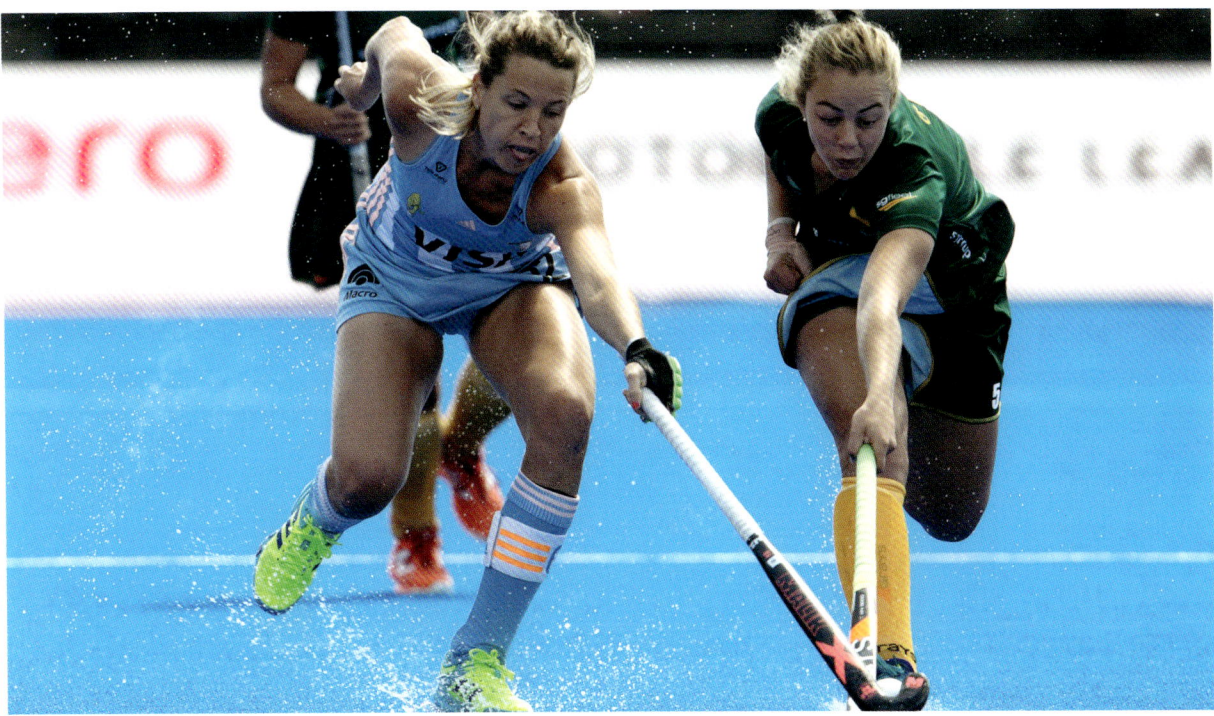

Leonas captain Delfina Merino fights for possession with Simone Gouws of South Africa. // *Rodrigo Jaramillo*

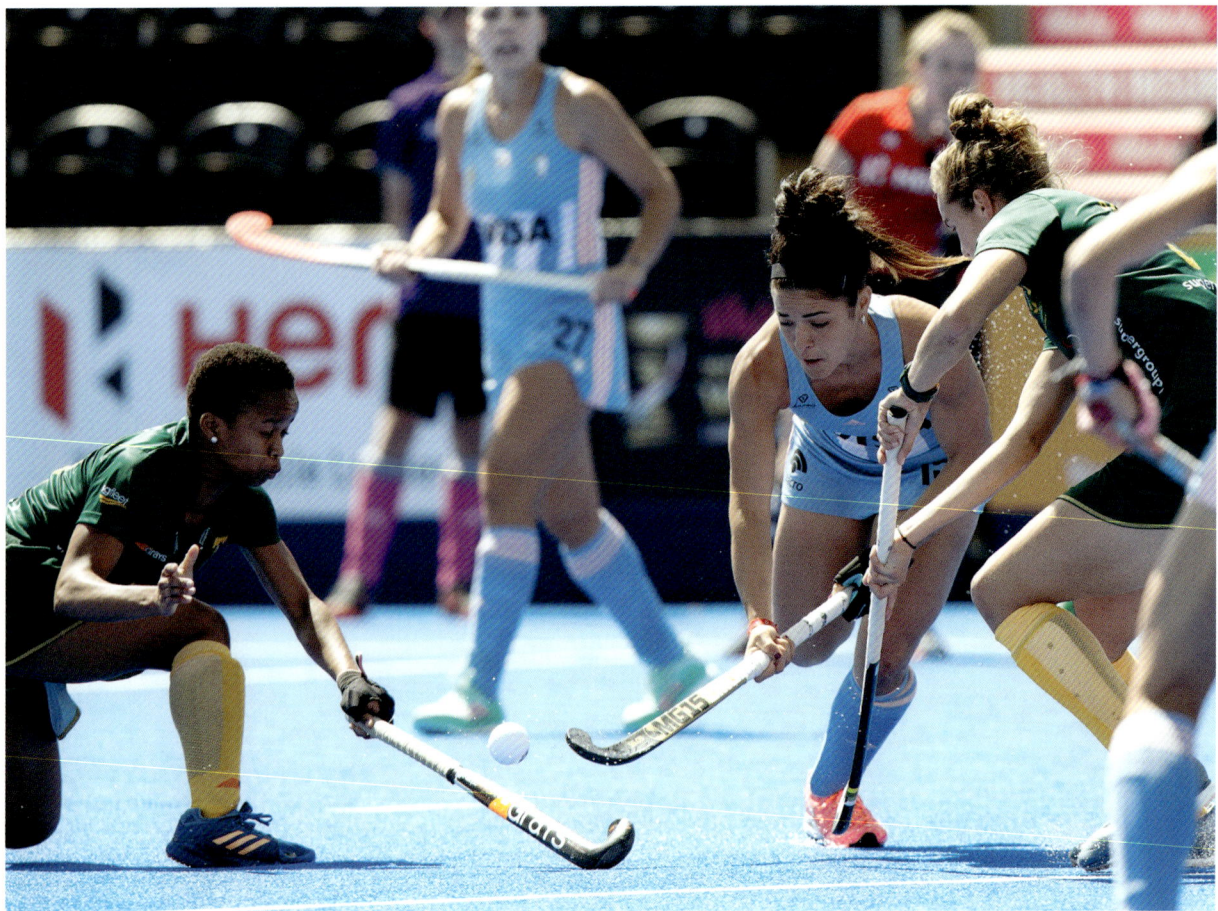

South Africa's continued efforts to stop the explosive Maria Granatto paid rich dividends as they earned a creditable draw against the 2010 world champions. // *Rodrigo Jaramillo*

a win would see them go to the cross-over stage of the competition and face the third-placed team from Pool D. It was not the situation they wanted and there was an air of tension in the Argentine squad that suggested they were desperate to put on a good performance, both for their loyal fans and for their own self-confidence.

The first half was a perfect example of a team setting up a defensive wall and stopping anything that came at it in its tracks. Argentina threw everything at the South Africa defence in the opening moments. Phumelela Mbande in South Africa's goal was in outstanding form and seemed to be reading the game faster than anyone else as she got behind every shot that came her way. She also had an element of luck on her side as she parried and blocked everything that was thrown at her, including a few shots that she couldn't have seen until the last second because of the melee of players in front of her.

One of the best opportunities fell to Maria Granatto after Agustina Albertarrio had burst down the right-hand side of the pitch and crossed in front of the South Africa goal. It perhaps summed up Argentina's performance in this match that even their hugely talented young forward was not able to convert that relatively simple chance into a goal.

And once again, this was the World Cup of surprises. No one could have predicted what would happen in the last two seconds of the first half. A break from South Africa found Lilian du Plesis, who struck a brilliant ball into the Argentina

circle. Jade Mayne was quickest to the bouncing ball. She chopped it down into the ground and both Argentina's defenders and South Africa's strikers watched as it squeaked past Belen Succi into the Argentina goal. All 22 players seemed stunned and then the South African players erupted into a wild celebration as the half-time whistle blew.

'That was a great moment,' said Nicolene Terblanche speaking after the game. 'When you saw that goal, the belief came flooding in. Moments like that just help you get momentum as a team.'

After the half-time break, Argentina resumed their position camped in the South Africa half of the pitch. They probed the opposing defence to try and find a way through but, even as the number of penalty corners racked up, the equaliser proved elusive.

The pressure mounted as the third quarter counted down. South Africa stood firm and protected their lead but the attacks from the blue and white shirts came thick and fast. The breakthrough came from a moment of brilliance from Maria Granatto, who latched on to a bouncing cross and turned it goalwards. The striker's celebrations loosened a little of the tension that had crept into the Argentina side.

By the end of the 60 minutes, Argentina had notched up 26 shots and 13 penalty corners in contrast to South Africa's two shots. It was a point about which Argentina head coach Agustin Corradini expressed some concern.

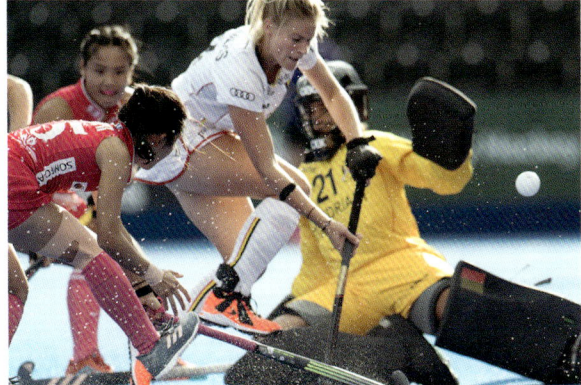
Belgium's defence stands firm. // *Frank Uijlenbroek*

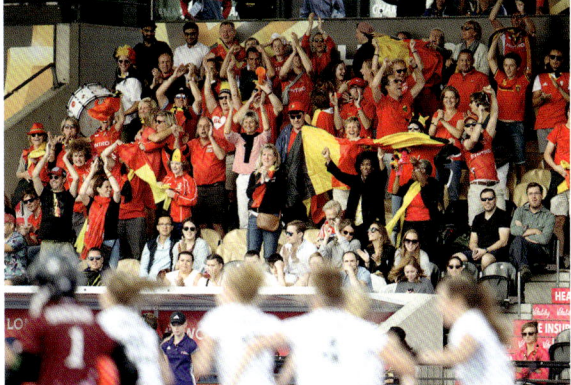
Fans of the Red Panthers revel in their team's outstanding result against the Cherry Blossoms. // *Rodrigo Jaramillo*

'What I saw out there was a team who had too much energy and no thinking. There was an air of desperation and going forward too quickly. We had 13 penalty corners and we didn't score. That is too many opportunities for only one outcome. We have to start putting those chances away.'

South Africa's captain, Nicolene Terblanche, explained that the team went on to the pitch determined to get a result from their final pool match. 'We had nothing to lose. We said to each other: "Flip guys, we need to be one-on-one solid defensively," and we did that. And our keeper, she was phenomenal today. In the first game we didn't do well, you cannot afford to start the tournament how we did. If you can play well from the first game then you get into a stronger position and you get momentum. We really didn't do that and we have suffered as a result.'

Verve, energy, innovation – Belgium had improved with every game and this was the Red Panthers at their best. Japan came to the party and played their role in a nine-goal thriller, but this was the performance that Belgium had been working towards.

As Anouk Raes acknowledged, at 15th in the world they were one of the lower-ranked teams but in this tournament, they had not looked out of place at any stage. 'We played very well against both New Zealand [lost 4-2] and Australia [0-0] but we had targeted this game because we are close to Japan in the rankings,' said the Belgium captain. 'If there was a match where we knew we were capable of getting three points, it was this one.'

The match was a must-win for Belgium who, despite drawing against Australia, were in danger of exiting the tournament because of other results. For Japan, a draw would suffice.

The match started at a high tempo that never really abated. It was Japan who put in the first serious attempt on goal. The shot from Shihori Oikawa was expertly saved by Aisling D'Hooghe in the Belgium goal, with the lithe keeper dropping to her right to stop the shot.

Japan had shown what they could do with a win over New Zealand and a close 3-2 encounter with Australia but, on this occasion, they were up against a Red Panthers team who had brought their A-game.

Belgium shot into a 2-0 lead before 20 minutes had passed. The first goal came from a slick penalty corner routine. Judith Vandermeiren was on the end of a three-pass move which left the Japanese defence chasing shadows.

The next two goals were all part of the Jill Boon show. If ever a player has mirrored her team, it is Boon. Always with the potential to be a game winner, at this tournament the Belgium forward stepped out of the shadows and demonstrated the striker's instinct that lay at the heart of her DNA. For her first piece of brilliance, she latched on to a ball that flew into the Japanese circle, her deflection sailing high into the goal, well out of reach of Megumi Kageyama. Her second contribution was to set up Anne-Sophie Weyns to score the third Belgium goal. Boon burst into the Japanese defending quarter, neatly wrong-footed a defender and thus cleared the way for a perfect pass to the waiting Weyns.

Kageyama went some way towards rectifying the error when she saved at point-blank range from Louise Versavel, but she was not able to do anything about Versavel's next move which saw her outwit the defence to fire home her second of the tournament.

Japan gave their World Cup dreams momentary hope when they

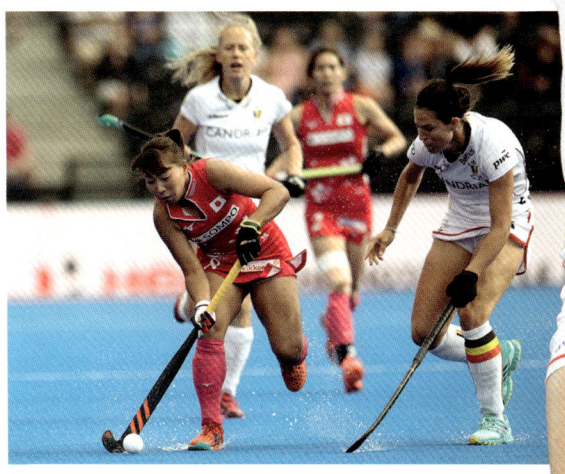
Yukari Mano in possession for Japan. // *Frank Uijlenbroek*

Anne-Sophie Weyns celebrates scoring Belgium's third goal against Japan. // *Rodrigo Jaramillo*

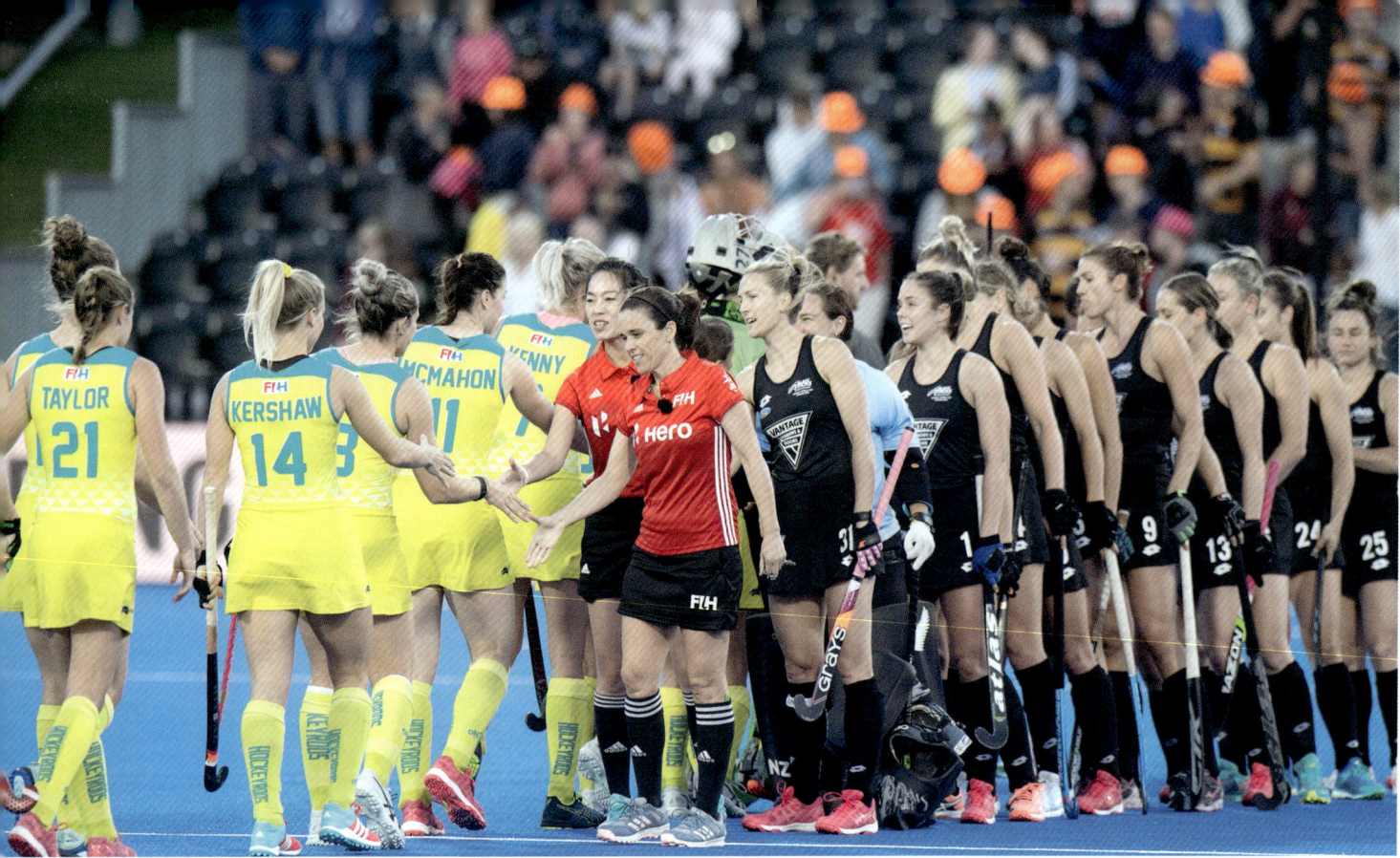

Australia and New Zealand prepare for Pool D's Oceania derby match. // *Frank Uijlenbroek*

scored a penalty corner after a great, flowing team move forced a foul in the circle. After the initial strike, Akiko Kato was on hand to slot the ball home.

Louise Versavel increased her tally five minutes later after she picked up a cross from Pauline Leclef. By now the striker knew exactly where the goal was and she slammed home with composure. Eight minutes later Versavel scored her hat-trick as she converted another Belgium corner.

One of the features of the World Cup was the innovative penalty corner routines, and Belgium produced a couple of beauties in this match.

Japan had delighted the spectators with their approach to the competition, and the neutrals in the crowd showed their appreciation when the Cherry Blossoms scored two more goals in the final ten minutes. First Kana Nomura strode into the circle and slammed a thumping penalty corner shot past D'Hooghe, and then Hazuki Nagai added her name to the score-sheet with a neatly finished penalty corner.

'We are so pleased,' said Anouk Raes after the match. 'Our goalkeeper was excellent and her first save provided the momentum for that performance. We came into the tournament with no pressure and we have played really well, even in the 4-2 loss to New Zealand. The team confidence is very high right now.'

The 6-3 result was Belgium's highest score in a World Cup, their previous was a 5-0 win over Italy in 1976, when they finished in fourth place.

The battle for supremacy between the two giants of Oceania had heated up in recent months. New Zealand had overtaken Australia in the FIH Hero World Rankings so the two teams now stood at four and five respectively. Australia failed to qualify for the Hockey World League Final,

which was held in Auckland while New Zealand finished second, to the delight of the home spectators. Australia then won the Oceania Cup but were left smarting after New Zealand snatched gold from them in their own backyard at the Gold Coast 2018 Commonwealth Games.

This pool match was always going to be an epic test of strength and resilience as both teams were seeking to establish themselves at the top of the standings. For Australia a draw was enough to secure passage straight through to the quarter-finals; for the Black Sticks, a win was the only option if they were to avoid a cross-over clash with Argentina.

It all started so well for New Zealand. They took the lead in the 13th minute when Olivia Merry pounced on a rebound after Rachael Lynch had saved from a fierce shot by Kelsey Smith. The joy was short-lived, however, as just five minutes later Emily Smith made a great run through the New Zealand defence and put the ball over Sally Rutherford in the Black Sticks' goal.

Samantha Harrison thought she had put her team ahead when she struck the ball high into the Hockeyroos' net, but on referral she was adjudged to have used the back of the stick.

A big half was called for from the players and, as so often with the Black Sticks, it was Stacey Michelsen who answered the call. The powerful midfielder strode through the ranks of Australia players to set up a shot for Samantha Harrison and it was Michelsen herself who nearly hit the rebound home – her shot fizzing wide of Lynch's goal.

Michelsen's example fired up those around her and the next player to test Lynch was Merry. A quick break – is there any other – from Anita McLaren, followed by a cross found Merry in front of goal and unmarked. Her shot was well saved by Lynch.

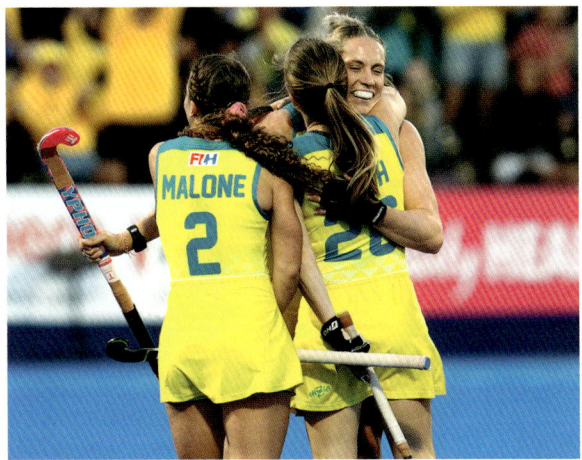

Australia hit back through team captain Emily Smith, whose 18th-minute strike would prove to be enough for the Hockeyroos to finish top of Pool D. // *Rodrigo Jaramillo*

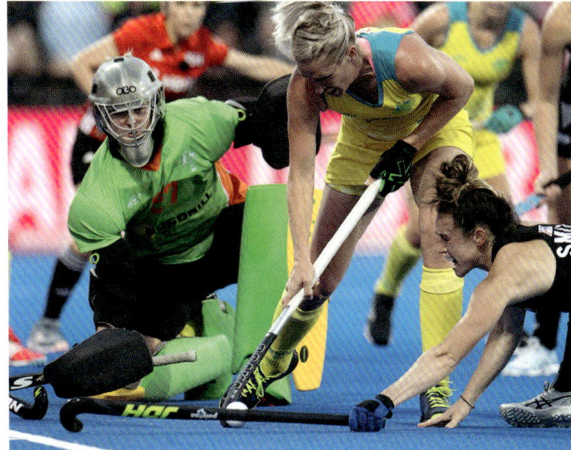

Australia's outstanding defensive line in action. // *Frank Uijlenbroek*

Jodie Kenny had the chance to put the game to rest as she stepped up to take a penalty corner after some good work by Emily Hurtz to win the corner. Kenny's shot was stopped by Rutherford and cleared by the Black Sticks' defence.

The resulting draw was just reward for two teams who really couldn't be separated. It was a point conceded by Maddy Fitzpatrick, who said the two teams knew each other so well that any encounter was always hard-fought and close. 'We had plenty of chances but then so did New

Zealand. It was never going to be pretty, because both sides are always just so keen to win this fixture.'

'We worked hard but the lines [between defence, midfield and forward] were perhaps a little too close so we couldn't play our game,' said Michelsen. New Zealand are renowned for bringing out the big game in the latter stages of a competition and there was steely determination in the eyes of the New Zealand captain as she declared that her team would be ready for Argentina on 30 July.

Results – Day 7 – Saturday 28 July 2018

Pool C

Spain   1-3   **Germany**
Maria Lopez 30m PC   Anne Schröder 5m PC
Selin Oruz 37m FG
Viktoria Huse 40m PC

Vitality Player of the Match: Franzisca Hauke (GER)

Argentina   1-1   **South Africa**
Maria Granatto 47m FG   Jade Mayne 30m FG

Vitality Player of the Match: Phumelela Mbande (RSA)

Pool D

Japan   3-6   **Belgium**
Akiko Kato 36m PC   Judith Vandermeiren 7m PC
Kana Nomura 50m PC   Jill Boon 17m FG
Hazuki Nagai 57m PC   Anne-Sophie Weyns 22m FG
Louise Versavel 33/39/47m FG

Vitality Player of the Match: Jill Boon (BEL)

New Zeland   1-1   **Australia**
Olivia Merry 13m FG   Emily Smith 18m FG

Vitality Player of the Match: Kelsey Smith (NZL)

Pool Standings – End of Day 7

Pool C – Final Standings

Pos	Team	Pld	W	D	L	GF	GA	GD	Pts
1	Germany	3	3	0	0	9	4	5	9
2	Argentina	3	1	1	1	9	6	3	4
3	Spain	3	1	0	2	10	10	0	3
4	South Africa	3	0	1	2	3	11	-8	1

Pool D – Final Standings

Pos	Team	Pld	W	D	L	GF	GA	GD	Pts
1	Australia	3	1	2	0	5	3	1	5
2	Belgium	3	1	1	1	8	7	1	4
3	New Zealand	3	1	1	1	6	5	1	4
4	Japan	3	1	0	2	7	10	-3	3

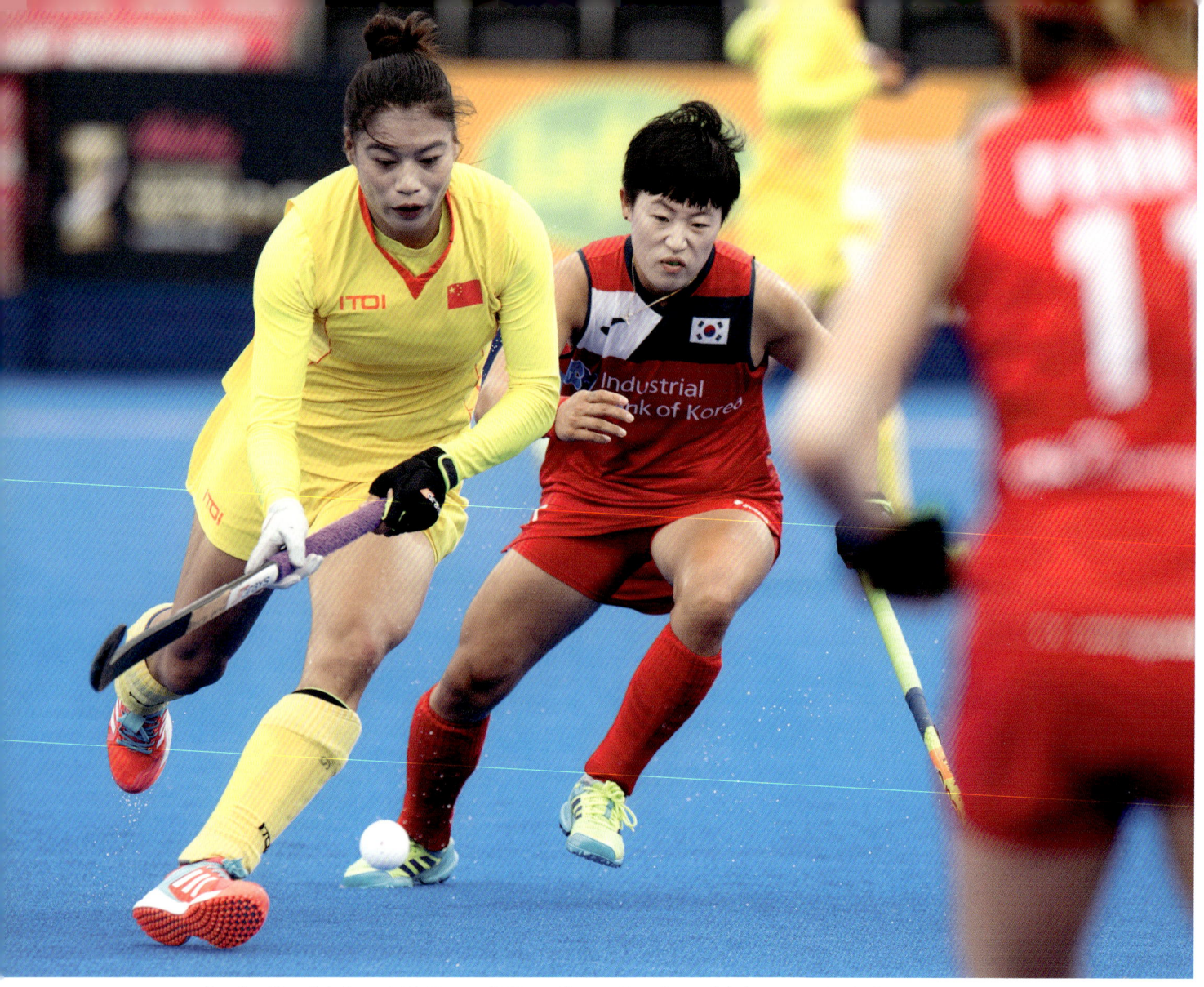

Korea (in red) knew that a draw against Pool A opponents China would be enough to see them qualify for the cross-over play-offs at the expense of their Asian rivals. // *Frank Uijlenbroek*

Day 8 – Sunday 29 July 2018

Dazzling Dutch break records while home favourites keep title hopes alive

After seven extraordinary days of hockey that contained far more shock results than anyone could have predicted, the concluding day of the pool phase at the Vitality Hockey Women's World Cup London 2018 had arrived. While Ireland, Germany and Australia had been confirmed as the respective winners of Pools B, C and D, earning a direct route to the quarter-finals, there was plenty of unfinished business.

The results of all four matches on the eighth day of competition would determine the fixtures for the knock-out phase, mapping out the exact route that each team would need to take in order to reach the final. For Italy and the Netherlands, the chance to top Pool A and earn a ticket to the quarter-finals – avoiding the rigours of an extra play-off match and gaining a couple of extra rest days – was understandably a coveted prize. For all other teams the primary goal was survival, and desperately avoiding a fourth-place pool finish that would see them join South

Africa and Japan, eliminated the previous day, on the plane home.

Korea and China were the first teams to enter the arena, kick-starting a first session that would finalise classification in Pool A. Both sides had suffered defeats at the hands of the Netherlands and Italy, but a marginally better goal difference meant that a draw would be just enough for Korea to hold on to third position and secure a place in the cross-over play-off matches. While it would mean an additional knock-out match ahead of the quarter-finals, it was an infinitely better option than the ejection from the event that came with finishing fourth.

China coach and former Germany international Jamilon Mülders. // *Frank Uijlenbroek*

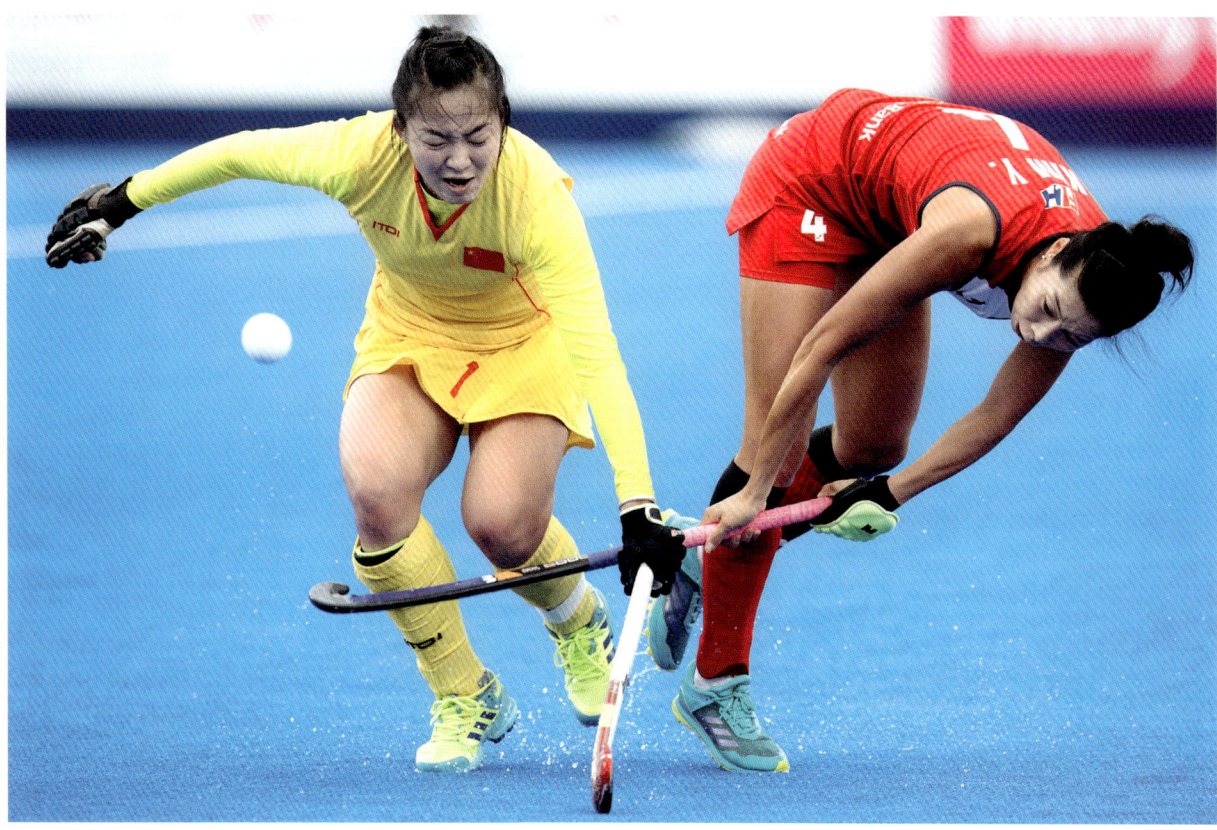

Korea captain Kim Youngran (in red) clears the danger as her team secured the point that they needed to progress from the pool phase. // *Frank Uijlenbroek*

Knowing that only a win was good enough, China started the game with intent, much to the delight of head coach Jamilon Mülders. His side were certainly the better team in the opening stages of the contest and were well worth the lead that they established in the fourth minute. Xhang Xiaoxue showed excellent movement in the Korean circle, evading her marker to collect a cross-field pass from the left before rattling home a backhand effort which significantly boosted China's hopes of staying in the competition at the expense of their Asian rivals. Korea would have found themselves even further behind were it not for the awareness of goalkeeper Hwang Hyeon, who produced a miraculous block to touch a goal-bound effort fractionally wide of the target.

The importance of Hwang's moment of brilliance became apparent in the very final second of the half, when Korea struck a dramatic equaliser. Kim Ok Ju was the scorer, showing a terrific determination to get in front of a static China defender before drilling a first-time slap-shot between the legs of helpless goalkeeper Kim Youngran.

Although Korea greatly improved as the half progressed, their leveller on the stroke of half-time was a

bitter pill to swallow for a China team that had produced their best hockey of the competition. It was a huge boost for Korea, who produced a supremely composed performance in the third and fourth quarters, largely inspired by an outstanding display from Korea central defender Tang Heesun, who was named Vitality Player of the Match. Despite China enjoying almost total dominance in the final 15 minutes of the match, they simply could not find the goal that they needed. Korea had finished third in Pool A and set up a cross-over play-off match against the team that would finish second in Pool B for a place in the quarter-finals.

'We played well but we didn't get the outcomes we had hoped for,' said China's Ou Zixia, reflecting on the contest. 'We have been doing a lot of preparation around penalty corners but we needed to get more structure to our attack to make that work. Our tactic was to do a lot of running to really stretch the pitch. Our coach asks us to work hard to the very last minute of the game. I think we did that today but it was not quite enough.'

With the third and fourth places in Pool A settled, focus switched to the contest between the highest, and

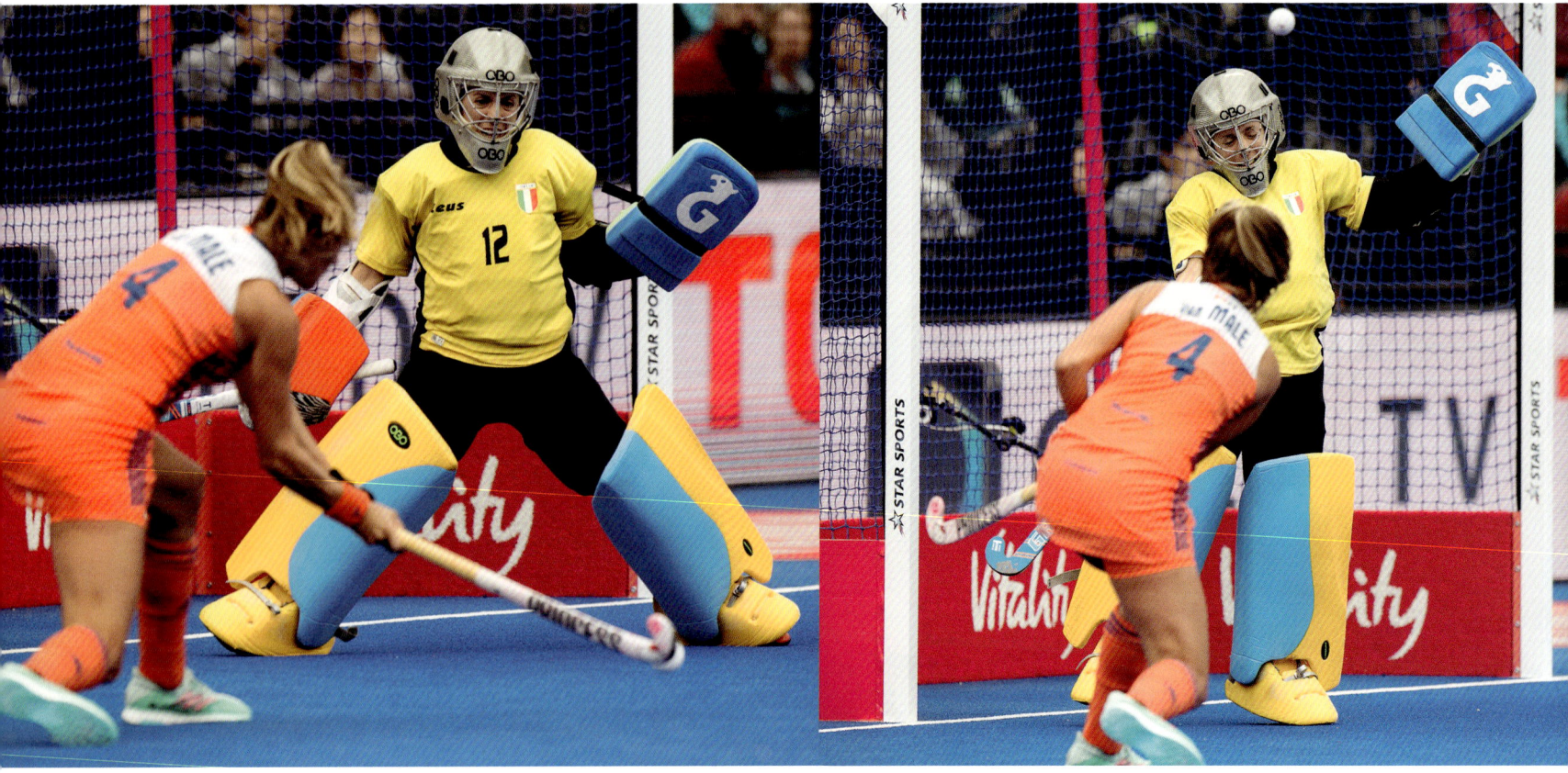

Kitty van Male smashes a glorious strike high into the Italian net before turning in celebration. It was one of four goals that Van Male registered in the contest.
// Frank Uijlenbroek

lowest-ranked teams competing at the Vitality Hockey Women's World Cup London 2018. While Italy had produced two wonderful performances in their defeats of supposedly superior opposition in China and Korea, claiming a result against Alyson Annan's extraordinary Netherlands team – who had scored 14 goals and conceded just once in their matches against Pool A's representatives from Asia – was an entirely different proposition.

The Italians showed plenty of spirit, but the Dutch were sensational in the opening two quarters and powered into a 5-1 half-time lead. Frederique Matla finished off a slick passing move to put the Netherlands ahead in the tenth minute, with Caia van Maasakker's unstoppable penalty corner drag-flick making it 2-0 just before quarter-time. Italy captain Chiara Tiddi smashed home a penalty corner early in the second period to give her team hope, but the dazzling Dutch turned on the style with Kelly Jonker, Margot van Geffen and Kitty van Male all making their mark on the score-sheet.

Rather than easing off, the Dutch somehow found a way to improve in the third and fourth quarters, adding another seven goals to claim a staggering final score of 12-1, setting a new all-time winning margin record at an FIH women's hockey World Cup. The Netherlands' captain Carlien Dirkse van den Heuvel marked her 200th international with two goals either side of blistering finishes from Van Male and Matla, pushing the score to 9-1 ahead of the final quarter. Van Male took her match tally to four with two strikes in the final quarter, with Kelly Jonker also adding another goal as the Netherlands topped Pool A with a quite remarkable scoreline.

'The start was not good enough, which Alyson [Annan] made clear at the break but we gradually got better

with our passes and the goals started to go in as a result,' said Netherlands ace Kitty van Male, who ended the day as the top scorer in the competition thanks to her tally of seven goals in just three games. 'Korea and China are good teams and we sometimes only win 1-0 against them, for example at Rio 2016, we only won by small margins. But our team spirit here is great and that is key to a good performance.'

The fact that the Oranje were crushing every opponent that stood in their way became a talking point for fans and media alike. The Dutch had reached the quarter-finals with consummate ease; they would now lie in wait for the winner of the cross-over play-off match which would be contested between Pool A runners-up Korea and the side that finished second in Pool B. Speculation was rife about how England, India and USA would be looking to avoid the Dutch at all costs, suggesting a third-place finish – which would mean a cross-over play-off match against Italy and a potential quarter-final clash with Ireland – would be a preferred option. However, there was no such discussion from head coaches Danny Kerry, Sjoerd Marijne and Janneke Schopman, who knew that if their teams failed to perform in their final Pool B matches, it would be a completely meaningless debate. All three nations could still finish fourth, ensuring that the threat of elimination loomed large. It served to focus the players' minds on what was the most important thing of all: staying in the competition.

Dutchman Marijne's India started the day level on points with compatriot Schopman's USA, but a slightly better goal difference in favour of the Eves meant that the Americans would need a victory to be absolutely certain of progressing through to the play-off phase at the expense of the Asian continental champions. To the delight of

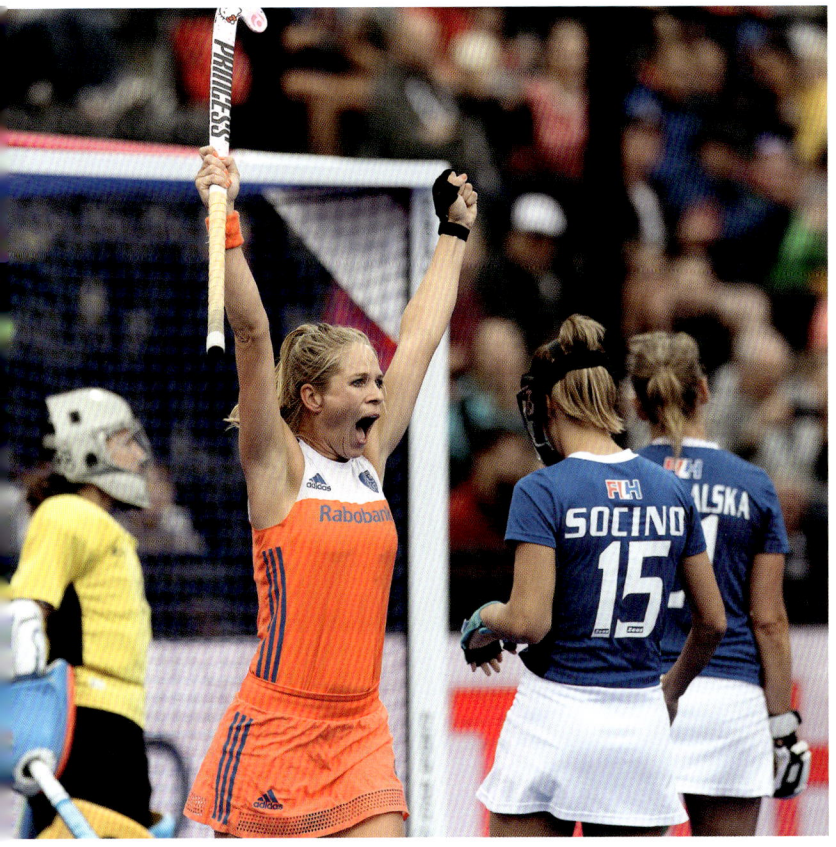

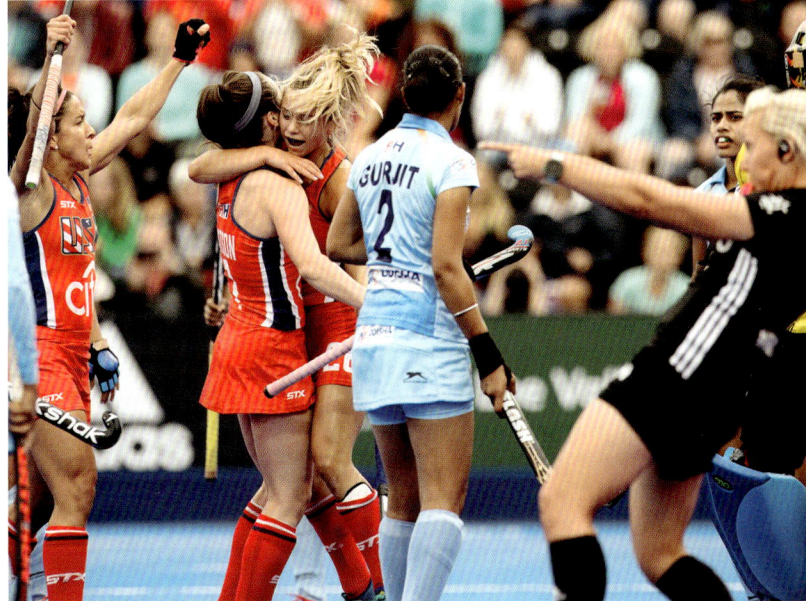

An 11th minute strike from Margaux Paolino gave USA the lead against India. // *Frank Uijlenbroek*

legendary Netherlands international Schopman, USA opened the scoring 11 minutes into a thrilling encounter thanks to 21-year-old attacker Margaux Paolino, who squeezed the ball between the legs of India goalkeeper Savita after excellent build-up play from outstanding teenager Erin Matson.

It was a lead that USA held until half-time, although with six shots and four penalty corners in the first two periods, India were doing everything in their power to swing the match back in their favour. The Eves were thwarted by USA goalkeeper Jackie Briggs, who pulled off some terrific saves to keep her side ahead.

India dragged themselves level just a minute into the third quarter, with the goal coming from a reliable source. Team captain and prolific scorer Rani – who limped off the field with an injured ankle just three minutes into the contest but later returned to the action, much to India's relief – restored parity with a low penalty corner strike, finally beating Briggs. Remarkably, it proved to be the final goal of the contest, with India getting the result they needed to secure a berth in the cross-over play-off matches.

'We have been playing well in all our games but we haven't been able to score,' said a battle-weary Rani after the match. 'Our coach just said, "believe in yourselves, you are doing very well, we just need an outcome". We went 1-0 down today but at half-time he said, "come on, you have just 30 minutes left. Let's put everything into the game." USA created a lot of chances but Savita and the defence played very well. It was a case of who wanted the game more and I think, today, we just wanted it that little bit more.'

While USA were clearly distraught about not getting the result they so desperately needed, mathematically they were still not out of it, as Pool B winners Ireland and host nation England took to the field in front of another huge crowd at the Lee Valley Hockey & Tennis Centre. If the home favourites suffered a 3-1 defeat against the Green Army, both England and USA would be on absolute parity in the Pool B table and a shoot-out would be required to decide which team would enter the play-offs. A 1-0 defeat for England at the hands of Ireland also had ramifications, with England then facing a shoot-out with India to decide the second and third placements in the pool. However, neither of those scenarios would come to fruition as England battled to a hard-fought 1-0 victory, confirming themselves as the second-place finisher in Pool B and ensuring that USA would play no further part in the event.

With 62 per cent possession, 39 circle penetrations and 15 penalty corners, England certainly deserved their victory over a stubborn, defensively brilliant Ireland. Not for the first time at this event, did Green Army goalkeeper Ayeisha McFerran make a string of saves for her side, keeping the scores locked at 0-0 until the breakthrough eventually arrived with seven minutes of the match remaining. The goal came from a penalty corner, with Giselle Ansley's powerful drag-flick taking a wicked

Deepika in possession for India.
// *Frank Uijlenbroek*

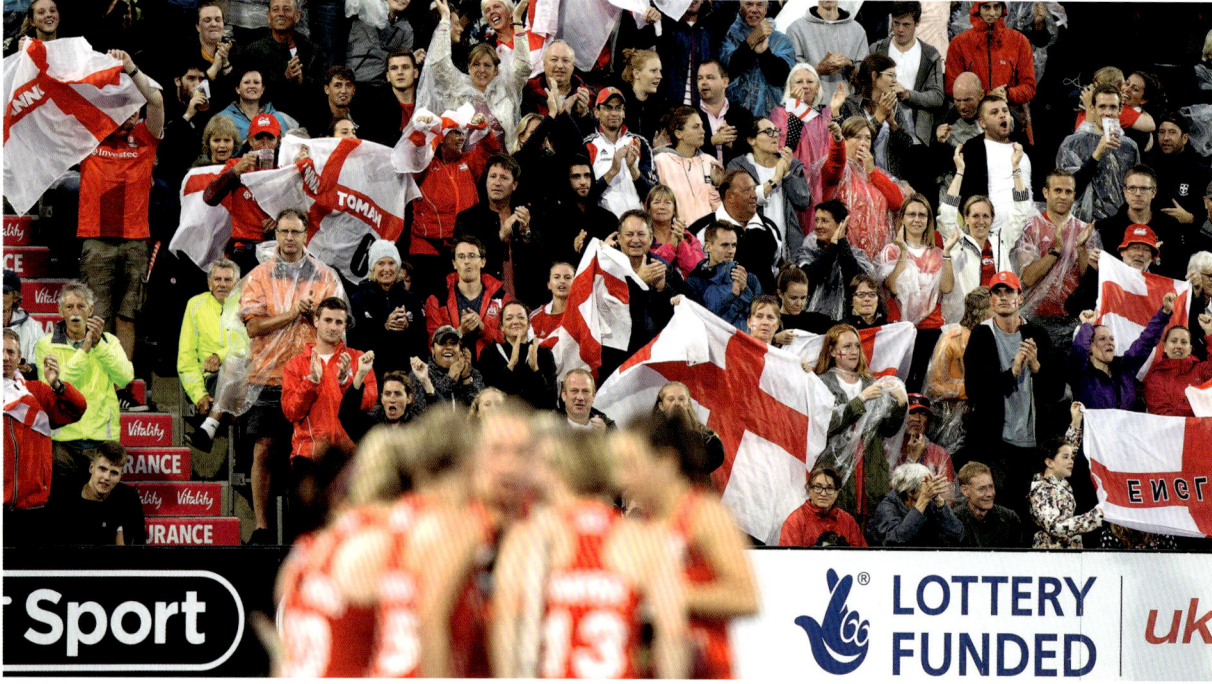

England fans applaud a first win of the competition for the host nation, with the team progressing safely through to the knock-out phase of the Vitality Hockey Women's World Cup London 2018. // *Frank Uijlenbroek*

deflection from the stick of Hannah Matthews. The crucial touch was enough to deceive McFerran, giving England their first win of the competition as the still undefeated hosts ended their pool campaign on a very positive note.

'We created a lot of chances and defended really well, as did Ireland,' said England defender Grace Balsdon after the match. 'Their goalkeeper Ayeisha McFerran had a brilliant game, but we stuck to it and got the goal in the end. We're really happy with the performance and hopefully we can take that through to our next game against Korea. We'll go away and look at the videos and focus on the next match.'

Despite the defeat, Ireland captain Katie Mullan was extremely proud of her team's display against the host nation in front of a partisan crowd. 'We came out today to give a performance and to try certain things ahead of our quarter-

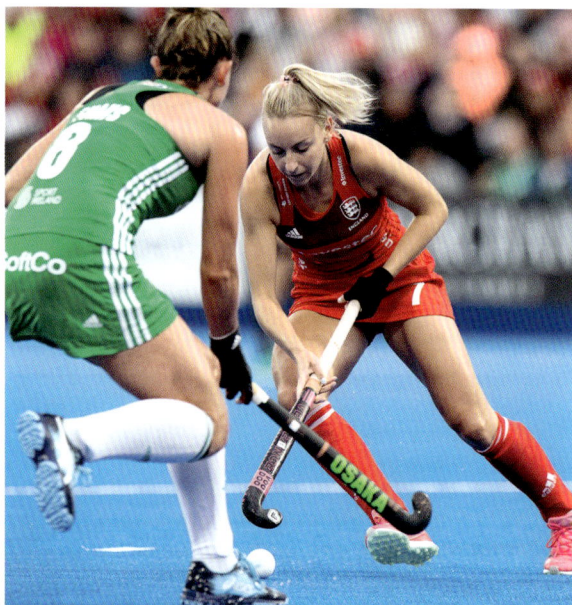

Ireland's Nicola Evans (in green) confronts England's Hannah Martin. // *Frank Uijlenbroek*

final,' said Mullan. 'There is plenty for us to work on, so we will recover and then look at the next match. Everyone worked so incredibly hard out there; our defence was awesome.'

A pool phase of shocks, surprises and a remarkable 102 goals in just 24 matches had come to an end, reducing 16 teams to 12 as South Africa, Japan, China and USA all fell at the first hurdle. The knock-out phase was about to begin, and there was plenty more drama ahead.

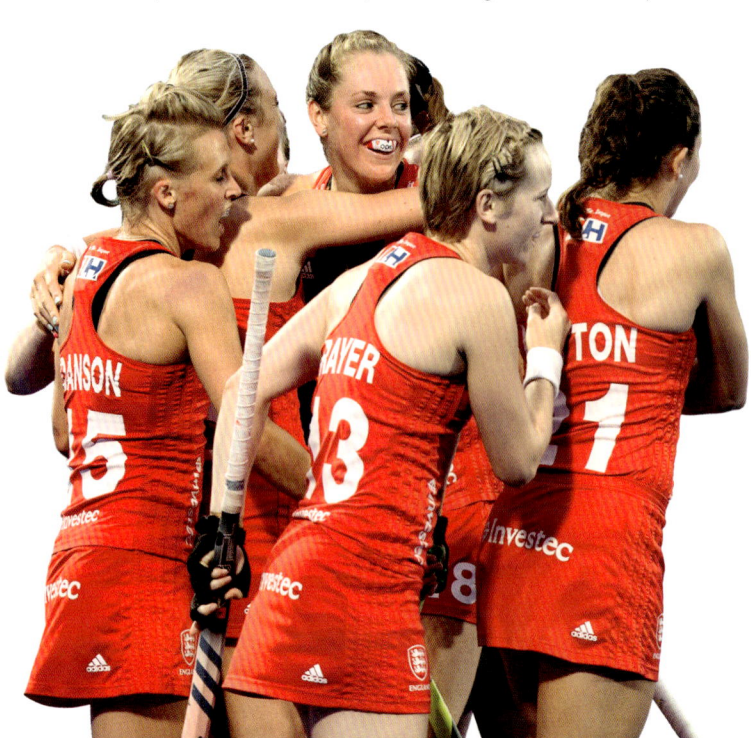

England players congratulate Giselle Ansley on her 53rd minute penalty corner goal. // *Frank Uijlenbroek*

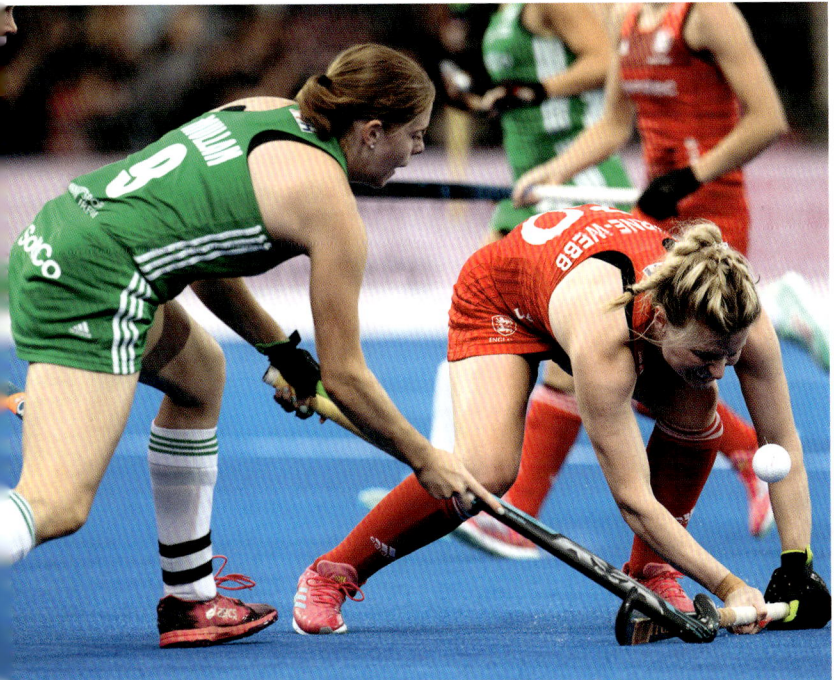

Katie Mullan of Ireland and England's Hollie Pearne-Webb show full commitment.
// Frank Uijlenbroek

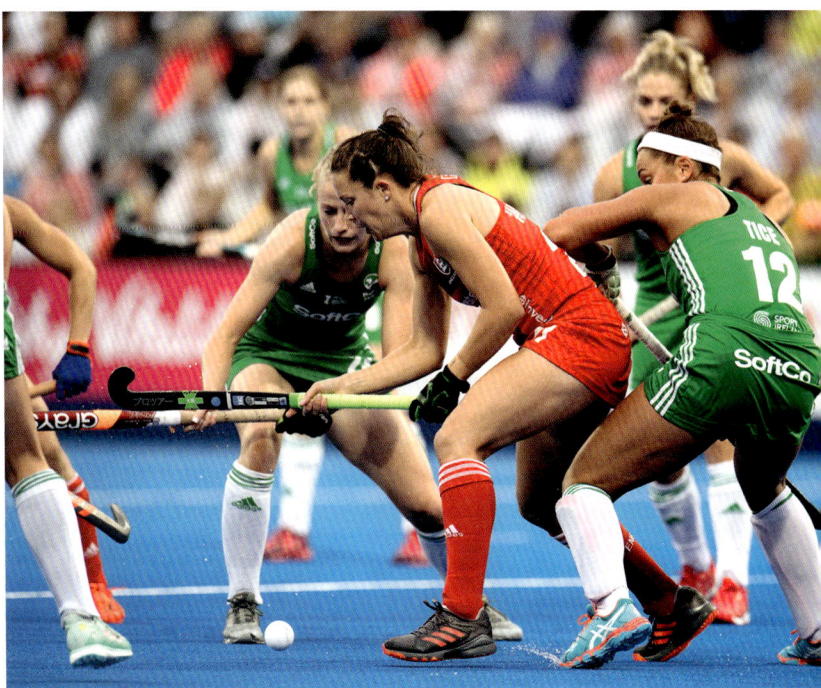

England's Ellie Watton attracts the attention of a trio of Irish players. // Frank Uijlenbroek

Results – Day 8 – Sunday 29 July 2018

Session 1

Pool A

Korea	1-1	China
Kim Ok Ju 15m FG		Zhang Xiaoxue 4m FG

Vitality Player of the Match: Tang Heesun (KOR)

Netherlands	12-1	Italy
Frederique Matla 10m FG, 44m PC		Chiara Tiddi 17m PC
Caia van Maasakker 13m PC		
Kelly Jonker 22m FG, 51m FG		
Margot van Geffen 26m PC		
Kitty van Male 28m FG, 41m PC,		
48m FG, 60m FG		
Carlien Dirkse van den Heuvel		
31m PC, 45m FG		

Vitality Player of the Match: Kitty van Male (NED)

Session 2

Pool B

India	1-1	USA
Rani 31m PC		Margaux Paolino 11m FG

Vitality Player of the Match: Kathleen Sharkey (USA)

Pool B

England	1-0	Ireland
Giselle Ansley 53m PC		

Vitality Player of the Match: Hollie Pearne-Webb (ENG)

Pool Standings – End of Day 8

Pool A – Final Standings

Pos	Team	Pld	W	D	L	GF	GA	GD	Pts
1	Netherlands	3	3	0	0	26	2	24	9
2	Italy	3	2	0	1	5	12	-7	6
3	Korea	3	0	1	2	1	9	-8	1
4	China	3	0	1	2	2	11	-9	1

Pool B – Final Standings

Pos	Team	Pld	W	D	L	GF	GA	GD	Pts
1	Ireland	3	2	0	1	4	2	2	6
2	England	3	1	2	0	3	2	1	5
3	India	3	0	2	1	2	3	-1	2
4	USA	3	0	2	1	3	5	-2	2

Fixtures – cross-over play-offs

Monday 30 July 2018

Belgium (2nd Pool D) v Spain (3rd Pool C).
Winner to play Germany in quarter-finals

Argentina (2nd Pool C) v New Zealand (3rd Pool D)
Winner to play Australia in quarter-finals

Tuesday 31 July 2018

Italy (2nd Pool A) v India (3rd Pool B)
Winner to play Ireland in quarter-finals

England (2nd Pool B) v Korea (3rd Pool A)
Winner to play Netherlands in quarter-finals

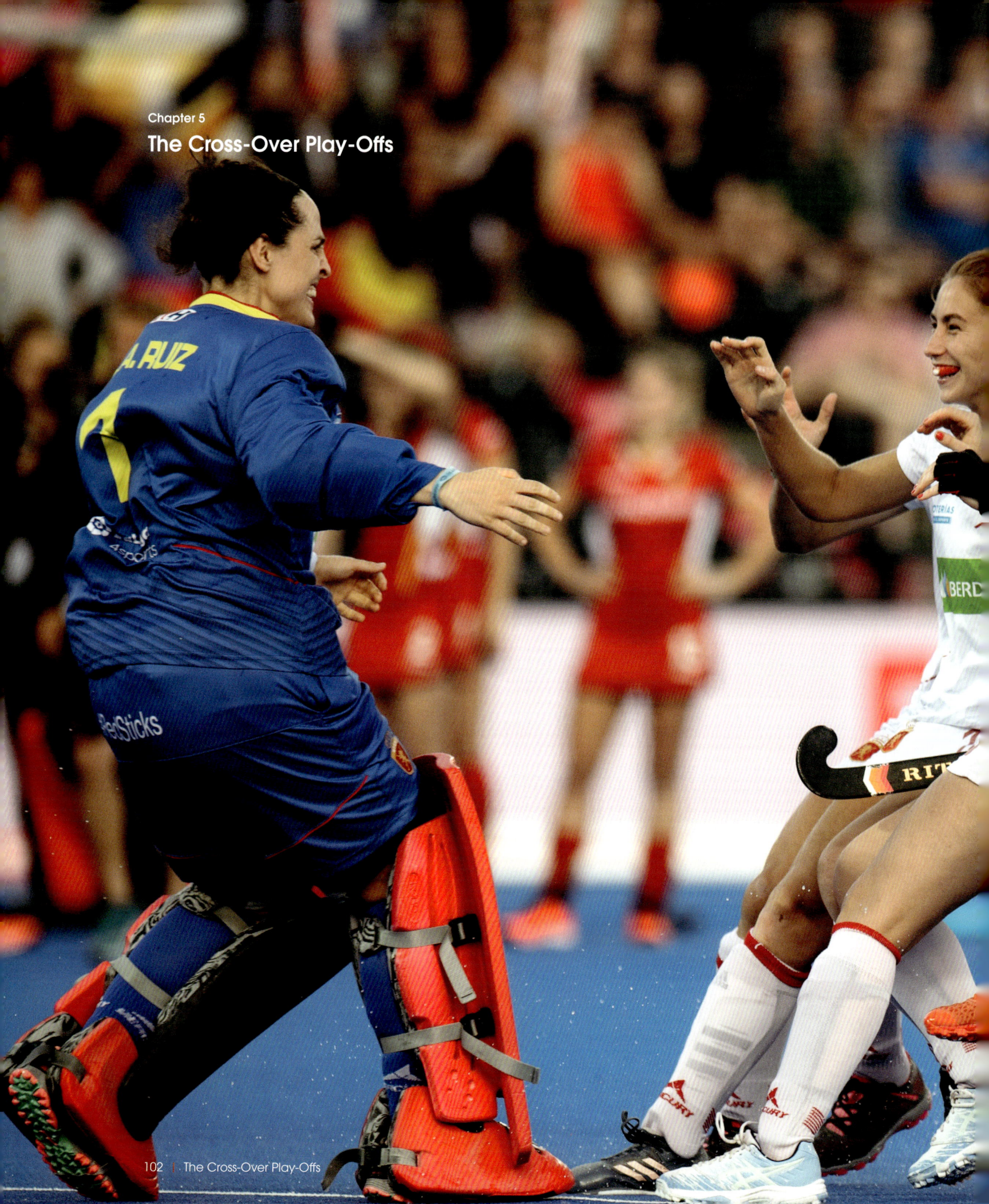

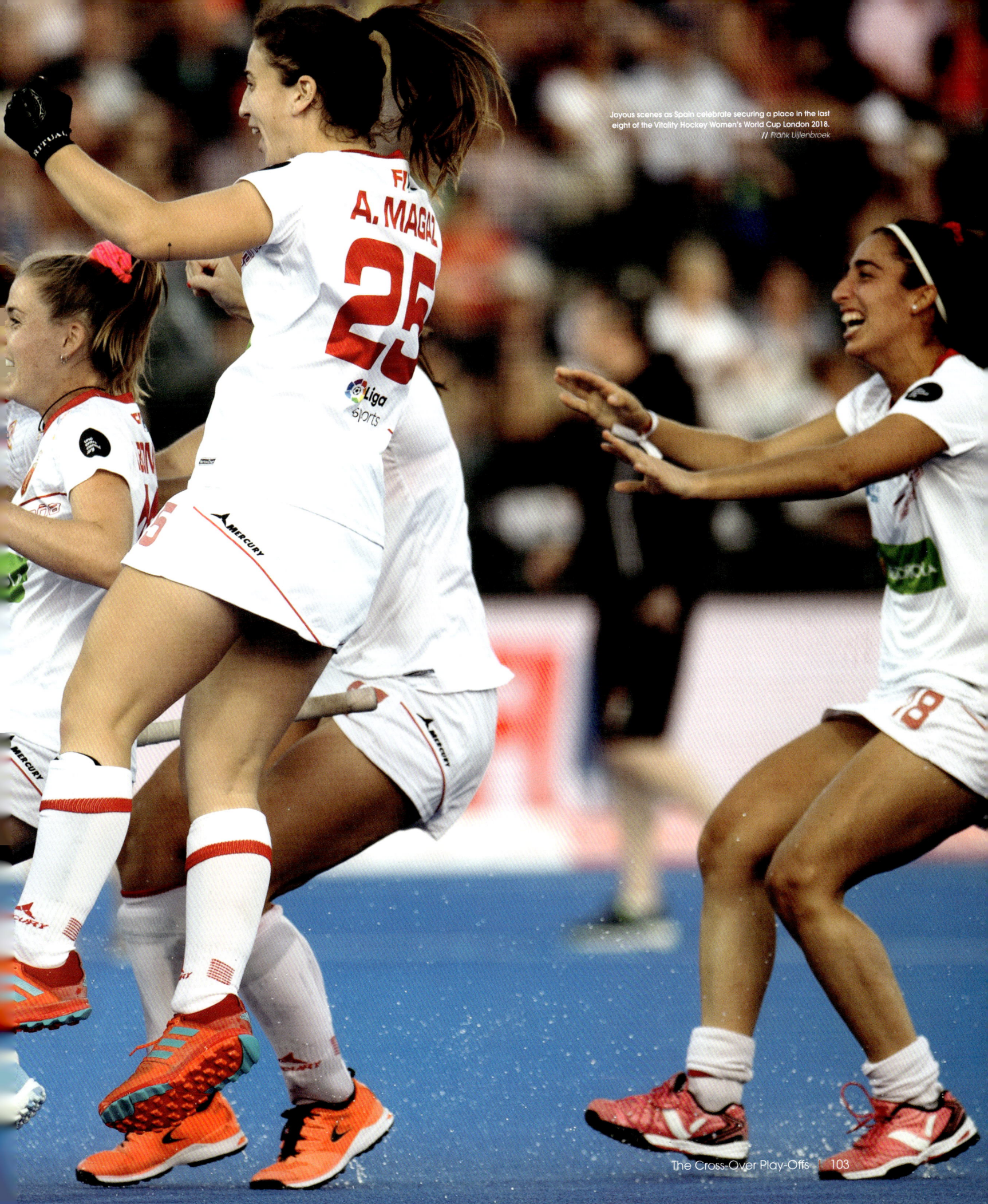

Joyous scenes as Spain celebrate securing a place in the last eight of the Vitality Hockey Women's World Cup London 2018.
// Frank Uijlenbroek

The Cross-Over Play-Offs

The knock-out stage of the Vitality Hockey Women's World Cup London 2018 started earlier for some than it did for others. While pool winners the Netherlands, Ireland, Germany and Australia were enjoying all of the added benefits that came with extra rest days, much of which would be spent learning as much as possible about the teams they might face in their respective quarter-final matches, it was an entirely different story for the eight other nations who had managed to progress from the pool phase.

To establish who would face the pool winners in the quarter-finals, the teams that finished second and third in the group phase would now have to negotiate their way through the cross-over play-offs. If teams had not been feeling the pressure to perform in the pool phase, they were certainly experiencing it now.

Aside from unbeaten host nation England, who had claimed two draws and a win in Pool B, all other teams competing in the cross-over play-offs had suffered at least one defeat in the pool phase. Italy, India, Argentina, Belgium and New Zealand were all beaten once, while Korea and Spain had managed to progress from their respective pools despite suffering two losses. However, from here on in there would be no second chances. The equation was simple: you lose, you go home. It was a fate that four of the eight teams competing in the cross-over play-offs were certain to suffer.

And as the competition got ever hotter, thousands of spectators yet again flocked to the Lee Valley Hockey & Tennis Centre to witness some of the world's finest teams battling for survival in what was turning out to be one of the most unpredictable women's hockey World Cup events in memory.

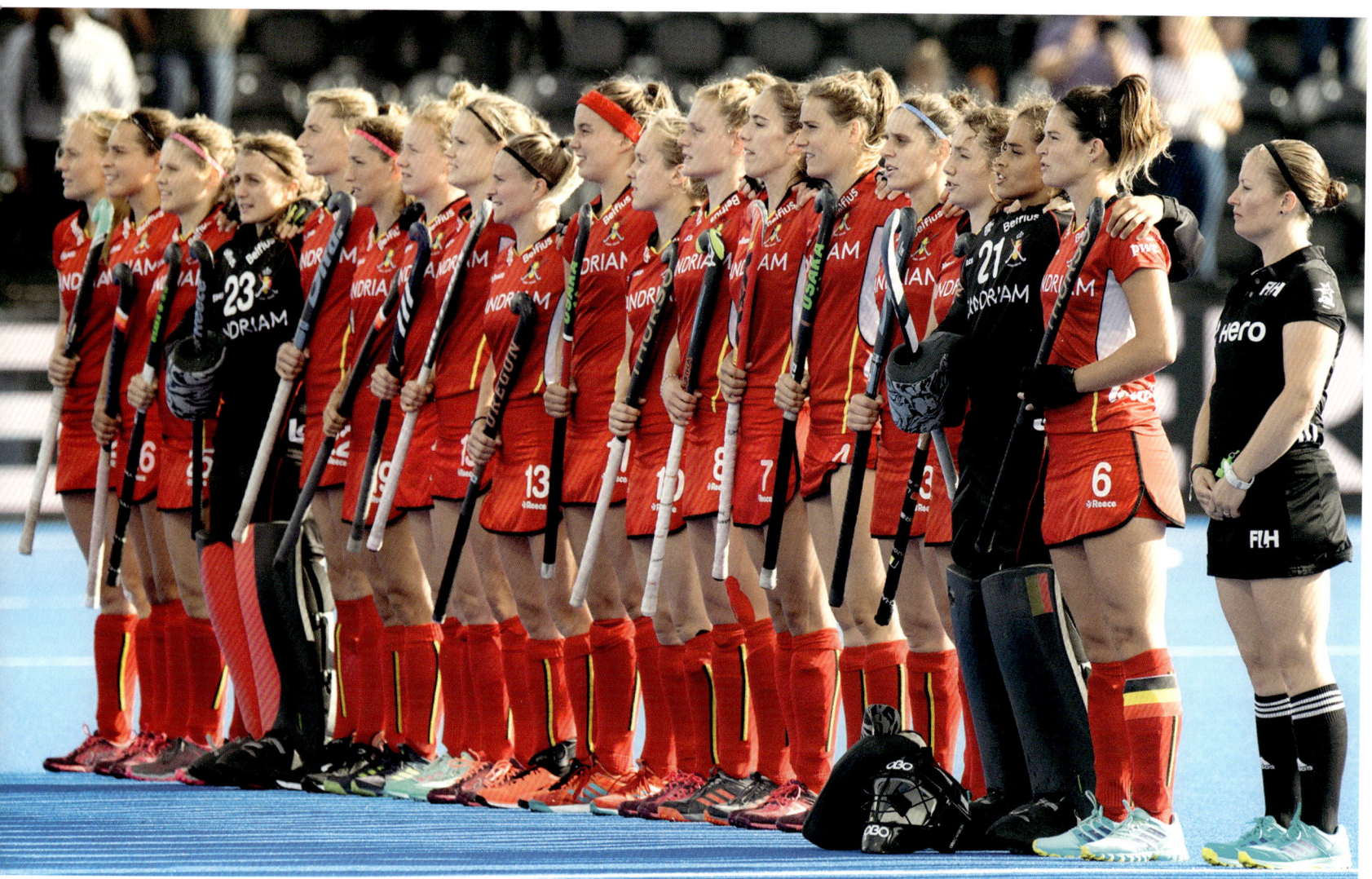

Belgium (in red) listen to their national anthem ahead of their cross-over match with Spain (opposite). // *Frank Uijlenbroek*

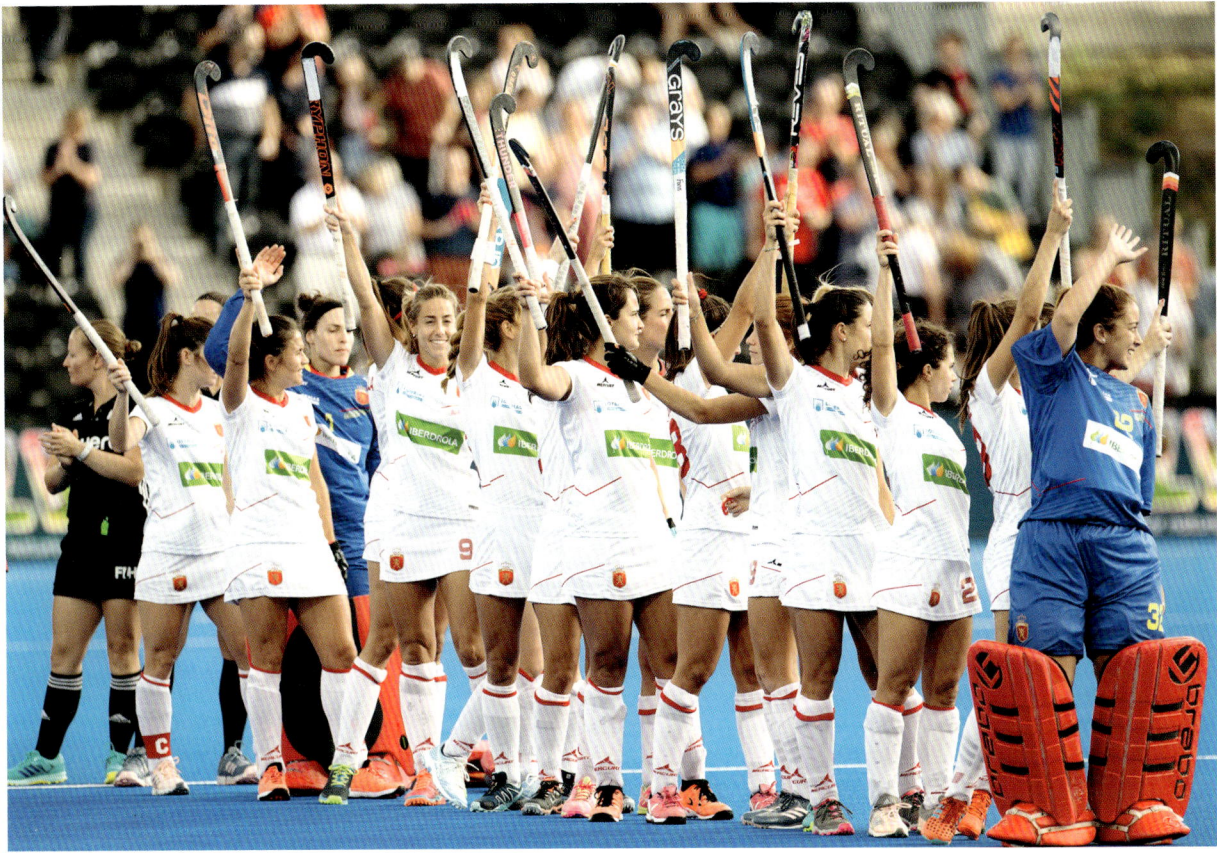

Spain salute their supporters ahead of their cross-over match against Belgium. // *Frank Uijlenbroek*

Day 9 – Monday 30 July 2018

Fiesta time for Red Sticks and Las Leonas

The first two of four cracking cross-over play-off matches took place on Monday 30 July, with Pool D runners-up Belgium facing Pool C's third-placed Spain before Argentina and New Zealand, who finished second and third in Pools D and C respectively, went head to head in a match that guaranteed the elimination of either the Pan American champions or the Commonwealth Games gold medallists.

With a quarter-final match against in-form Germany – 3-1 winners against Spain in their Pool C meeting – the reward, the battle between Belgium's Red Panthers and the Red Sticks of Spain was, unsurprisingly, tense and cagey. Both teams were conservative in their attacking play, reluctant to commit players forward, out of fear of being exposed at the back and running the risk of conceding.

While excellent defensive organisation from the Belgian and Spanish back lines kept genuine scoring chances to a minimum, there were occasional moments when it seemed the deadlock between the two European nations might be broken. A weaving run and shot from Spain's Begoña Garcia forced a decent but comfortable save from Belgium goalkeeper Aisling D'Hooghe in the first

quarter, while the defences of both teams used smart video referrals to overturn penalty corners awarded against them in the second period.

Belgium – who as European silver medallists from the summer of 2017 entered the match as marginal favourites despite sitting two places below their opponents in the FIH Hero World Rankings – were perhaps the better team as half-time neared, with Stephanie Vanden Borre having two penalty corner strikes charged down before a late Spanish counter-attack brought another fine save from D'Hooghe.

The two nations continued to cancel each other out in the third and fourth quarters, although the two best opportunities arguably fell the way of a Spanish side showing plenty of self-belief. Lola Riera sent a penalty corner drag-flick over the crossbar despite having clear sight of goal, before Garcia wasted a glorious chance to score a late winner when she crashed an off-target backhand strike into the body of a Belgian defender.

Garcia's miss left Spain coach Adrian Lock holding his head in his hands, with the Englishman well aware that a goal at such a late stage in the game would surely have

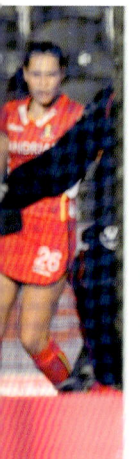

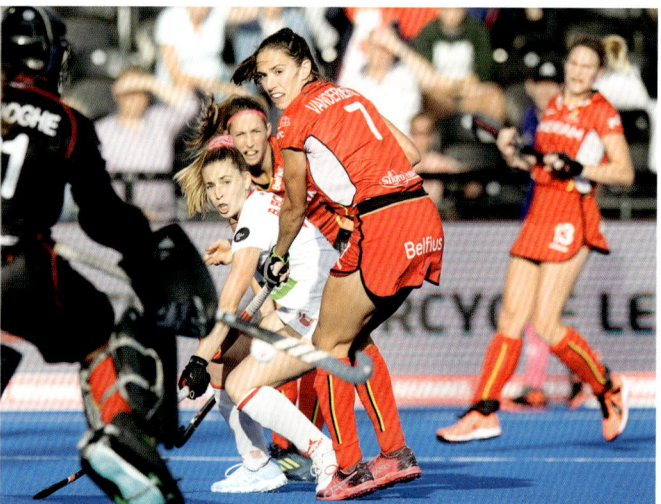

Red Sticks' attacker Berta Bonastre (in white) gets ahead of Belgium's Judith Vandermeiren to force a save from goalkeeper Aisling D'Hooghe. // *Frank Uijlenbroek*

been enough for a place in the quarter-finals, avoiding the inevitable anxiety and stress that comes with a shoot-out.

The nervousness of the attacking players involved in the subsequent one-on-ones was evident throughout, although masterful performances from two world-class goalkeepers in Belgium's D'Hooghe and Maria Luiz of Spain certainly played their part. Only four players – Louise Versavel and Pauline Leclef for Belgium coupled with Spanish duo Lola Riera, who converted a penalty stroke after a foul on Beatriz Perez, and Berta Bonastre – found the target from ten attempts to trigger sudden death.

The defining moment arrived after Perez, the Vitality Player of the Match, made it 3-2 with a supremely cool effort, piling the pressure on Belgium's Louise Versavel, who now needed to score to keep her team in the competition. It proved to be a heartbreaking moment for Versavel, who was

adjudged to have fouled Red Sticks goalkeeper Luiz before she could even get her shot away. The decision handed Spain a dramatic 3-2 win in the shoot-out. The European silver medallists were out, while Spain confirmed a rematch against Pool C rivals Germany in the quarter-finals of the Vitality Hockey Women's World Cup London 2018.

'That was a difficult game,' said a relieved Berta Bonastre in the moments immediately following the end of the match. 'We are two teams who know each other well. We have been talking about reaching this level for a number of years and working hard to achieve it. We really deserve this because we did a great job out there.'

While Spain were enjoying the taste of victory, the talented Belgium women's team were enduring the pain of defeat that had been immeasurably magnified by the drama of the shoot-out. 'In the first half we were really good and again in the third quarter,' said Belgium captain Anouk Raes. 'But Spain are very tough to play, they have a good structure, good creativity and some really excellent players, who stopped us playing our lines. We have come a long way but this is not the first time we have lost a shoot-out,' she continued, possibly making reference to her team's defeat at the hands of Spain in the FINTRO Hockey World League Semi-Final 2017 on home soil in Brussels. 'We need to keep practising.'

On reaching the quarter-finals, Spain were now assured of a top-eight finish at the event and therefore guaranteed to outperform their 11th position in the FIH Hero World Rankings.

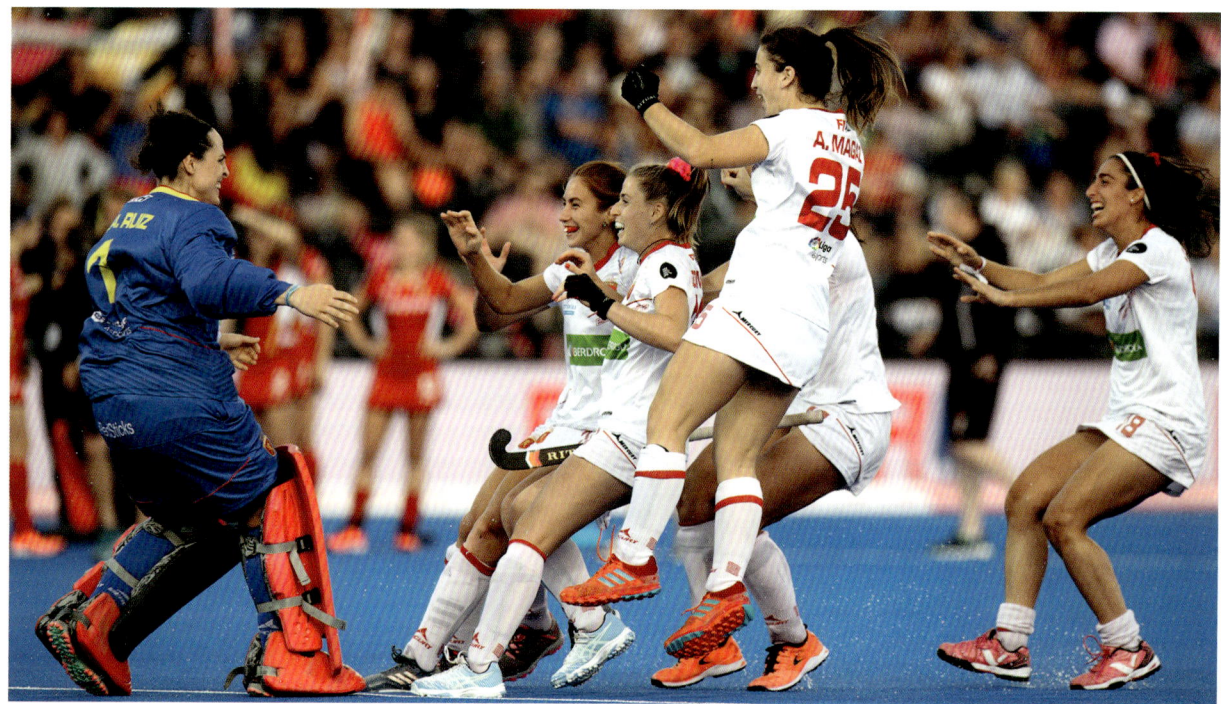

Joyous scenes as Spain celebrate securing a place in the last eight of the Vitality Hockey Women's World Cup London 2018. // *Frank Uijlenbroek*

The same could not be said for the opponents of the second cross-over play-off match on day nine, as two genuine title contenders faced a massive challenge to avoid falling at a relatively early stage of the event.

Pool C runners-up Argentina, the champions of Pan America and third in the world rankings, faced fourth-ranked New Zealand, the Commonwealth Games champions who finished third in Pool D. A quarter-final meeting with Oceania champions Australia was the prize awaiting the winner, while the losing team would be eliminated. With both Las Leonas and the Black Sticks being cited as potential winners prior to the start of the event, the fact that one was now certain to be eliminated before the quarter-finals was definitely not in the script.

After a passionate rendition of the anthems – with superstar goalkeeper Belen Succi being moved to tears during the 'Hymno Nacional Argentino' – the two sides went at each other as if their lives depended on it. However, it was Argentina, and extraordinary Leonas captain Delfina Merino in particular, who were fastest out of the blocks. The 2017 FIH Player of the Year was at her brilliant best from the start, producing a wonderful individual performance that would see her named as the Vitality Player of the Match come the end of the contest.

Merino and Rocio Sanchez both fired early warning shots over the crossbar of the New Zealand goal before the Black Sticks began to create some chances of their own, with Madison Doar going close after being set up by some magical stickwork from Stacey Michelsen, New Zealand's world class midfielder and inspirational captain.

The ferocious speed and intensity on display certainly befitted the occasion, as two of the finest teams on the planet showed all of the grit and desire you would expect in a World Cup knock-out match.

The breakthrough came five minutes before half-time and went the way of the South Americans. New Zealand goalkeeper O'Hanlon produced an excellent save from a penalty corner strike so powerful it forced the shot-stopper's glove off her hand. Quite bizarrely, the glove fell directly into

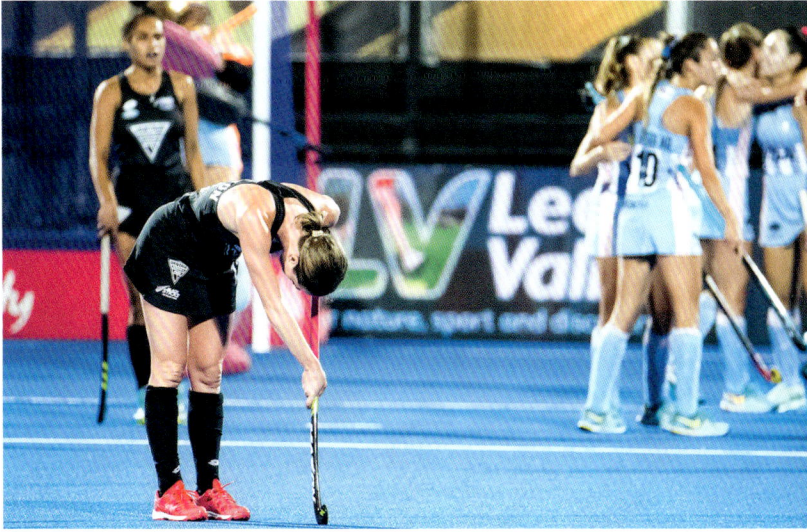
New Zealand show their disappointment while Argentina celebrate Barrionuevo's strike. // *Koen Suyk*

the path of Agustina Habif, who was denied a certain goal when she connected with the stray goalkeeping equipment rather than the ball with the goal at her mercy. Argentina appealed to the video umpire and were awarded a penalty stroke that was dispatched with ease by veteran defender Noel Barrionuevo, despite O'Hanlon's best efforts to deny the 2010 World Cup winner.

The action continued to swing rapidly from one end of the field to the other throughout the third and fourth quarters. New Zealand searched desperately for an equaliser but could not find a way past the inspired Belen Succi, another member of the World Cup winning squad from the 2010 event in Rosario alongside Merino and Barrionuevo.

At the other end, Argentina saw a trio of penalty corner chances foiled by O'Hanlon and her rapid defence.

The key moment arrived with just over 11 minutes of the match remaining, as Argentina finally found that crucial second goal to give themselves some much needed breathing space. Delfina Merino was the scorer, finishing off an intricate penalty corner routine from close range with the deftest of touches, to give New Zealand a mountain to climb in the final stages. The Black Sticks threw caution to the wind and replaced O'Hanlon with an outfield player, but it was to no avail. After some stuttering displays, Argentina had not just set up a quarter-final meeting with Australia, they had produced the kind of performance that would make all other teams sit up and take note.

It was a tough blow to take for New Zealand head coach Mark Hager, who felt that the Black Sticks' slow start to the competition ended up costing his side dearly. 'We didn't hit our game in the pool matches. No one wants a game with Argentina at this stage. We only have ourselves to blame for earlier results.'

Argentina's Rocio Sanchez confessed that their head coach Agustin Corradini had put the team through a gruelling physical training session the day before the New Zealand game, such was his dissatisfaction with the below par performances earlier in the competition. However, Sanchez was relieved that her team had finally shown the world 'the real Argentina'. 'I think we wanted to play tonight, we were inspired and very determined and that was a huge improvement.'

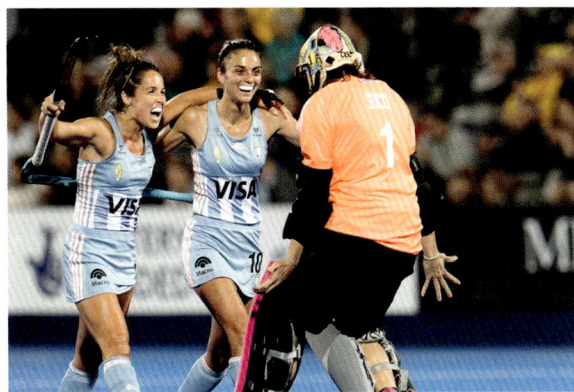
Rocio Sanchez and Magdalena Fernandez share the moment with goalkeeper Belen Succi. // *Frank Uijlenbroek*

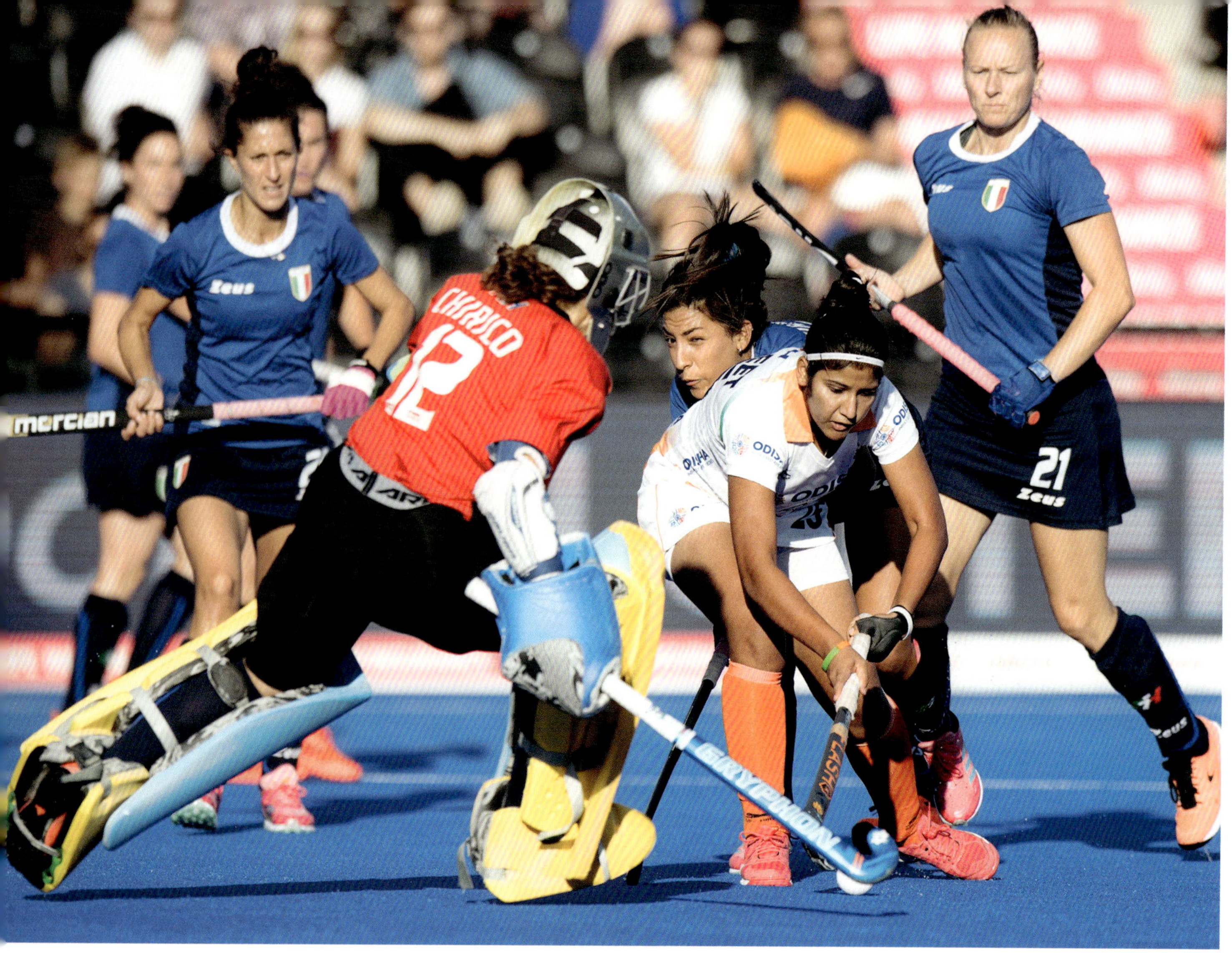

Navneet Kaur shows wonderful skills to move past Italy goalkeeper Martina Chirico but could only find the side of the goal with her shot. // *Frank Uijlenbroek*

Day 10 – Tuesday 31 July 2018

India and England rise to the occasion

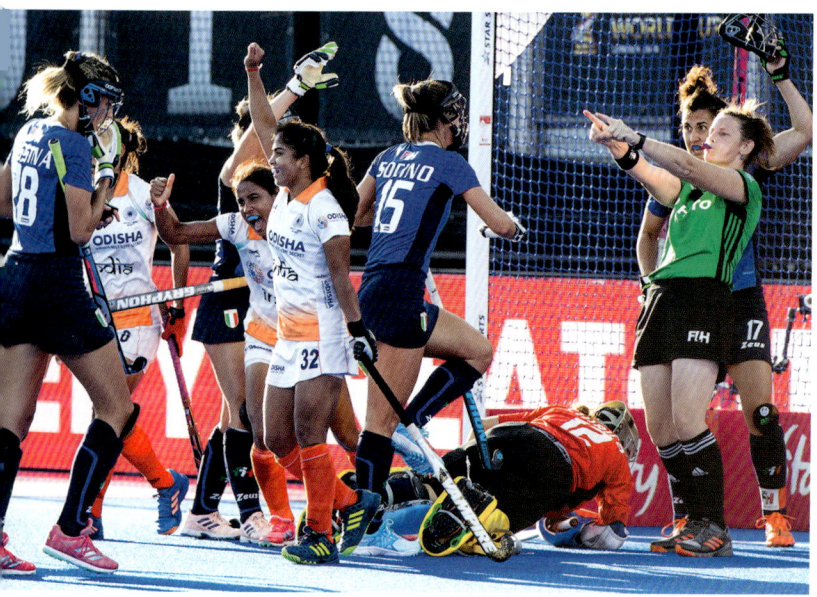

Umpire Kelly Hudson (right, in green) signals the goal as Neha Goyal (#32) scores from close range. // *Koen Suyk*

With two of the four quarter-final matches now confirmed, the complete line-up for the last eight would be decided on Tuesday 31 July. Italy and India would play off for a quarter-final showdown with Pool B winners Ireland, while Pool A winners and reigning world champions the Netherlands would await either England or Korea.

Aside from their heavy defeat at the hands of the Netherlands in their final Pool A match, few could dispute that Italy's performances in London had massively surpassed all expectations. Entering the event as 17th in the world, the lowest-ranked team in the competition claimed victories over China and Korea to finish in second place behind the Dutch. The victories over two of Asian hockey's most successful teams were richly deserved, but Italy would need to rediscover that early form if they were to defeat India, the continental champions of Asia.

With tenth-ranked India only finishing third in Pool B with a tally of just two points from three matches, it would have been easy to dismiss their chances against an Italian team that had claimed six points from nine in their pool

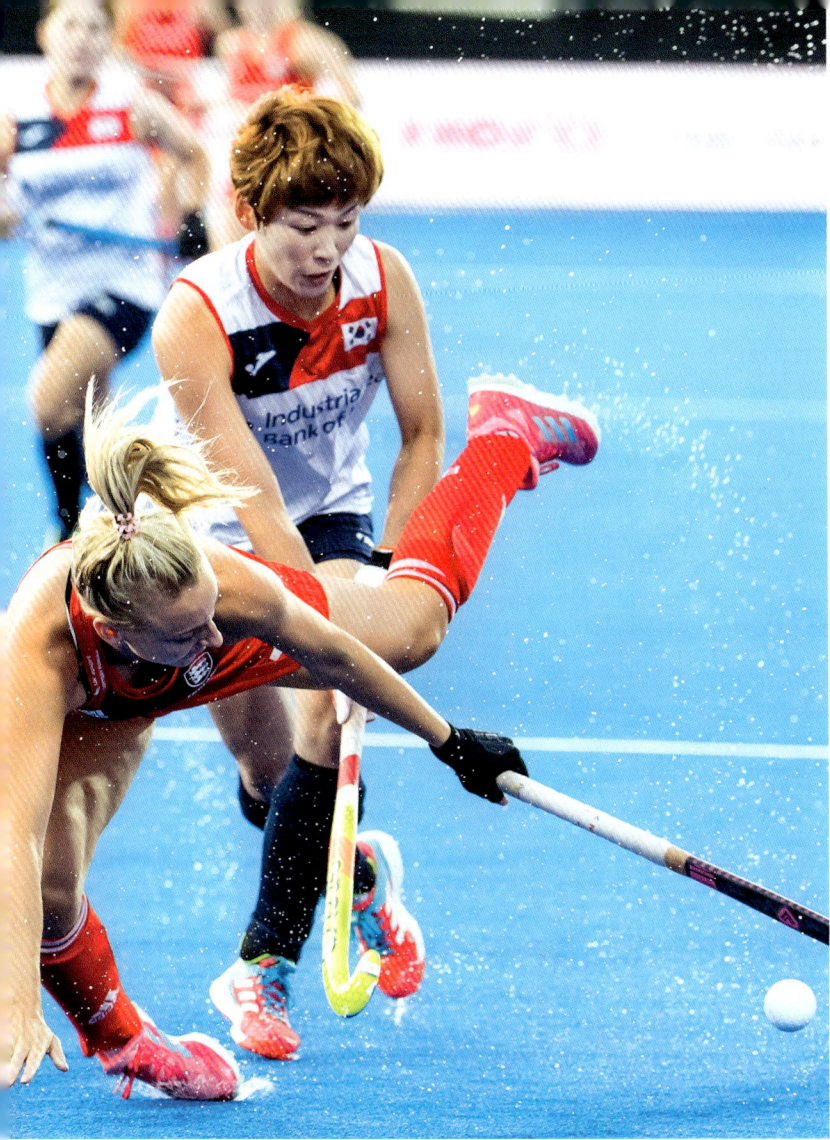

Hannah Martin in action during the second cross-over play-off match of the day as England took on Korea. // *Koen Suyk*

campaign. However, India's performances in the pool phase had also turned heads, earning draws against higher-ranked opponents England (WR:2) and USA (WR:7). The result against host nation England was achieved in front of 10,500 fans desperate to see a triumph for the home side, while their tie against the USA was achieved with tenacity and a steely resilience, getting the required result to see the Eves reach the knock-out phase ahead of their American opponents.

The outcome of the meeting between India and Italy became more and more obvious as the match progressed, with the Asian champions showing a level of speed, skill and agility that the Italians struggled to contain. While Italy could not be faulted for the bravery of their defending, the Indian attackers were proving hard to handle and it came as little surprise when the inevitable opening goal arrived. A quick free hit unlocked the Italian defence, with Vitality Player of the Match Lalremsiami on hand to lift the ball past Martina Chirico in the Italian goal after the ball was quickly switched across the circle by Vandana Katariya.

'Lalremsiami is the youngest player in our team [19 years old] and I remember how, when I was 15, I played in my first World Cup and it was just so exciting,' said captain Rani, post-match, remembering her own stunning World Cup debut when she was named as FIH Young Player of the Tournament at Rosario 2010. 'She brings an extra energy that we feed off.'

India's lead was nearly extended at the start of the second quarter as Lalremsiami was again found in plenty of space. However the talented teenager was unable to get the ball under enough control to beat the rapidly advancing Chirico.

Italy were reinvigorated after the half-time break, producing the attacking hockey that had served them so well during the pool phase. Jasbeer Singh and Lara Oviedo were both instrumental in creating chances for dangerous striker Valentina Braconi, although she could not find a way past the impressive Lilima Minz at the heart of the India defence.

Despite the Italian resurgence, India remained the better side and certainly the most threatening in front of goal. Their hard work was eventually rewarded by a penalty corner in the final minute of the third quarter, with Chirico doing her best to save Gurjit Kaur's drag-flick before the ball was eventually forced over the line from close range by Neha Goyal. It was a goal celebrated wildly by the Indian players and coaching staff alike, who all knew that India were within touching distance of a quarter-final meeting with Ireland.

The result was finally put beyond doubt five minutes from the end thanks to Vandana Katariya, who got the crucial touch on Gurjit's penalty corner drag-flick to guide the ball beyond the stranded Chirico, who had little chance of saving. A 3-0 scoreline was no more than India deserved, giving head coach Sjoerd Marijne the chance to gain a measure of revenge over an Irish team that had beaten them 1-0 in the pool phase. It was an encounter that Rani was anticipating with relish.

'We have gained confidence throughout this tournament,' she said. 'Early in the tournament we didn't do the one thing we needed to do – score goals. But we have found the net now and we can definitely push on with our journey. We do not see that journey ending on Thursday.'

Notwithstanding the loss and subsequent World Cup exit, Italy's captain Chiara Tiddi was justifiably proud of her team's first World Cup campaign since the 1976 competition in West Berlin.

'We have created history and, more importantly, we have shown that we are more than capable of competing at this level,' said the experienced defender, who had been so instrumental in Italy's rapid development in recent years.

'We need to push on now and build on all we have learnt. We have more confidence in our ability now. I hope that we will now see more investment into Italian hockey so we can keep competing at the top level. We have definitely not been out of place here. I am very proud of the whole team.'

The fourth and final cross-over play-off match was one that the vast majority of a sell-out crowd at the Lee Valley Hockey & Tennis Centre had turned up to witness. Pool B runners-up England taking on Pool A's third-placed Korea for a place in the quarter-finals against the Netherlands was an understandably attractive prospect for England fans, who

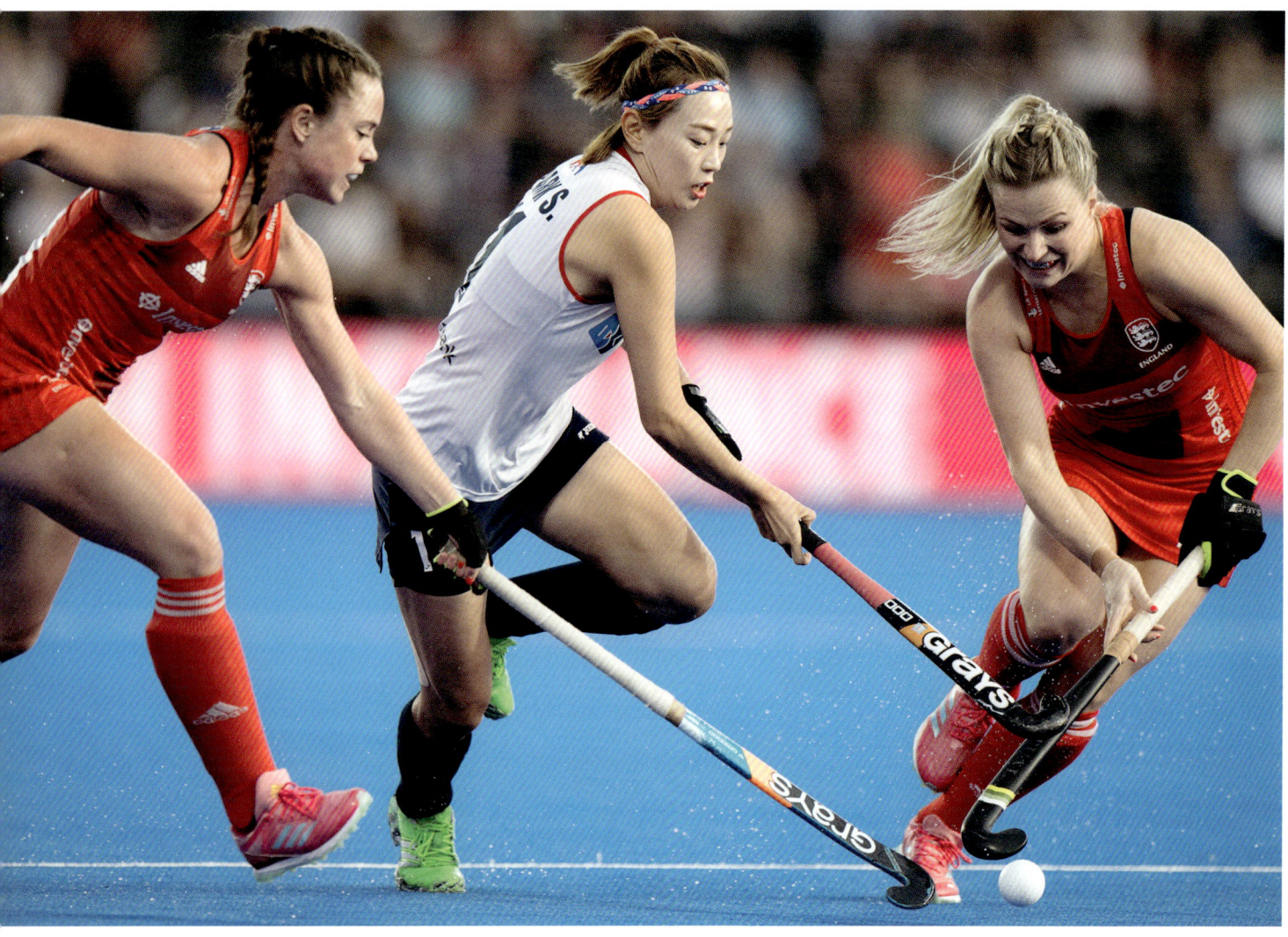

Korea's Park Seunga comes under pressure from England's Grace Balsdon (left) and Holly Pearne-Webb. // *Frank Uijlenbroek*

arrived at the stadium full of optimism following England's victory over pool winners Ireland two days earlier.

They were not to be disappointed, as Danny Kerry's team produced their performance of the competition, one that contained all of the intensity and fluidity that some of their earlier matches had been missing. Suddenly the passes were connecting, the runs were better-timed and chances were being created. It was all starting to click into place.

England's hopes were boosted by the news that Korea's iconic striker Park Mi Hyun would be forced to watch the action from the sidelines due to injury. With the 32-year-old forward having been Korea's stand-out attacking talent for over a decade, it was a huge blow for the team ranked ninth in the world and one that certainly affected their potency in front of goal.

Cheered on by another sell-out crowd, England made an electric start and created some excellent chances early in the contest. Korea's goalkeeper Hwang Hyeon was called into action in the opening minutes, although some impressive early saves from the shot-stopper quickly demonstrated that beating her was certainly not going to be an easy task.

Korea's defence buckled under the intense English pressure in the ninth minute of the match, leading to a goal that was excellent in its creation and determined in its finish. Speedy forward Sarah Haycroft, who was later named Vitality Player of the Match, showed wonderful technique to bring a long, high pass from defence perfectly under her control before setting up the chance for Rio 2016 Olympic gold medallist Sophie Bray. Bray's first effort was brilliantly blocked by the glove of Hwang, who then denied Haycroft before the ball once again fell into the path of Bray, who made no mistake at the second time of asking.

As the stadium erupted in celebration of Bray's crucial strike, a new sense of confidence seemed to surge through the England team. At half-time, many people were wondering how England were only one goal ahead in a contest that had seen them enjoy 65 per cent possession and ten shots in anger. At the other end of the pitch, England goalkeeper Maddie Hinch had not been troubled at any stage.

England remained completely in charge after the break, continuing to press for that all-important second goal that, despite their numerous opportunities, was proving hard to find. Korea gave England a scare midway through the

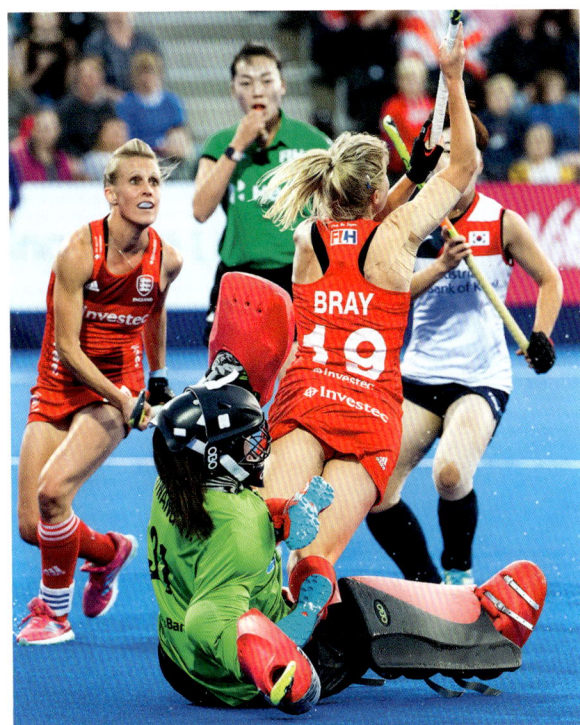

Sophie Bray takes a tumble over Korea goalkeeper Hwang Hyeon, with England captain Alex Danson looking on. // *Koen Suyk*

third quarter when Cheon Seul Ki rattled a shot into the pads of Hinch, who had remained fully aware of the counter-attacking threat posed by Korea and sprung into life when she was required to do so.

Hinch was called into action twice more in the dying stages, with the 2016 and 2017 FIH Goalkeeper of the Year making crucial blocks to keep her side ahead. Her save from An Hyoju was particularly special, with the Korean player's fierce shot destined for the bottom right corner before Hinch showed remarkable reflexes to instinctively kick out with her left foot to deny the opportunity.

To their great credit, England remained calm under pressure and eventually got the second goal that they richly deserved. Lily Owsley was the scorer, coolly passing into an unguarded net after Korea goalkeeper Hwang was replaced with an outfield player by head coach Huh Sang Young in one final attempt to salvage something from the contest. England had made it to the quarter-finals of their home World Cup, much to the delight of team captain Alex Danson.

'It was a really professional performance against a fantastic Korean side, and once again the crowd were absolutely outstanding,' said Danson. 'We stuck to the task, did the job and I'm absolutely delighted to progress through.'

When asked about facing the Dutch – a team England defeated in the final of the EuroHockey Championships in 2015 at Lee Valley – and the need to execute the opportunities created, Danson said: 'Of course. We need to go away and do our homework now. That is the wonderful thing about a World Cup, it is one game at a time. We are delighted to meet the Dutch in the next round. We'll be prepared and ready to go.'

Results – Cross-over play-offs

Monday 30 July 2018

2nd Pool D v 3rd Pool C

Belgium	0-0	Spain

Shoot-out	2-3	
Jill Boon – No Goal		Begoña García – No Goal
Louise Versavsel – Goal		Beatriz Perez – Goal (PS – Lola Riera)
Stephanie Vanden Borre – No Goal		Alicia Magaz – No Goal
Anouk Raes – No Goal		Berta Bonastre – Goal
Pauline Leclef – Goal		Lola Riera – No Goal
Louise Versavel – No Goal		Beatriz Perez – Goal

Vitality Player of the Match: Beatriz Perez (ESP)

2nd Pool C v 3rd Pool D

Argentina	2-0	New Zealand
Noel Barrionuevo 25m PS		
Delfina Merino 49m PC		

Vitality Player of the Match: Delfina Merino (ARG)

Tuesday 31 July 2018

2nd Pool A v 3rd Pool B

Italy	0-3	India
		Lalremsiami 20m FG
		Neha Goyal 45+m PC
		Vandana Katariya 55m PC

Vitality Player of the Match: Lalremsiami (IND)

2nd Pool B v 3rd Pool A

England	2-0	Korea
Sophie Bray 9m FG		
Lily Owsley 59m FG		

Vitality Player of the Match: Sarah Haycroft (ENG)

Quarter-final line-up

Wednesday 1 August 2018

Germany v Spain
Australia v Argentina

Thursday 2 August 2018

Ireland v India
Netherlands v England

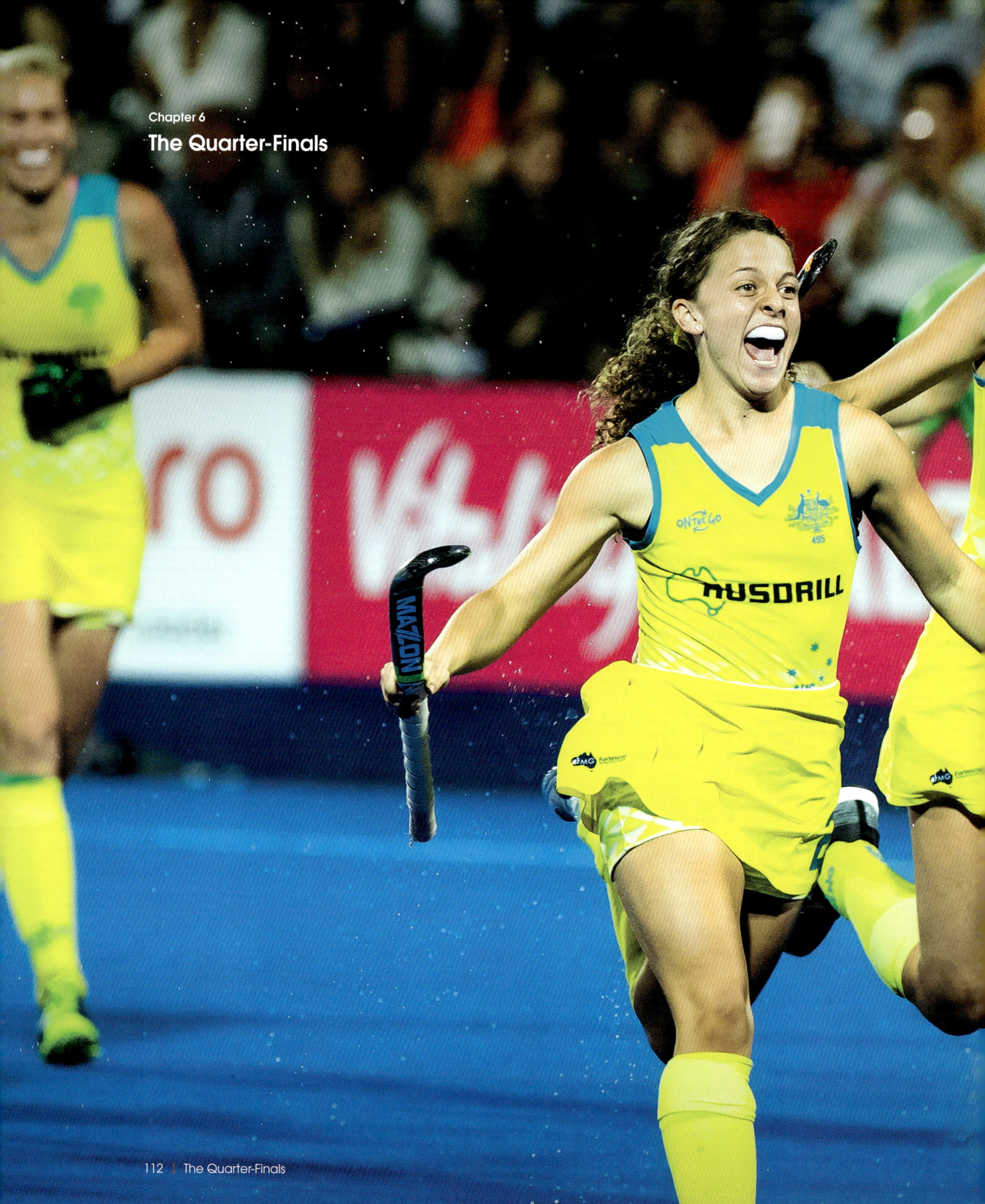

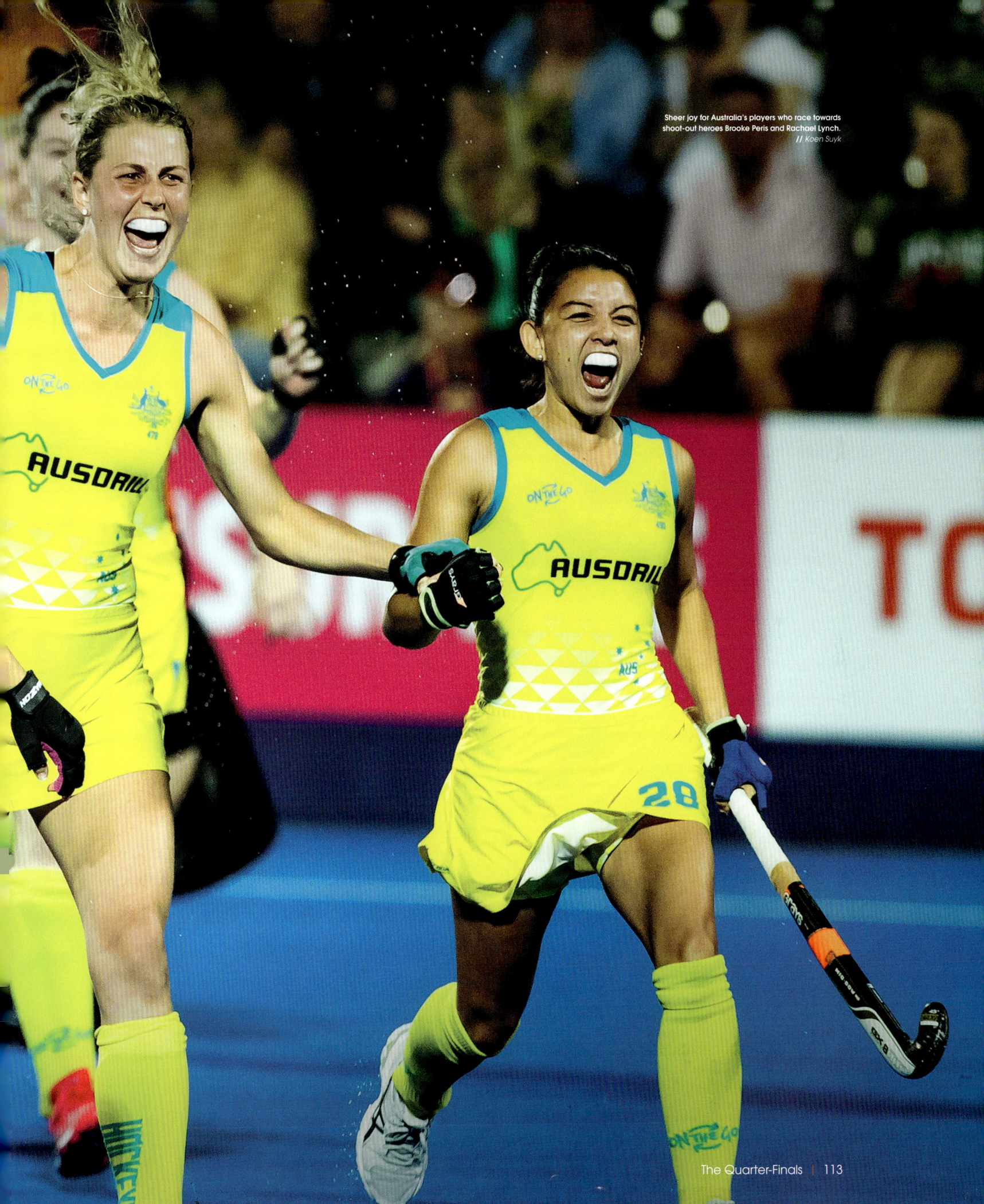

Sheer joy for Australia's players who race towards shoot-out heroes Brooke Peris and Rachael Lynch.
// Koen Suyk

Chapter 6

The Quarter-Finals

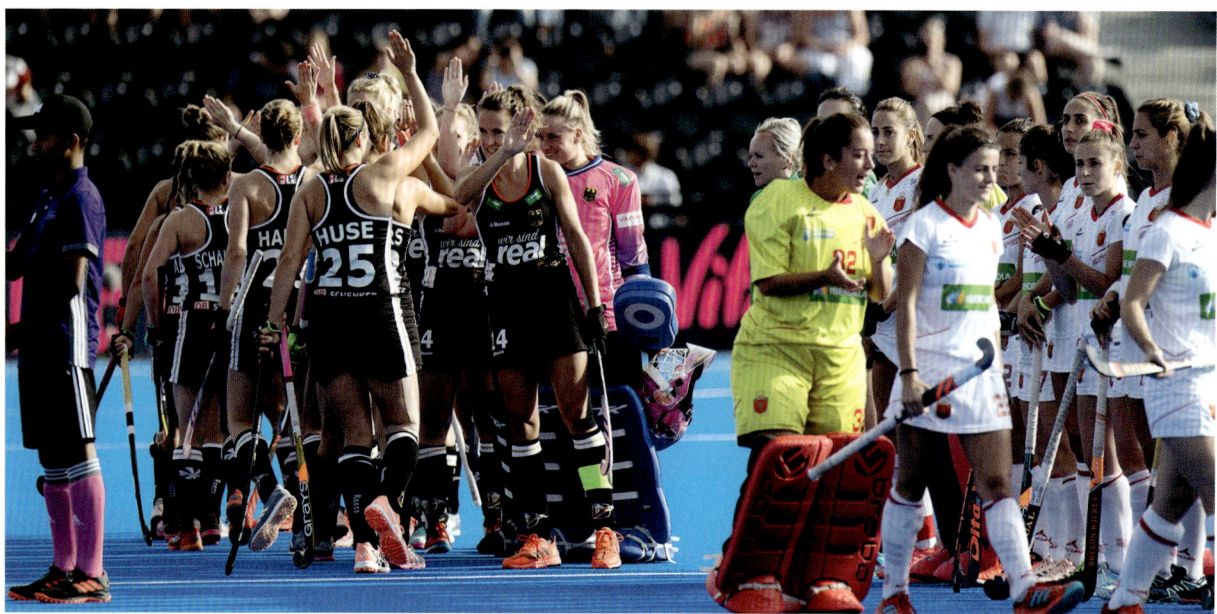

High fives all round as Germany (black) and Spain (white) prepare for their quarter-final meeting. // *Frank Uijlenbroek*

While the line-up for the quarter-finals of the Vitality Hockey Women's World Cup London 2018 contained some surprises, no one could dispute the fact that all eight teams had categorically earned the right to be there. A failure to win their respective pools meant Spain, Argentina, India and England had been forced to do it the hard way, battling through the cross-over play-off matches to secure a place in the last eight and set up meetings against four nations that were feeling pretty good about themselves. As the winners of the four pools, their confidence was entirely justified.

The format of the quarter-finals, which were being used for the first time in the history of the women's hockey World Cup, triggered two rematches from the pool phase. Following their hard-earned cross-over play-off triumph over Belgium, Adrian Lock's Spain would once again take on Germany, a team that had comfortably beaten the Red Sticks 3-1 on their way to finishing top of the standings in Pool C. India – winners in the cross-over phase against Italy – would also go head to head against a familiar foe, with shock Pool B winners Ireland blocking their path to a place in the semi-finals. Fascinatingly, the winners of the Spain versus Germany and India versus Ireland contests would play each other in the semi-final. With all four nations placed outside of the top five in the FIH Hero World Rankings – sixth-placed Germany were the highest-ranked team on this side of the draw – it was now guaranteed that the showpiece final on Sunday 5 August would contain at least one 'surprise' team.

On the other side of the draw, things looked very different indeed, with four of the top five-ranked teams in the world set to go head to head in eliminators. A 2-0 win over 2018 Commonwealth Games gold medallists New Zealand in the cross-overs meant that third-ranked Argentina would now face the other giant of Oceania hockey, with Pool D winners and fifth-ranked Australia – silver medallists at the Rabobank Hockey World Cup 2014 in The Hague, Netherlands – set to provide a stern test for Las Leonas. However, it was at least preferable to the task confronting host nation England, who now had to overcome the mother of all challenges in order to keep their own World Cup title hopes alive. A richly deserved 2-0 cross-over victory against Korea earned the second-ranked home favourites an earlier-than-hoped for meeting with the Netherlands, the defending champions and the top-ranked team in world hockey. With 26 goals scored and just two conceded in a Pool A campaign that included a 7-0 victory over a Korean team that England had only managed two goals against, the Dutch masters were absolutely flying and quite rightly regarded as clear favourites not only to win the match but also successfully defend their world title.

Despite the magnitude of the challenge, England head coach Danny Kerry was firm in his assessment that his team, bolstered by the atmosphere generated by the 10,500 fans that would cram into the Lee Valley Hockey & Tennis Centre for the fixture, were more than capable of rising to the occasion. 'We've been watching the Dutch here and have had some good results against them in recent years,' said Kerry, referencing England's shoot-out victory over the Dutch at the Lee Valley Hockey & Tennis Centre in the final of the Unibet EuroHockey Championships 2015, as well as Great Britain's monumental gold-medal triumph at the Rio 2016 Olympic Games. 'We've got a few things up our sleeves, so we'll see what happens.'

Day 11 – Wednesday 1 August 2018

Spain continue to live the dream while Australia dig deep to overcome Argentina

Remaining true to the spirit of this most unpredictable of competitions, the quarter-finals of the Vitality Hockey Women's World Cup London 2018 continued to tear up the FIH Hero World Rankings before our very eyes. The first two of the four quarter-final matches took place on Wednesday 1 August 2018, with Germany versus Spain and Australia versus Argentina taking centre stage on another captivating day of action.

Germany came into their quarter-final meeting with Spain feeling confident about their chances of claiming a fourth successive match victory in London, and with good reason. They had, at times, played some exceptional hockey in their triumphs over South Africa, pre-tournament pool-favourites Argentina and quarter-final opponents Spain to deservedly finish top of Pool C. Also, in sensational attacker Charlotte Stapenhorst, they had a player who was producing potential match-winning moments of brilliance with startling

regularity. They now found themselves just two wins away from a first women's hockey World Cup final since the 1986 event in Amstelveen, Netherlands, where they finished second to the host nation. And those two games would both be against lower-ranked teams. It seemed that the stars were aligning for Die Danas. However, at a World Cup where very little was following the script, it was never going to be that simple.

Germany sparkled in the early stages of the contest, forcing the 11th-ranked Spaniards to defend deep in their own territory to stop the Rio 2016 Olympic Games bronze medallists from putting the first mark on the scoreboard. Marie Mävers fired an early warning at the Spanish goal before Red Sticks' shot-stopper Maria Ruiz was called into action to confidently kick away a penalty corner slap-shot from Germany captain Janne Müller-Wieland.

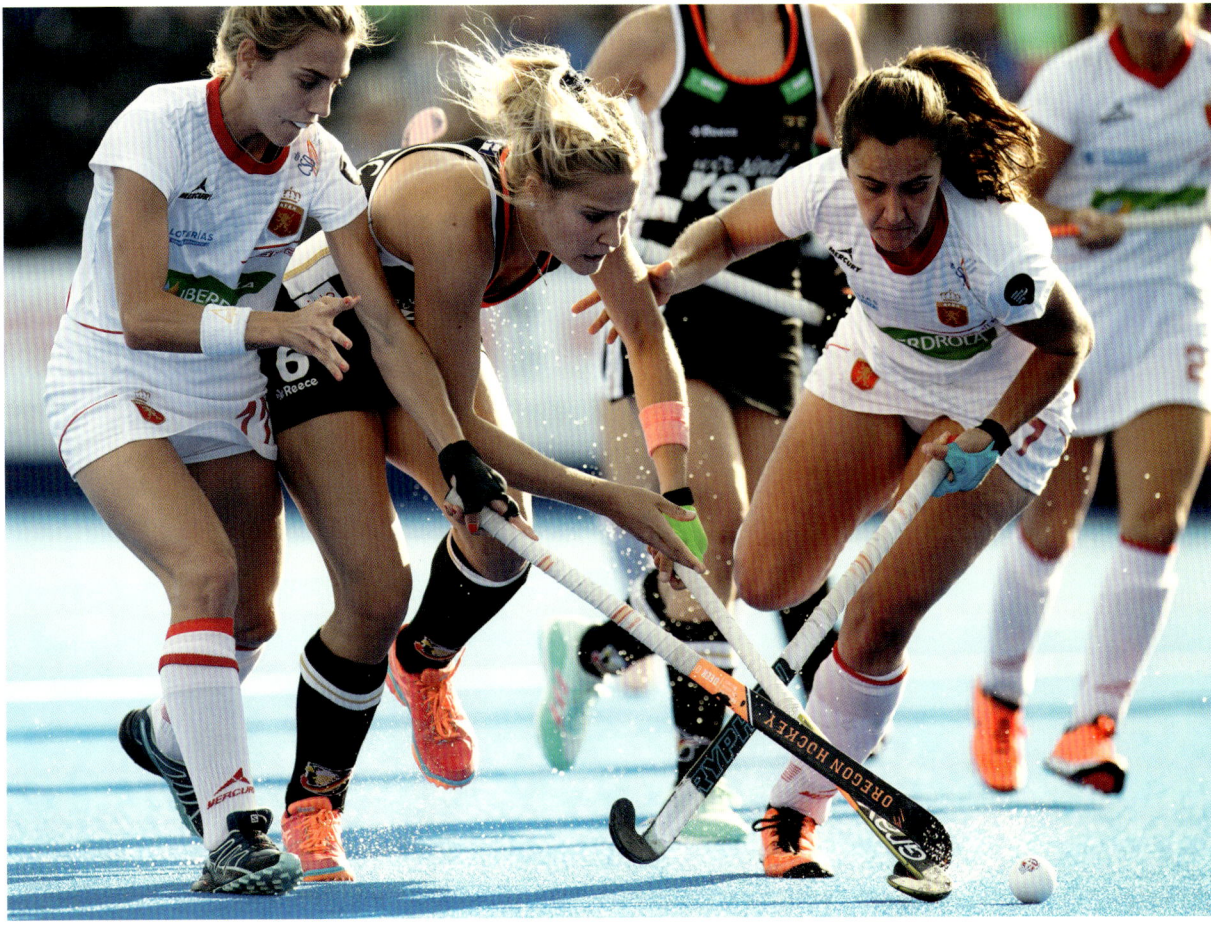

Spain's Cristina Guinea and Lola Riera challenge Germany's Hannah Gablac. // *Frank Uijlenbroek*

While Germany were dominant and certainly looked the most likely to score – the opening quarter saw Die Danas have five shots on target compared to Spain's one – it was certainly not all one-way traffic. Adrian Lock had set his team up to deliberately soak up the German pressure and catch their high-pressing opponents out with a swift counter-attack. It was a tactic that came close to paying rich dividends when gifted attacking midfielder Berta Bonastre made a brilliant interception, but her subsequent pass forward was just out of the reach of Alicia Magaz, who was denied the chance to score on her 100th senior international appearance in Spanish colours.

As had been expected, the skill, speed and deception of Charlotte Stapenhorst was proving to be a near constant thorn in the side of the Spanish team. Stapenhorst came close to scoring a wonderful individual goal three minutes before the end of the first quarter, bursting from her own half to skip past numerous Spanish challenges before seeing her backhand strike blocked by the gloves of Ruiz.

While Carmen Cano and Maialen Garcia both had good chances for Spain in the second quarter, the momentum remained very much with Germany. However, when Lisa Altenburg and Mävers again came painfully close to opening the scoring in the third period, Germany head coach Xavier Reckinger may have started to wonder whether this really was to be his team's day.

While Germany had arguably been the better team for much of the contest, Spain's wonderful efforts in containing one of the most devastating attacking sides in the competition had been nothing short of heroic, laying the

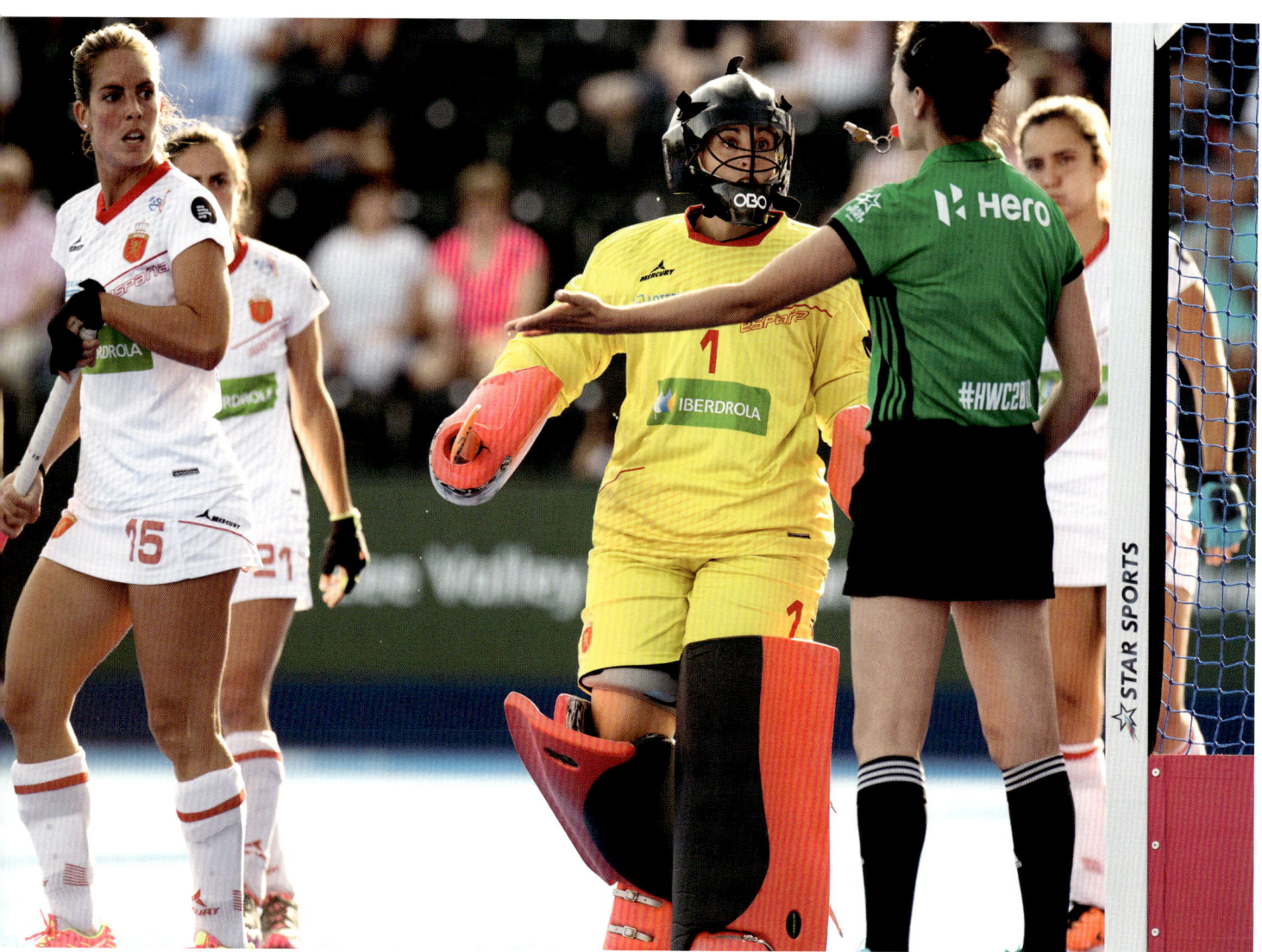

Spain goalkeeper Maria Ruiz in discussion with umpire Liu Xiaoying of China. // *Frank Uijlenbroek*

foundations for another stunning shock at the Vitality Hockey Women's World Cup London 2018.

Against both the run of play and all expectations, it was the defensively superb Spaniards who finally broke the deadlock with six minutes of the match remaining. Carmen Cano was the scorer, volleying into the roof of the Germany goal after some persistent play down the right from Carlota Petchame, who simply would not let Die Danas clear their lines.

It was a stunning blow from Spain, a sucker punch that left a team considered by many as potential champions with just six minutes to avoid elimination. Petchame went from hero to villain when she was sent from the field for a yellow card offence with less than two minutes remaining, intensifying an already pressurised situation as the Germans laid siege to the Spanish circle.

With just seconds of the contest left to play, Germany's big chance arrived in the shape of a penalty corner, causing the entire stadium to hold their breath in anticipation as Janne Müller-Wieland waited at the top of the circle ready to flick for goal. When the Germany captain's effort sailed past the left post, the sense of relief among the Spanish contingent on the field and in the stadium was palpable, while the scene that greeted the final hooter was one of unrestrained joy. Adrian Lock hugged his coaching staff and bench players, who then burst on to the field in celebration. Having reached the final four of the women's hockey World Cup for only the second time in their history – their only other semi-final appearance being at the 2006 event on home soil in Madrid – it was an accomplishment well worth celebrating.

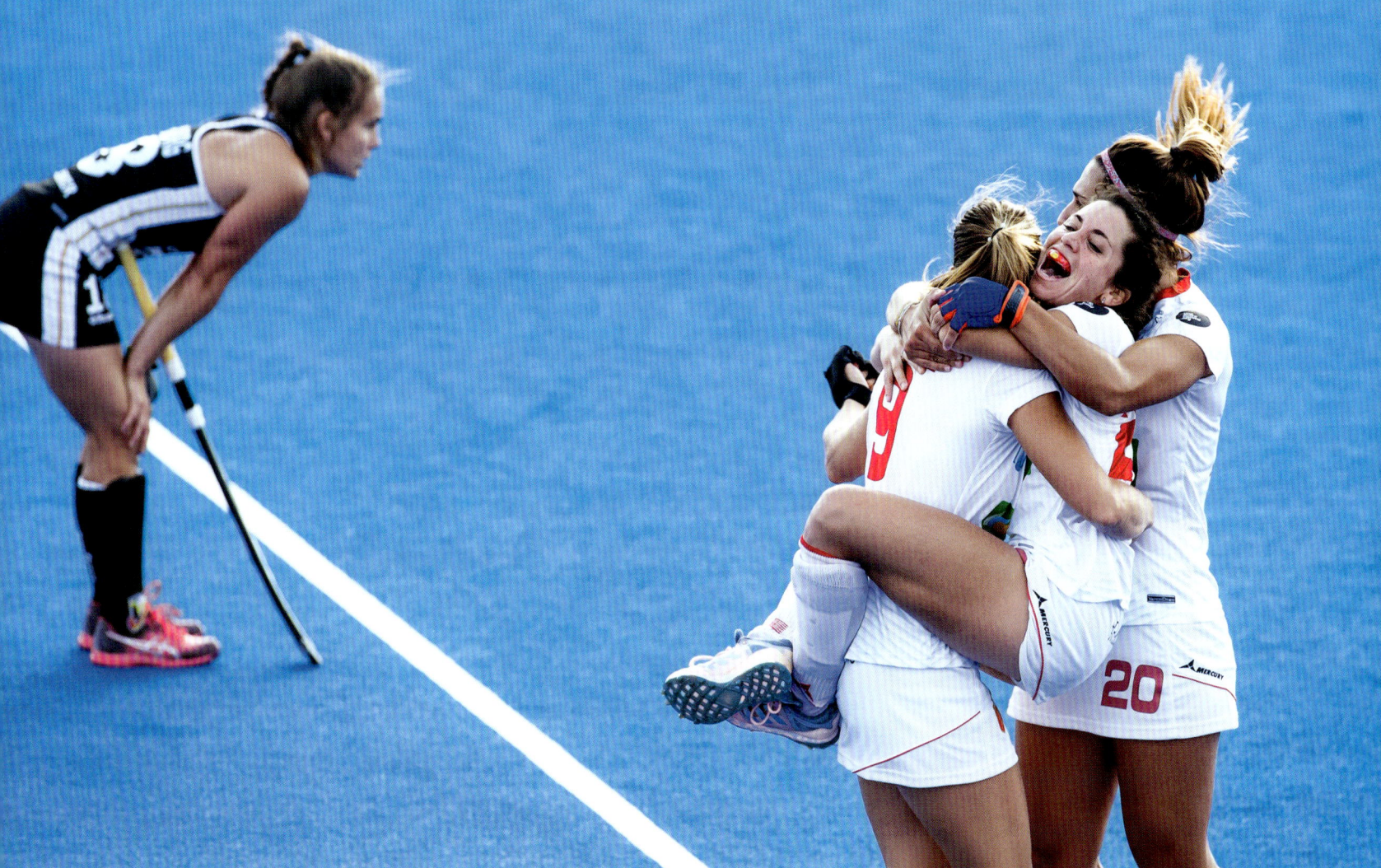

Highs and lows: Maria Lopez, Georgina Oliva and Xantal Gine show their delight at Carman Cano's late strike, with Germany's Lisa Altenburg in the background. // *Koen Suyk*

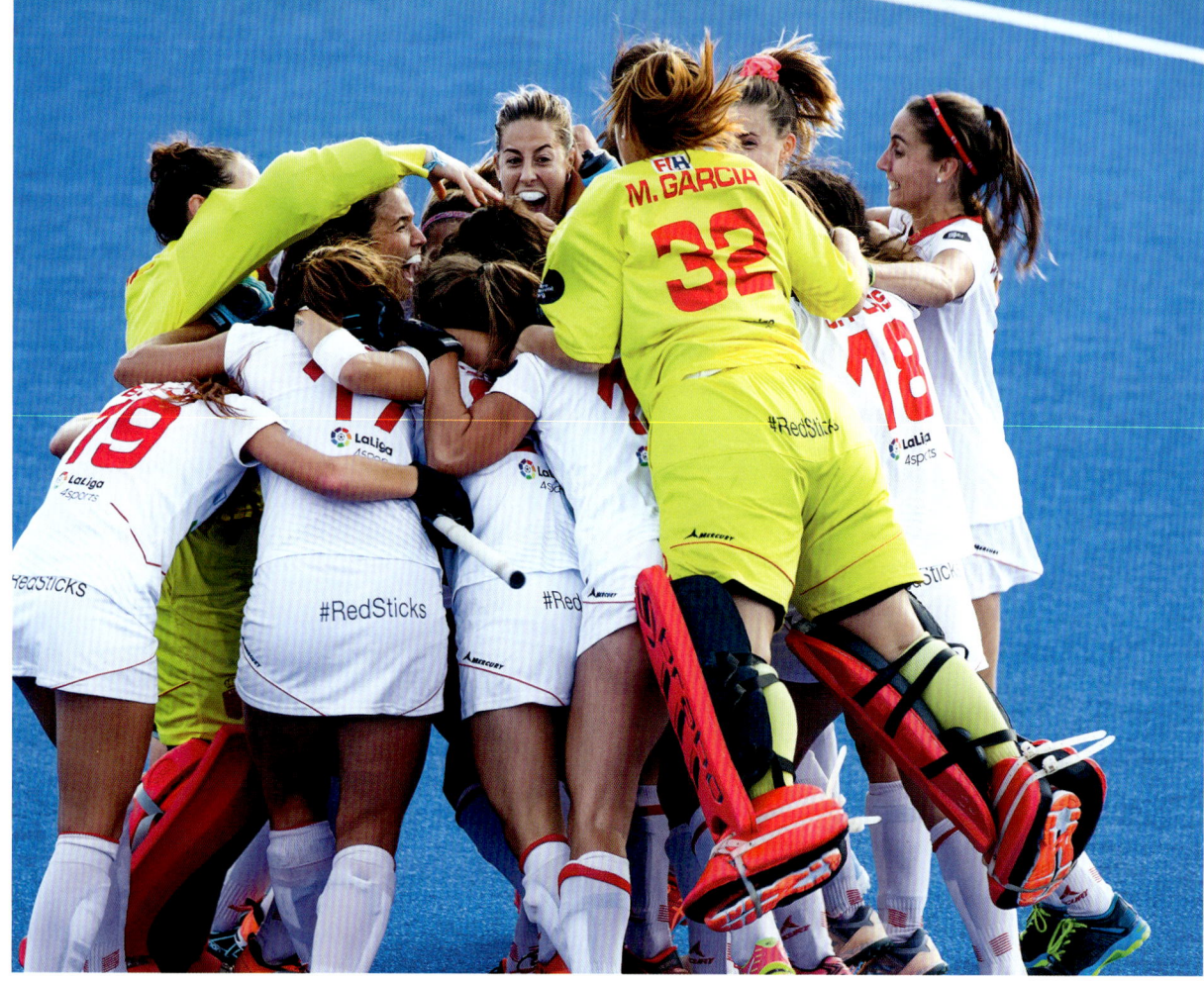

Spain celebrate reaching the World Cup semi-finals for the first time since the 2006 event on home soil in Madrid. // *Frank Uijlenbroek / Koen Suyk*

'There were no stars out there today, we all played for each other,' said a relieved but ecstatic Berta Bonastre after the match. 'We have worked so long for this and all too often it is "we are making progress", but tonight all our hard work paid off.'

For Germany, it was very much a case of reflecting on what might have been. 'If you don't score you don't win,' said an understandably disappointed Xavier Reckinger, providing a simple yet perfect summary of the situation. His sentiments were echoed by Charlotte Stapenhorst, who reiterated the importance of turning opportunities into goals. 'Spain gave us no space to play our game, so we needed to take chances when we could. That didn't happen tonight and then one moment of switching off and they scored. That is quarter-final hockey.'

While Spain – who now faced a semi-final clash at the weekend against either Ireland or India, who were set to play their quarter-final match on Thursday 2 August – continued their festivities back in the changing room and long into the evening, there was plenty more drama still ready to take place on the field at the Lee Valley Hockey & Tennis Centre as two former world champions squared up to each other.

Australia and Argentina, the respective silver and bronze medallists from the Rabobank Hockey World Cup 2014 in The Hague, Netherlands, had long been two of hockey's major powerhouses, and their form coming into this quarter-final meeting ensured that this match would be difficult to predict. The fifth-ranked Hockeyroos – world champions in 1994 and 1998 – had excelled by claiming a first-place finish in Pool D ahead of Belgium and, significantly, Oceania rivals New Zealand. Meanwhile, the performances of third-ranked Argentina in their Pool C campaign had been mixed to say the least, ranging from hammering Spain 6-2 before losing to pool winners Germany and then drawing with bottom-of-the-table South Africa. It was just enough for the 2002 and 2010 world champions to claim a second-place finish behind Germany, setting up a cross-over play-off game against New Zealand. It was a match where Las Leonas produced their most complete performance of the competition, with captain and 2017 Player of the Year Delfina Merino inspiring the Pan American champions to a thoroughly deserved 2-0 win over the Black Sticks, a team that Australia themselves had only managed to draw against when the two sides met in Pool D.

The match itself proved to be every bit as close as expected, with head coaches Paul Gaudoin and Agustin Corradini deliberately setting up their teams to keep scoring chances to an absolute minimum. Both teams showed unswerving discipline in defence: Corradini's Argentina were restricted to just four shots in anger to Australia's two in what was a cagey opening 30 minutes of hockey. This was chess on a hockey field, a contest between two nations fully aware of the potential threat posed by the other.

The second half saw both teams start to explore the attacking options a little less tentatively. Australia's Ambrosia Malone and Renee Taylor both had shots that tested the Leonas's defence, while Delfina Merino, Agustina Albertarrio and the effervescent Maria Granatto all forced some brave defending from the Hockeyroos. Teenage star Julieta

Jankunas was also becoming a growing influence on the contest, but the rock-steady Australian defence, where Vitality Player of the Match Georgina Morgan was one of the stars, continued to thwart the danger.

Australia's best chance came in the 37th minute when striker Kathryn Slattery created space for herself before unleashing a fierce backhand effort towards the roof of the Argentina goal, only for Leonas shot-stopper Belen Succi to bat the ball away to safety.

The first penalty corner of the game came late in the third quarter, with Argentina winning another in the 50th minute which ended up in the back of the net, but Bianca Donati's strike was disallowed for being above the backboard.

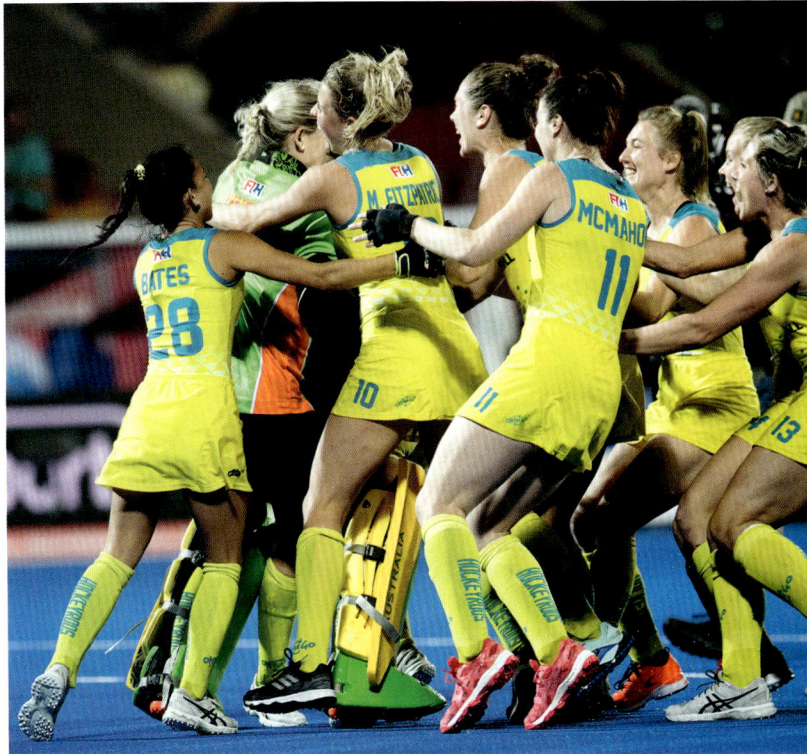

Brooke Peris and Rachael Lynch are mobbed by their team-mates. // *Frank Uijlenbroek*

Australia won their first and only penalty corner of the match seven minutes from the end, a deflected shot from Slattery which Succi was quick to clear.

The contest finished with the score deadlocked, ensuring the match would need to be settled by a shoot-out that would take 14 attempts on goal before the winner would eventually be revealed. Both Succi and Lynch were heroic in goal, Merino thought she had scored but was timed out, there was a penalty stroke after Succi brought Kenny down. In the end it was gladiatorial as Brooke Peris faced Succi. The Australian held her nerve and scored, and seconds later she was mobbed by a sea of yellow shirts as Succi lay sobbing and inconsolable on the floor.

'I just focused on what I needed to do,' said shoot-out hero Peris, speaking to Hockey Australia. 'She's a very good goalkeeper. I had a plan in mind and I just did what I wanted to do. I got the result so I'm pretty happy. I'm very proud of the girls. It was a very tough performance.

'We hung in there. It does come down to one-on-ones sometimes and you've got to get the job done.'

'We knew we had to keep a really strong defence,' added Edwina Bone. 'And then we have someone like her [Rachael Lynch] on our side and she was brilliant tonight.'

As well as being a memorable day for Australia, it would also prove an unforgettable one for Belgian umpire Laurine Delforge, who officiated her 100th senior international match and was presented with her Golden Whistle afterwards to mark the occasion.

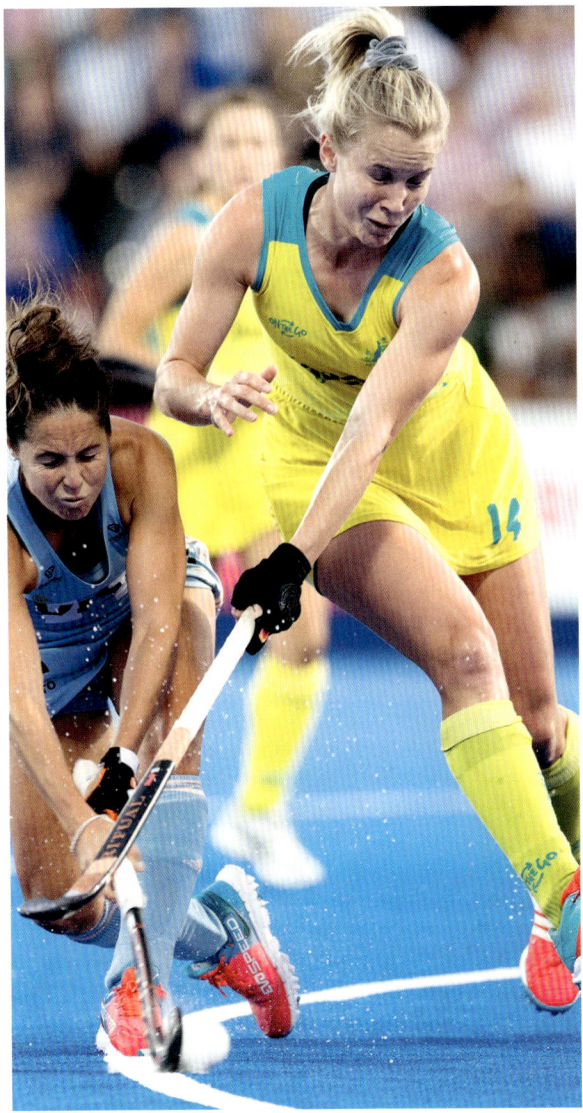

Argentina's Rocio Sanchez gets her shot away despite the presence of Australia's Stephanie Kershaw. // *Frank Uijlenbroek*

Day 12 – Thursday 2 August 2018

Green Army march on while Netherlands deliver knock-out blow to England

With a previous best finish at a women's hockey World Cup of 11th, achieved at the 1990 event in Sydney, Australia, Ireland had already created history by simply reaching the quarter-final phase. The Green Army had entered the competition sitting 16th in the FIH Hero World Rankings but were now absolutely guaranteed a top-eight finish. However, the team coached by Graham Shaw were determined to ensure that their staggering run in London was not about to end when they faced a quarter-final clash against tenth-ranked India – another team that had surpassed all expectations – in the first of two last eight matches that would be played on Thursday 2 August.

Ireland's 1-0 win over the Eves in Pool B was certainly reason to believe that they could secure a dream place in the semi-finals, although India's excellent 3-0 cross-over play-off victory against Italy on Tuesday ensured that the Asian continental champions were equally confident about

their own chances of claiming a win. Were India to reach the semi-finals they would, at worst, match the fourth-place finish achieved 44 years previously at the 1974 Women's Hockey World Cup in Mandelieu, France. Whatever the outcome, history would be made. Furthermore, with the winner setting up a semi-final meeting against Spain, the gold-medal match at the Vitality Hockey Women's World Cup London 2018 was guaranteed to contain at least one first-time finalist.

The match itself, played on another sizzling evening in London, was finely balanced throughout with genuine scoring opportunities few and far between. India head coach Sjoerd Marijne had clearly done his homework, putting in place an excellent defensive strategy to reduce the effectiveness of Ireland's potent counter-attacking style. Ireland striker Anna O'Flanagan – scorer of the winning goal against India in the pool phase – had two chances in

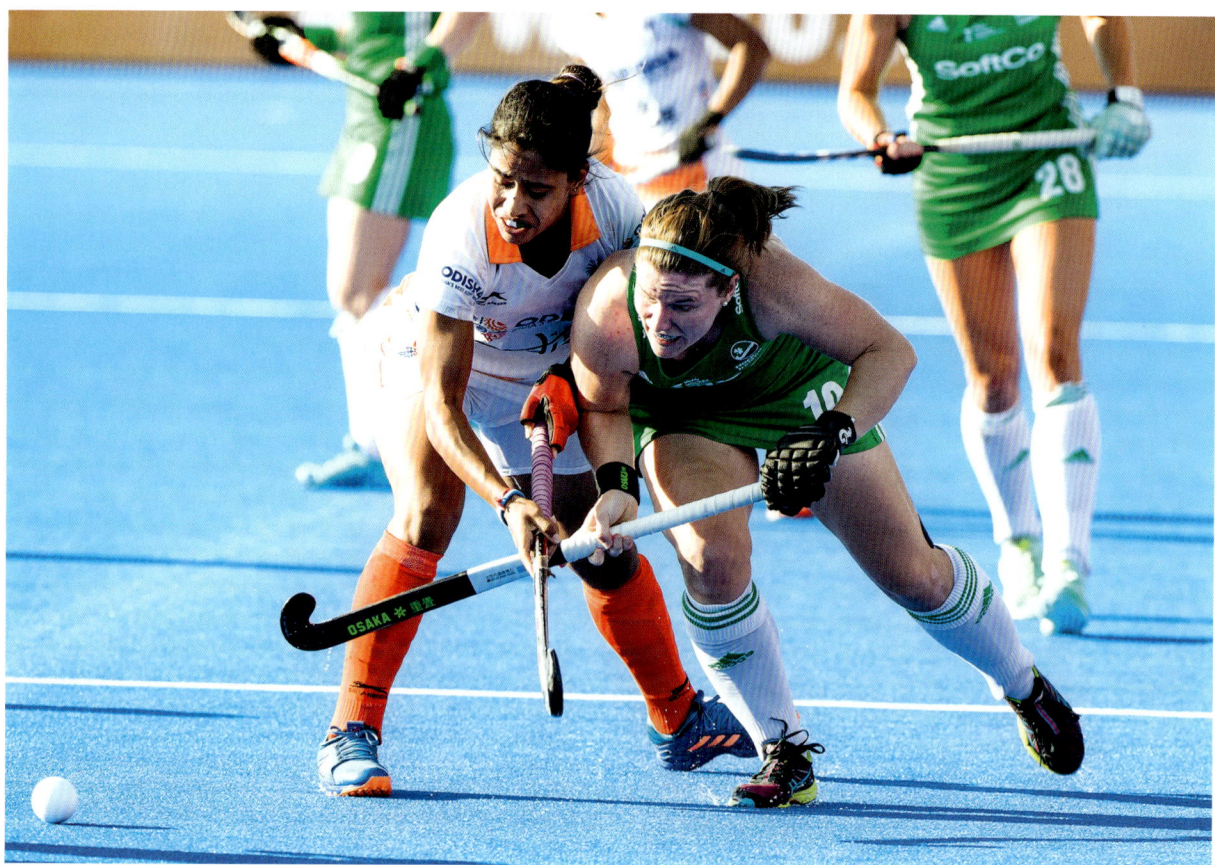

Ireland's vastly experienced defender Shirley McCay makes a crucial interception. // *Koen Suyk*

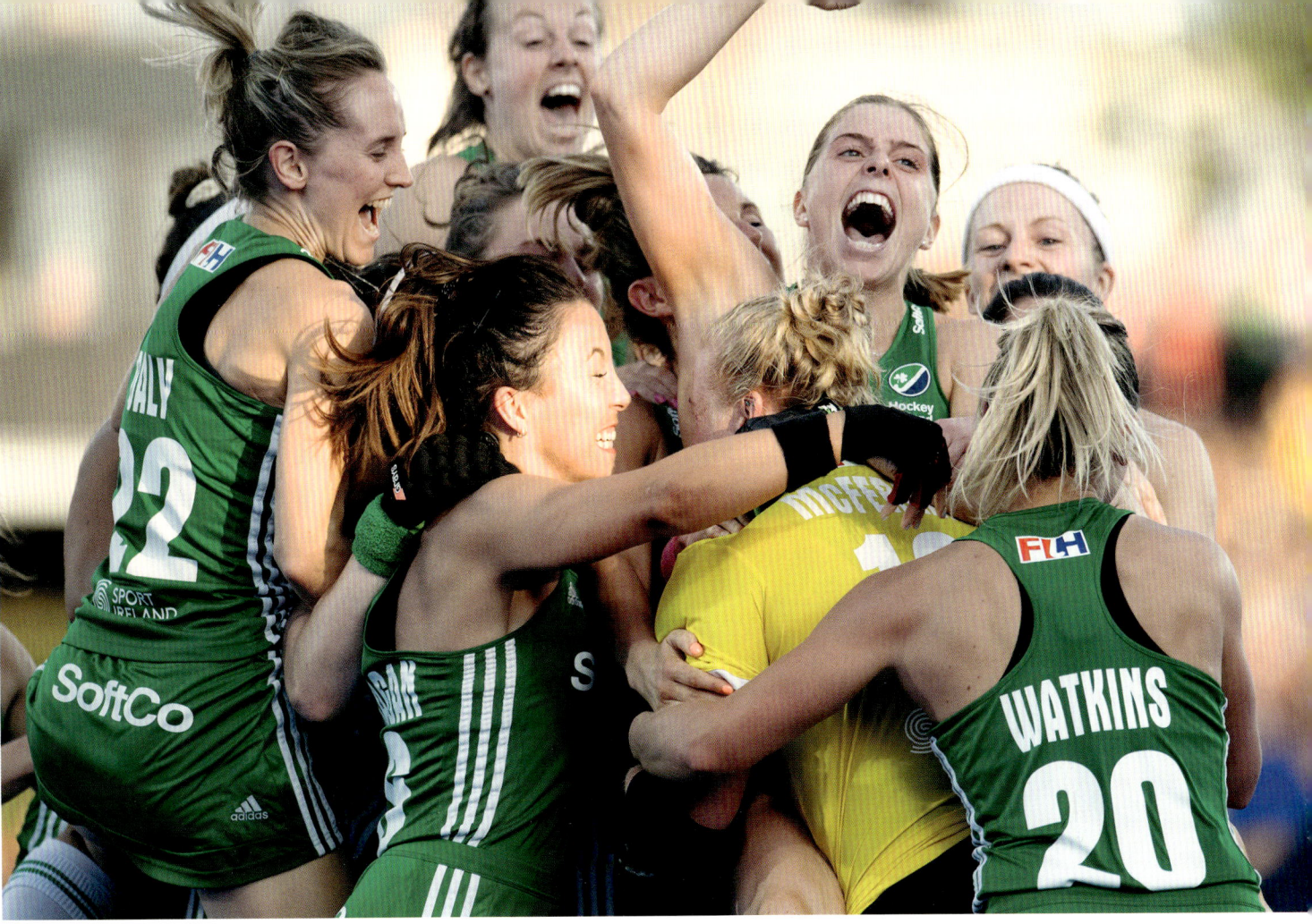

Semi-finals here we come! Ireland's celebrations begin. // *Frank Uijlenbroek*

quick succession in the second quarter but failed to test India's ever impressive shot-stopper Savita, while Green Army goalkeeper Ayeisha McFerran was a spectator for much of the half thanks to the discipline shown by the vastly experienced Shirley McCay and her fellow defenders.

India's biggest and best chance to score came in the final quarter when captain Rani drilled a penalty corner shot into the pads of McFerran before Elena Tice showed a cool head to clear the ball away to safety. It was the only penalty corner of a game which always seemed destined to be decided by a shoot-out, and what a one-on-one contest it proved to be, for Ireland and McFerran in particular.

The 22-year-old goalkeeper from Ulster had already established herself as one of the standout performers in London, but was astonishing in the shoot-out, denying captain Rani and Navjot Kaur with wonderful saves while forcing Monika to shoot wide.

McFerran's goalkeeping heroics were capitalised on by Roisin Upton and Alison Meeke who both scored to make it advantage Ireland. Meeke's effort was audacious in the extreme, showing quick hands to shift Savita out of position before casually reverse flicking the ball between the goalkeeper's legs to leave Ireland one goal away from a place in the semi-finals.

Alison Meeke scored an outrageous goal in the shoot-out.
// *Frank Uijlenbroek*

Reena Khokhar did her very best to keep India in the contest when her cool finish made the score 2-1, but it only served to delay the inevitable. A silent stadium erupted with a deafening noise when Chloe Watkins showed a zen-like level of calm that completely betrayed the enormity of the occasion, spinning brilliantly to leave Savita stranded before passing into an empty net and wheeling away in celebration at a monumentally significant moment in Irish hockey history. The second lowest-ranked team in the entire competition were into the final four. Against all the odds, the Green Army were marching on.

'We knew we had the best keeper in the game at these (shoot-outs),' said Chloe Watkins, who was named Vitality Player of the Match after the game. 'I just knew she would keep them out. We all had faith in her, and she just kept blocking and blocking. When it came to mine we had been practising and practising them. I knew what I was going to do, and thankfully it came off. It was a really tight game and all credit to India, they played really well and have had a great tournament, but we just stuck at it. When it came down to the one-on-ones we were confident.'

For Elena Tice, the atmosphere generated by the 10,500 fans packed into

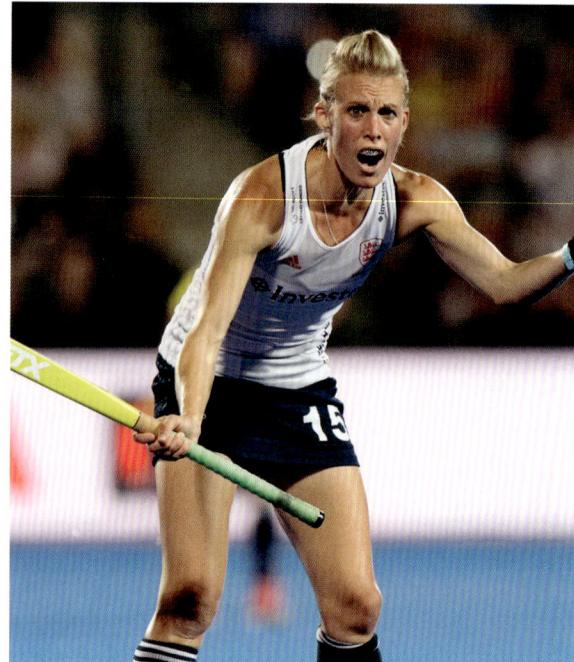

England captain Alex Danson makes her feelings known in her team's quarter-final clash against the Netherlands. // *Frank Uijlenbroek*

the Lee Valley Hockey & Tennis Centre had certainly made a big impact. 'It was absolutely unbelievable out there. It felt like it was all Ireland and when our legs began to ache, the crowd really got us going. We try to go into every game without fear. We are the underdog every time we play but we want to push on, become a top-ten team and expect to win.'

While it was not the outcome that India had desired, head coach Sjoerd Marijne felt that the experience gained in London would be hugely beneficial to his team, especially in relation to their participation in an event that was only weeks away: the Asian Games 2018. With tickets to the Tokyo 2020 Olympic Games on offer to the winners, the importance of success at the multi-sport event in Indonesia was obvious.

'I think the girls will be proud of what they achieved so they will have lots of confidence [for the Asian Games],' said Dutchman Marijne, who would go on to coach his team to a silver medal in Indonesia. 'Now they don't feel that, but they soon will. This has given them the experience of playing on the big stage, doing shoot-outs under high pressure. They will take all of that to the Asian Games.'

While the sell-out crowd had certainly made themselves heard throughout the first quarter-final of the day, the decibel count considerably increased in the build-up to arguably the most eagerly anticipated match of the competition thus far, as the two highest-ranked teams in the game went head to head.

As the reigning world champions and the top-ranked team in the game, it came as little surprise that, despite being the 'away' team, the Netherlands came into their last eight match against second-ranked England as heavy favourites to reach the semi-finals. While a match against the host nation in front of a mammoth home crowd would present an entirely different set of challenges to those

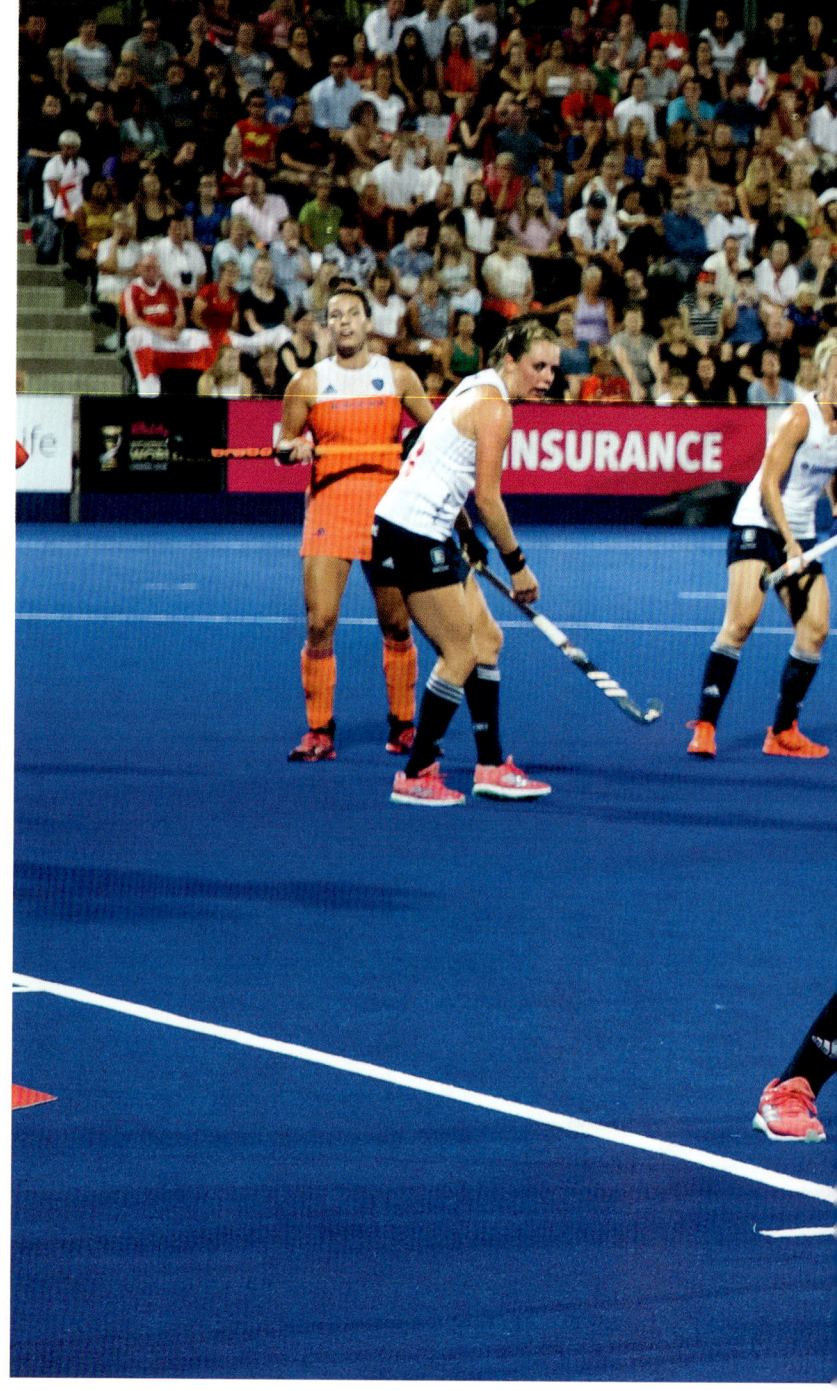

Netherlands captain Carlien Dirkse van den Heuvel evades the challenges in the English circle. // *Koen Suyk*

experienced in their demolitions of Korea, China and Italy in Pool A, their outstanding form in London meant that the 'favourites' tag given to Alyson Annan's team was completely justified. With three gold and three silver medals from the last six editions of the women's hockey World Cup, history was also very much on their side. Could Danny Kerry, who had famously master-minded England and Great Britain's respective European and Olympic title successes over the Netherlands, really do it again?

Not on this occasion. The Dutch were absolutely on fire in the opening period, putting the England defence under huge pressure from the very first minute. England goalkeeper Maddie Hinch produced a superb block to deny Kelly Jonker's backhand strike before Caia van Maasakker issued a warning when she rattled England's crossbar with a fierce penalty corner effort, drawing a gasp of relief from a packed

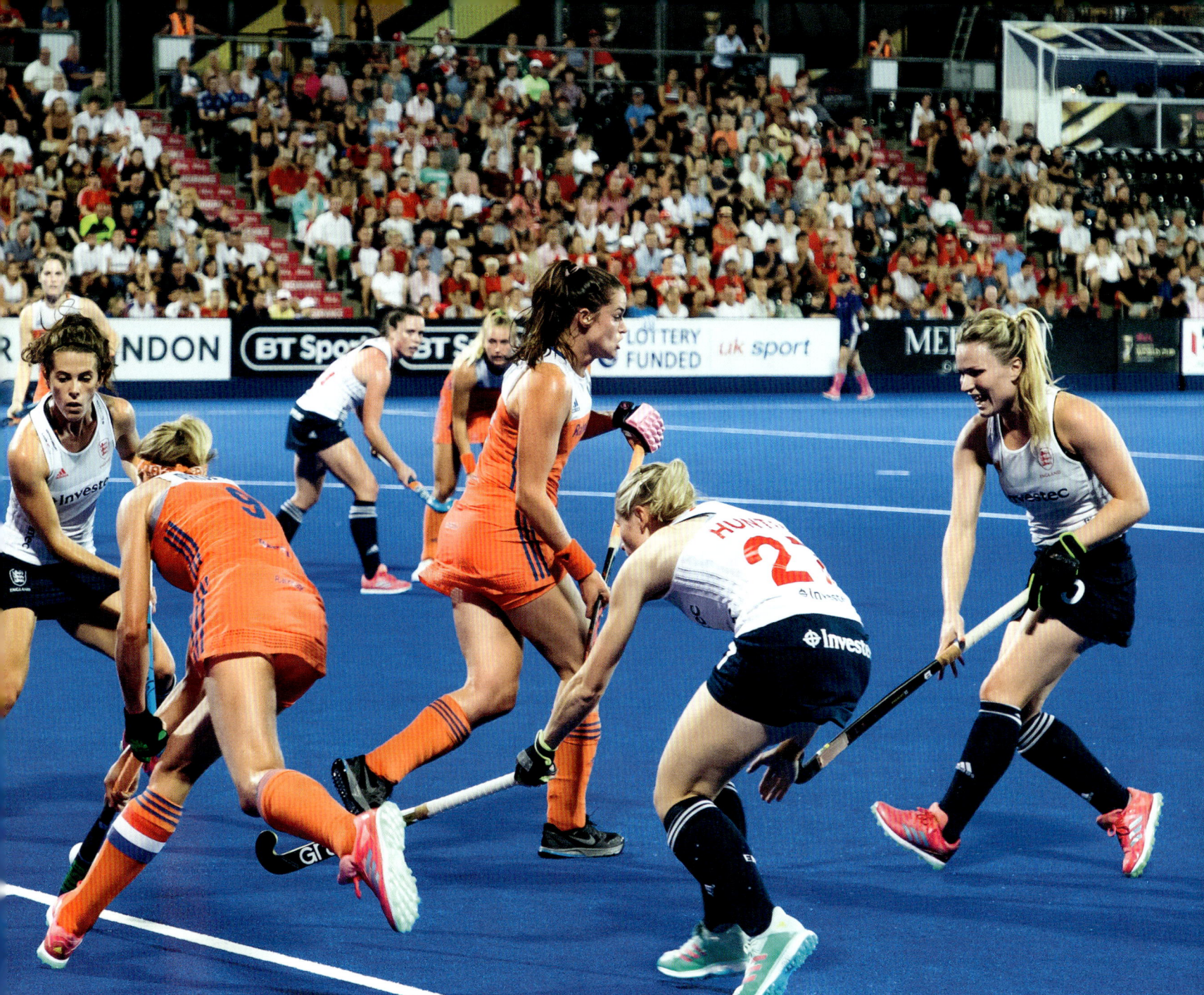

house watching on. It seemed only a matter of time before the opening goal would come, which it duly did in the 14th minute through 2015 Hockey Stars Player of the Year Lidewij Welten. Xan de Waard was the creator, sending a perfectly weighted pass into the path of Welten who squeezed a first-time strike between the legs of Hinch.

The relentless Dutch pressure continued in the second period, with Hinch again called into action before Suzy Petty cleared a goal-bound shot off the line to keep the score at 1-0 going into half-time.

However, that all changed one minute after the break when the extraordinary quality of the Dutch attacking line again resurfaced. This time Welten – deserving recipient of the Vitality Player of the Match award after the game – was the creator, splitting the English defence with a precision pass to Frederique Matla, who in turn eliminated Hinch with

a square pass for Laurien Leurink to tap into an open goal.

Much to the appreciation of the home crowd, England gave an excellent showing in the final quarter and threw everything they had at their opponents. However, it was to no avail as the Dutch showed that their defensive capabilities were equal to their attacking prowess. It was a heartbreaking defeat for the hosts, but few could argue that the Netherlands were anything other than worthy winners and had further cemented their position as red-hot favourites to claim an eighth women's hockey World Cup title.

For the England players trooping off the pitch, the support from the crowd was overwhelming for many, with tears running freely down the faces of several players as they applauded the capacity crowd.

An emotional head coach, Danny Kerry, said: 'I told the players I was really proud. We have had a tough

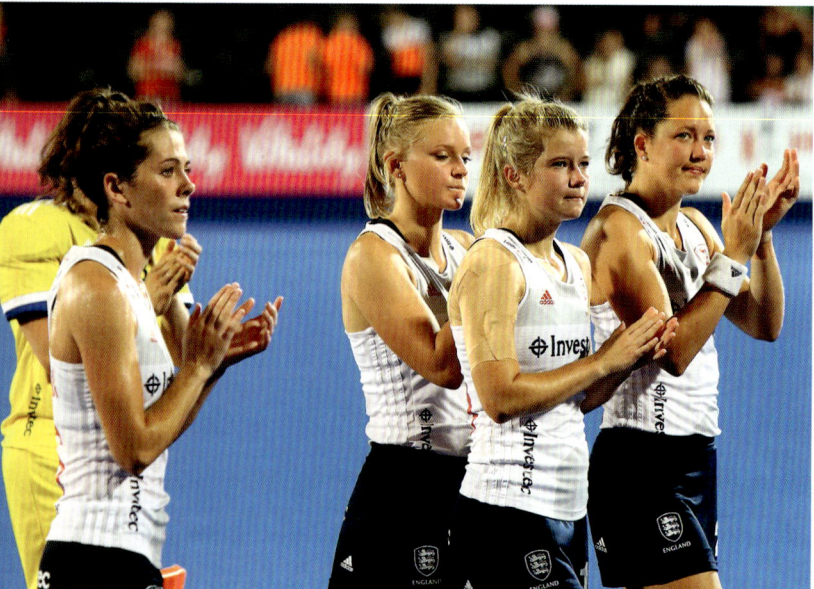

England's players thank the crowd for their tremendous support. // *Rodrigo Jaramillo*

tournament with injury and for all sorts of reasons. One of our players played the entire tournament with a broken big toe but they all gritted it out and carried on.

'The Netherlands were the better team and they deserved the win. Other than two great passes, we defended well, but we didn't hold on to the ball long enough so we weren't going to create much. That will come.'

'We kept a tight ship in defence and that worked well for us,' said Netherlands ace Caia van Maasakker after the match. 'They made us work hard for it. It is amazing, so cool, to play here in this stadium so we are pretty happy with the result.' When asked about the processes behind the consistently excellent performances that the Oranje were currently producing, Van Maasakker said that desire, hunger and working tirelessly for each other were all key to the team's success. 'They are all crucial. Our passing and keeping the pace high are at the heart of our game. We have some great skills and we try to always keep the pace as high as we possibly can.'

Although England's World Cup journey had come to an end, experienced defender Hollie Pearne-Webb was pragmatic about her team's performances in London and was confident that their new-look squad would learn important lessons from the event. 'Looking back, we have had a fairly good tournament, although we should have got better outcomes from the first two games,' said Pearne-Webb, acknowledging that a second-place finish in Pool B had proved costly. 'We need to learn to turn up for the pool games. We only conceded one penalty corner today and for us that is the best defensive performance we have had against them [the Netherlands]. Now we must look at when we win the ball and making more of our chances.'

Looking to the future, Pearne-Webb said that she was full of optimism. 'We are missing some experience in the squad and the new girls are still finding their feet. They will grow in confidence. The hurt and disappointment of this loss will put extra fire in all our bellies.'

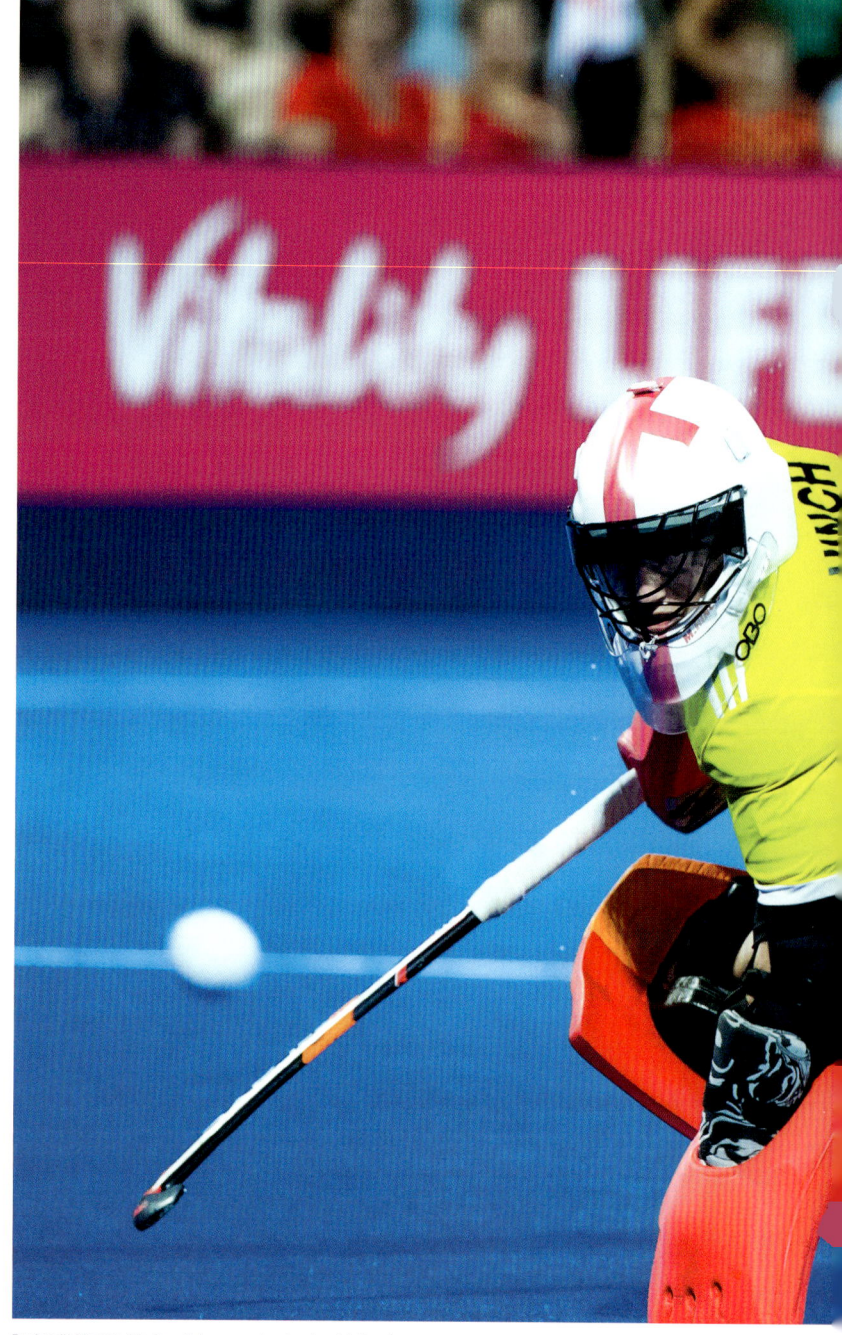

England's Maddie Hinch watches on as Laurien Leurink fires home a perfect pass from Frederique Matla to put the Netherlands into a commanding 2-0 lead. // *Koen Suyk*

Results – Quarter-finals

Wednesday 1 August 2018

Germany	**0-1**	**Spain**
		Carman Cano 54m FG

Vitality Player of the Match: Georgina Oliva (ESP)

Australia	**0-0**	**Argentina**
Shoot-out	4-3	
Booke Peris – No Goal		Delfina Merino – No Goal
Kristina Bates – Goal		Lucina von der Heyde – Goal
Maddy Fitzpatrick – No Goal		Agustina Albertarrio – Goal
Ambrosia Malone – Goal		Julia Gomes – Goal
Jodie Kenny – Goal (PS – Karri McMahon)		Magdalena Fernandez – No Goal
Sudden Death		
Kristina Bates – No Goal		Agustina Albertarrio – No Goal
Brooke Peris – Goal		Delfina Merino – No Goal

Vitality Player of the Match: Georgina Morgan (AUS)

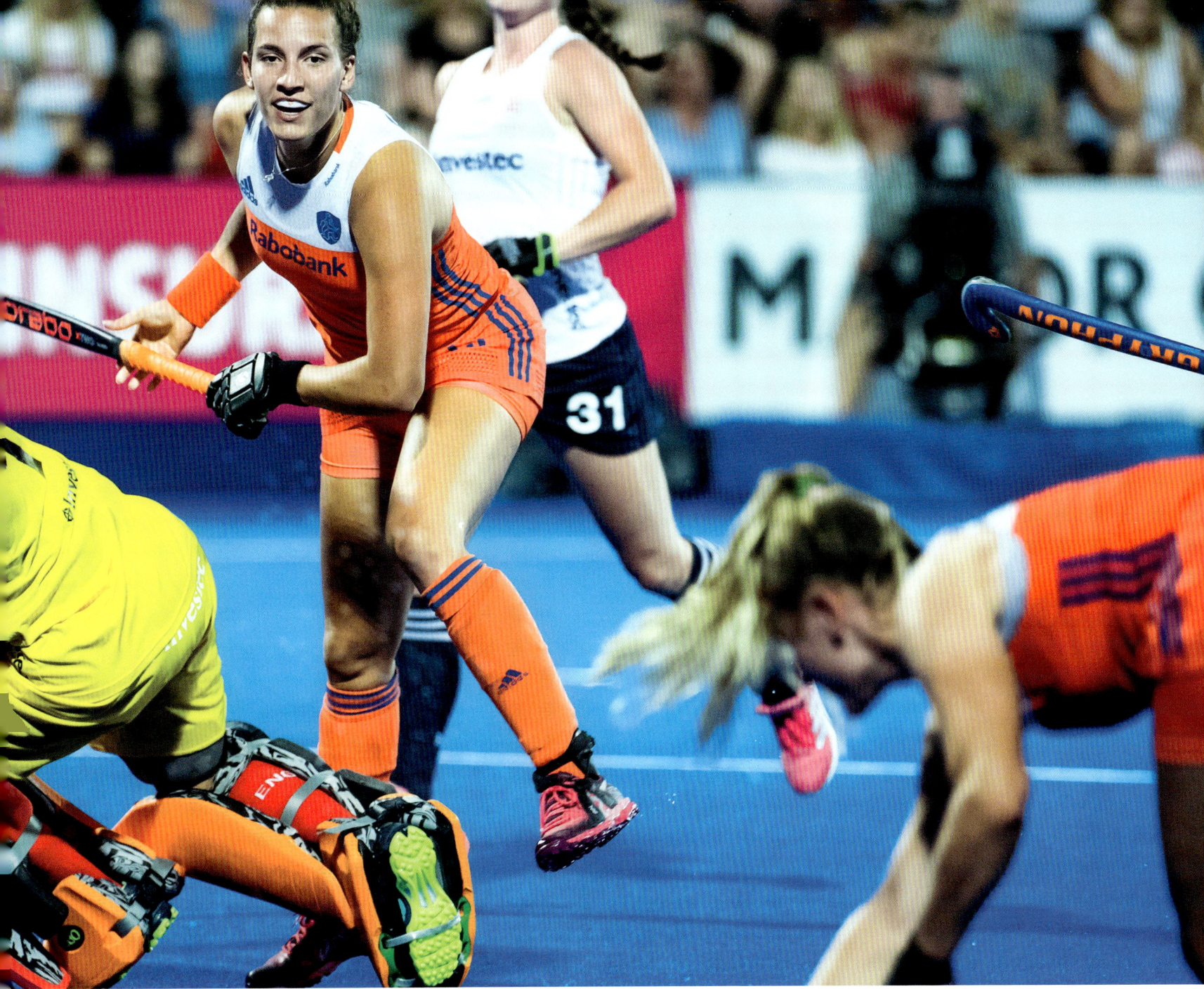

Thursday 2 August 2018

Ireland	0-0	India

Shoot-out	3-1	
Nicola Daly – No Goal		Rani – No Goal
Anna O'Flanagan – No Goal		Monika – No Goal
Roisin Upton – Goal		Navjot Kaur – No Goal
Alison Meeke – Goal		Reena Khokhar– Goal
Chloe Watkins – Goal		

Vitality Player of the Match: Chloe Watkins (IRL)

Netherlands	2-0	England
Lidewij Welten 14m FG		
Laurien Leurink 31m FG		

Vitality Player of the Match: Lidewij Welten (NED)

Semi-final line-up
Saturday 4th August 2018

Ireland v Spain
Netherlands v Australia

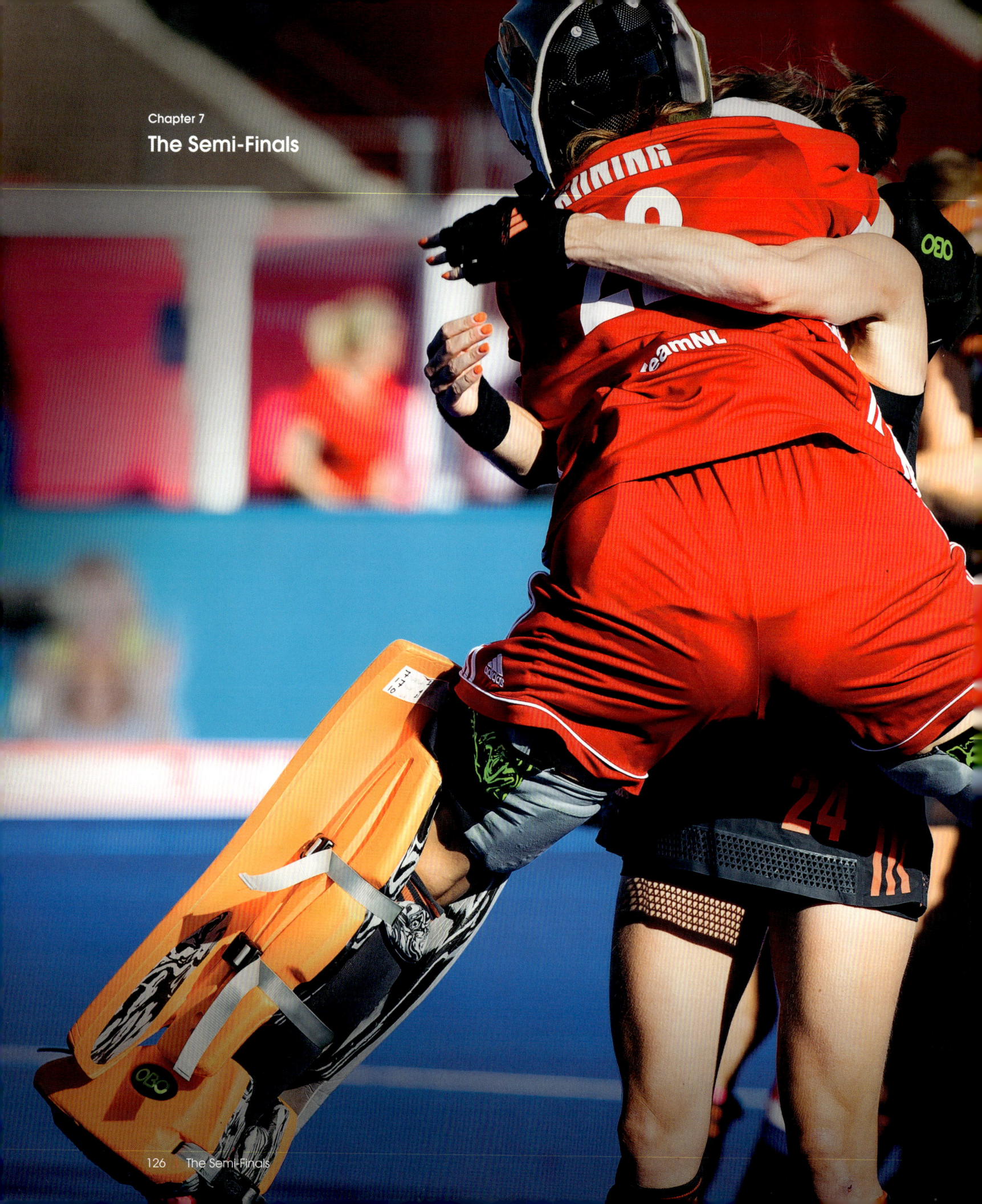

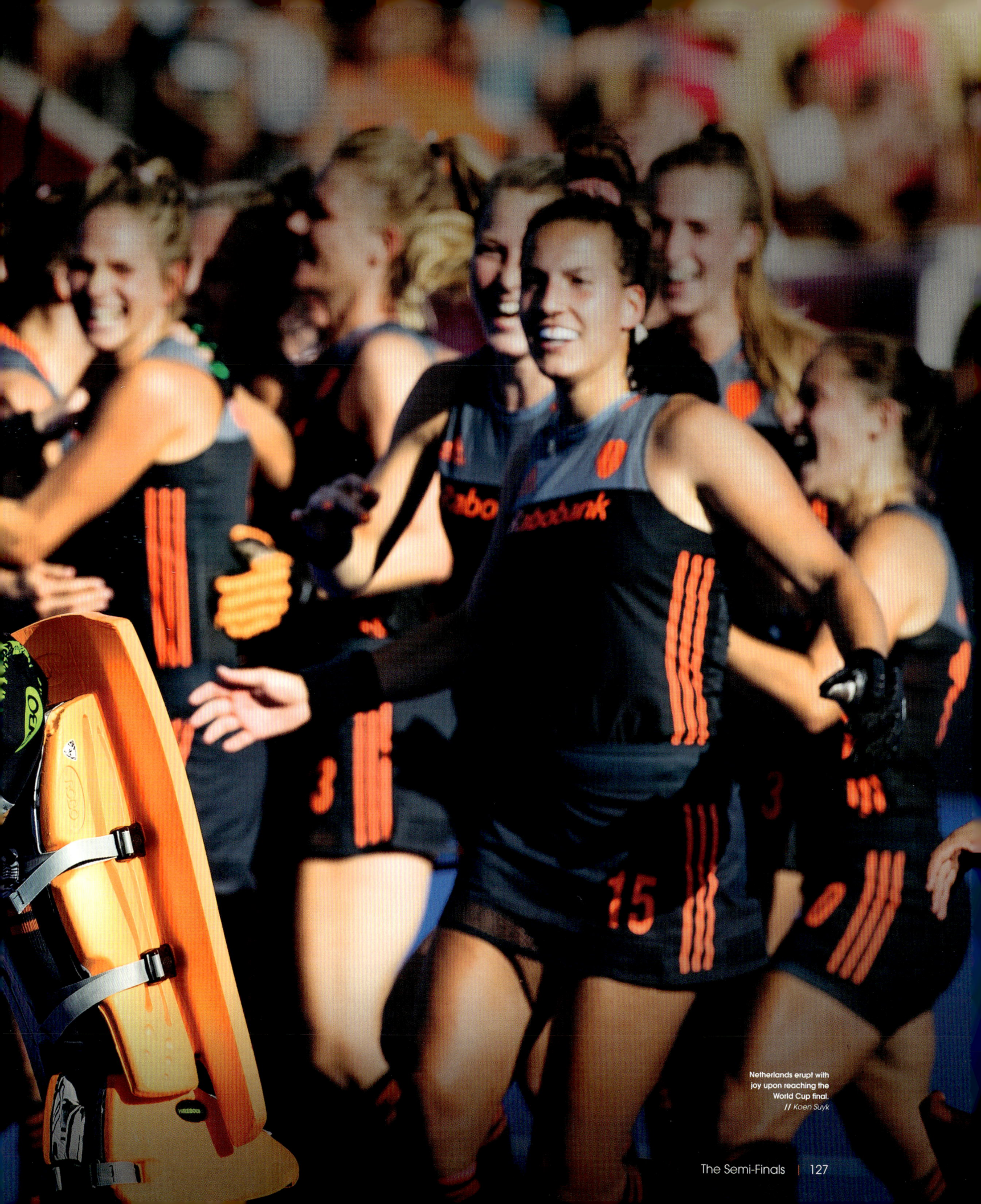

Netherlands erupt with
joy upon reaching the
World Cup final.
// Koen Suyk

The Semi-Finals

Day 13 – Saturday 4 August 2018

Ireland and the Netherlands take the shoot-out route to the final

Semi-finals day opened with the Games Maker Choir being joined by thousands of spectators belting out 'Ireland's Call' – the song used by many Irish sports teams that represent the whole of Ireland. Two weeks prior, when the choir was practising, it is highly unlikely that they would have spent much time learning the words to the anthem. Ireland, ranked 16th, on paper at least, had little chance of reaching a semi-final. But here they were and the capacity crowd sang their hearts out as the teams took to the field. Around the stadium the four stands were a sea of green as it seemed the whole of Ireland had come to cheer their team on to a place in a World Cup final. Remarkably, if Ireland won, they would be the first Irish team, men's or women's, in any sport, to make it to a World Cup final.

Speaking before the match, Spain's head coach Adrian Lock was full of praise for Ireland and their coach, Graham Shaw. The two men had led their teams on similar journeys and under similar financial constraints. Neither coach had been able to spend as much time with their respective teams as they would have liked, but both coaches were astute tacticians who knew how to get the best from their players. They were also both former high-performance players who knew what it meant to play on a stage like this. It was with real feeling that Lock said: 'Both teams have great spirit and it is a real shame that one team won't make it to the final.'

Ireland had been rewriting hockey history since they arrived in London. They were the lowest-ranked team in Pool C and yet they won it, with victories over USA and India and a narrow loss to England. They then met India again in the quarter-finals and held their nerve to win the match in a shoot-out. Now they were facing Spain, another team with a higher ranking and with some highly talented players in their midst.

Graham Shaw had revealed their approach in an interview in the lead-up to the World Cup: 'A lot of the players have been chasing this for a long time, so there will be a lot of emotion, which we will have to manage. A lot of players have been after this moment all their lives. Every match in our pool will be like a final. They are three different teams, with three styles of play, so we will have a different plan for each game.'

So far the plans had worked, but could the Shaw magic take the Green Army one step further?

For Adrian Lock and his Spanish Red Sticks, this was a moment they had also been working towards for a long time. In the interview following Spain's incredible defeat of the world number-six side, Germany, Berta Bonastre had spoken of the frustration the players felt at being 'nearly' there on so many occasions. This was a team with ambitions to be a top-ten side, with real medal prospects whenever they played a competition and, for as long as they hovered around the world number-11 mark, players such as Bonastre, Beatriz Perez, Georgina Oliva and Carola Petchame would feel that they were underachieving. Yes, Spain getting to the semi-finals of this edition of the World Cup may have been a surprise, but this was the start of a whole new era in Spanish hockey was the message from the passionate midfielder.

Her coach agreed: 'For too long in Spanish hockey it has been about short-term fixes,' said Lock. 'We have worked hard over the past five years to create a certain culture that underpins everything. If you get the culture right, then the fitness, the skills, the tactics, they all fit into one whole, but that takes time. I think we are beginning to see the outcome of all that hard work now.'

And so the match got underway. The Green Army started with the ball but immediately conceded possession, with Spain stealing the ball and racing up the pitch. Ireland quickly regrouped and started playing with the energy and confidence that has been core to their performances throughout the World Cup. They won a penalty corner just three minutes into the game after captain Katie Mullan fired

Spain's Red Sticks salute the crowd ahead of their Vitality Hockey Women's World Cup semi-final clash with Ireland. // *Frank Uijlenbroek*

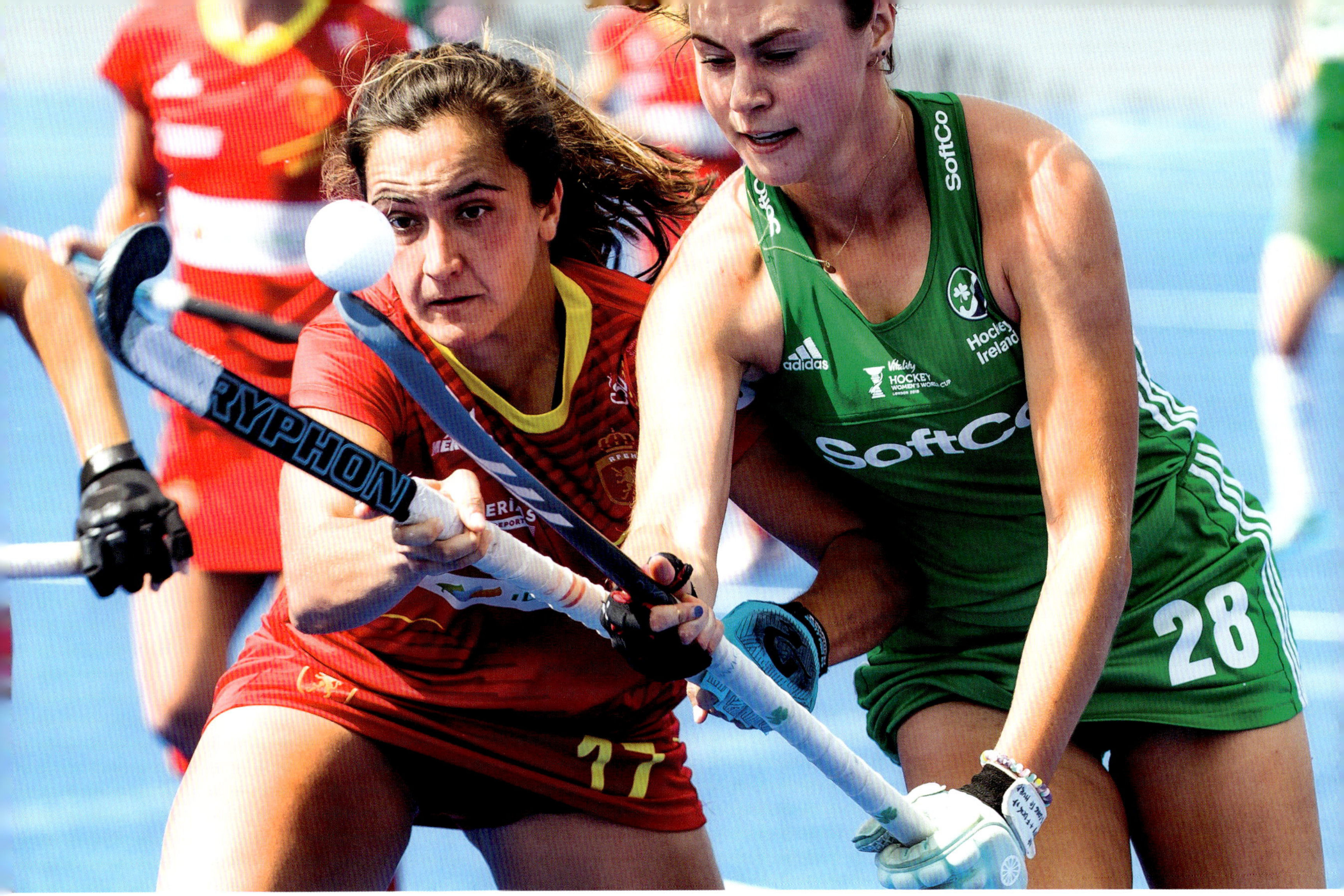

Ireland's Deirdre Duke shows exceptional 3D skills to move past Spain's Lola Riera. // *Koen Suyk*

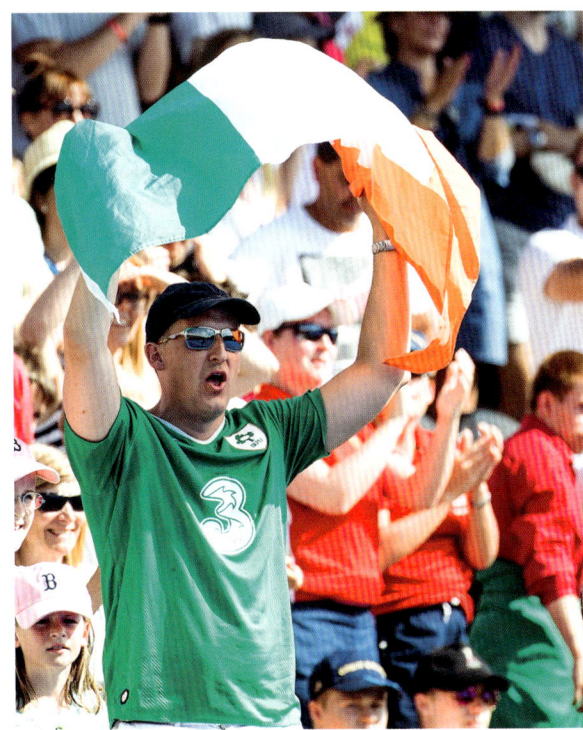

Ireland fans knew that they had witnessed something quite extraordinary at the Lee Valley Hockey & Tennis Centre. // *Koen Suyk*

a speculative pass into the Spain circle. That ball struck a Spanish foot to win the corner. Shirley McCay's strike was deflected by Anna O'Flanagan through the pads of Maria Ruiz in the Spain goal to give the Green Army an early lead.

'We only created that penalty corner routine a few days ago,' revealed Shaw after the game. 'We were going to use it against India but we didn't win a penalty corner to use it.'

Most of the opening quarter was all about Ireland as Spain struggled to come to terms with the enormity of the occasion. That dynamic changed as the time counted down and, in the final minute, Spain issued their first warning that they were also here to win. Rocio Gutierrez glided up the pitch, slipping the ball to Carola Salvatella, who was unlucky to tip the ball just around the corner of the goal.

'We are definitely not going to sit back and consolidate,' said Graham Shaw at the quarter-break interview with BT Sport, the host broadcaster. 'It's not something we are very good at, we want to go out and score as many goals as we can.'

Spain had other plans, though, as they continued where they left off, piling pressure on the Ireland defence. The largely Irish crowd groaned as the ball was hammered into the circle by Beatriz Perez and flew into the net but, fortunately for Ireland, it was off the stick of Katie Mullan and Perez's hit had been struck outside the circle.

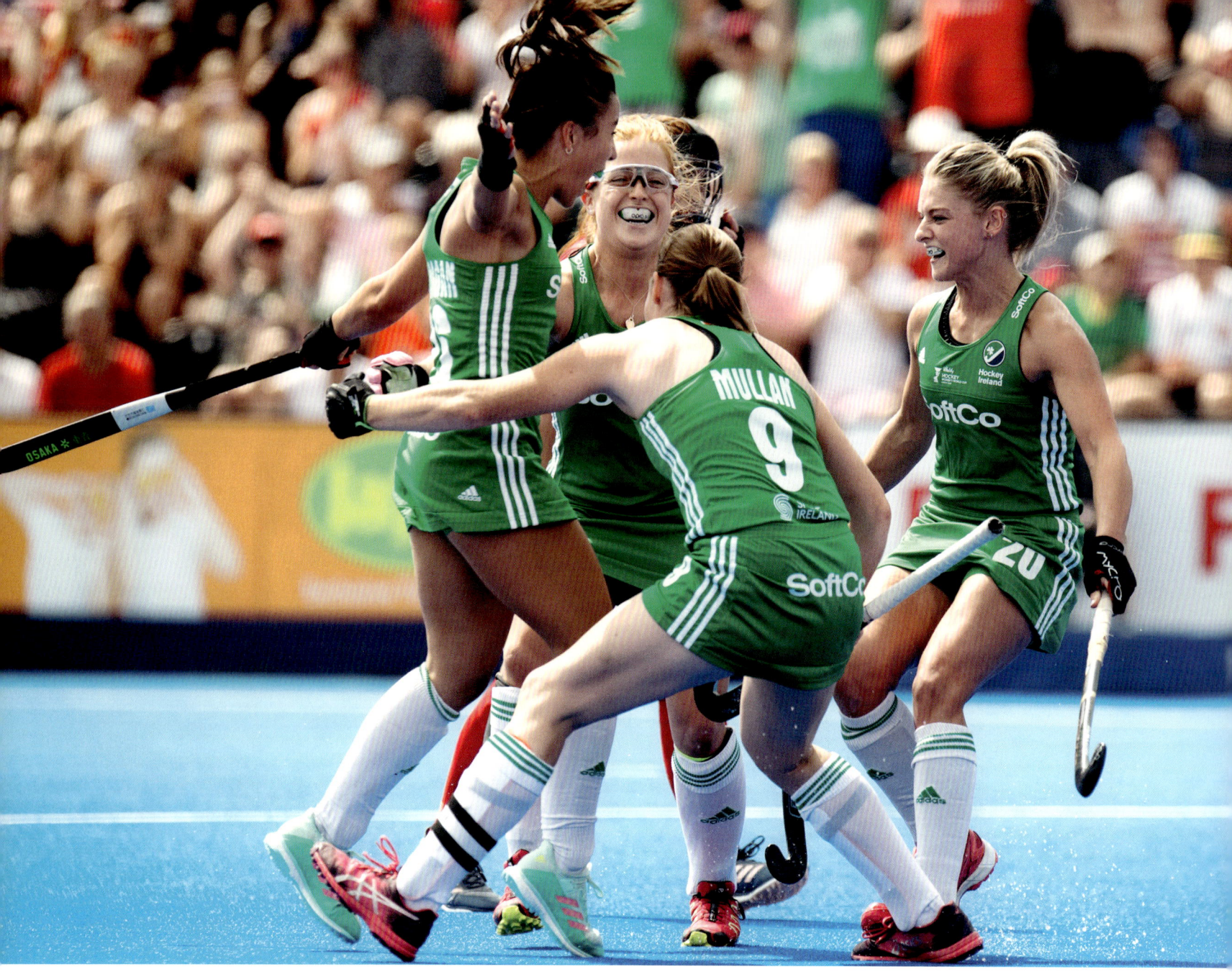

Ireland captain Katie Mullan (#9) leads the charge to congratulate O'Flanagan on her strike. // *Frank Uijlenbroek*

There were more chances for both sides as the players shook off the shackles of big-match nerves and played the free-flowing, exciting hockey that had been part of their World Cup campaigns. Xantal Gine nearly scored the most audacious goal of the competition as she chopped the ball backwards through her legs. Fortunately for Ireland the move was anticipated by Ayeisha McFerran in the Ireland goal and she reacted swiftly to clear the danger. At the other end of the pitch, Deirdrie Duke was unlucky not to put her team two ahead after Nicola Daly and O'Flanagan worked the ball swiftly down the Irish right-hand side of the pitch. McCay touched the ball to Duke but her backhand shot flew just wide.

Ireland won their third penalty corner of the game when Nicola Evans put in a shift in the Spanish circle to force the ball on to a Spanish player's foot. The shot was chased down but the Irish would have been pleased to have instigated an attack after an onslaught by their opponents for most of the quarter.

The wonderful stick skills of the Spanish players were very much in evidence as the Red Sticks tightened their grip on the game in the second half. Desperately trying to find the equaliser, the Spanish players probed and prodded to find gaps in the Irish defence. The breakthrough came as Georgina Oliva played in a pass that found Perez. She cleverly dodged the Irish sticks and found Alicia Magaz, who made no mistake as she slotted the ball past McFerran – only the third goal during match play that the Irish keeper had conceded all tournament.

With the teams locked at 1-1 there were just 15 minutes left for either side to create their own hockey history. The tension on the pitch translated into a few spilled passes, and turnovers by both teams were rapid. Nicola Evans had a great opportunity to set Alison Meeke on her way but the pass that evaded the Spanish defence was also just too far ahead of the midfielder.

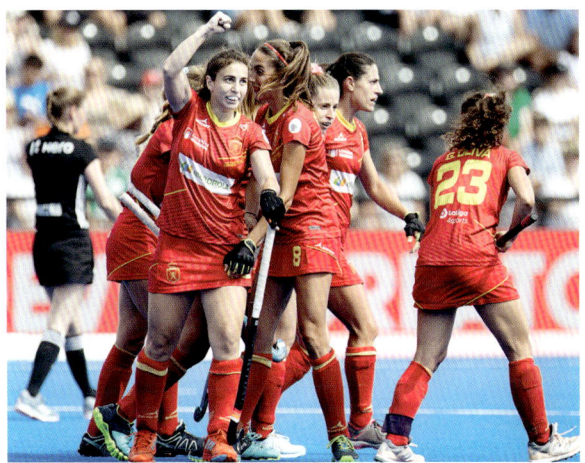

Spain showed their class by deservedly levelling the scores in the 39th minute thanks to Alicia Magaz. // *Frank Uijlenbroek*

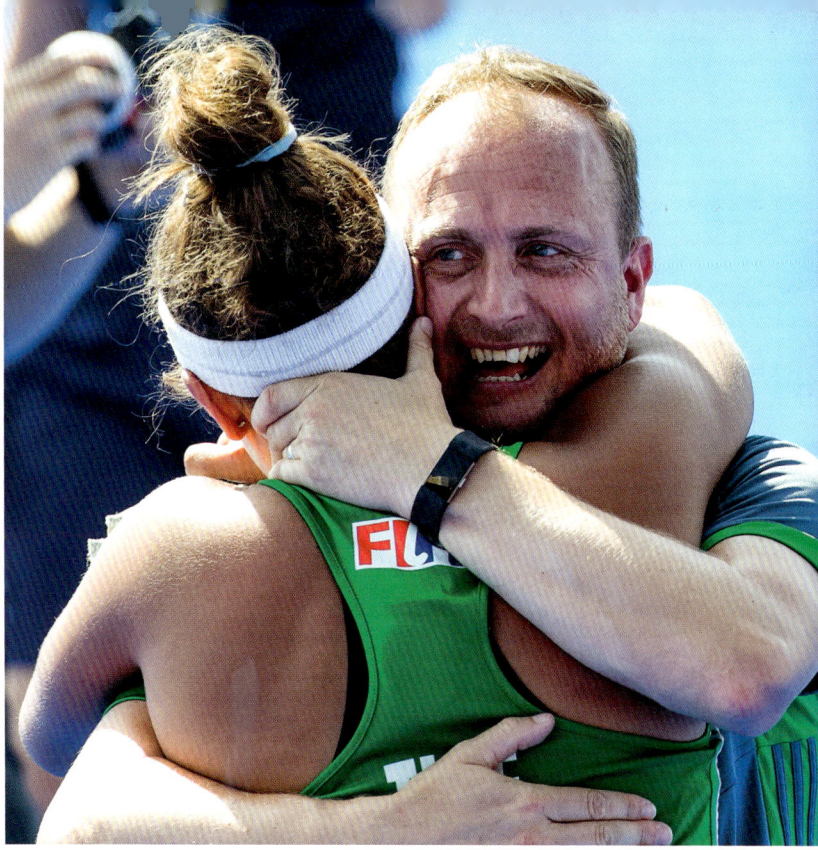

Elena Tice and Graham Shaw share a joyous embrace at reaching the World Cup final. // *Koen Suyk*

A neutral observer would probably have backed Spain to provide the breakthrough at this point in the match. Georgina Oliva was controlling the centre of the pitch and her clever passes were constantly putting the Irish defence under pressure, and it was only the stoic efforts of the Irish defence that prevented the Red Sticks from taking the game. At the heart of the defence was the excellent Shirley McCay. A blow to the face, rather than dampening her resolution, served as yet another incentive to push forwards as the multi-capped player rallied her team, and continued to urge them forwards.

Fortunately for the Irish, the sting was taken out of their opponent's attack when Oliva was sent off with a green card. This was a crucial loss to Spain as the diminutive midfielder had been at the epicentre of all Spain's attacking play. The drama intensified further as Ireland won a penalty corner in the final two minutes. Ruiz was unable to save the shot but, fortunately for the keeper, Gutierrez was on hand to clear the ball out.

And so to the shoot-out. These two teams had both won shoot-outs earlier in the competition, with Spain beating Belgium and Ireland defeating India. The psychological advantage of having won a shoot-out was a little nullified by the fact that both teams now had knowledge of each other's tactics.

In an attempt to do the unexpected, head coach Shaw changed personnel, adding Gillian Pinder to the line-up of five players who would take on Ruiz in a one-on-one. Not only was this Pinder's first shoot-out at the World Cup, Shaw also made her the first to go. Pinder stepped up and showed nerves of steel to flick the ball over Ruiz and get Ireland off to the best of starts.

Later Graham Shaw admitted that sending Pinder into the heat of a shoot-out had been a gamble. 'That took serious guts and bottle on her part, when she hadn't taken one in the quarter-final,' he said.

Next up was Begoña Garcia, who found herself in the unenviable position of facing the hugely talented McFerran. As so often, McFerran stood tall and refused to let the Spanish player get a sight of the goal. Instead, she danced around the circle, matching Garcia turn for turn. With an air of resignation as the clock counted down, Garcia took her shot and watched it go wide.

The next three attempts by O'Flanagan, Perez, and Upton all missed, but Oliva made no mistake as she shot home to bring the scores level.

Chloe Watkins put Ireland back ahead with a solid effort but the most audacious shoot-out goal, particularly in light of the pressured situation, was scored by Lola Riera who, seeing there was no way round the keeper, lobbed the ball over McFerran's head.

That took serious guts and bottle on her part, when she hadn't taken one in the quarter-final.

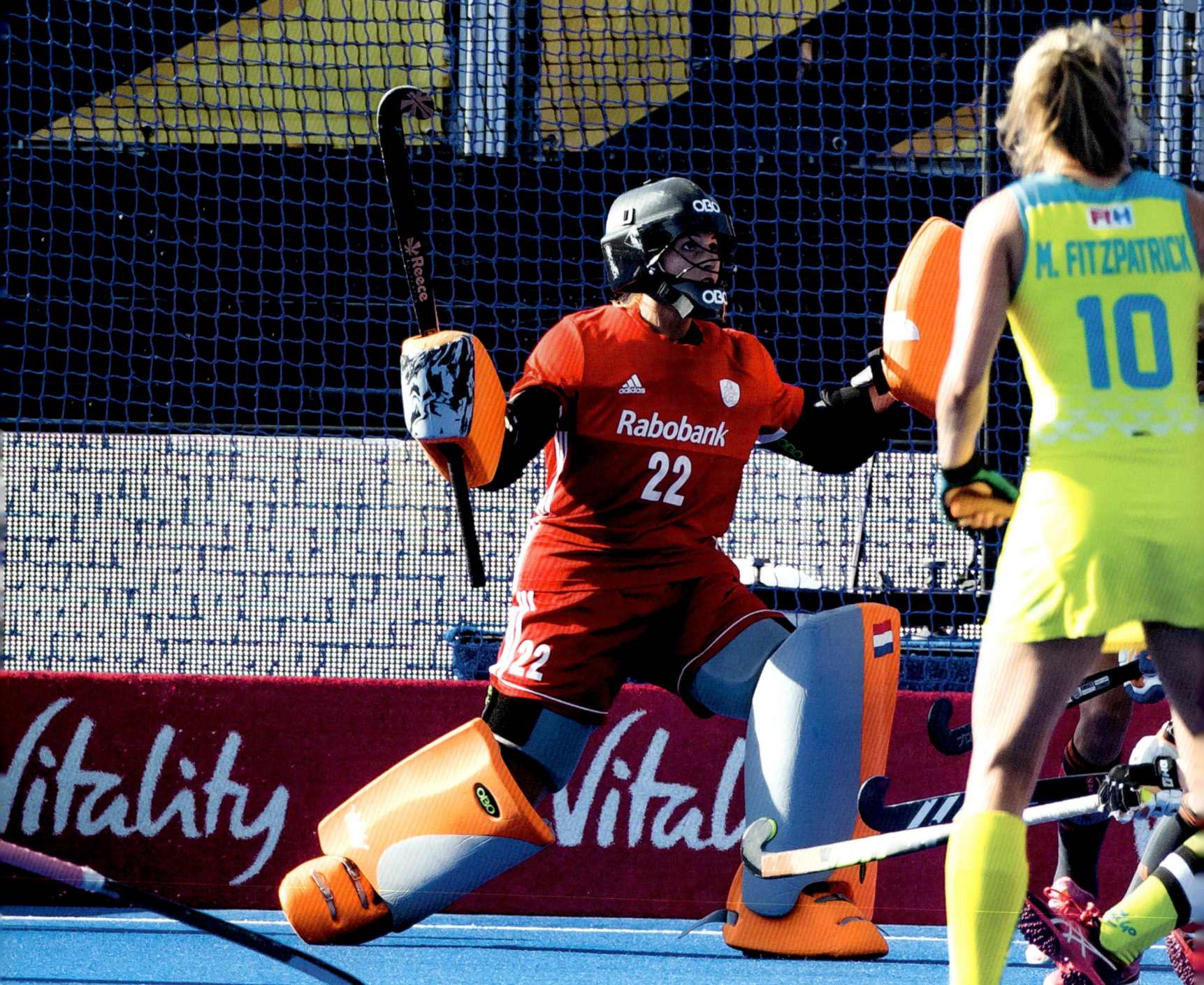

Dutch goalkeeper Josine Koning, who replaced Anne Veenendaal at the start of the second half, is called into action. // *Koen Suyk*

With the scores level, the match went to sudden death. McFerran pulled off a magnificent save using her stick to pull the ball out of mid-air and then it was all on Pinder's shoulders to put her team through to the final. As the entire stadium held its breath, Pinder coolly slotted home and Ireland were through.

'She is brilliant, she is like twinkle toes,' said Shaw as he praised the excellence of McFerran. 'She's not the biggest keeper in the world, but she is lightning off the mark. It played into the Spanish heads and they were questioning being near her.'

A speechless Elena Tice, the youngest player on the Irish team, could only say: 'It was unbelievable.' Once she gathered her composure she added: 'In every single game we have battled tooth and nail. We have executed our goals when it mattered, defended our goal when it mattered. We

just said in this tournament it was important that we defended from the front.

'We are a young team and we have had to learn quickly. Our forwards set the tone with their energy and our midfield team are so hard working. We are the underdog in every game and in every game it is like we have won the World Cup. Whoever we play tomorrow, we are going to fight tooth and nail. The last bit of our soul will be out on the pitch tomorrow.'

And as the Spanish players huddled in an exhausted circle at the other end of the pitch, Irish defender Zoe Wilson struggled for the words to express her joy. 'I just want someone to pinch me,' she said. 'Oh it feels amazing, absolutely amazing. I can't believe we are in the final of the World Cup.'

Who would be facing Ireland came down to a clash between two hockey powerhouses who knew each other

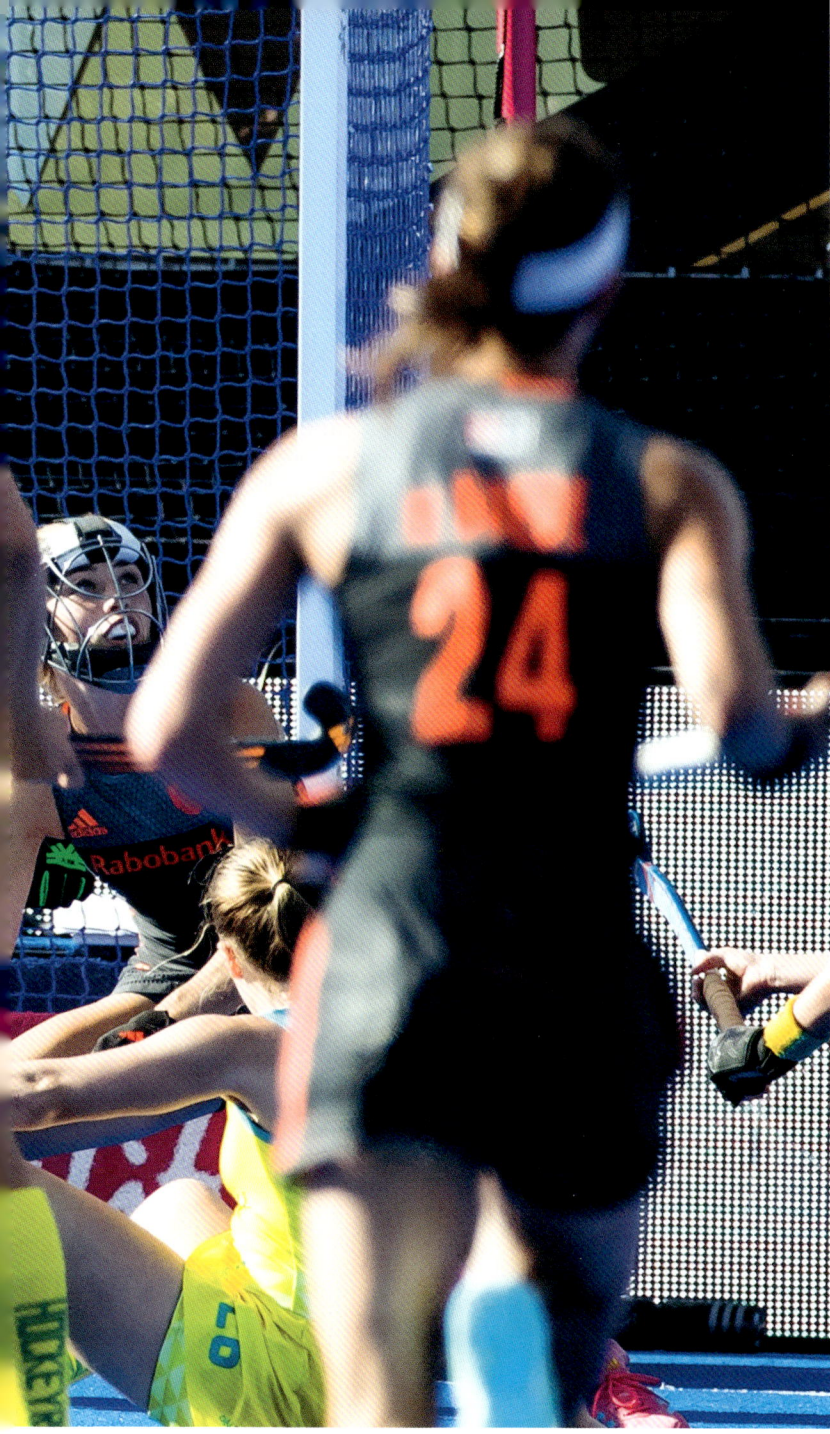

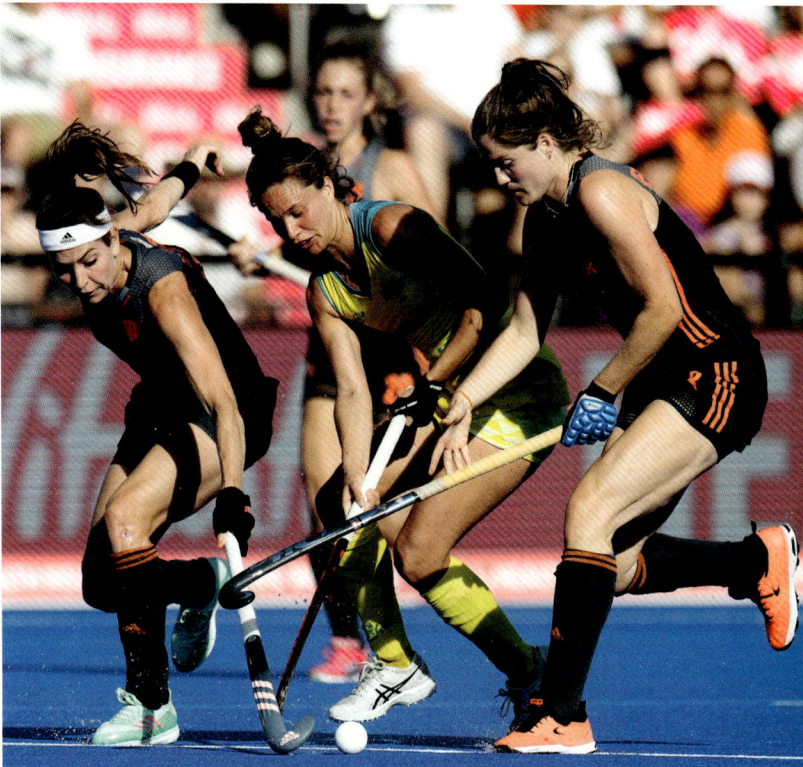

Australia forward Brooke Peris cannot find a way past Netherlands' duo Eva de Goede and Marloes Keetels. // *Frank Uijlenbroek*

well. The Netherlands and Australia were old foes who both had great traditions in World Cup history. With Alyson Annan's unerring eye for goal and precocious talent as a forward, the Hockeyroos of the 1990s and early 2000s had transformed women's hockey. Now the same World Cup hero was seeking to lead her Dutch charges to an unprecedented eighth title, at the expense of her country of birth. It was also the eve of the anniversary of Annan's brother's death, seven years earlier from a heart attack, and in a social media post the head coach revealed that this was something that was very much on her mind. 'Dear big brother,' the coach wrote just hours before turning her attention to a World Cup final. 'Seven years ago. I miss and love you so much.'

Both teams had reached this stage of the competition undefeated, although the Netherlands had enjoyed the far easier route, sailing serenely through the pool matches, scoring 28 goals and conceding just two. Australia, by contrast, had won only one match in regulation time and their quarter-final match against Argentina had been won in a shoot-out.

But Australia are a team that will always rise to the occasion and so it proved this time. Three penalty corners in the opening five minutes of the game was the sign that the Hockeyroos had no intention of letting the Netherlands dominate this match in the same way they had all their previous games. Unfortunately for Paul Gaudoin's side, both Jodie Kenny and Georgina Morgan's fearsome penalty corner strike routines were slightly below par and the Netherlands' defence was let off the hook.

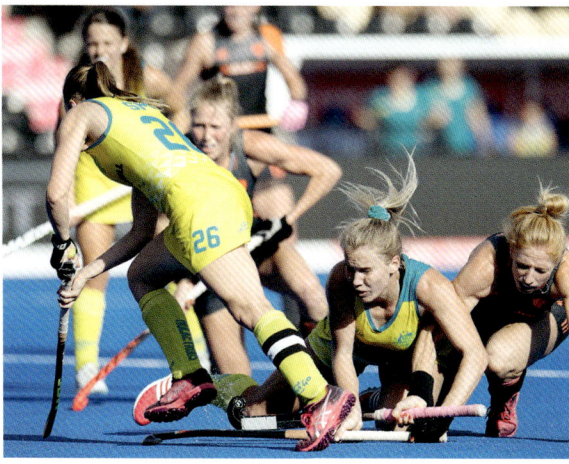

Australia captain Emily Smith (#26) takes the ball away from danger. // *Frank Uijlenbroek*

As the quarter progressed, so the Netherlands began to work their way into the game and it was the Hockeyroos who started to wilt under the pressure. As was so often the case, it was Lidewij Welten who provided the skill that unlocked the defence and Kelly Jonker was able to slam the ball home past Rachael Lynch in the Australia goal.

This was a rare lapse for the Hockeyroos' defence. Led by the terrific Lynch, the defence stood tall against the Dutch attacks and had clearly done their homework on the penalty corner routines – Caia van Maasakker's usually reliable drag flick was coolly dealt with on each occasion and the Dutch began to look like a team searching for new ideas.

The importance of maintaining the gap at just one goal was highlighted a few minutes later when Australia scored the equaliser. Chances to score against the Dutch were rare, so when Georgina Morgan stepped up to strike a penalty corner past Josine Koning in the Dutch goal, the relief among the Australia contingent on the pitch, the bench and in the crowd was palpable.

There were now seven minutes left to play and Australia suddenly had verve and an energy that had many wondering if Lee Valley was about to see yet another shock result. However, the Netherlands forward line might have stolen the plaudits in the earlier games but in this game it was the defence who had to play their part. As Xan de Waard later explained, under Annan, every member of the squad saw themselves as responsible for defence when the Oranje were not on the ball and so it was in this match. As Australia tried to gain momentum, so they found themselves sucked into pockets of Dutch defence and all too often the Australian ball carrier was suddenly isolated and surrounded by three Dutch players. It was relentless and, as the seconds ticked by, so a shoot-out became more and more likely.

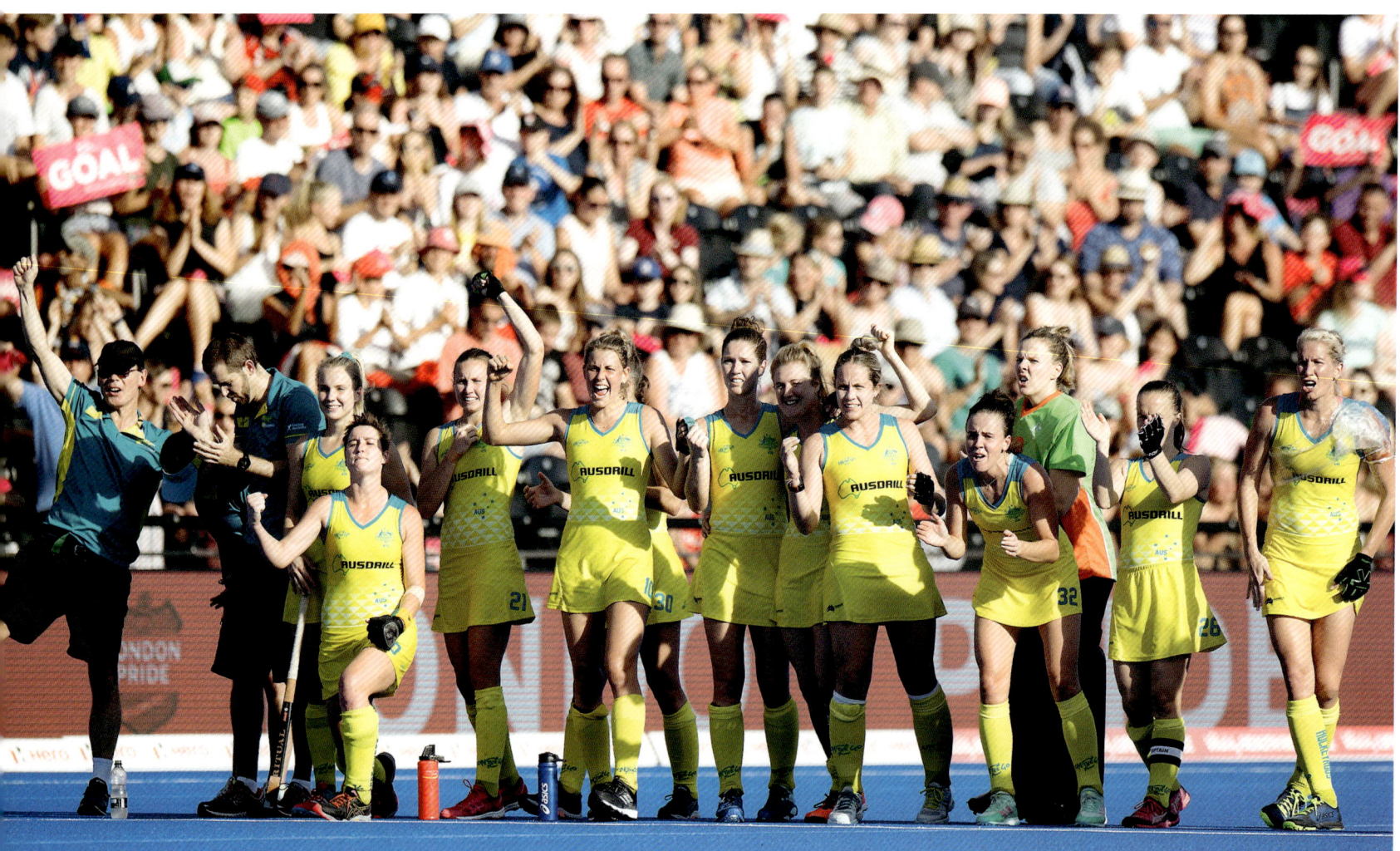

Australia players revel in Lynch's save, but their joy would be short-lived. // *Frank Uijlenbroek*

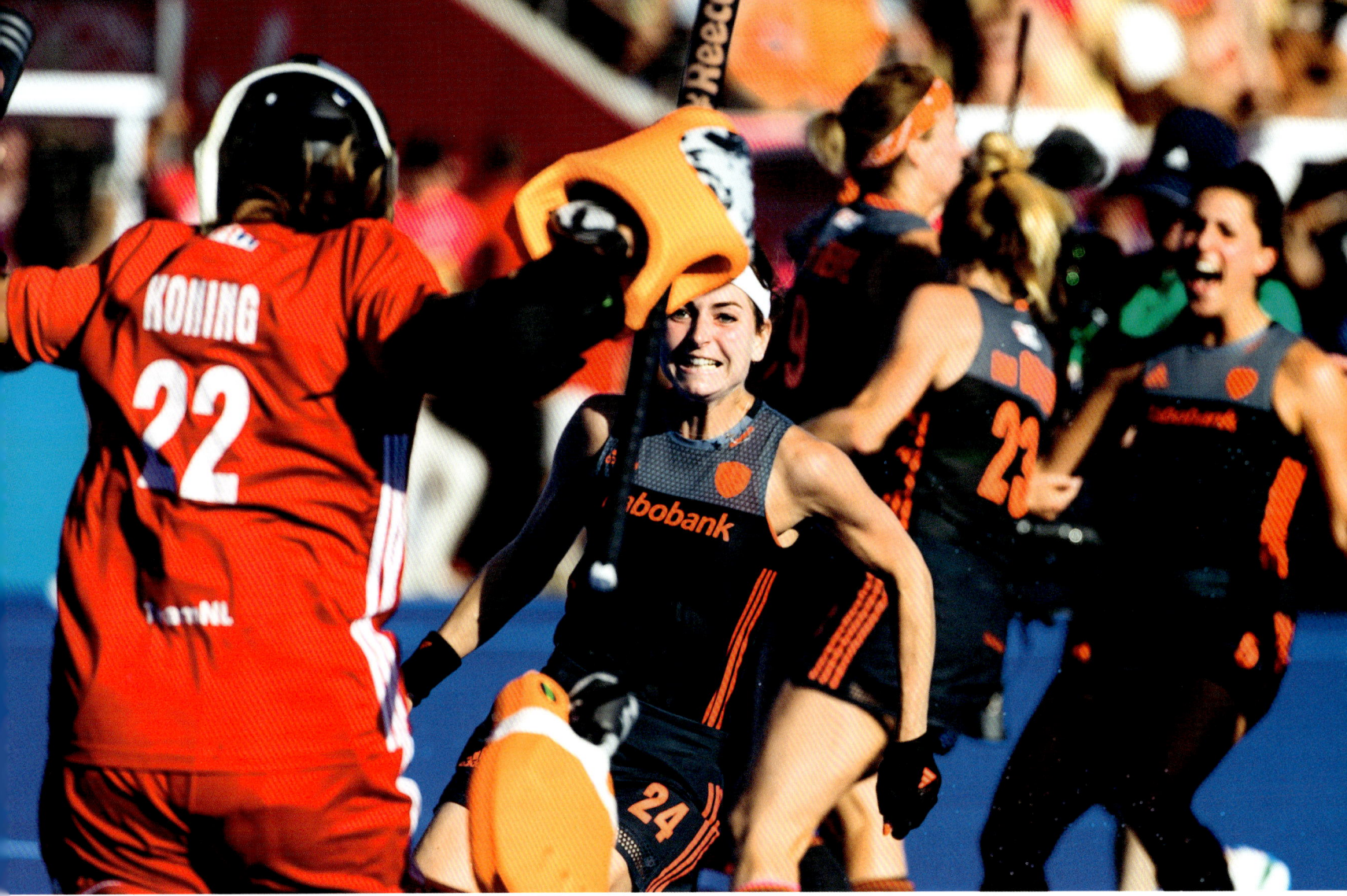

Netherlands goalkeeper Josine Koning brilliantly saves Karri McMahon's shoot-out effort to put the Dutch into their sixth successive World Cup final. // *Koen Suyk*

Prior to the tournament, Rachael Lynch had spoken of her love of the shoot-out situation. 'As a goalkeeper, it is a fantastic opportunity for me to stand up and show just what I can do,' she said. 'My team all think I am crazy but, for me, I would like every match to end in a shoot-out.'

If Lynch loved the pressure of the shoot-out, so too did Frederique Matla. The young Netherlands' forward took the ball wide of Lynch and then fired home to give her team the lead. Australia's Kristina Bates followed suit and placed the ball past Koning. Both goalkeepers then managed to keep out the next two efforts: Carlien Dirkse van den Heuvel and Margot van Geffen both found themselves out-witted by Lynch, but Australia's Brooke Peris, Kaitlyn Nobbs and Karri McMahon were similarly foiled by Koning. Xan de Waard then gave the Netherlands a 2-1 lead and the match was wound up by Welten who, it seemed, could do no wrong during this tournament.

And so the Irish watching in the stand knew who they would be facing in less than 24 hours. For Graham Shaw, it was the dream final: 'I've been after a fixture against the Dutch for months. Now they have no bloody choice in the matter,' the Irishman joked.

Results – Semi-finals
Saturday 4 August 2018

Ireland	1-1	Spain
Anna O'Flanagan 3m PC		Alicia Magaz 39m FG

Shoot-out	3-2	
Gillian Pinder – Goal		Begoña Garcia – No Goal
Anna O'Flanagan – No Goal		Beatriz Perez – No Goal
Roisin Upton – No Goal		Georgina Oliva – Goal
Alison Meeke – No Goal		Carlota Petchame – No Goal
Chloe Watkins – Goal		Lola Riera – Goal

Sudden Death		
Gillian Pinder – Goal		Georgina Oliva – No Goal

Vitality Player of the Match: Anna O'Flanagan (IRL)

Netherlands	1-1	Australia
Kelly Jonker 22m FG		Georgina Morgan 54m PC

Shoot-out	3-1	
Frederique Matla - Goal		Kristina Bates - Goal
Carlien Dirkse van den Heuvel – No Goal		Brooke Peris – No Goal
Margot van Geffen – No Goal		Kaitlin Nobbs – No Goal
Xan de Waard – Goal		Karri McMahon – No Goal
Lidewij Welten – Goal		

Vitality Player of the Match: Rachael Lynch (AUS)

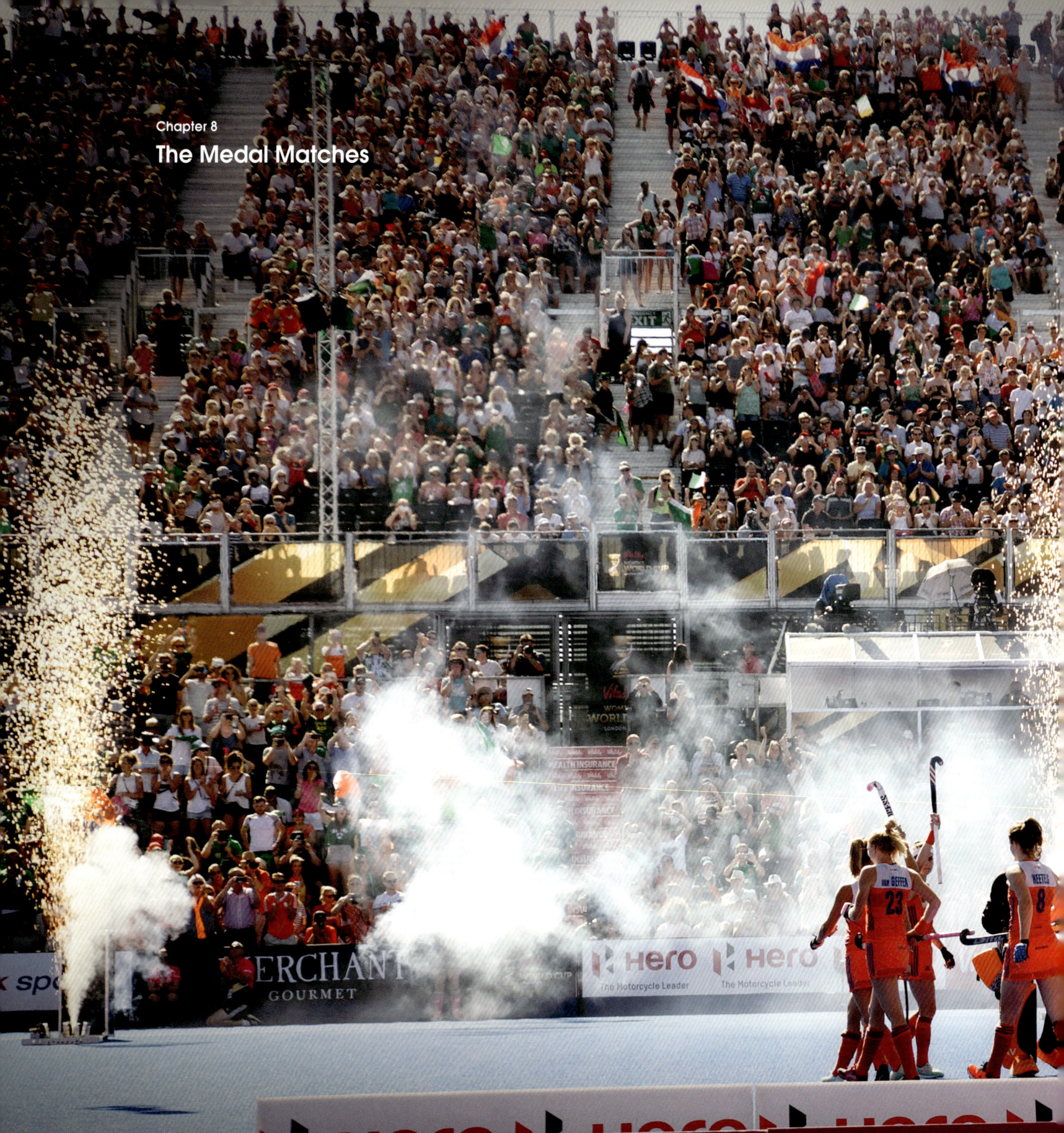

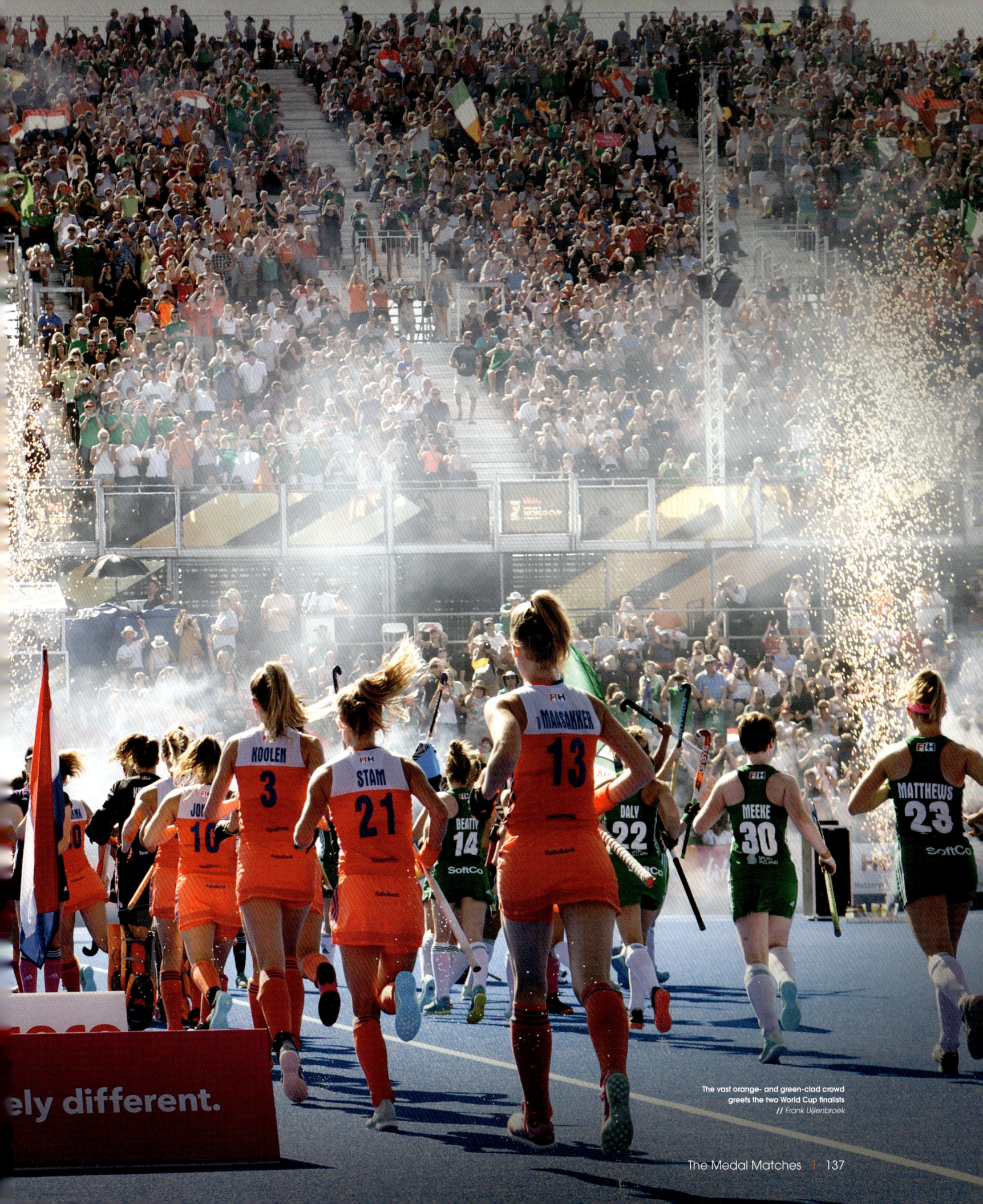

The vast orange- and green-clad crowd
greets the two World Cup finalists
// Frank Uijlenbroek

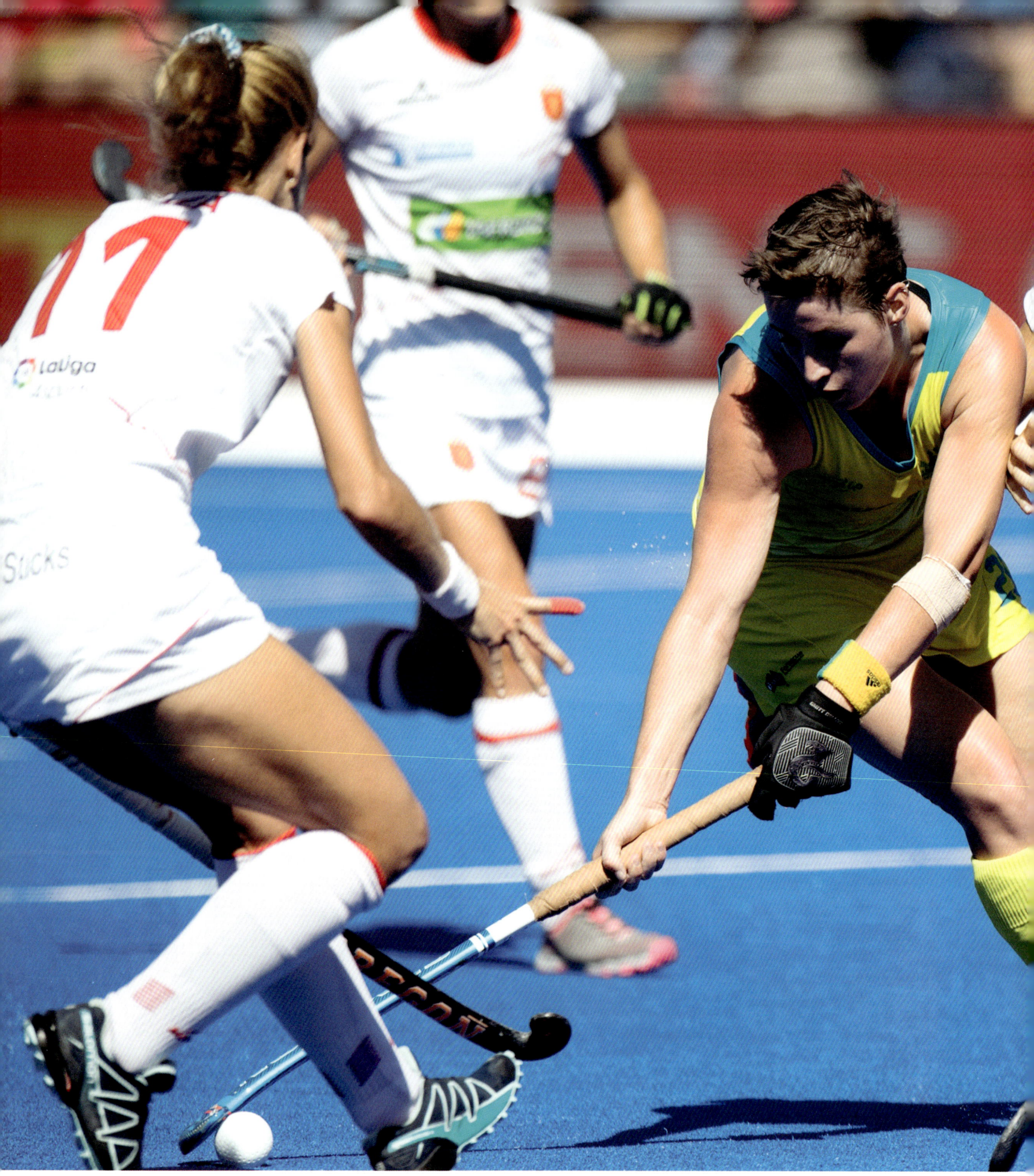

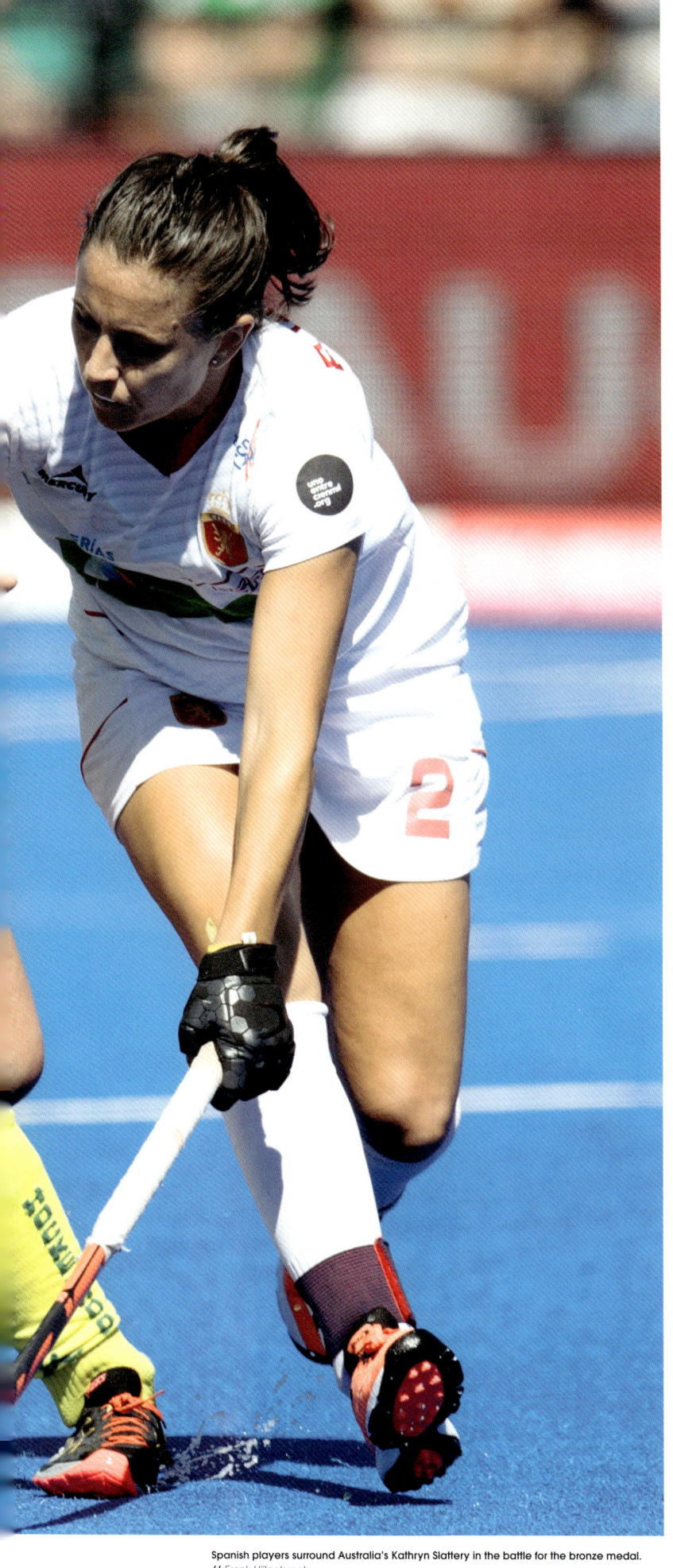

Spanish players surround Australia's Kathryn Slattery in the battle for the bronze medal.
// *Frank Uijlenbroek*

Day 14 – Sunday 5 August 2018

Green Army is no match for sublime Netherlands, but Spain enjoy their moment in the sun

The final day of the Vitality Hockey Women's World Cup burnt as hot as every other day of the two-week competition. London had not seen weather like this for years; hockey had not seen an encounter like this…ever. Fourteen days earlier, Spain and Ireland had turned up for their first World Cup games with few expectations beyond a possible quarter-final place. True, Adrian Lock had talked of the 'surprises' this World Cup might spring, but even the laconic Englishman would have had to admit that this event had produced more upsets and intrigue than anyone could have foreseen.

And now, here was his team battling one of the powerhouses of hockey for a bronze medal, while later in the day, the biggest surprise of all would see Ireland facing the Netherlands in the gold-medal match. Ireland's astonishing run had brought stresses of its own to the family, friends and sports fans in Ireland: a mad rush for tickets, purchased from disgruntled supporters of the other, higher-ranked teams; last minute hotel bookings and website searches for flights had all resulted in an Irish-dominated crowd at the Lee Valley Hockey & Tennis Centre.

When the gates opened an hour before the bronze-medal match, it was the green of the Irish and the orange of the Netherlands that decorated the sun-drenched stands, although there was also plenty of support for Australia and Spain in the first match of the day.

For Spain, who had lost a gruelling battle with Ireland the day before, this was still a chance to write their own history. A bronze medal would be Spain's highest ever finish – no mean return for the team who entered the tournament ranked 11th in the world.

Australia, by contrast, had lost in nail-biting circumstances to the Netherlands. Once the quarter-finals had finished, Australia had seemed the only team capable of living with the Dutch and had fallen just short in the semi-finals. For the Hockeyroos, 2014 silver medallists and twice World Cup winners, bronze was a very meagre consolation prize. The question was: could Paul Gaudoin lift his team to put in one last winning performance?

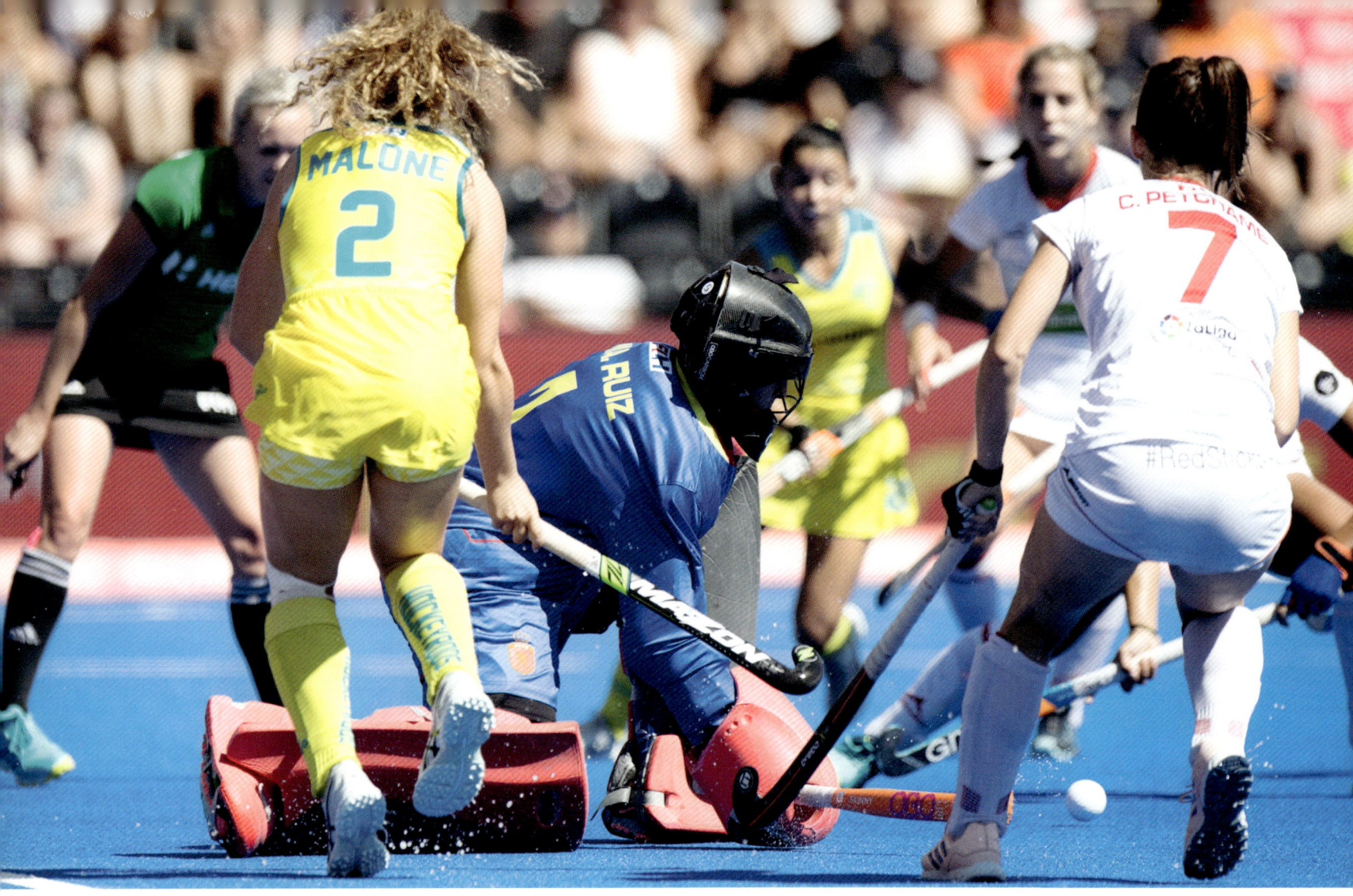

Spain goalkeeper Maria Ruiz makes yet another crucial save to deny Australia. // *Frank Uijlenbroek*

Australia certainly looked the more battered of the two teams contesting the bronze medal. Jodie Kenny was sporting heavy strapping on her shoulder, following a bruising encounter with Argentina's Belen Succi in the quarter-finals, and Renee Taylor was unable to play, so Lily Brazel had come into the squad as a replacement.

Spain in contrast looked lively as they came flying out of the blocks and were rewarded with a goal just ten minutes into the game. Maria Lopez was the scorer after yet another innovative penalty corner routine saw Lynch unable to react to the quick switch of play.

Australia were still looking flat as Spain kept pushing and pushing for a second goal. While Australia were seeking to play the ball wide and up the sides, the Spain side were happy to create and push forwards through the middle of the pitch, where Georgina Oliva was able to spark several attacks with her defence-splitting passing options.

For the Hockeyroos, both Rosie Malone and Brooke Peris showed their own determination to leave this World Cup with a medal as they made several bursting runs from the midfield, but every Australia attack was met by a stoic and disciplined Spanish defence.

It was this strength in the defence that led to the second goal. Australia attacked but lost possession. The ball was cleared and was collected by Beatriz Perez, who in turn found Berta Bonastre. Bonastre, who had been so devastated after her team's loss to Ireland the previous day, fired home and doubled her team's lead.

As the teams re-emerged into the sweltering hot arena after the half-time break, Bonastre said: 'We know it is not how we start the game but how we finish it. We are here to win a medal, we really deserve it.'

The third quarter saw Spain attempt to increase their lead; again their defence was solid as the Australia midfield and attack tried to unpick it. The breakthrough eventually came as Emily Hurtz found Emily Smith. The Hockeyroos' captain's shot was goal bound anyway but Kathryn Slattery was on hand to make sure the ball found the back of the net. The deficit was halved and suddenly the match was very much anyone's. In a swift change in momentum, the Spanish team looked less confident while Australia regained some of their swagger as they pushed for the equaliser.

As the fourth quarter counted down, both teams seemed to be suffering from the heat and the previous day's exertion. Spain had withstood the Australia onslaught and, in yet another shift in momentum, the Red Sticks stole the ball in midfield – again following excellent work by Oliva – and Alicia Magaz elegantly struck the ball home to extend the lead to 3-1.

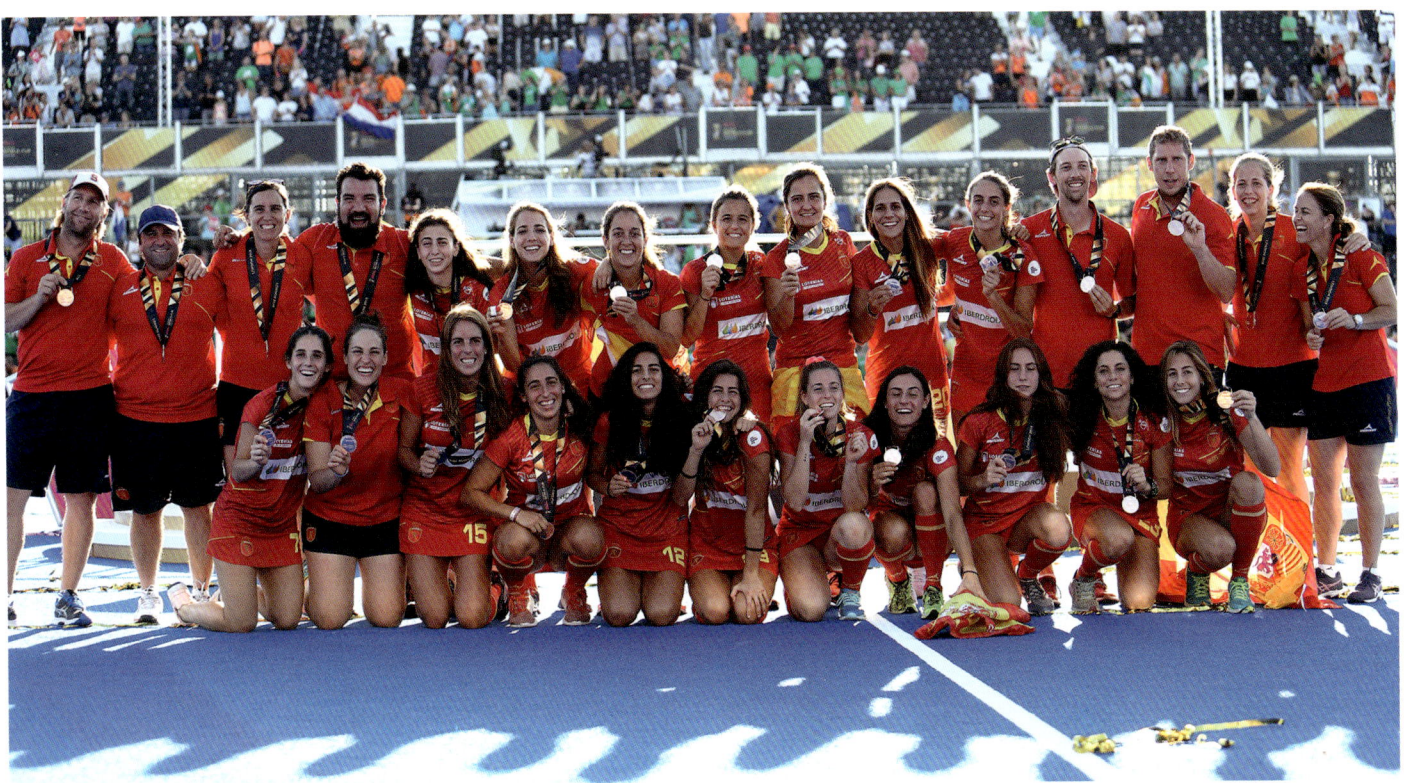

Spain's Red Sticks, the Vitality Hockey Women's World Cup London 2018 bronze medallists. // *Rodrigo Jaramillo*

Australia's head coach Paul Gaudoin replaced goalkeeper Rachael Lynch with an extra field player to increase pressure on the Spanish defence. Slattery and Maddy Fitzpatrick both ran at the Red Sticks' defence but found the wall impenetrable.

The last chance for Australia came with just seconds left. A penalty corner was taken by Georgina Morgan but her shot was not strong enough to give Smith the chance of a deflection. As the clock counted down a jubilant Rocio Gutierrez played the ball out of defence and her team celebrated their first major international medal.

'We didn't put in a performance yesterday, the girls were gutted and they wanted to put it right today,' said Adrian Lock. 'We took it to Australia. The goals went in and once they went in we weren't going to let that go.

'We talked about the opportunity to do something that no one has ever done before. We wanted to make our own history. We have played Australia five times this year; true, we hadn't beaten them but we drew four times. We knew we could win today,' he added.

Australia's head coach Paul Gaudoin said: 'Spain were very good today and we weren't quite there. We will learn a lot from today's performance. We can't use yesterday's match as an excuse for today.'

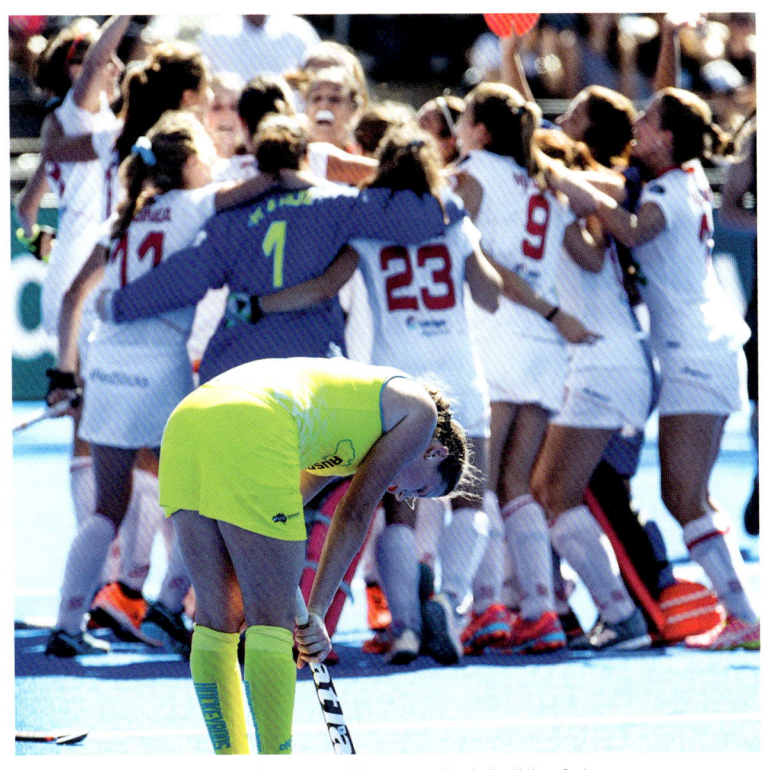

Contrasting emotions as Spain revel in their success at the expense of Australia. // *Koen Suyk*

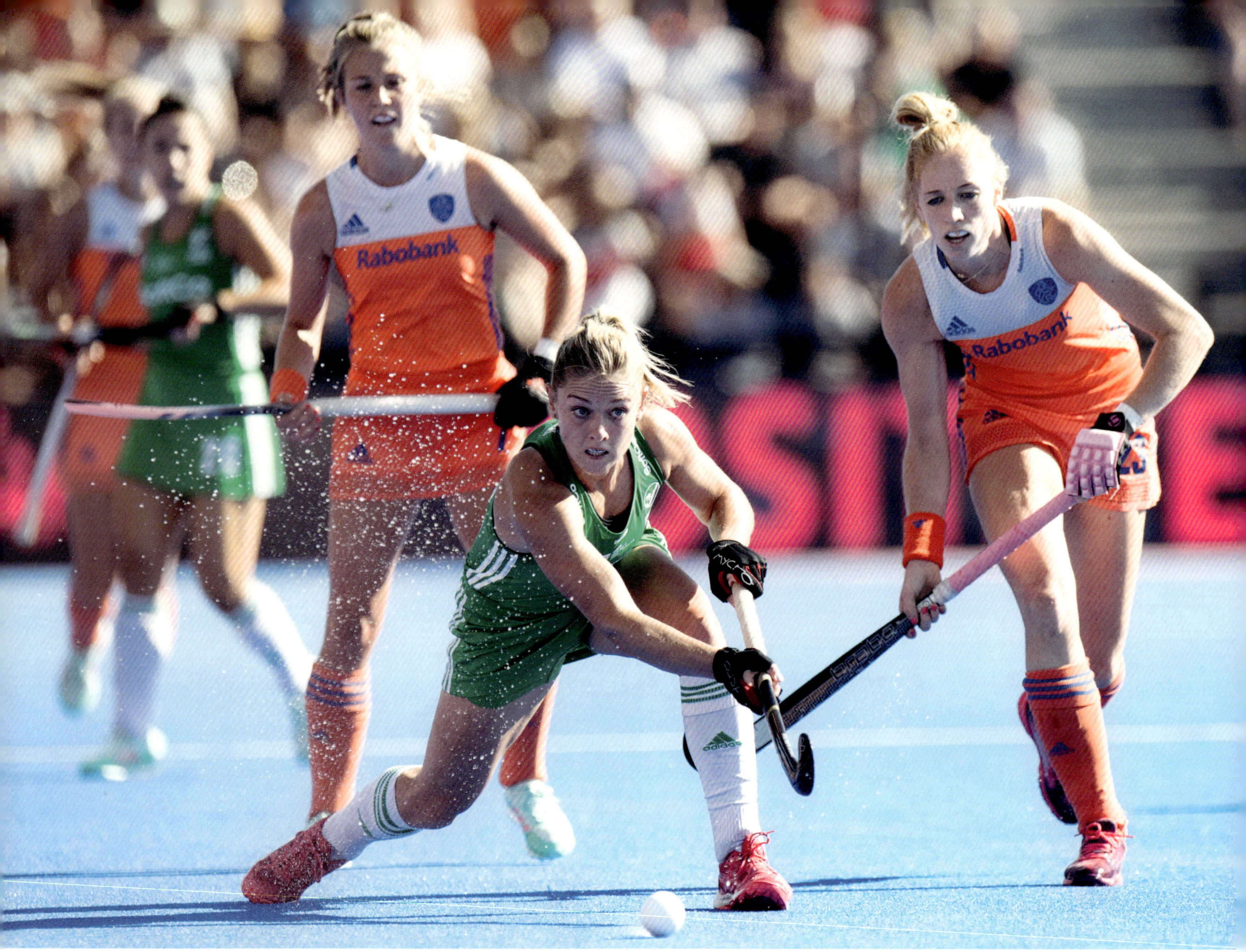

Ireland's Chloe Watkins under pressure from Margot van Geffen. // *Frank Uijlenbroek*

Could all Ireland's Christmas wishes come true?

Passers-by who happened to be around central London when the Ireland squad were doing their mobility and stretching exercises on a patch of grass near their hotel might have been surprised by the choice of music.

A squad of 18 female hockey players, plus a team of coaching staff, all singing along to Mariah Carey's 'All I Want for Christmas is You', might have gathered some odd glances. The tune's seasonal inappropriateness was further emphasised by the fact that London was experiencing a three-month heat wave. But the song was just part of the team's ritual and was key to their togetherness.

In an interview with the sporting website The42, midfielder Nicola Daly explained further: 'When some of the younger girls in the squad said they felt like it was Christmas Eve because of the excitement and anticipation surrounding the opening game, it led to a chorus of Mariah Carey's famous festive hit. It became a recurring bonding exercise.'

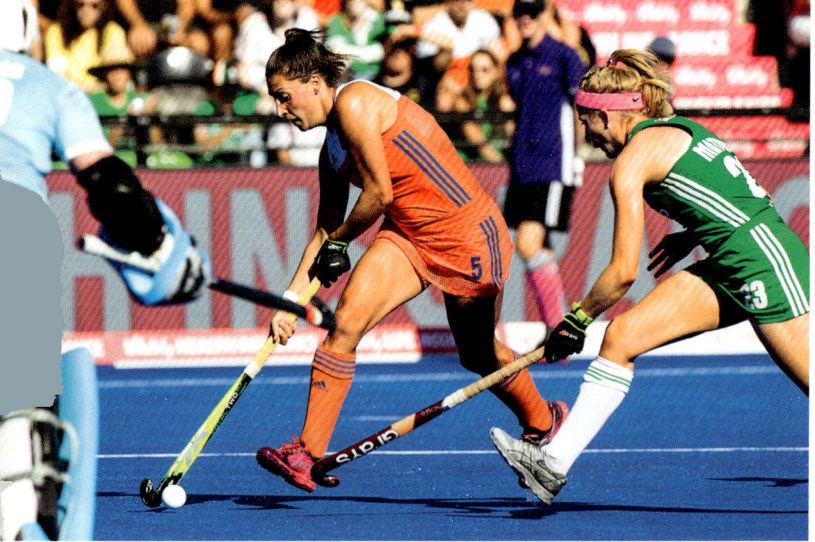

The Netherlands' Malou Pheninckx evades the reach of Ireland's Hannah Matthews. // *Koen Suyk*

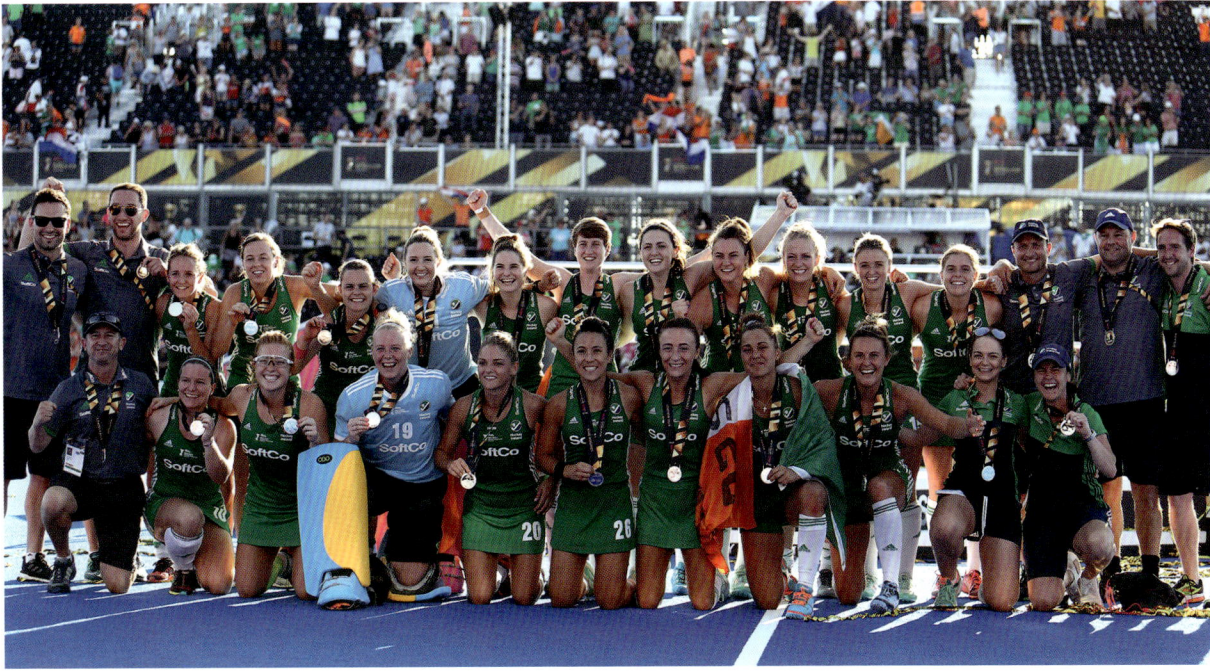

The Irish celebrate their historic World Cup silver medal. // *Rodrigo Jaramillo*

'The more it went on the more exciting it got because we were getting further and further in the tournament. It was something that stuck with the team and when we were doing our mobility exercises in the centre of London, all the commuters on their way to work would stop and listen to us singing "All I Want For Christmas Is You". Some would be wondering what was going on but others would embrace it and recognise who we were and wish us well.'

It was just one more example of the inexplicable squad doing inexplicable things, on and off the pitch. And the watching world was devouring every second of this fairy-tale sporting adventure.

And central to the Green Army's success was the entire squad's approach to each game as a final in its own right. Nikki Evans summed it up: 'We promised we would go out for every game and enjoy it. We promised ourselves that we would have no regrets in this competition and leave everything on the pitch, and at the end of the day we could look back at the scoreline and accept it.'

At the Lee Valley Hockey & Tennis Centre, as the excitement that surrounded Spain's victory subsided, the spectators took their seats for the main event. Two teams walked out on to an electric blue pitch – seeing a team in orange in a hockey final was no surprise; seeing a team in green in a final was totally new. No Irish sports team, male or female, had ever appeared in a World Cup final before. The first whistle of the match had yet to be blown but Ireland women had already made history.

Despite the mountain the team faced as they prepared to play out the final chapter of their fascinating World Cup journey, the Irish supporters were in buoyant and vocal mood. They sang their chosen national anthem with a pride and a passion that moved even the most neutral of spectators and the Netherlands were, for just a moment, a sideshow to the main event. As the Irish team hugged their neighbour's shoulder and sang, the camera panned on to the faces of each player. There were undoubtedly nerves but there were also expressions that ranged from fierce determination to put up a good show to an unequivocal delight that they had found themselves on this great sporting stage.

As if the pressure wasn't enough, for Ireland's Chloe Watkins and the Netherland's Eva de Goede, this final was even more special as both players were representing their respective nations for the 200th time. Both received rapturous applause from the crowd as they stepped forward to acknowledge the milestone.

Then the action started on the pitch. Every Irish pass was greeted with a roar of approval and for the opening minutes it was Ireland who seemed to have the upper hand. When Caia van Maasakker was forced into crudely halting a break by Anna O'Flanagan there were faint hopes that the girls in green could follow the example of Spain. Then, in the seventh minute, Welten, finding a gap between the legs of the otherwise excellent Ayeisha McFerran, broke through and the reasons for Ireland to sweat in 28C heat began mounting up.

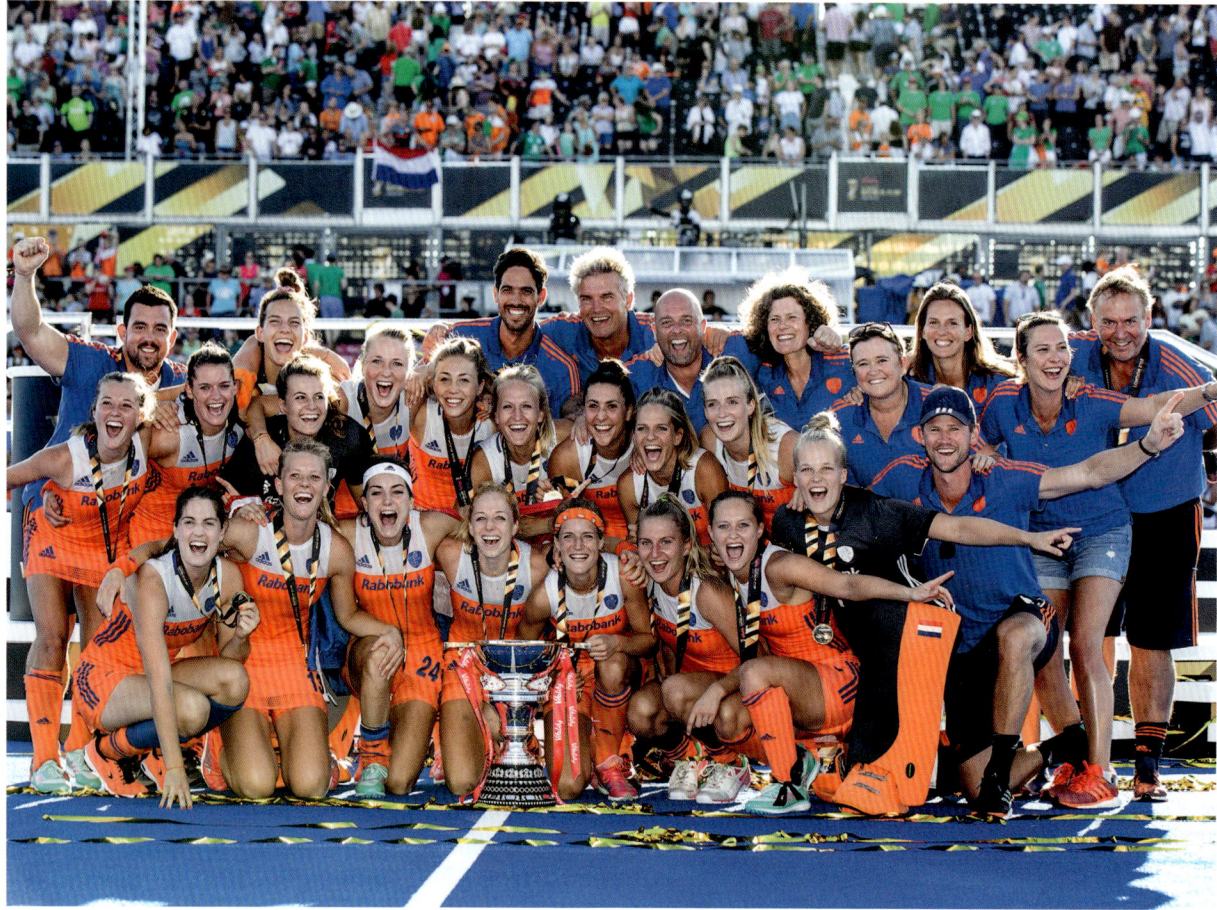

World-title winning Netherlands' team and coaching staff pose with the trophy. // *Koen Suyk*

After the quarter break it was a sweeping team move that doubled that lead. Frederique Matla took the ball down the Dutch right-hand side of the pitch, before slipping to Xan de Waard. De Waard's shot was weak and dealt with easily by McFerran but the rebound fell to sharp-shooter Kelly Jonker who made no mistake as she hit home with a clipped backhand strike.

The Netherlands began to turn up the pressure, winning two penalty corners in quick succession. Unusually for the world number one team the shots failed to produce goals, but this was rectified a few minutes later when Kitty van Male pounced on a rebounded effort from van Maasakker and shot home for her eighth goal of the tournament.

With just 30 seconds left of the first half, Malou Pheninckx unleashed a shot from the edge of the circle that flew into the top corner of the Ireland goal. McFerran, who had been so excellent all tournament, could do nothing about that rocket of a shot – Pheninckx's third goal for her nation and her third of this tournament.

The half-time break gave Graham Shaw a chance to regroup his shattered troops but it also gave Alyson Annan an opportunity to put her foot on the pedal even more firmly.

The Netherlands came out with every intention of making each attack count and just two minutes into the second half, Marloes Keetels was on hand to knock the ball into the goal after another defence-splitting run by Welten.

Caia van Maasakker finally found her groove as she scored from the penalty corner – her third of the tournament.

The shot was perfectly placed just out of McFerran's reach.

Irish hopes were lifted for a moment when a Netherlands' penalty corner broke down and a quick move saw Deirdrie Duke alone with just one Dutch defender to beat. A lot had been said about the Netherlands' magnificence in attack, but on this occasion it was the defence that showed its class. Irene van Assem made the tackle and the danger was averted with composure.

There were no further goals in the final quarter and, on paper, the 6-0 win will look like a walkover, but only the most stony-hearted of sports critics could dismiss this World Cup final as a one-sided, one-dimensional affair. The 6-0 win was a record for a World Cup final and the Dutch really were that good, but Ireland held their own for periods of the game and the back story to this final, combined with the undimmed spirit of the spectators, meant that this encounter was as much a spectacle as any other World Cup climax. And the excellence of the Dutch performance alone made for compelling viewing.

As is her wont, Alyson Annan was reserved in her reflections straight after the game: 'We deservedly won, we played the best hockey throughout the tournament and this was shown today,' said the Australian, adding, 'There are things we have taken from this tournament that are not good enough and we need to improve on those.

'There are some attacking things and our finishing also needs to be improved upon and there are some things in the defence that still need to be worked on. But, yes, we

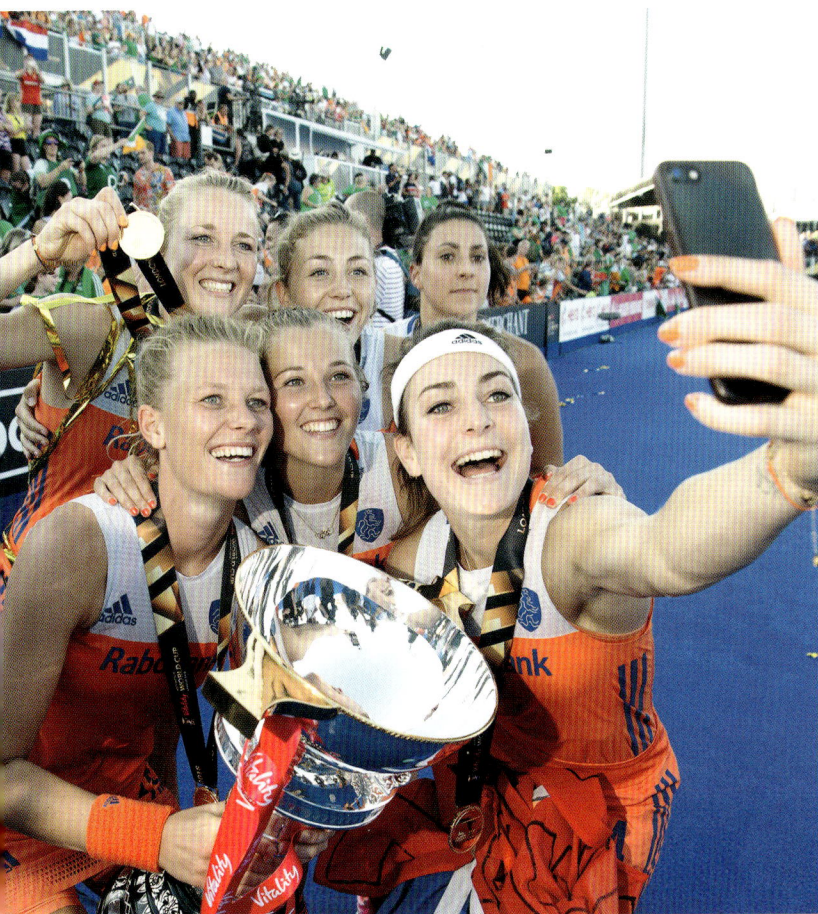

Selfie time. // *Frank Uijlenbroek*

are looking good right now. I have a lot of players with very different skills and abilities and it is a question of moulding them into one team. I have players with exceptional 3-D skills, there are others who are strong and steady. There is a place for many types of player in one team.'

Reigning World Cup champions, number one-ranked team in the world, and a style of hockey that had set the bar so high that the rest of the world could only play catch-up: this might have been the World Cup of surprises but it was also a World Cup that provided a spectacular showcase for the most prodigiously talented sports team in the world.

Sunday 5 August 2018

Bronze

Australia	1-3	Spain
Kathryn Slattery 40m FG		Maria Lopez 11m PC
		Berta Bonastre 14m FG
		Alicia Magaz 51m FG

Vitality Player of the Match: Beatriz Perez (ESP)

Gold

Netherlands	6-0	Ireland
Lidewij Welten 7m FG		
Kelly Jonker 19m FG		
Kitty van Male 28m PC		
Malou Pheninckx 30m FG		
Marloes Keetels 32m FG		
Caia van Maasakker 34m PC		

Vitality Player of the Match: Marloes Keetels (NED)

Vitality Hockey Women's World Cup London 2018

Final Standings
1: Netherlands
2: Ireland
3: Spain
4: Australia
5: Germany
6: England
7: Argentina
8: India
9: Italy
10: Belgium
11: New Zealand
12: Korea
13: Japan
14: USA
15: South Africa
16: China

Individual award winners
Vitality Best Player: Lidewij Welten (NED)
Best Goalkeeper: Ayeisha McFerran (IRL)
Best Young Player: Lucina von der Heyde (ARG)
Hero Top Scorer: Kitty van Male (NED – 8 Goals)

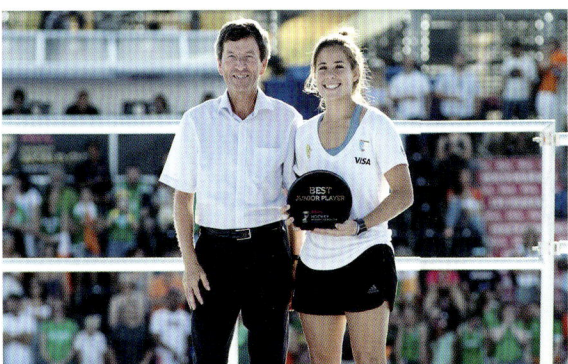

Argentina's Lucina von der Heyde being presented with her Best Junior Player award by England Hockey non-executive director Andy Tapley. // *Frank Uijlenbroek*

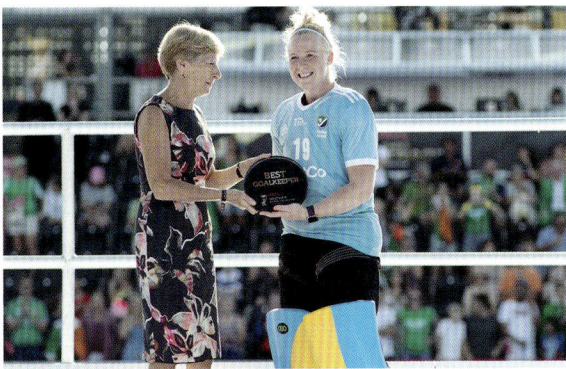

Ayeisha McFerran's stunning performances for Ireland saw her named Best Goalkeeper. She was presented with her award by Liz Nicholl, chief executive of UK Sport. // *Frank Uijlenbroek*

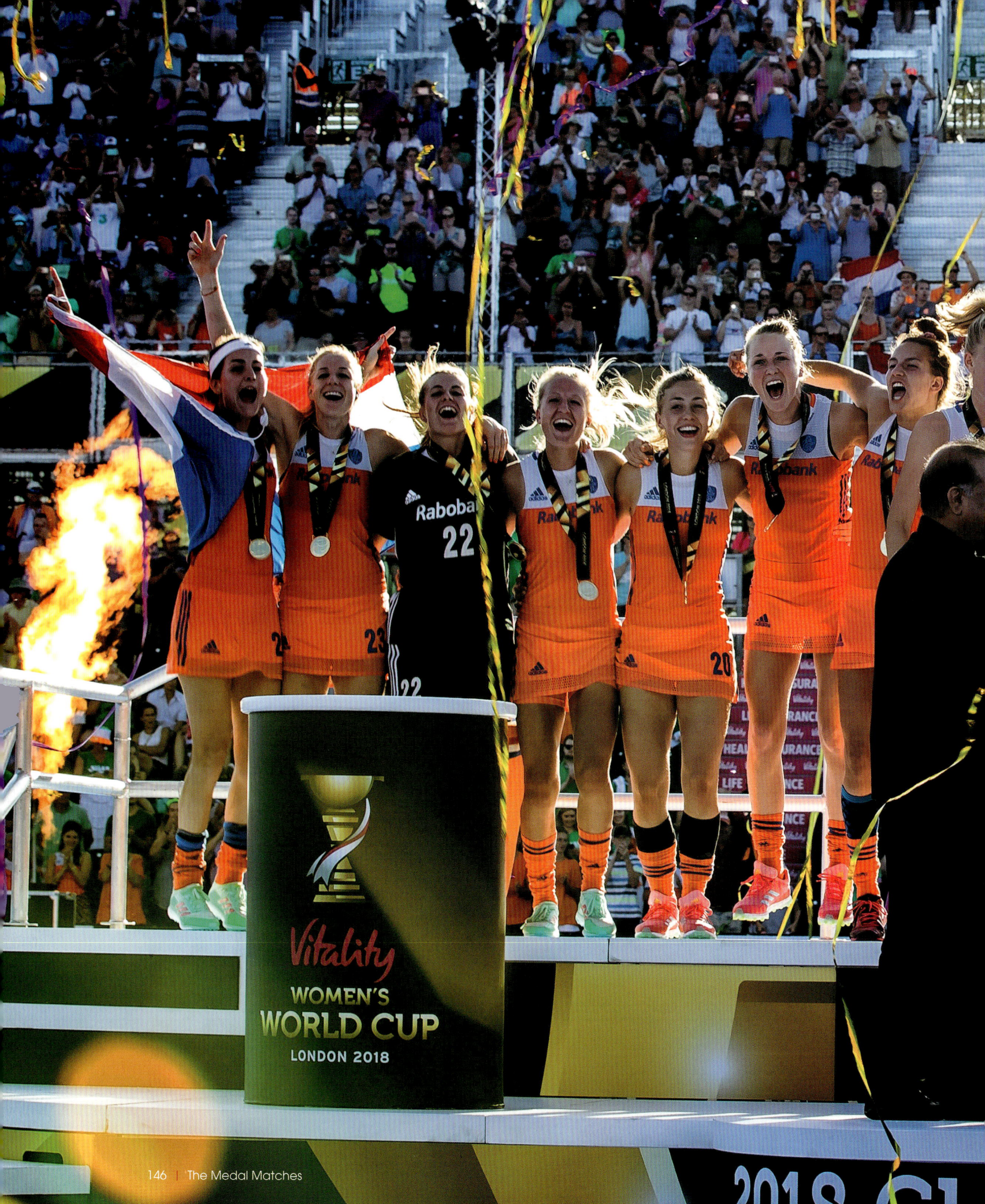

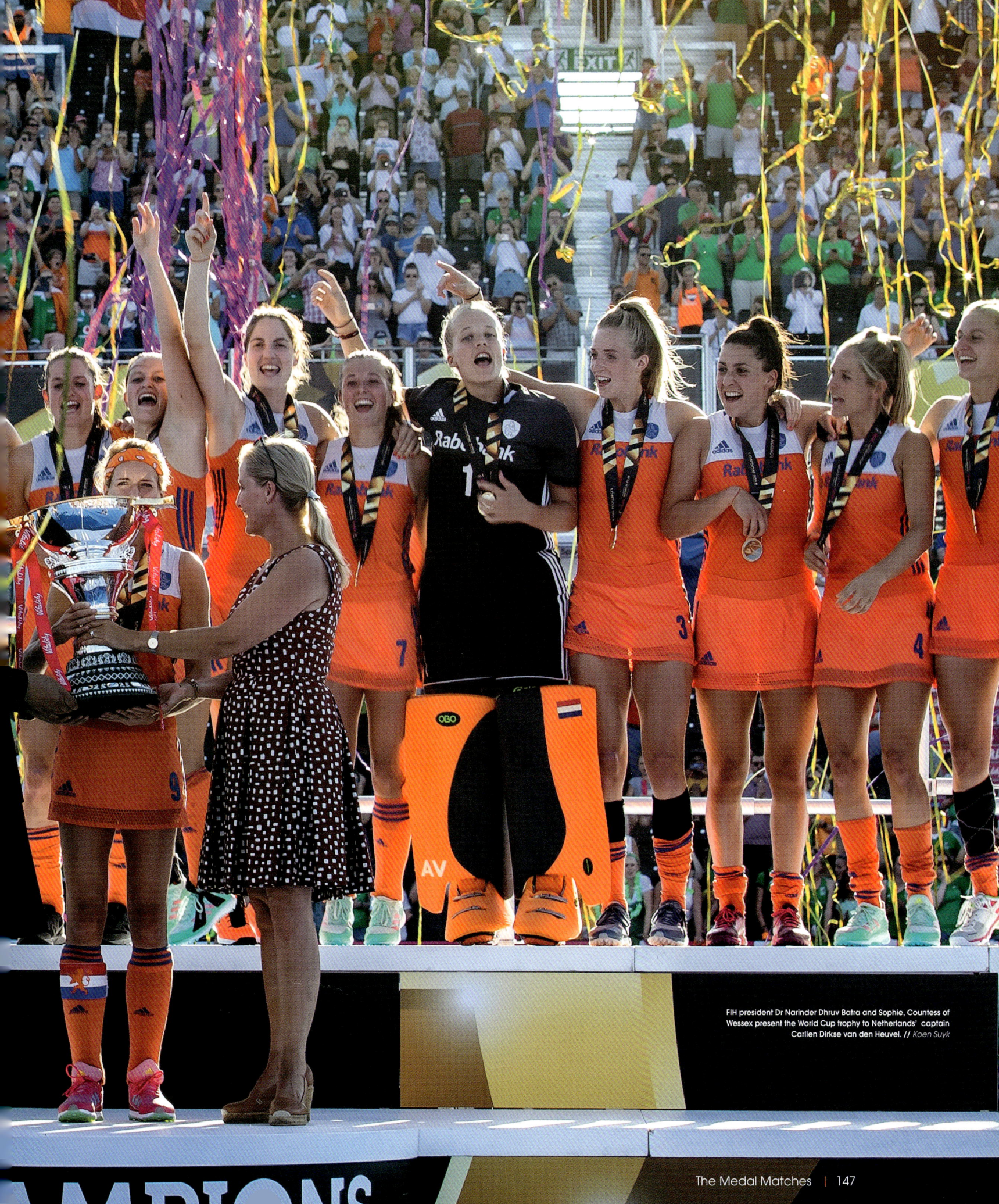

FIH president Dr Narinder Dhruv Batra and Sophie, Countess of Wessex present the World Cup trophy to Netherlands' captain Carlien Dirkse van den Heuvel. // *Koen Suyk*

Chapter 9

Aftermath and Reflections

As the laborious process of dismantling the huge West Stand began and the volunteer Hockey Makers were called upon one more time to help remove every clue that a World Cup had even taken place at the Lee Valley Hockey & Tennis Centre, so the players and coaches began to reflect upon the two weeks that had, in many cases, changed their lives.

For some players, such as USA stars Melissa Gonzalez and Jackie Briggs, as well as England's Ellie Watton, it was a farewell to the international scene. For others, such as Germany's Charlotte Stapenhorst and Ireland's Anna O'Flanagan, the World Cup had proved to be the catalyst that turned them from national players into household names.

For the coaches, too, it was a moment of reflection and change. Danny Kerry sparked discussion in the British papers when the news broke that he would be leaving the England and Great Britain women's team to take up the position of head coach of Great Britain and England men. A few weeks later Jamilon Mülders announced that he would be leaving the role as China's head coach and taking a sabbatical from the game. Sheldon Rostron followed Kerry and Mülders when his contract with South Africa women ended as planned and he chose not to apply to continue in the role.

An event that had been five years in the making was not just going to cause ripples in the months to come. For many of the characters in the story it was going to be a game-changer. For some teams and players the change was for the good; for others, the ramifications of a poor World Cup performance were going to be felt in the harshest of ways.

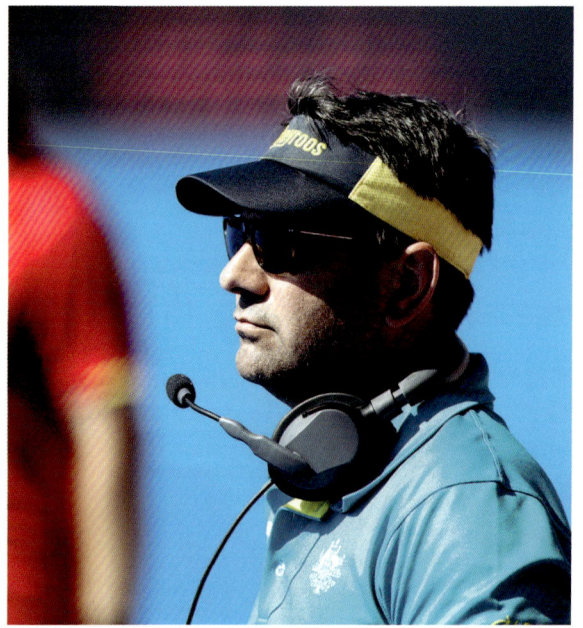

Paul Gaudoin guided Australia's Hockeyroos to a fourth place finish in London. // *Frank Uijlenbroek*

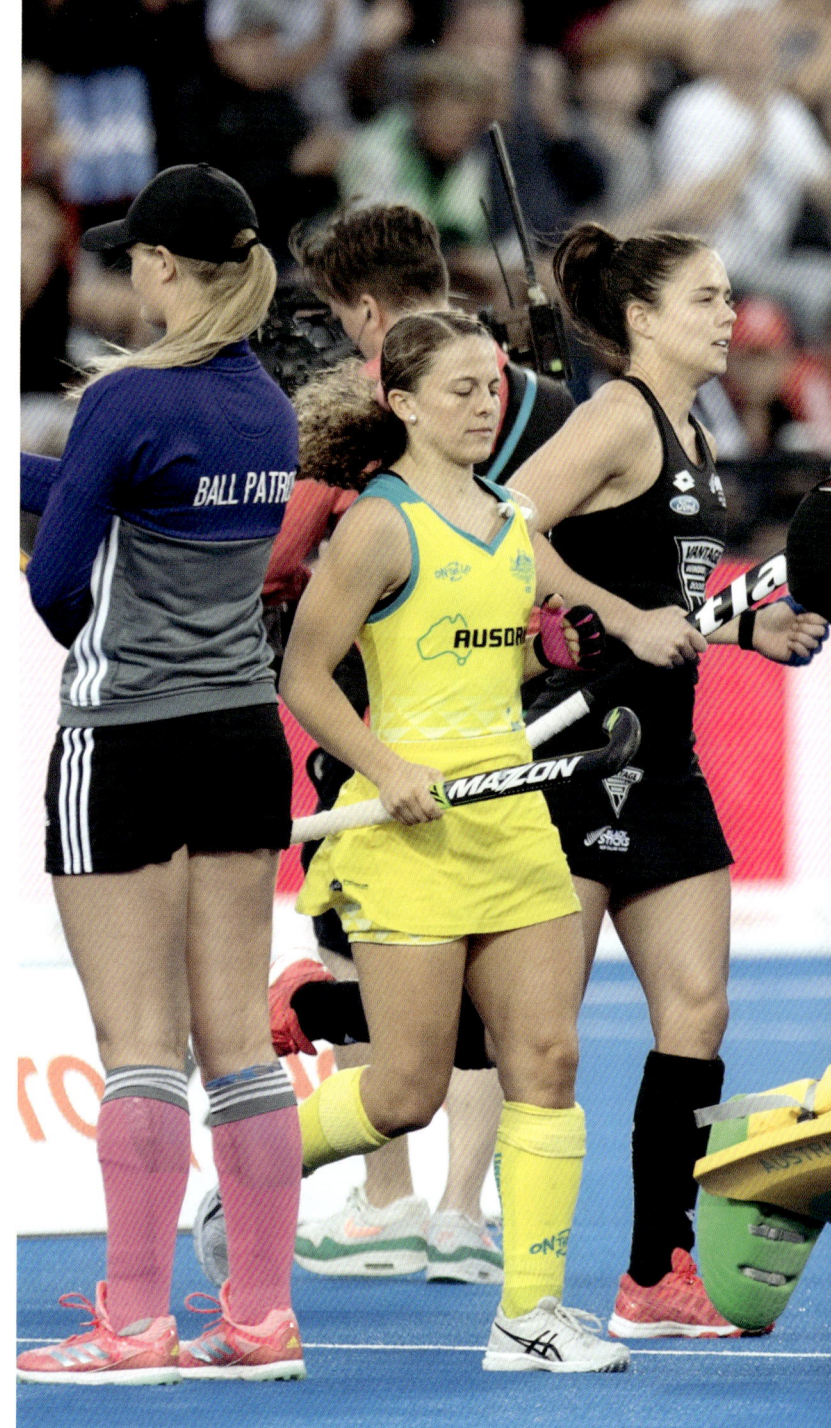

Oceania's big two have mixed fortunes

At the start of the World Cup, New Zealand were probably most people's choice to be the team from Oceania who would get closest to the gold medal. As it turned out, Australia were the side who nearly managed to overcome the might of the Dutch.

Despite an under par performance against Spain, which saw them miss out on the medals, the Hockeyroos' fourth-place finish saw them move to third in the FIH Hero World Rankings, leap-frogging Argentina and New Zealand in the process.

Reflecting on the semi-final when they came within touching distance of beating the Netherlands, head coach Paul Gaudoin said: 'If you're pushing the number one team in the world to a shoot-out after the normal time, I think that

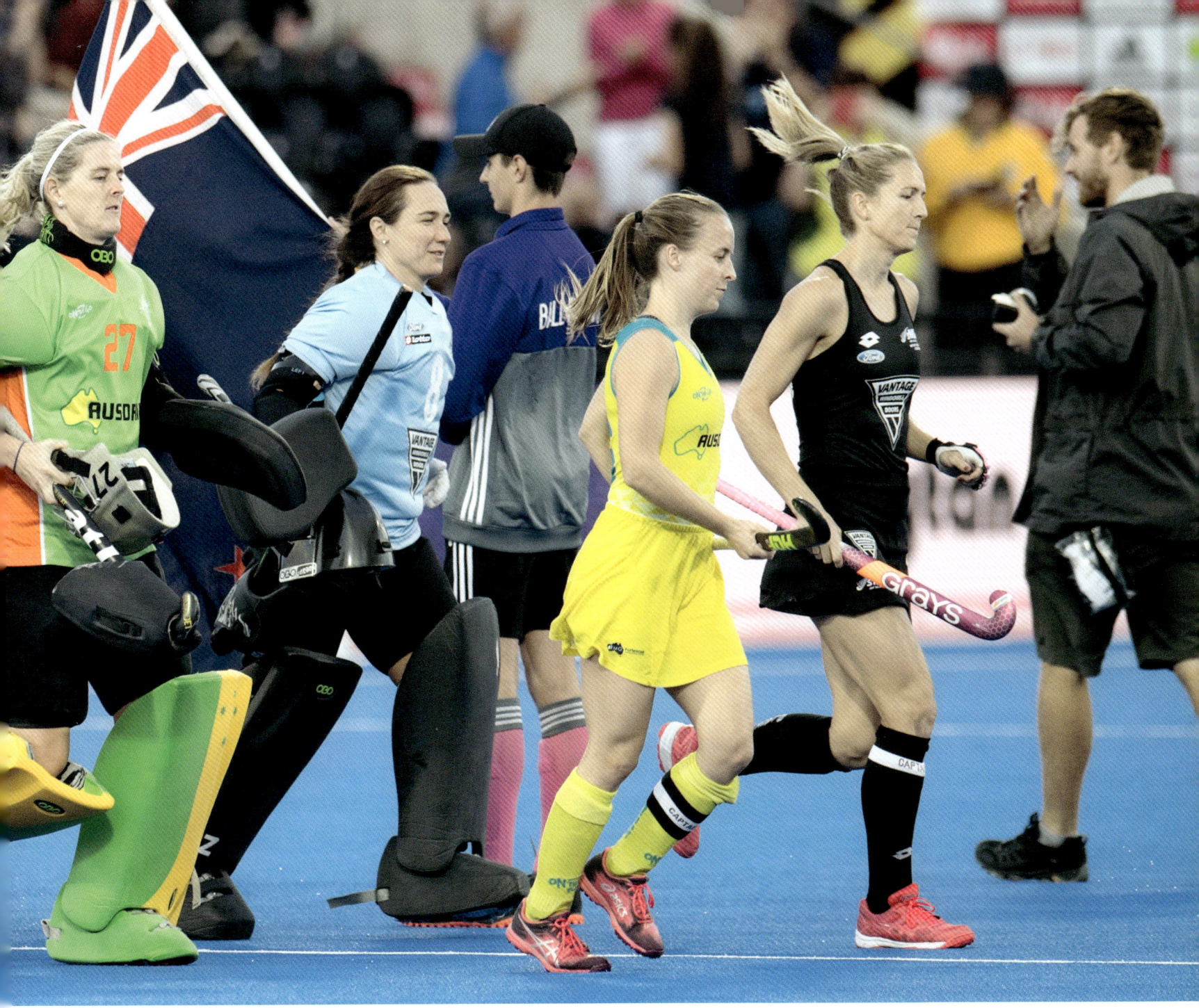

The respective performances of Australia and New Zealand sparked very different conversations in the weeks following the competition in London. // *Frank Uijlenbroek*

gives us great belief in what we can achieve. There's no question we still have an awful lot to do, but it allows us to dream big and believe we can do.'

Gaudoin's achievements in the previous few months could not be overlooked. He picked up a team low on morale and suffering a lack of trust in the team's management. Slowly, the team, under his care, was finding its way again. Fourth place in the World Cup was evidence of this but it remained a long way from the glory days of the 1990s and the opening years of the 21st century.

In conversation with the Australian *Daily Telegraph*, Hockeyroos' captain Emily Smith said: 'It hasn't been an easy rebuild, but things are starting to click. Everyone is starting to work together now and it's the same as any

new relationship, you have to work on it and be constantly learning about each other and knowing what works for each other.

'I think we've come a long way. I won't say it was smooth sailing from the start but we didn't think it would be.

'Paul had never coached a women's team and we're 30 women who are really passionate and organised and want everything to be written out for us, as you can imagine. This is our life and our goal and we want to know and need to be organised…he quickly learnt that we need to know all the details well in advance.'

For Gaudoin, the few months following the World Cup would be crucial, and he would be seeking to build on his players' growing confidence and preparation for Tokyo

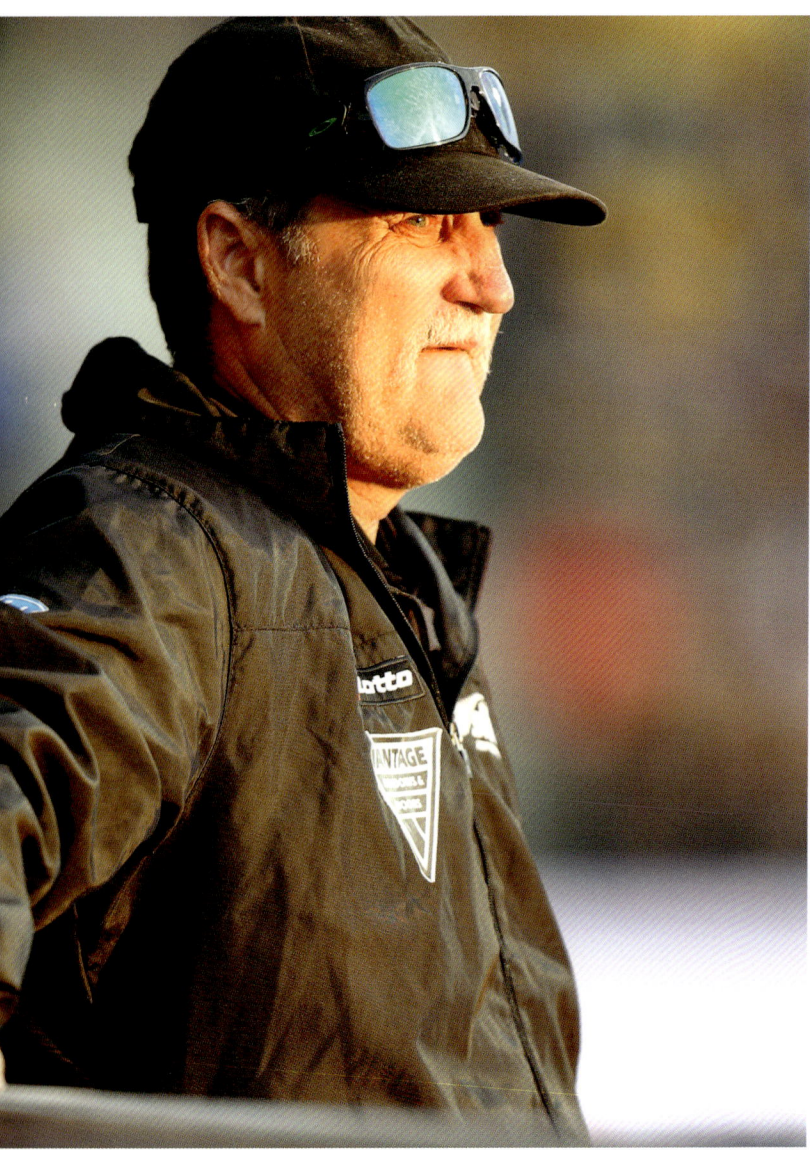

New Zealand head coach Mark Hager. // *Rodrigo Jaramillo*

It says something about the new-found belief that both coach and captain were clearly looking ahead to Tokyo 2020 with unmistakable relish.

Over in New Zealand, Mark Hager encountered a storm when an email was leaked to the press in which the head coach had been forthright about his players' levels of fitness during the World Cup.

The fall-out from this, combined with a poor performance in London, gave the long-serving head coach a headache for a few weeks. Hager issued an apology via Hockey New Zealand and then prepared for the usual, if potentially uncomfortable, team review.

What would have cheered Hager up immensely was the alacrity with which many former and current internationals leapt to his defence. An open letter, with signatories including multi-capped Olympians Katie Glynn, Krystal Forgesson and Bianca Russell, highlighted the tough environment that was part of being an international hockey player.

The letter said: 'High performance sport is extremely tough. Hockey in New Zealand has very limited funding and support in comparison to other competitive hockey countries around the world. The environment was tough and players had to make many sacrifices to be part of it, but for us, it was not a sacrifice – it was a choice and we all committed.

'To become a better team, to climb up the rankings and compete with the best in the world, we needed to work harder than we had ever done before.

'Mark is a person of high integrity and has always created a high-pressure training environment, designed to challenge players physically and mentally. Mark never allows the group to become complacent, and he always has every player in the squad pushing and challenging for selection.

'Through Mark's high expectations and low tolerance of complacency, this became ingrained in us as individuals, and we were constantly striving for better performances and demanding more of ourselves in both trainings and in games – this essentially led us to being successful, strong and resilient as a group. These high expectations and constant goals to get better have essentially helped us all immensely in life after sport.'

Unsavoury as it was, the New Zealand experience served to highlight the fragile nature of elite sport. While the whole of New Zealand had celebrated a glorious gold medal at the Gold Coast 2018 Commonwealth Games, an 11th-place finish at the World Cup, resulting in a drop in world rankings, was the catalyst for internal wrangling and a split among a previously cohesive bunch of players.

2020. 'At the moment, certainly, everyone is having the ability to centralise; footage and knowledge of what other teams are doing is via the net etc., everything is out there and a lot more readily available…it's created a bigger group of teams vying for spots in the top few positions.'

So the Hockeyroos needed to adapt, a point on which Smith was clear: 'You have to be innovative and try new things. It's very close [between the top teams] and I'm not sure what we're going to do that is going to be the difference but I guess that's for us and our coaching staff to work hard and have a good think about what we need to do.'

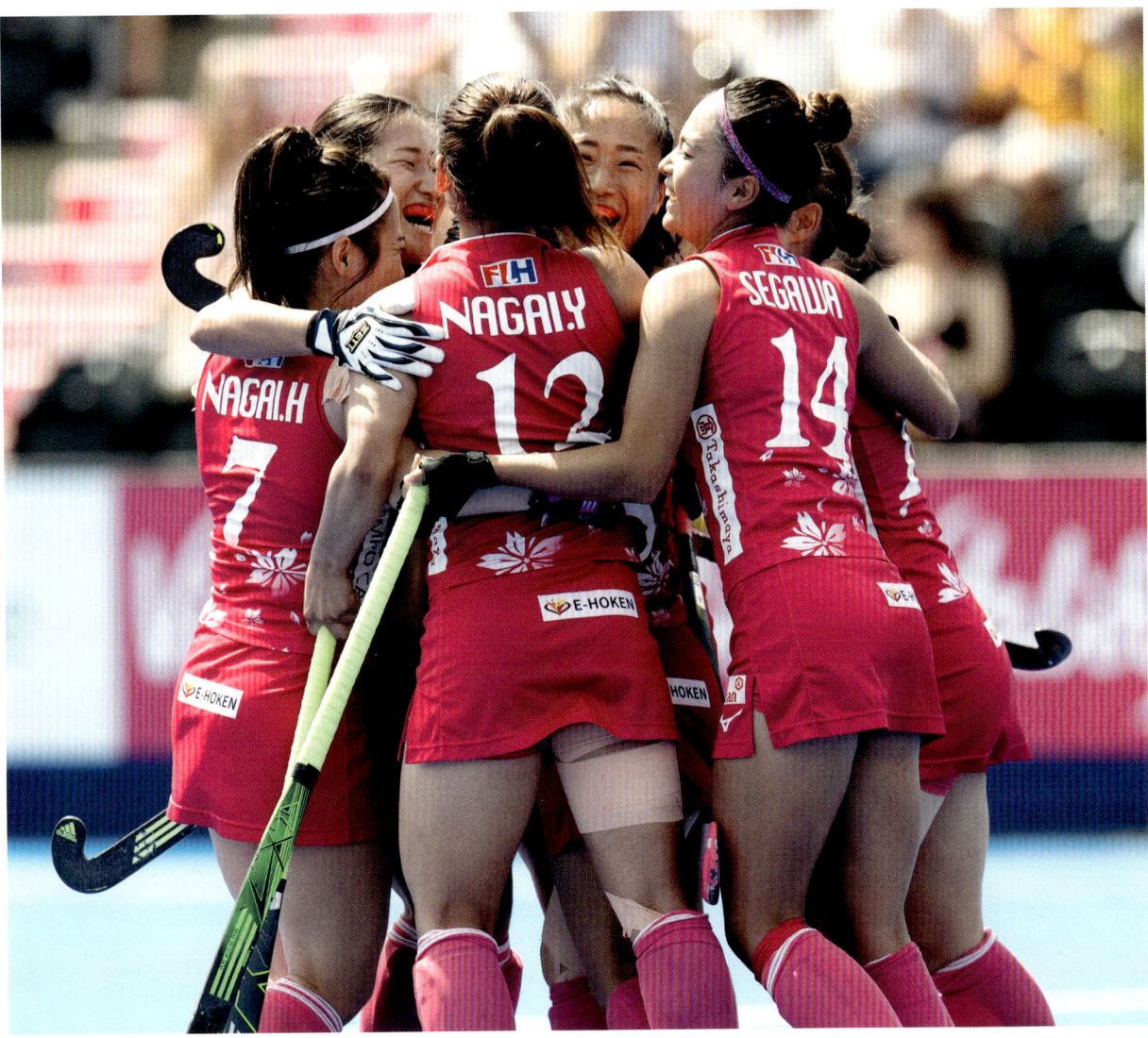

Japan's experiences in London laid the foundation for a glorious success at the Asian Games 2018 in Jakarta, Indonesia. // *Frank Uijlenbroek*

Japan blossoms at Asian Games

Like New Zealand, Japan left the World Cup at the cross-over play-off stage but, rather than it having a negative impact on subsequent performances, the Cherry Blossoms, under the leadership of head coach Anthony Farry, went on to make their own piece of history.

At the Asian Games, Japan were in fine form, building on the performances that had impressed hockey fans in London. Playing with a fast, free-flowing style, Japan swept to the top of their pool in Jakarta, Indonesia and set up a semi-final encounter with higher-ranked Korea. This they won 2-0, a stoic defence holding off the Korea attack before two goals in the latter stages of the game won Japan a place in the final against India.

India had been another team who had produced some exciting hockey in London, their journey ending in the quarter-finals as they lost a shoot-out to Ireland. Head coach Sjoerd Marijne was hoping that the Asian Games would provide India with their ticket to the 2020 Tokyo Olympic Games, but instead Japan secured a tight 2-1 victory to take their first gold medal at the event.

While the result left Japan eyeing the top prize in the home Games in two years' time, their Australian coach remained realistic: 'The Netherlands remain a step above everyone else, but the difference between the number two in the world, down to the number 16 or 17, well that is close.'

England's Kerry takes on new role

'As a head coach you often find that you don't get the chance to take in just how spectacular an event is. You come away from an Olympics or a World Cup and everyone says it was amazing but you have had your head down and not really taken it in at the time.' So said England head coach Danny Kerry as he reflected on his last competition at the helm of England before he moved to pastures new with the England and Great Britain men's team.

'For me, I think it hit home when we went as a team to Fan Central on the medal-match day. That experience will stay with me for a long time. It is a demonstration of just how far the sport has come since I have been involved. It's gone from one man and his dog to this spectacular event – and it was spectacular – with thousands of people watching and thousands wanting to get autographs. And that was even though we weren't playing for a medal. That was a special moment.'

Kerry's final outing with England women didn't achieve the medal-winning outcome that the thousands of fans pouring into the Lee Valley Hockey & Tennis Centre might have hoped for, but it did provide the coach and his players with a chance to progress further along the way to defending their gold medal at Tokyo 2020.

The innovative coach had never been afraid to learn from other sports and coaches and, in explaining why London offered more positives than might have appeared

at first sight, he quoted Dave Brailsford, the hugely successful cycling coach and General Manager of Team Sky. Brailsford had created the concept of the Triangle of Change, which said that for learning and change to occur, three elements had to be in place: the suffering or reward had to be great enough for players to seek change; the players had to be 'psychologically minded' – to think that change could occur; and the players had to be committed to change. In Kerry's eyes, the World Cup offered a unique environment that provided the catalyst for change among his players.

'I think the biggest thing we learnt was how much the little things matter. If just one of our results had been slightly different, the whole World Cup might have looked very different.'

Kerry was referring in part to the missed opportunities that saw his side rack up numerous scoring chances in their three pool games only to draw with USA and India and beat Ireland 1-0 – despite having 14 penalty corners in the Ireland match.

Against Korea, England put in a far better performance and Kerry cited the Korean tactic of throwing massive aerial balls into the England defending area as a great learning opportunity for his players. 'You just saw some of the players grow during that game,' he says.

At the tournament, the Netherlands, who England met in the quarter-finals, were the best side in the world but, said Kerry, Australia showed that the Dutch were beatable. 'Holland have to deliver under a huge amount of pressure. If you can stay with them in the game, then a gap can occur. We defended brilliantly against them in that quarter-final, probably better than we did in the Olympic final. They didn't penetrate our circle for 20 minutes in the second half.

'At the moment I would say that Argentina have the players who could beat the Dutch and there are four or five other teams who are capable of beating them. This was a strange tournament, though. Argentina had a strange tournament as did New Zealand – but they are both teams who can beat the Netherlands – and I would put us there too.'

Kerry did not believe that the landscape of hockey had been changed hugely by the topsy-turvy results of the World Cup. 'It was great for the sport but I'm not convinced there has been a change in the status quo,' he said. 'The same teams are still at the top – Netherlands, Australia, Argentina, Germany and us. Japan, with Tokyo in mind, might make a semi-final in a major competition but I don't think there has been a seismic shift.'

As Kerry took his leave of the women's squad to join the men's outfit he reflected upon the state of the team. 'Looking at the bigger picture, the group is in a good place. There are some extremely good young players, I would

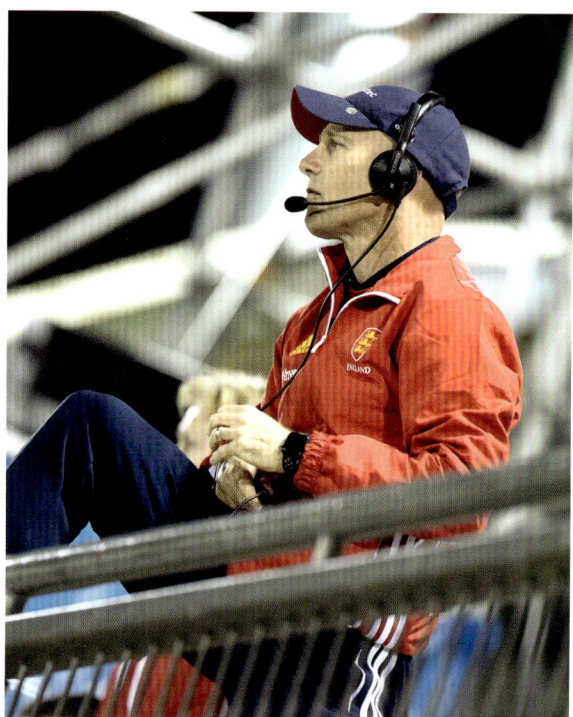

After a hugely successful stint with his country's women's team, head coach Danny Kerry has taken charge of England and Great Britain's men's sides. // *Frank Uijlenbroek*

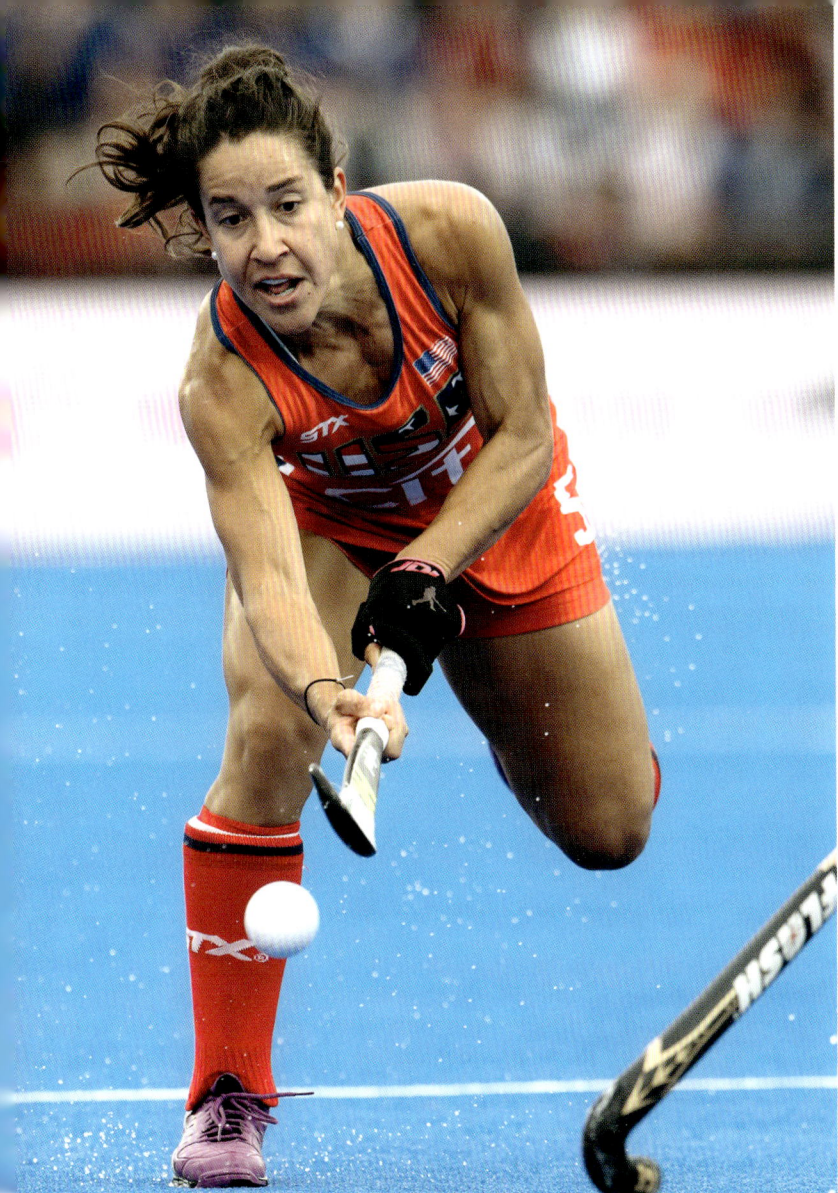

USA's midfield dynamo Melissa Gonzalez has called time on a stellar international career. // *Frank Uijlenbroek*

say veering towards world class. I hope that Nic White and Shona McCallin return from their concussion injuries because they are also truly great players. The squad is definitely capable of competing for medals in Tokyo.

'Of course, there are also some players who are still asking themselves if they want to do it all again and some people are struggling with some aspects. People think there is a rosy aura around a gold-medal squad, but that is not always the case. I think new leadership will reinvigorate the squad. So yes, the squad are at number two in the world, with world-class players coming through the junior ranks and a major sponsor – I think that is a good place.'

USA say goodbye to two stalwarts

Between them USA stalwarts Jackie Briggs and Melissa Gonzalez had amassed 425 caps for their national team and had played for the senior side since 2010. They were part of the team that caused an upset in the 2011 Pan American Games when they beat pre-tournament favourites Argentina in the final. For Briggs this was made even more special as she had been flown in as a last-minute replacement in the squad.

It was a tragedy that brought Melissa Gonzalez to hockey. She had been on the point of choosing to major as a soccer player in junior school when her father died. The prospect of playing the sport he had loved so passionately was something that the teenager couldn't face and so she turned her focus to hockey.

With Briggs and Gonzalez as key members of the USA squad, the team improved rapidly after the surprise Pan Am Games success. Over the next few years they won gold at the 2014 Champions Challenge and came fourth at the 2014 Rabobank Hockey World Cup. They then won gold at the 2015 Pan Am Games, bronze at the 2016 Champions Trophy and gold at the Hockey World League Semi-Final in Johannesburg, South Africa.

For Briggs, the 2018 World Cup seemed like a keeper finishing right at the top of her game. She was one of the short-listed goalkeepers for the FIH Goalkeeper of the Year award and, in the words of USA head coach Janneke Schopman: 'She is still getting better. Jackie is one of the most competitive people I have worked with…She will be missed.'

As captain, Gonzalez was an inspirational figure for USA. Like Briggs, she was one of six individuals short-listed for the 2017 FIH Player of the Year award. She was renowned for her work rate but with the retirement of Lauren Crandall in 2016, Gonzalez proved herself to be a great leader as well as a fierce competitor. She was also one of the game's most engaging personalities and had a ready smile. There was never a dull moment when she was around.

Both Briggs and Gonzalez moved into coaching after the event, with Briggs returning to her post as assistant coach at the University of North Carolina and Gonzalez taking up the position of assistant coach at Wake Forest University in Winston Salem, North Carolina.

2010 World Cup winner Carla Rebecchi returned to the Argentina set-up in the months following the showpiece event in London. // *Frank Uijlenbroek*

Argentina turn clock back in search of Tokyo gold

As Argentina crashed out of the World Cup in the quarter-finals at the hands of Australia, several Argentinian journalists were shaking their heads sadly. The new squad, formed under head coach Agustin Corradini had promised much but was still not the finished article. 'Tokyo is the target,' said Florencia Grunfeld, director of hockey website Hockey Mobile, 'They are two years from reaching their potential.'

Even as the match went to a shoot-out, another journalist, Gabriela Faccenini, had predicted Las Leonas's exit. 'We are just no good at these anymore,' she said.

And so, while keeping an eye firmly on the future, Corradini allowed himself to look backwards as he recalled one of Argentina's all-time greats.

Carla Rebecchi quit the national team in 2016 after the 2016 Rio Olympics to start a family with her Olympian husband Jorge Lombi. In February 2018 Vera Lombi made her entry into the world and a few months later Rebecchi was tempted back to the international game.

'Agustin called after the World Cup,' explained the star striker, who has competed in three World Cups and three Olympic Games. 'He was talking about the project from here until Tokyo 2020. What excited me most and what prompted me to make the decision, beyond the fact that wearing the Argentina shirt is beautiful, is to have another opportunity, another dream to play at an Olympic Games.

'It is a young team with a lot of talent,' she added. 'From my part, I can contribute experience. After so many years I learnt a lot, even being away for a year and a half that makes you see differently. I want to add something to help the team grow and keep getting better. I want to demonstrate, for example, all the values that were taught to me and that I think are key for the team.'

Ireland's silver lining

A silver medal has probably never been more passionately celebrated than the one that the Ireland women's hockey team brought back to Dublin Airport on Monday 6 August.

As reported in the *Irish Times*: 'If only Sunday's World Cup final had been a singing competition not a hockey match, the medals brought home by the Irish team would have been gold and not silver.'

True, the team had been thrashed 6-0 in a consummate Dutch performance, but that wasn't the point for Ireland women and their thousands of supporters. Their story was one of an underdog defying all the odds to take to the greatest stage of all. They were the Seabiscuit of the hockey world, the little guy taking on the giant; and the rolling stone that had begun to gather momentum as they recorded their first win of the World Cup over the USA was by now careering almost out of control.

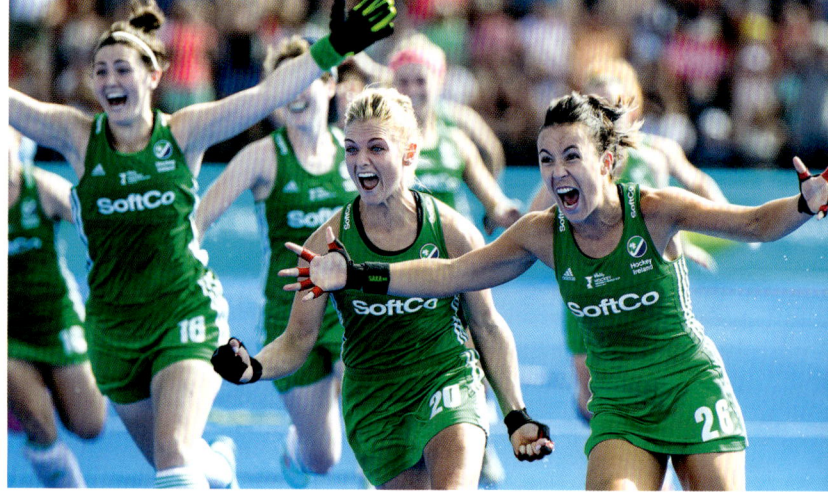

Ireland's joyous celebrations in London will live long in the memory. // *Koen Suyk*

As the plane touched down, among the 5,000 waiting to greet the team was sports minister, Shane Ross, who announced that there would be a further €1.5 million available to fund teams preparing for the 2020 Tokyo Olympics, and a substantial share of that would go to Hockey Ireland.

Now, the key thing for Irish hockey was how they could capitalise on the explosion in positive PR and how the funding could be used to improve results and bring more success.

For one of the jubilant squad, goalkeeper Ayeisha McFerran, the party came to an end on Saturday 11 August as she boarded a plane back to the USA. The 22-year-old goalkeeper was a student at the University of Louisville and her coach wanted her back training with the squad. But the goalkeeper's return to her college side was later than coach Justine Sowry expected, as McFerran explained: 'Justine took one look at our World Cup draw and thought we would be out by the cross-over matches.'

When Ireland not only got past the cross-over matches but into the quarter-finals as pool leaders, Sowry hopped on a plane and came to watch. As Ireland's journey continued, so the head coach resigned herself to the fact that her keeper would not be back for a few weeks.

McFerran might have been an unknown to many of the teams and spectators in London prior to the World Cup, but in the USA she was already a star. In December 2017 McFerran was picked, for the second year running, by the National Field Hockey Coaches Association for their 'All-American' team of the year, the highest honour in US college sport.

She had just one year left at Louisville, where she went on a hockey scholarship in 2015, majoring in Health and Human Performance, but she was already giving some thought to the future.

'I have to, really, because I need to start thinking about what I'll do next year, so I'll look at clubs and see what options there are for me, maybe think about playing abroad [in one of the major European leagues] if that was possible. But right now I'll enjoy the moment and enjoy my season with the girls in America, I love being with them.

'Of course Tokyo is the dream, and I hope we've made it a bigger possibility by what we did in London. And I think that's the most important thing we've done, kind of putting Irish hockey on the map and, hopefully, helping make hockey in Ireland even bigger than it is.'

Peerless Netherlands continue striving for perfection

And what of the Netherlands? Having obliterated all the opposition with a near-faultless performance, consolidated their position as the world number one team and claimed an unprecedented eighth World Cup medal, what was next for the team in orange?

'The next few years will be interesting,' mused head coach Alyson Annan. 'We have the new Pro League, which will call for an expansion in the team. Qualifying for the Tokyo 2020 Olympics will be our main priority, though, along with introducing more youngsters on the international circuit.'

And the coach was not one to sit on her laurels, and was already thinking about ways that the team could improve upon its performance in London and stay one or two steps ahead of the opposition. 'I was impressed with the resilience we showed at the World Cup, but there are always areas to improve and that is what we are looking at now,' she said.

'We were confident without being arrogant and we played a fast game which sought to utilise all the players. But sure, there are things on and off the pitch that can be improved further. My homework, if you like, is to try and put myself in the shoes of the other coaches and ask "How would I beat the Netherlands?"'

The Netherlands did not run a full-time national hockey programme so from the following August to October Annan would not see her players. 'I just told them to go and have some fun,' she said. 'They go back to their clubs now and I won't see them for two months.'

Annan's attitude perhaps went a long way to explaining why the Netherlands were dominating world hockey. Having achieved greatness, she simply got on with the task of setting the bar even higher. Her players, having won gold, were simply on the hunt for more trophies to adorn their glittering careers in the sport. 'If we didn't always want to win, if we didn't absolutely hate losing, then it would be time to stop playing the game,' said captain Carlien Dirkse van den Heuvel.

Yes, the final score that decided the crown in the 2018 World Cup was a 6-0 drubbing, but never will such a large winning margin have brought such delight to all parties. For Ireland, it was an exceptional campaign with a fairy-tale outcome; for world hockey and international sport it was the moment a squad of female hockey players and an outstanding coach secured their position as one of the finest sports teams on the planet.

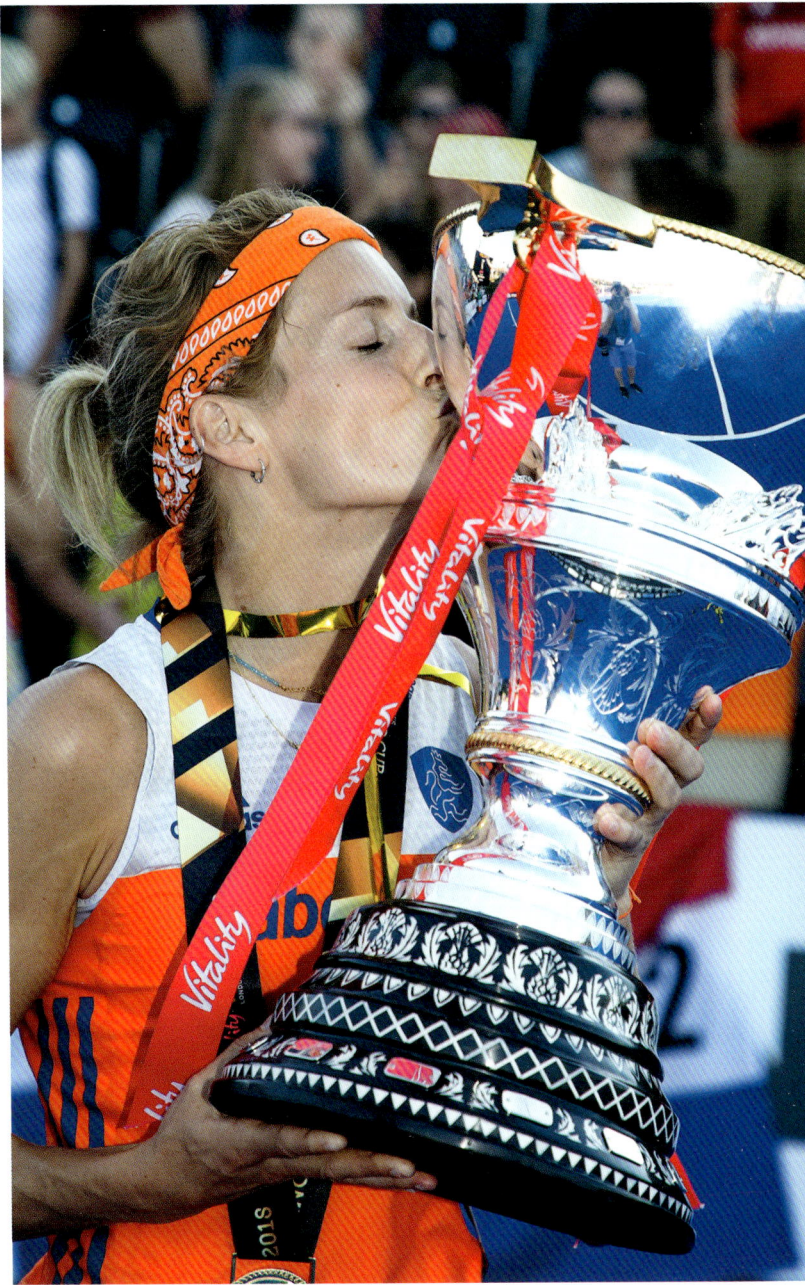

Captain's kiss: Carlien Dirkse van den Heuvel with the World Cup trophy. // *Koen Suyk*

Teams and Officials - Vitality Hockey Women's World Cup London 2018

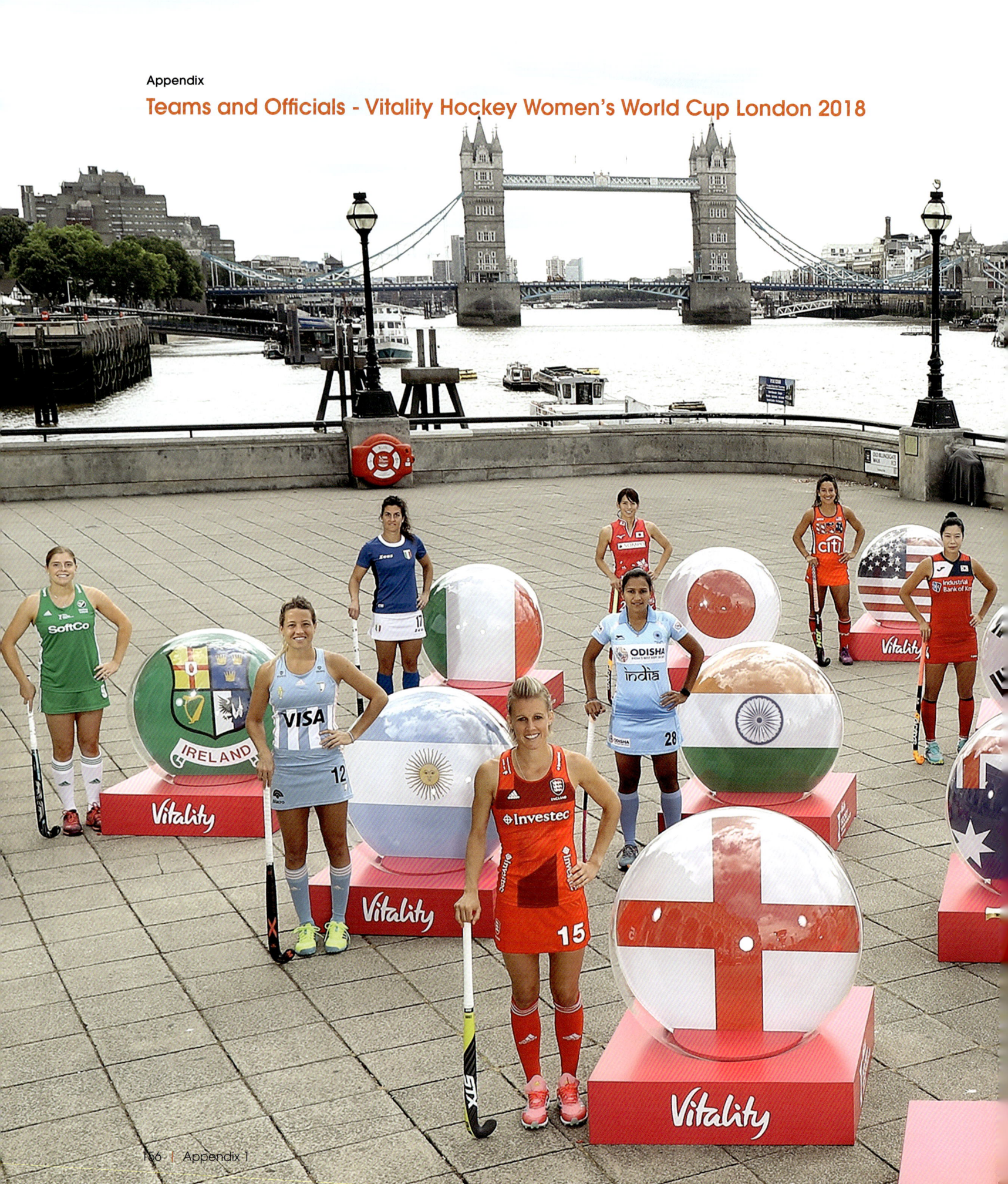

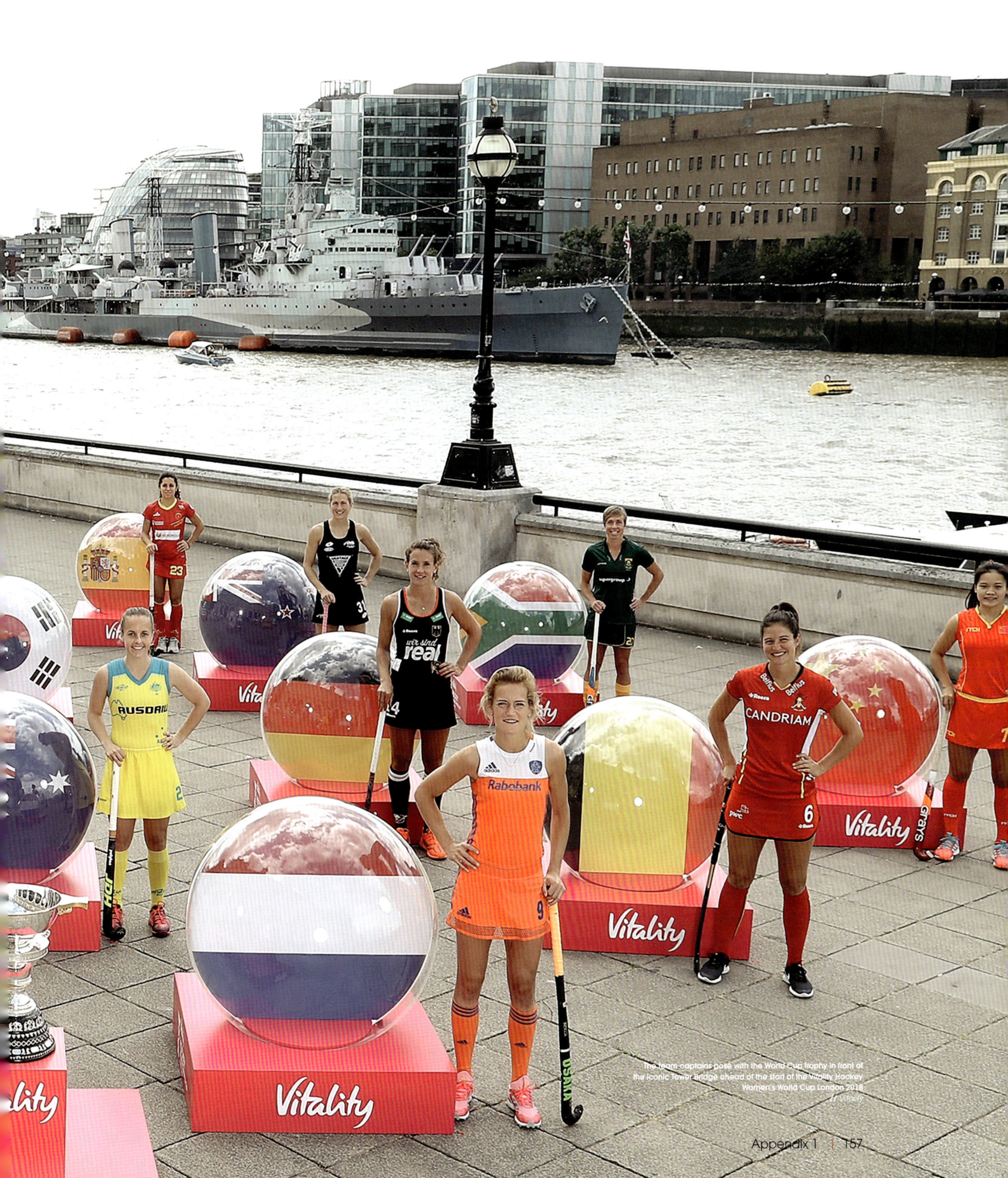

The team captains pose with the World Cup trophy in front of the iconic Tower Bridge ahead of the start of the Vitality Hockey Women's World Cup London 2018
Vitality

1.1: Teams (listed in order of final standings)

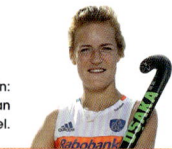

1: The Netherlands

Captain: Carlien Dirkse van den Heuvel.

Shirt	Player	Age [1]	Goals [2]	Matches [3]	Caps [4]
1	VEENENDAAL Anne (GK)	22	0	6	41
3	KOOLEN Sanne	22	0	6	15
4	van MALE Kitty	30	8	6	116
5	PHENINCKX Malou	26	1	6	62
6	LEURINK Laurien	23	3	6	68
7	de WAARD Xan	22	1	6	117
8	KEETELS Marloes	25	1	6	128
9	DIRKSE van den HEUVEL Carlien (C)	31	2	6	203
10	JONKER Kelly	28	6	6	153
12	WELTEN Lidewij	28	5	6	187
13	van MAASAKKER Caia	29	3	6	160
15	MATLA Frederique	21	4	6	45
17	van den ASSEM Ireen	28	0	6	51
20	NUNNINK Laura	23	0	6	87
21	STAM Lauren	24	0	6	53
22	KONING Josine (GK)	22	0	6	38
23	van GEFFEN Margot	28	1	6	168
24	de GOEDE Eva	29	0	6	200

Team Staff

KOOIJMAN Femke – Team Manager
JUDGE Lucas – Assistant Coach
MANENSCHIJN Albert – Assistant Coach
HOOGEWERFF Stefan – Physiotherapist/Stand-in Manager
BACKELANDT Franc – Physiotherapist/Stand-in Manager
EYLES Matthew – Physical Trainer
GILLHAUS Lars – Video Technician

ANNAN Alyson – Head Coach
ZYP Simon – Assistant Coach
van der POL Carmen – Medical Doctor

van der LAAN Doris – Physical Trainer
BITTERLING Joost – Video Technician

2: Ireland

Captain: Katie Mullan.

Shirt	Player	Age [1]	Goals [2]	Matches [3]	Caps [4]
1	O'FLANAGAN Grace (GK)	29	0	1	35
4	O'BYRNE Yvonne	26	0	6	119
8	EVANS Nicola	28	0	6	169
9	MULLAN Katie (C)	24	0	6	157
10	McCAY Shirley	30	1	6	273
11	FRAZER Megan*	27	0	5	133
12	TICE Elena	20	0	6	74
14	BEATTY Emily*	24	0	1	88
15	PINDER Gillian	26	0	6	143
18	UPTON Roisin	24	0	6	45
19	McFERRAN Ayeisha (GK)	22	0	6	79
20	WATKINS Chloe	26	0	6	200
21	COLVIN Lizzie	28	0	6	166
22	DALY Nicola	30	0	6	169
23	MATTHEWS Hannah	27	0	6	114
26	O'FLANAGAN Anna	28	2	6	114
27	WILSON Zoe	21	0	6	114
28	DUKE Deirdre	26	2	6	109
30	MEEKE Alison	27	0	6	120

Team Staff

BOYLES Arlene – Team Manager
HENDERSON Nigel – Assistant Coach
STEWART Colin – Assistant Coach
KENNA Darren – Physical Trainer
KAVANAGH Mark – Video Technician

SHAW Graham – Head Coach
GRUNDIE Gareth – Assistant Coach
MURPHY Roisin – Physiotherapist
ONGWELL Gary – Psychologist

* Emily Beatty came into the squad in place of Megan Frazer, who was withdrawn due to an injury sustained during competition.

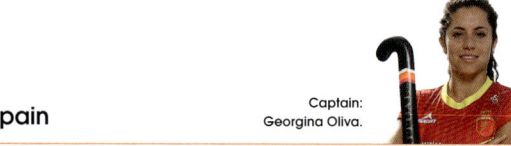

3: Spain

Captain: Georgina Oliva.

Shirt	Player	Age [1]	Goals [2]	Matches [3]	Caps [4]
1	RUIZ Maria (GK)	28	0	7	127
2	GUTIERREZ Rocio	33	0	7	151
7	PETCHAME Carlota	28	2	7	171
8	SALVATELLA Carola	24	2	7	117
9	LOPEZ Maria	28	2	7	171
10	BONASTRE Berta	26	3	7	169
11	GUINEA Cristina	25	0	7	136
12	CANO Carmen	25	1	7	56
15	GARCIA Maialen	28	0	7	90
17	RIERA Lola	27	2	7	156
18	PONS Julia	23	0	7	141
19	GARCIA Begoña	23	0	7	113
20	GINE Xantal	25	0	7	149
21	PEREZ Beatriz	27	1	7	177
23	OLIVA Georgina (C)	28	0	7	209
25	MAGAZ Alicia	24	2	7	102
29	JIMMENEZ Lucia	21	0	7	97
32	GARCIA Melanie (GK)	27	0	0	50

Team Staff

DEO Santiago – Team Leader
GOMEZ Raul – Stand-in Manager
LOCK Adrian – Head Coach
MORENCOS Esther – Assistant Coach
MORENO Berta – Physiotherapist

RUIZ Alberto – Team Manager
MONDO Andres – Stand-in Manager
WILSON Andrew – Assistant Coach
MUNOZ Silvia – Medical Doctor
CARREIRA Marco – Psychologist

4: Australia

Captain: Emily Smith.

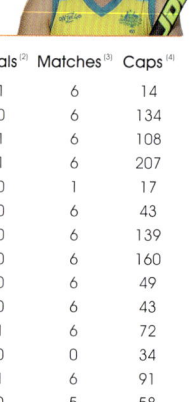

Shirt	Player	Age [1]	Goals [2]	Matches [3]	Caps [4]
2	MALONE Ambrosia	20	1	6	14
3	PERIS Brooke	25	0	6	134
4	HURTZ Emily	28	1	6	108
7	KENNY Jodie	30	1	6	207
9	BRAZEL Lily*	23	0	1	17
10	FITZPATRICK Maddy	21	0	6	43
11	McMAHON Karri	26	0	6	139
13	BONE Edwina	30	0	6	160
14	KERSHAW Stephanie	23	0	6	49
15	NOBBS Kaitlin	20	0	6	43
17	MORGAN Georgina	25	1	6	72
19	BARTRAM Jocelyn (GK)	25	0	0	34
20	SLATTERY Kathryn	24	1	6	91
21	TAYLOR Renee*	21	0	5	58
23	COMMERFORD Kalindi*	24	0	3	17
26	SMITH Emily (C)	25	1	6	206
27	LYNCH Rachael (GK)	32	0	6	188
28	BATES Kristina	22	0	6	30
30	STEWART Grace	21	0	6	54
32	FITZPATRICK Savannah*	23	0	3	31

Team Staff

GREY Melissa – Team Manager
ALLEN Katie – Team Manager
ANDREWS Stephanie – Stand-in Manager
GAUDOIN Paul – Head Coach

APPLEBY Brendyn – Physical Trainer
LOCKE Vance – Psychologist
MAGUIRE Matthew – Video Technician
BASS Tim – Physiotherapist

* Savannah Fitzpatrick and Lily Brazel came into the squad in place of Renee Taylor and Kalindi Commerford, who were withdrawn due to injuries sustained during the competition.

(1) Age at the start of the event. (2) Goals scored at the HWC2018. (3) Matches played at the HWC2018. (4) Caps at the end of the event

5: Germany

Shirt	Player	Age [1]	Goals [2]	Matches [3]	Caps [4]
3	WORTMANN Amelie	21	0	4	24
4	LORENZ Nike	21	0	4	83
5	ORUZ Selin	21	1	4	69
6	GABLAC Hannah	23	1	4	58
8	SCHRÖDER Anne	23	1	4	114
9	GRÄVE Elisa	21	0	4	43
11	MICHEEL Lena	20	0	4	14
12	STAPENHORST Charlotte	23	3	4	84
14	MÜLLER-WIELAND Janne (C)	31	0	4	277
15	KUBALSKI Nathalie (GK)	24	0	0	6
17	TESCHKE Jana	27	0	4	166
18	ALTENBURG Lisa	28	0	4	120
19	SCHAUNIG Maike	22	0	4	17
20	CIUPKA Julia (GK)	26	0	4	31
21	HAUKE Franzisca	28	0	4	150
22	PIEPER Cecile	23	0	4	91
23	MÄVERS Marie	27	0	4	196
25	HUSE Viktoria	22	3	4	27

Team Staff

KNUF Heino – Team Leader
KELLER Florian – Stand-in Manager
BOUCHOUCHI Akim – Assistant Coach
LUDWIG Dominik – Assistant Coach
STRIEGL Evi – Physiotherapist
HAUMANN Stephan – Video Technician

KEANEY Donna – Team Manager
RECKINGER Xavier – Head Coach
LEWIS James – Assistant Coach
MANDRYKA Boris – Medical Doctor
JAUBE Anne – Physiotherapist

6: England

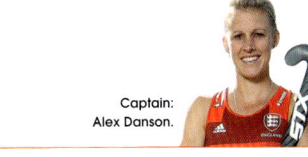

Shirt	Player	Age [1]	Goals [2]	Matches [3]	Caps [4]
1	HINCH Maddie (GK)	29	0	5	133 *(88/45)**
3	LANE Kathryn	23	0	5	12
4	UNSWORTH Laura	30	0	5	229 *(140/89)**
5	HAYCROFT Sarah	27	0	5	82 *(63/17)**
6	TOMAN Anna	25	0	5	41 *(36/5)**
7	MARTIN Hannah	23	0	5	39 *(35/4)**
9	TOWNSEND Susannah	28	0	5	140 *(88/52)**
11	PETTY Suzy	26	0	5	22 *(18/4)**
13	RAYER Elena	21	0	5	30 *(25/2)**
15	DANSON Alex (C)	33	1	5	306 *(203/103)**
18	ANSLEY Giselle	26	1	5	124 *(84/39)**
19	BRAY Sophie	28	1	5	128 *(86/42)**
20	PEARNE-WEBB Hollie	27	0	5	146 *(93/53)**
21	WATTON Ellie	29	0	5	77 *(50/27)**
23	TENNANT Amy (GK)	23	0	0	10
26	OWSLEY Lily	23	2	5	118 *(78/40)**
27	HUNTER Jo	27	0	5	38 *(33/5)**
31	BALSDON Grace	25	0	5	35 *(31/4)**

Caps for England/GBR

Team Staff

SOUYAVE Maggie – Team Manager
KERRY Danny – Head Coach
MOGHAL Moiz – Medical Doctor
LUZAR Amber – Video Technician

REVINGTON Paul – Stand-in Manager
RALPH David – Assistant Coach
BATCHELOR Emma – Physiotherapist

7: Argentina

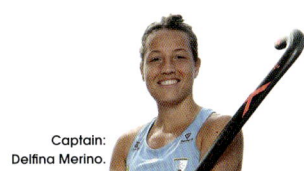

Shirt	Player	Age [1]	Goals [2]	Matches [3]	Caps [4]
1	SUCCI Belen (GK)	32	0	5	207
4	TRINCHINETTI Eugenia	21	0	5	58
5	ALONSO Agostina	22	0	5	47
6	DONATI Bianca	23	0	5	35
7	CAVALLERO Martina	28	0	5	198
10	FERNANDEZ Magdalena	23	0	5	56
12	MERINO Delfina (C)	28	2	5	271
14	HABIF Agustina	26	0	5	133
15	GRANATTO Maria	23	1	5	90
16	HABIF Florencia	24	1	5	179
17	SANCHEZ Rocio	29	0	5	227
19	ALBERTARRIO Agustina	25	1	5	127
20	von der HEYDE Lucina	21	0	5	68
26	ORTIZ Maria	21	3	5	77
27	BARRIONUEVO Noel	34	2	5	320
28	JANKUNAS Julieta	19	1	5	55
29	GOMES Julia	26	0	5	147
31	MUTIO Maria (GK)	33	0	0	64

Team Staff

CONNA Walter – Team Manager
CORRADINI Agustin – Head Coach
FEIJO Pable – Medical Doctor
PESCI Eduardo – Physical Trainer

del VALLE Carolina – Stand-in Manager
BERTHOLD Martin – Assistant Coach
FIORONI Patricia – Physiotherapist
MUÑOZ Carlos – Video Technician

8: India

Shirt	Player	Age [1]	Goals [2]	Matches [3]	Caps [4]
1	KAUR Navjot	23	0	5	138
2	KAUR Gurjit	22	0	5	60
3	EKKA Deep	24	0	5	169
4	MONIKA	24	0	5	122
6	KHOKHAR Reena	25	0	5	19
8	PRADHAN Nikki	24	0	5	74
11	SAVITA (GK)	28	0	5	174
13	ETIMARPU Rajani (GK)	28	0	0	74
16	KATARIYA Vandana	26	1	5	206
17	DEEPIKA	31	0	5	224
18	UDITA	20	0	5	20
19	TOPPO Namita	23	0	5	154
20	LALREMSIAMI	18	1	5	30
25	KAUR Naveet	22	0	5	45
26	LAKRA Sunita	27	0	5	137
28	RANI (C)	23	1	5	218
31	MINZ Lilima	24	0	5	121
32	GOYAL Neha	21	2	5	41

Team Staff

KUMAR C.R. – Team Manager
MARIJNE Sjoerd – Head Coach
SUDANE Sonika – Physiotherapist

JOHN David – Stand-in Manager
WONINK Erik – Assistant Coach
PERUMAL Amuthaprakash – Video Technician

(1) Age at the start of the event. (2) Goals scored at the HWC2018. (3) Matches played at the HWC2018. (4) Caps at the end of the event

9: Italy

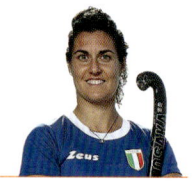

Captain:
Chiara Tiddi.

Shirt	Player	Age [1]	Goals [2]	Matches [3]	Caps [4]
2	TRAVERSO Celina	32	0	4	77
7	BRACONI Valentina	27	2	4	76
8	BIANCHI Eugenia	28	0	3	30
9	GARRAFFO Maria	24	0	4	49
10	MIRABELLA Dalila	23	0	4	106
12	CHIRICO Martina (GK)	30	0	4	92
14	PACELLA Elisabetta	24	0	4	107
15	SOCINO Maria	28	0	4	30
17	TIDDI Chiara (C)	29	1	4	148
18	CARTA Federica	18	0	3	22
20	SINGH Jasbeer	31	0	4	73
21	WYBIERALSKA Agata	40	0	4	124 *(98/26)**
22	CUSINAMO Clara (GK)	17	0	0	6
23	VYNOHRADOVA Maryna	35	0	4	15 *(9/6)***
25	RUGGIERI Giuliana	27	1	4	62
27	OVIEDO Lara	30	1	4	26 *(4/22)****
28	PESSINA Ivanna	28	0	4	20 *(10/10)****
32	CASALE Marcela	31	0	4	55

*Caps for Italy/Poland **Caps for Italy/Ukraine ***Caps for Argentina/Italy*

Team Staff

MIGNARDI Sergio – Team Leader
FIGUS Fabio – Stand-in Manager
LIVOLI Tommaso – Assistant Coach
GORJAO Margarida – Medical Doctor
MEDDA Enrico – Psychologist

FABRIZIO Luca – Team Manager
CARTA Roberto – Head Coach
MATTEI Fabrizio – Assistant Coach
BALZANI Francesca – Physiotherapist
ANGIUS Luca – Video Technician

10: Belgium

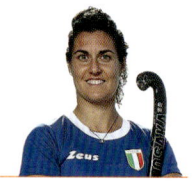

Captain:
Anouk Raes.

Shirt	Player	Age [1]	Goals [2]	Matches [3]	Caps [4]
2	LIMAUGE Sophie	20	0	4	42
3	CAVENAILE Louise	29	0	4	230
4	FOBE Aline	25	0	4	161
6	RAES Anouk (C)	29	0	4	279
7	VANDERMEIREN Judith	23	1	4	135
8	PUVREZ Emma	20	0	4	99
10	VERSAVEL Louise	23	4	4	157
11	PEETERS Joanne	22	0	4	82
13	GERNIERS Alix	25	0	4	179
15	WEYNS Anne-Sophie	23	1	4	67
17	STRUIJK Michelle	20	0	4	27
19	NELEN Barbara	26	0	4	224
21	D'HOOGHE Aisling (GK)	23	0	4	162
22	VANDEN BORRE Stephanie	20	0	4	104
23	SOTGIU Elena (GK)	23	0	0	33
25	LECLEF Pauline	23	0	4	63
26	HILLEWAERT Lien	20	0	4	42
27	BOON Jill	31	2	4	276

Team Staff

PECHE Muriel – Team Manager
THIJSSEN Niels – Head Coach
LETCHFORD Simon – Assistant Coach
BAYER Steve – Physical Trainer

AGACHE Hannes – Stand-in Manager
WIJBENGA Frank – Assistant Coach
STEURS Lien – Physiotherapist
COSMA Michael – Video Technician

11: New Zealand

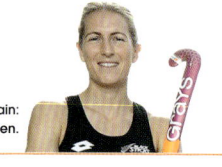

Captain:
Stacey Michelsen.

Shirt	Player	Age [1]	Goals [2]	Matches [3]	Caps [4]
1	DAVEY Tarryn	22	0	3	37
2	HARRISON Samantha	26	0	4	156
4	MERRY Olivia	26	3	4	205
5	DAVIES Frances	21	0	4	57
6	ROBINSON Amy	22	0	4	56
8	RUTHERFORD Sally (GK)	37	0	3	170
9	NEAL Brooke	26	0	4	154
12	GUNSON Ella	29	0	4	196
13	CHARLTON Samantha	26	0	4	226
15	O'HANLON Grace (GK)	25	0	1	39
16	THOMPSON Liz	23	0	4	173
24	KEDDELL Rose	24	0	4	183
25	SMITH Kelsey	23	1	4	86
28	GLOYN Shiloh	28	1	4	75
29	DOAR Madison	19	0	4	30
30	TUILOTOLAVA Louisa	22	0	3	12
31	MICHELSEN Stacey (C)	27	0	4	261
32	McLAREN Anita	30	1	4	271

Team Staff

MENEZES Jude – Team Manager
HAGER Mark – Head Coach
MEYER Jessica – Physiotherapist

DANCER Sean – Stand-in Manager
LESLIE Chris – Assistant Coach
HICKS Ian – Video Technician

12: Korea

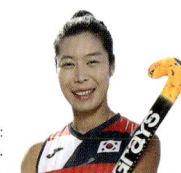

Captain:
Kim Youngran.

Shirt	Player	Age [1]	Goals [2]	Matches [3]	Caps [4]
2	CHOI Su Ji	25	0	4	7
4	KIM Youngran (C)	32	0	4	141
5	LEE Yurim	23	0	4	11
6	BAE Sora (GK)	26	0	1	7
8	AN Hyoju	30	0	4	124
10	PARK Mi Hyun	32	0	2	254
11	PARK Seunga	27	0	4	95
12	LEE Youngsil	31	0	4	116
13	CHO Eunji	28	0	4	102
14	CHO Yun Kyoung	26	0	4	80
16	CHEON Seul Ki	29	0	4	124
17	KIM Ok Ju	30	1	4	133
28	KIM Bomi	32	0	4	112
19	CHO Hyejin	23	0	4	61
21	SHIN Hyejeong	26	0	4	34
22	JANG Heesun	32	0	4	31
23	LEE Yuri	23	0	4	54
31	HWANG Hyeon A (GK)	23	0	4	9

Team Staff

HONG Kyung Suep – Team Manager
HUH Sang Young – Head Coach
KIM Jieung – Video Technician

KIM Yoon – Stand-in Manager
BAE Eun Hee – Physiotherapist

(1) Age at the start of the event. (2) Goals scored at the HWC2018. (3) Matches played at the HWC2018. (4) Caps at the end of the event

13: Japan

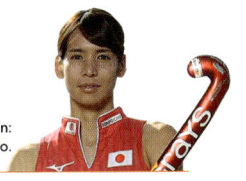

Captain:
Natsuki Naito.

Shirt	Player	Age [1]	Goals [2]	Matches [3]	Caps [4]
1	KAGEYAMA Megumi (GK)	25	0	3	44
2	NAITO Natsuki (C)	27	0	3	37
3	ONO Mayumi	33	0	3	234
5	ASAI Yu	22	0	3	50
7	NAGAI Hazuki	23	1	3	135
8	MANO Yukari	24	0	3	86
9	KATO Akiko	30	2	3	54
10	SHIMIZU Minami	25	1	3	65
11	NOMURA Kana	28	1	3	107
12	NAGAI Yuri	26	0	3	143
13	KOZUKA Miki	22	0	3	38
14	SEGAWA Maho	22	0	3	29
15	ISHIBASHI Yui	22	0	3	18
16	OIKAWA Shihori	29	1	3	106
20	KARINO Mami	22	0	3	34
22	KAWAMURA Motomi	22	1	3	59
27	YAMADA Aki	25	0	3	13
30	AKAYA Erika (GK)	27	0	1	16

Team Staff

NAKAMURA Mari – Team Manager
FARRY Anthony – Head Coach
MOGI Jun – Physiotherapist
SHEAHAN John – Stand-in Manager
MIURA Keiko – Assistant Coach
DRAKE Greg – Video Technician

14: USA

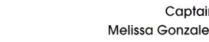

Captain:
Melissa Gonzalez.

Shirt	Player	Age [1]	Goals [2]	Matches [3]	Caps [4]
1	MATSON Erin	18	1	3	44
2	FEE Stefanie	28	0	3	114
5	GONZALEZ Melissa (C)	29	0	3	241
9	VITTESE Michelle	28	0	3	211
10	FUNK Jill	26	0	3	139
12	MAGADAN Amanda	23	0	3	43
13	HOFFMAN Ashley	21	0	3	39
14	YOUNG Julia	23	0	3	22
19	MOYER Lauren	23	0	3	40
20	FROEDE Ali	25	0	3	56
21	WOODS Nicole	22	0	3	27
22	BLAZING Lauren (GK)	25	0	0	11
23	VITTESE Tara	22	0	3	10
24	SHARKEY Kathleen	28	0	3	141
26	PAOLINO Margaux	21	2	3	12
28	van SICKLE Caitlin	28	0	3	116
29	MANLEY Alyssa	24	0	3	89
31	BRIGGS Jackie (GK)	30	0	3	184

Team Staff

MILLER Christa – Team Leader
WILLIAMSON David – Stand-in Manager
SHEDD Nick – Assistant Coach
HIGGINS David – Medical Doctor
FRY Christopher – Video Technician
LANGFORD Maren – Team Manager
SCHOPMAN Janneke – Head Coach
EDWARDS Phil – Assistant Coach
KIMURA-KOENIG Yuko – Physiotherapist

15: South Africa

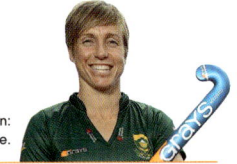

Captain:
Nicolene Terblanche.

Shirt	Player	Age [1]	Goals [2]	Matches [3]	Caps [4]
4	WALRAVEN Nicole	23	0	3	45
5	GOUWS Simone	19	0	3	4
8	PATON Kristen	21	0	3	15
10	JONES Shelley	31	0	3	276
11	BOTES Kara-Lee	28	1	3	41
12	CHAMBERLAIN Dirkie	31	0	3	225
13	DEETLEFS Lisa-Marie	30	1	3	250
16	HUNTER Erin	26	0	3	41
17	MANUEL Candice	27	0	3	61
19	du PLESSIS Lilian	25	0	3	119
20	TERBLANCHE Nicolene (C)	30	0	1	215
21	MALI Ongeziwe	19	0	3	10
24	MBANDE Phumelela (GK)	25	0	3	35
27	MAYNE Jade	29	1	3	146
28	BOBBS Quanita	24	0	3	114
29	GLASBY Tarryn	23	0	3	30
30	DAMONS Sulette (C)	28	0	3	198
31	Van TONDER Marlise (GK)	21	0	1	17

Team Staff

ELOFF Maryke – Team Manager
CERFONTEIN Kurt – Assistant Coach
SPARKS Martinique – Physical Trainer
le ROUX Jacques – Physical Trainer
ROSTRON Sheldon – Head Coach
NURGER Salmina – Physiotherapist
BAKKER Niels – Physical Trainer
HENDRICKS Wayne – Video Technician

16: China

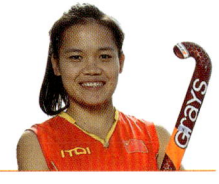

Captain:
Cui Qiuxia.

Shirt	Player	Age [1]	Goals [2]	Matches [3]	Caps [4]
2	GU Bingfeng (C)	24	0	3	55
3	SONG Xiaoming	24	0	3	24
7	CUI Qiuxia (C)	27	0	3	141
9	XU Wenyu	22	0	3	41
10	PENG Yang	26	0	3	164
12	GUO Qiu	22	0	3	39
16	OU Zixia (C)	22	0	3	66
17	YONG Jing	24	1	3	23
19	ZHANG Xiaoxue	25	1	3	110
20	HE Jiangxin	20	0	3	14
21	LIU Meng	22	0	3	28
22	CHEN Yi (GK)	19	0	0	10
24	WANG Shumin	24	0	3	23
26	CHEN Yang	21	0	3	45
27	TU Yidan	21	0	3	39
28	WU Qiong	29	0	3	49
31	ZHONG Jiaqi	18	0	3	27
32	YE Jiao (GK)	23	0	3	40

Team Staff

WALTER Julia – Team Manager
MÜLDERS Jamilon – Head Coach
FIEBER Lukas – Assistant Coach
Li TIANZUO – Medical Doctor
HUO Kelin – Video Technician
BOCKHORST Tillmann – Stand-in Manager
GARCIA Carlos – Assistant Coach
HUANG Yongsheng – Assistant Coach
GEITER Anna – Physiotherapist

(1) Age at the start of the event. (2) Goals scored at the HWC2018. (3) Matches played at the HWC2018. (4) Caps at the end of the event

1.2: Competition Officials

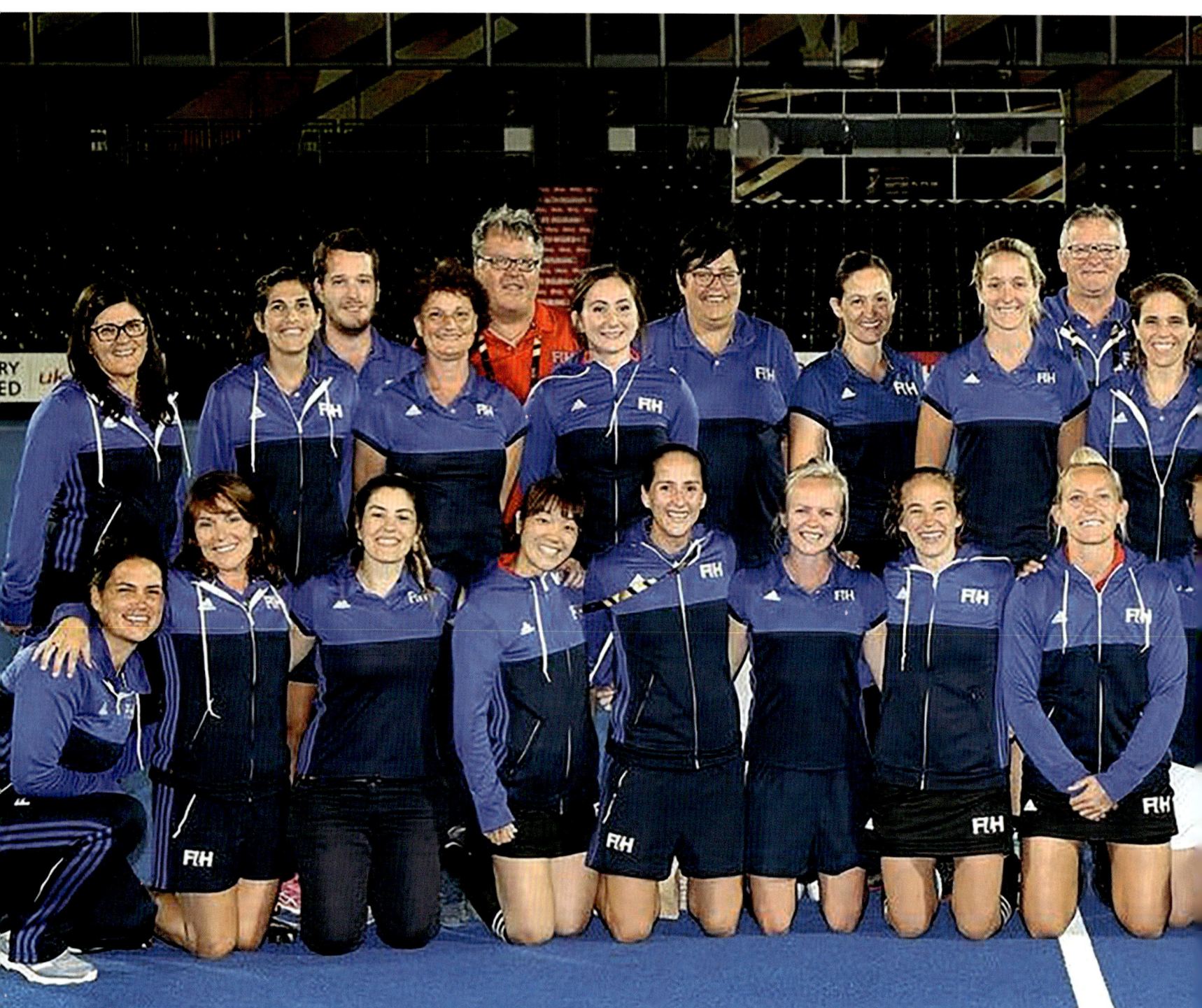

The competition officials for the Vitality Hockey Women's World Cup London 2018. // *Submitted*

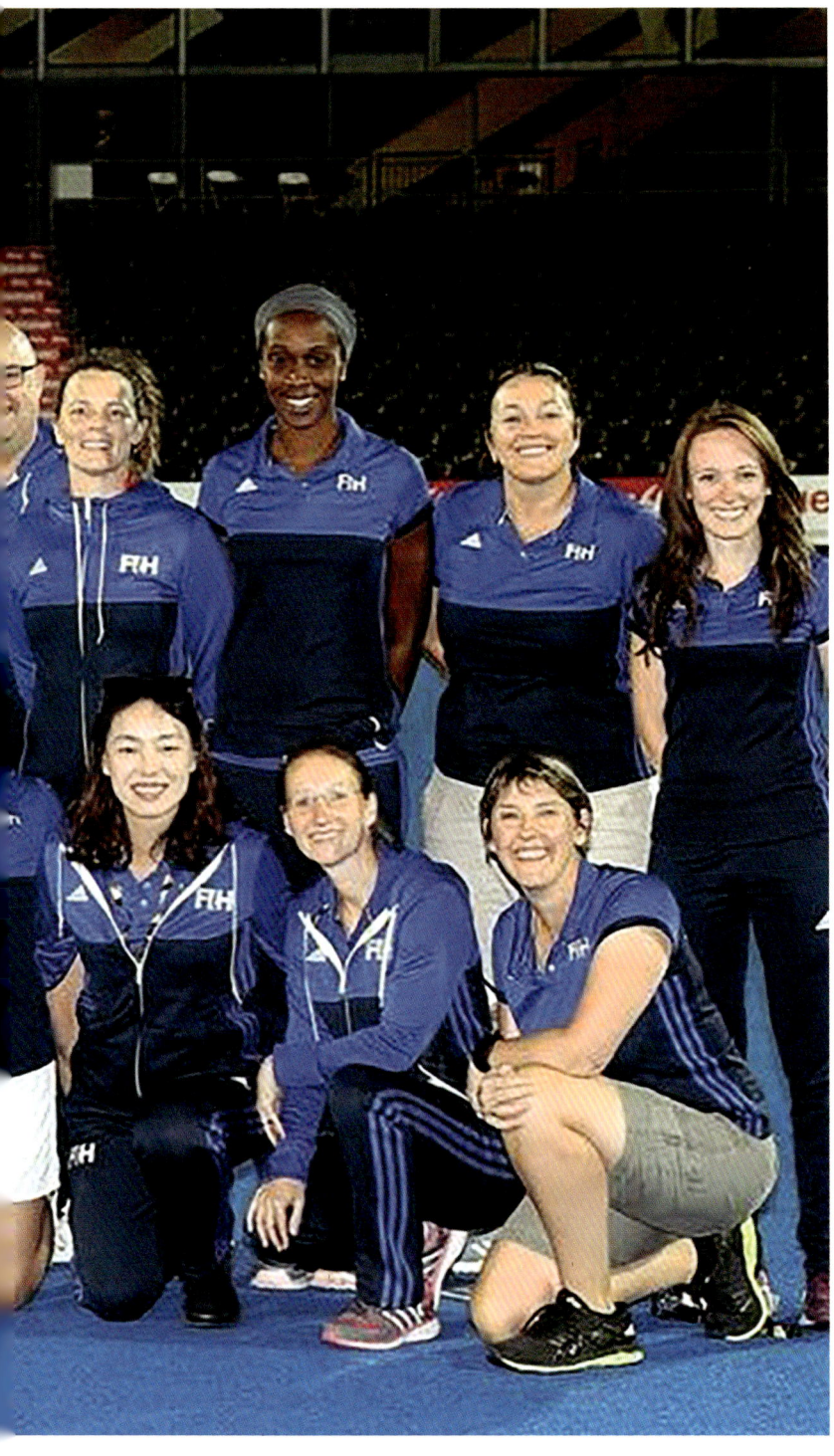

Tammy Standley (AUS) Technical Delegate
Elisabeth Fuerst (AUT) Technical Official
Gavin Hawke (NZL) Technical Official
Lorena Rinaldini (ARG) Technical Official
Sam Stickland (ENG) Technical Official
Marie van Rensburg (RSA) Technical Official
Rene Zelkin (USA) Technical Official
Dr Leigh Gordon (RSA) FIH Medical Officer
Marelize de Klerk (RSA) Umpires Manager
Ray O'Connor (IRL) Umpires Manager
Amber Church (NZL) Umpire
Carolina de la Fuente (ARG) Umpire
Laurine Delforge (BEL) Umpire

Maggie Giddens (USA) Umpire
Kelly Hudson (NZL) Umpire
Michelle Joubert (RSA) Umpire
Alison Keogh (IRL) Umpire
Liu Xiaoying (CHN) Umpire
Ayanna McClean (TTO) Umpire
Michelle Meister (ARG) Umpire
Alesha Neumann (AUS) Umpire
Irene Presenqui (ARG) Umpire
Annelize Rostron (RSA) Umpire
Sarah Wilson (SCO) Umpire
Emi Yamada (JPN) Umpire
Carol Metchette (IRL) Video Umpire Coach

Official Results and Statistics
Vitality Hockey Women's World Cup London 2018

2.1: Results and Tables

Pool A

22 July 2018

China	0-3	Italy
		Valentina Braconi 17m FG
		Lara Oviedo 32m PC
		Giuliana Ruggieri 45m FG

Netherlands	7-0	Korea
Frederique Matla 1m FG, 11m FG		
Lidewij Welten 4m FG		
Kitty van Male 9m FG, 23m FG		
Kelly Jonker 14m FG		
Laurien Leurink 17m FG		

27 July 2018

China	1-7	Netherlands
Yong Jing 57m FG		Caia van Maasakker 13m PC
		Kelly Jonker 15m FG
		Laurien Leurink 24m FG
		Lidewij Welten 30m FG, 37m FG
		Kitty van Male 56m FG
		Xan de Waard 59m FG

Korea	0-1	Italy
		Valentina Braconi 60m FG

29 July 2018

Korea	1-1	China
Kim Ok Ju 15m FG		Zhang Xiaoxue 4m FG

Netherlands	12-1	Italy
Frederique Matla 10m FG, 44m PC		Chiara Tiddi 17m PC
Caia van Maasakker 13m PC		
Kelly Jonker 22m FG, 51m FG		
Margot van Geffen 26m PC		
Kitty van Male 28m FG, 41m PC, 48m FG, 60m FG		
Carlien Dirkse van den Heuvel 31m PC, 45m FG		

Pool A – Final Standings

Pos	Team	Pld	W	D	L	GF	GA	GD	Pts	Qualification
1	Netherlands	3	3	0	0	26	2	24	9	Quarter-finals
2	Italy	3	2	0	1	5	12	-7	6	Quarter-final play-offs
3	Korea	3	0	1	2	1	9	-8	1	Quarter-final play-offs
4	China	3	0	1	2	2	11	-9	1	Eliminated

Points awarded for Win: 3, Draw: 1, Loss: 0

Pool B

21 July 2018

England	1-1	India
Lily Owsley 54m PC		Neha Goyal 25m FG

USA	1-3	Ireland
Margaux Paolino 15m PC		Deirdre Duke 5m FG, 41m FG
		Shirley McCay 12m PC

25 July 2018

USA	1-1	England
Erin Matson 39m FG		Alex Danson 34m FG

26 July 2018

India	0-1	Ireland
		Anna O'Flanagan 13m PC

29 July 2018

India	1-1	USA
Rani 31m PC		Margaux Paolino 11m FGG

England	1-0	Ireland
Giselle Ansley 53m PC		

Pool B – Final Standings

Pos	Team	Pld	W	D	L	GF	GA	GD	Pts	Qualification
1	Ireland	3	2	0	1	4	2	2	6	Quarter-finals
2	England	3	1	2	0	3	2	1	5	Quarter-final play-offs
3	India	3	0	2	1	2	3	-1	2	Quarter-final play-offs
4	USA	3	0	2	1	3	5	-2	2	Eliminated

Points awarded for Win: 3, Draw: 1, Loss: 0

Pool C

21 July 2018

Germany   **3-1**   **South Africa**
Viktoria Huse 14m FG, 54m PS   Lisa-Marie Deetlefs 40m PC
Charlotte Stapenhorst 32m FG

22 July 2018

Argentina   **6-2**   **Spain**
Julieta Jankunas 8m PC   Carola Salvatella 3m FG
Maria Ortiz 15m FG, 28m FG   Beatriz Perez 49m PC
Agustina Albertarrio 22m FG
Delfina Merino 31m FG
Noel Barrionuevo 48m PS

25 July 2018

Germany   **3-2**   **Argentina**
Hannah Gablac 6m FG   Florencia Habif 16m PC
Charlotte Stapenhorst 20m FG, 25m FG   Maria Ortiz 30m FG

26 July 2018

Spain   **7-1**   **South Africa**
Lola Riera 2m PC, 48m PC   Kara-Lee Botes 35m PC
Berta Bonastre 10m FG, 55m PC
Carlota Petchame 37m FG, 42m FG
Carola Salvatella 45m FG

28 July 2018

Spain   **1-3**   **Germany**
Maria Lopez 30m PC   Anne Schröder 5m PC
   Selin Oruz 37m FG
   Viktoria Huse 40m PC

Argentina   **1-1**   **South Africa**
Maria Granatto 47m FG   Jade Mayne 30m FG

Pool C – Final Standings

Pos	Team	Pld	W	D	L	GF	GA	GD	Pts	Qualification
1	Germany	3	3	0	0	9	4	5	9	Quarter-finals
2	Argentina	3	1	1	1	9	6	3	4	Quarter-final play-offs
3	Spain	3	1	0	2	10	10	0	3	Quarter-final play-offs
4	South Africa	3	0	1	2	3	11	-8	1	Eliminated

Points awarded for Win: 3, Draw: 1, Loss: 0

Pool D

21 July 2018

Australia   **3-2**   **Japan**
Ambrosia Malone 17m PC   Motomi Kawamura 36m FG
Emily Hurtz 22m FG   Akiko Kato 60m FG
Jodie Kenny 35m PC

22 July 2018

New Zealand   **4-2**   **Belgium**
Kelsey Smith 24m PC   Louise Versavel 28m FG
Shiloh Gloyn 32m PC   Jill Boon 30m FG
Olivia Merry 32m FG, 54 PS

24 July 2018

Japan   **2-1**   **New Zealand**
Shihori Oikawa 35m PC   Anita McLaren 52m PS
Minami Shimizu 48m FG

Australia   **0-0**   **Belgium**

28 July 2018

Japan   **3-6**   **Belgium**
Akiko Kato 36m PC   Judith Vandermeiren 7m PC
Kana Nomura 50m PC   Jill Boon 17m FG
Hazuki Nagai 57m PC   Anne-Sophie Weyns 22m FG
   Louise Versavel 33m FG,
   39m FG, 47m FG

New Zealand   **1-1**   **Australia**
Olivia Merry 13m FG   Emily Smith 18m FG

Pool D – Final Standings

Pos	Team	Pld	W	D	L	GF	GA	GD	Pts	Qualification
1	Australia	3	1	2	0	4	3	1	5	Quarter-finals
2	Belgium	3	1	1	1	8	7	1	4	Quarter-final play-offs
3	New Zealand	3	1	1	1	6	5	1	4	Quarter-final play-offs
4	Japan	3	1	0	2	7	10	-3	3	Eliminated

Points awarded for Win: 3, Draw: 1, Loss: 0

Cross-over Play-off Matches

30 July 2018
2nd Pool D v 3rd Pool C

Belgium   **0-0**   Italy

Shoot-out   2-3

Jill Boon – No Goal   Begoña Garcia – No Goal
Louise Versavel – Goal   Beatriz Perez – Goal (PS – Lola Riera)
Stephanie Vanden Borre – No Goal   Alicia Magaz – No Goal
Anouk Raes – No Goal   Berta Bonastre – Goal
Pauline Leclef – Goal   Lola Riera – No Goal

Sudden Death
Louise Versavel – No Goal   Beatriz Perez - Goal

_____

30 July 2018
2nd Pool C v 3rd Pool D

Argentina   **2-0**   Italy
Noel Barrionuevo 25m PS
Delfina Merino 49m PC

_____

31 July 2018
2nd Pool A v 3rd Pool B

Italy   **0-3**   **India**
                               Lalremsiami 20m FG
                               Neha Goyal 45+m PC
                               Vandana Katariya 55m PC

_____

31 July 2018
2nd Pool B v 3rd Pool A

England   **2-0**   Korea
Sophie Bray 9m FG
Lily Owsley 59m FG

....

Quarter-finals - 1 August 2018

Germany   **0-1**   **Spain**
                               Carman Cano 54m FG

Australia   **0-0**   **Argentina**

Shoot-out   4-3

Brooke Peris – No Goal   Delfina Merino – No Goal
Kristina Bates – Goal   Lucina von der Heyde – Goal
Maddy Fitzpatrick – No Goal   Agustina Albertarrio – Goal
Ambrosia Malone – Goal   Julia Gomes – Goal
Jodie Kenny – Goal (PS – Karri McMahon) Magdalena Fernandez – No Goal

Sudden Death
Kristina Bates – No Goal   Agustina Albertarrio – No Goal
Brooke Peris – Goal   Delfina Merino – No Goal

Quarter-finals – 2 August 2018

Ireland   **0-0**   **India**

Shoot-out   3-1

Nicola Daly – No Goal   Rani – No Goal
Anna O'Flanagan – No Goal   Monika – No Goal
Roisin Upton – Goal   Navjot Kaur – No Goal
Alison Meeke – Goal   Reena Khokhar – Goal
Chloe Watkins – Goal

Netherlands   **2-0**   **England**
Lidewij Welten 14m FG
Laurien Leurink 31m FG

_____

Semi-finals – 4 August 2018

Ireland   **1-1**   **Spain**
Anna O'Flanagan 3m PC   Alicia Magaz 39m FG

Shoot-out   3-2

Gillian Pinder – Goal   Begoña Garcia – No Goal
Anna O'Flanagan – No Goal   Beatriz Perez – No Goal
Roisin Upton – No Goal   Georgina Oliva – Goal
Alison Meeke – No Goal   Carlota Petchame – No Goal
Chloe Watkins – Goal   Lola Riera – Goal

Sudden Death
Gillian Pinder – Goal   Georgina Oliva – No Goal

Netherlands   **1-1**   **Australia**
Kelly Jonker 22m FG   Georgina Morgan 54m PC

Shoot-out   3-1

Frederique Matla – Goal   Kristina Bates – Goal
Carlien Dirkse van den Heuvel – No Goal Brooke Peris – No Goal
Margot van Geffen – No Goal   Kaitlin Nobbs – No Goal
Xan de Waard – Goal   Karri McMahon – No Goal
Lidewij Welten – Goal

_____

Bronze - 5 August 2018

Australia   **1-3**   **Spain**
Kathryn Slattery 40m FG   Maria Lopez 11m PC
                               Berta Bonastre 14m FG
                               Alicia Magaz 51m FG

_____

Gold – 5 August 2018

Netherlands   **6-0**   **Ireland**
Lidewij Welten 7m FG
Kelly Jonker 19m FG
Kitty van Male 28m PC
Malou Pheninckx 30m FG
Marloes Keetels 32m FG
Caia van Maasakker 34m PC

2.2: Final Standings
(FIH Hero World Ranking at Time of Competition)

1: **Netherlands** *(1)*

2: **Ireland** *(16)*

3: **Spain** *(11)*

4: **Australia** *(5)*

5: **Germany** *(6)*

6: **England** *(2)*

7: **Argentina** *(3)*

8: **India** *(10)*

9: **Italy** *(17)*

10: **Belgium** *(13)*

11: **New Zealand** *(4)*

12: **Korea** *(9)*

13: **Japan** *(12)*

14: **USA** *(7)*

15: **South Africa** *(14)*

16: **China** *(8)*

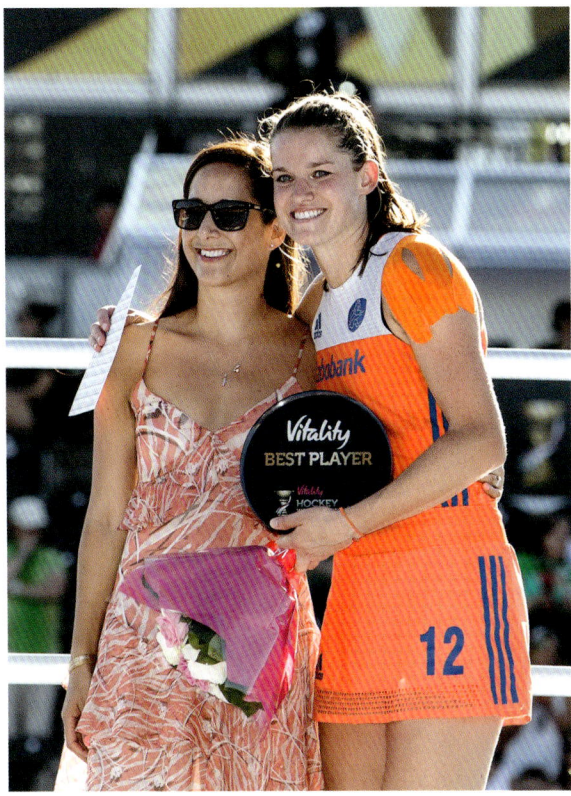

Lidewij Welten being presented with the Vitality Best Player award by Kelly Thomas, Head of Marketing at Vitality UK. *// Koen Suyk.*

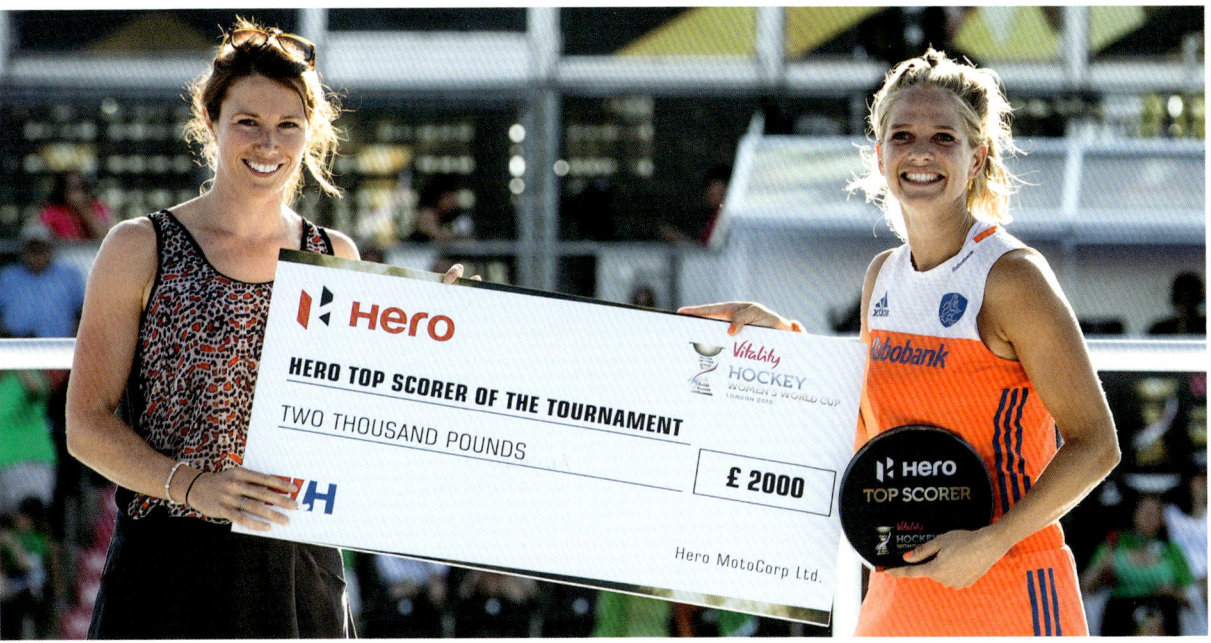

Netherlands' Kitty van Male scored eight goals to take the Hero Top Scorer award, which was presented by Annie Panter, co-chair of the FIH Athletes' Committee. *// Koen Suyk.*

2.3: Individual Award Winners

Vitality Best Player: **Lidewij Welten** (NED)

Best Goalkeeper: **Ayeisha McFerran** (IRL)

Best Young Player: **Lucina von der Heyde** (ARG)

Hero Top Scorer: **Kitty van Male** (NED – 8 goals)

2.4: Top Scorers

Player	Team	FG	PC	PS	Goals
van MALE Kitty	Netherlands	6	2	0	8
JONKER Kelly	Netherlands	6	0	0	6
WELTEN Lidewij	Netherlands	5	0	0	5
MATLA Frederique	Netherlands	3	1	0	4
VERSAVEL Louise	Belgium	3	1	0	4
BONASTRE Berta	Spain	2	1	0	3
HUSE Viktoria	Germany	1	1	1	3
LEURINK Laurien	Netherlands	3	0	0	3
MERRY Olivia	New Zealand	2	0	1	3
ORTIZ Maria	Argentina	3	0	0	3
STAPENHORST Charlotte	Germany	3	0	0	3
van MAASAKKER Caia	Netherlands	0	3	0	3
BARRIONUEVO Noel	Argentina	0	0	2	2
BOON Jill	Belgium	2	0	0	2
BRACONI Valentina	Italy	2	0	0	2
DIRKSE van den HEUVEL Carlien	Netherlands	1	1	0	2
DUKE Deirdre	Ireland	2	0	0	2
GOYAL Neha	India	1	1	0	2
KATO Akiko	Japan	1	1	0	2
LOPEZ Maria	Spain	0	2	0	2
MAGAZ Alicia	Spain	2	0	0	2
MERINO Delfina	Argentina	1	1	0	2
O'FLANAGAN Anna	Ireland	0	2	0	2
OWSLEY Lily	England	1	1	0	2
PAOLINO Margaux	USA	1	1	0	2
PETCHAME Carlota	Spain	2	0	0	2
RIERA Lola	Spain	0	2	0	2
SALVATELLA Carola	Spain	2	0	0	2
ALBERTARRIO Agustina	Argentina	1	0	0	1
ANSLEY Giselle	England	0	1	0	1
BOTES Kara-Lee	South Africa	0	1	0	1
BRAY Sophie	England	1	0	0	1
CANO Carmen	Spain	1	0	0	1
DANSON Alex	England	1	0	0	1
de WAARD Xan	Netherlands	1	0	0	1
DEETLEFS Lisa-Marie	South Africa	0	1	0	1
GABLAC Hannah	Germany	1	0	0	1

Name	Country	FG	PC	PS	Total
GLOYN Shiloh	New Zealand	0	1	0	1
GRANATTO Maria	Argentina	1	0	0	1
HABIF Florencia	Argentina	0	1	0	1
HURTZ Emily	Australia	1	0	0	1
JANKUNAS Julieta	Argentina	0	1	0	1
KATARIYA Vandana	India	0	1	0	1
KAWAMURA Motomi	Japan	1	0	0	1
KEETELS Marloes	Netherlands	1	0	0	1
KENNY Jodie	Australia	0	1	0	1
KIM Ok Ju	Korea	1	0	0	1
LALREMSIAMI	India	1	0	0	1
MALONE Ambrosia	Australia	0	1	0	1
MATSON Erin	USA	1	0	0	1
MAYNE Jade	South Africa	1	0	0	1
McCAY Shirley	Ireland	0	1	0	1
McLAREN Anita	New Zealand	0	0	1	1
MORGAN Georgina	Australia	0	1	0	1
NAGAI Hazuki	Japan	0	1	0	1
NOMURA Kana	Japan	0	1	0	1
OIKAWA Shihori	Japan	0	1	0	1
ORUZ Selin	Germany	1	0	0	1
OVIEDO Lara	Italy	0	1	0	1
PEREZ Beatriz	Spain	0	1	0	1
PHENINCKX Malou	Netherlands	1	0	0	1
RANI	India	0	1	0	1
RUGGIERI Giuliana	Italy	1	0	0	1
SCHRÖDER Anne	Germany	0	1	0	1
SHIMIZU Minami	Japan	1	0	0	1
SLATTERY Kathryn	Australia	1	0	0	1
SMITH Emily	Australia	1	0	0	1
SMITH Kelsey	New Zealand	0	1	0	1
TIDDI Chiara	Italy	0	1	0	1
van GEFFEN Margot	Netherlands	0	1	0	1
VANDERMEIREN Judith	Belgium	0	1	0	1
WEYNS Anne-Sophie	Belgium	1	0	0	1
YONG Jing	China	1	0	0	1
ZHANG Xiaoxue	China	1	0	0	1
Totals		**78**	**43**	**5**	**126**

Legend: FG – Field Goal, PC – Penalty Corner, PS – Penalty Stroke

Historical Results and Statistics
Vitality Hockey Women's World Cup London 2018

Note: while global gatherings of elite women's hockey teams have been taking place since 1933, thanks to the wonderful events organised by the International Federation of Women's Hockey Associations (IFWHA), the information detailed in Appendix 3 covers the competitions recognised by the International Hockey Federation (FIH) as official women's hockey World Cups. The authors wish to place on record their thanks to renowned hockey statistician B.G. Joshi for taking the time to verify these statistics and for supplying us with the details in appendix 3.6.

3.1: Snapshot Summary

Number of editions: 14

Number of teams participated: 27 – Argentina, Australia, Austria, Belgium, Canada, Czechoslovakia, China, England, France, Germany (including West Germany), India, Ireland, Italy, Japan, Korea, Mexico, Netherlands, New Zealand, Nigeria, Russia (including the USSR), Scotland, South Africa, Spain, Switzerland, Ukraine, USA, Wales.

Most titles: 8 – Netherlands

Most podium finishes: 13 – Netherlands (8 gold, 4 silver, 1 bronze)

Previous winners

Netherlands: 8 – 1974, 1978, 1983, 1986, 1990, 2006, 2014, 2018

Argentina: 2 – 2002, 2010

Australia: 2 – 1994, 1998

Germany*: 2 – 1976, 1981 *As West Germany

3.2: Medal-Winning Nations

Edition	Venue	Gold	Silver	Bronze
2018	London (ENG)	Netherlands	Ireland	Spain
2014	The Hague (NED)	Netherlands	Australia	Argentina
2010	Rosario (ARG)	Argentina	Netherlands	England
2006	Madrid (ESP)	Netherlands	Australia	Argentina
2002	Perth (AUS)	Argentina	Netherlands	China
1998	Utrecht (NED)	Australia	Netherlands	Germany
1994	Dublin (IRL)	Australia	Argentina	USA
1990	Sydney (AUS)	Netherlands	Australia	Korea
1986	Amstelveen (NED)	Netherlands	West Germany	Canada
1983	Kuala Lumpur (MAS)	Netherlands	Canada	Australia
1981	Buenos Aires (ARG)	West Germany	Netherlands	Soviet Union
1978	Madrid (ESP)	Netherlands	West Germany	Argentina / Belgium*
1976	West Berlin (FRG)	West Germany	Argentina	Netherlands
1974	Mandelieu (FRA)	Netherlands	Argentina	West Germany

*Argentina and Belgium shared the bronze medal at the 1978 World Cup.

3.3: All-Time Women's Hockey World Cup Placements

London 2018: 1: Netherlands, 2: Ireland, 3: Spain, 4: Australia, 5: Germany, 6: England, 7: Argentina, 8: India, 9: Italy, 10: Belgium, 11: New Zealand, 12: Korea, 13: Japan, 14: USA, 15: South Africa, 16: China

The Hague 2014: 1: Netherlands, 2: Australia, 3: Argentina, 4: USA, 5: New Zealand, 6: China, 7: Korea, 8: Germany, 9: South Africa, 10: Japan, 11: England, 12: Belgium

Rosario 2010: 1: Argentina, 2: Netherlands, 3: England, 4: Germany, 5: Australia, 6: Korea, 7: New Zealand, 8: China, 9: India, 10: South Africa, 11: Japan, 12: Spain

Madrid 2006: 1: Netherlands, 2: Australia, 3: Argentina, 4: Spain, 5: Japan, 6: USA, 7: England, 8: Germany, 9: Korea, 10: China, 11: India, 12: South Africa

Perth 2002: 1: Argentina, 2: Netherlands, 3: China, 4: Australia, 5: England, 6: Korea, 7: Germany, 8: Spain, 9: USA, 10: Japan, 11: New Zealand, 12: Scotland, 13: South Africa, 14: Ukraine, 15: Ireland, 16: Russia

Utrecht 1998: 1: Australia, 2: Netherlands, 3: Germany, 4: Argentina, 5: Korea, 6: New Zealand, 7: South Africa, 8: USA, 9: England, 10: Scotland, 11: China, 12: India

Dublin 1994: 1: Australia, 2: Argentina, 3: USA, 4: Germany, 5: Korea, 6: Netherlands, 7: China, 8: Spain, 9: England, 10: Canada, 11: Ireland, 12: Russia

Sydney 1990: 1: Netherlands, 2: Australia, 3: Korea, 4: England, 5: Spain, 6: China, 7: New Zealand, 8: West Germany, 9: Argentina, 10: Canada, 11: Japan, 12: USA

Amstelveen 1986: 1: Netherlands, 2: West Germany, 3: Canada, 4: New Zealand, 5: England, 6: Australia, 7: Argentina, 8: Soviet Union, 9: USA, 10: Scotland, 11: Spain, 12: Ireland

Kuala Lumpur 1983: 1: Netherlands, 2: Canada, 3: Australia, 4: West Germany, 5: England, 6: USA, 7: New Zealand, 8: Scotland, 9: Argentina, 10: Soviet Union, 11: India, 12: Wales

Buenos Aires 1981: 1: West Germany, 2: Netherlands, 3: Soviet Union, 4: Australia, 5: Canada, 6: Argentina, 7: Japan, 8: Belgium, 9: France, 10, Spain, 11: Mexico, 12: Austria

Madrid 1978: 1: Netherlands, 2: West Germany, 3*: Belgium, 3*: Argentina, 5: Canada, 6: Japan, 7: India, 8: Spain, 9: Czechoslovakia, 10: Nigeria

West Berlin 1976: 1: West Germany, 2: Netherlands, 3: Argentina, 4: France, 5: Spain, 6: Belgium, 7: Austria, 8: Italy, 9: Switzerland, 10: Mexico, 11: Nigeria

Mandelieu 1974: 1: Netherlands, 2: Argentina, 3: West Germany, 4: India, 5: Belgium, 6: France, 7: Spain, 8: Austria, 9: Switzerland, 10: Mexico

*Argentina and Belgium shared the bronze medal at the 1978 World Cup.

3.4: All-Time Women's Hockey World Cup Medallists by Team

Country	Gold	Silver	Bronze	Total
Netherlands	8	4	1	13
Argentina	2	3	3**	8
Australia	2	3	1	6
Germany*	2	2	2	6
Canada	0	1	1	2
Ireland	0	1	0	1
Belgium	0	0	1**	1
China	0	0	1	1
England	0	0	1	1
Korea	0	0	1	1
Soviet Union	0	0	1	1
Spain	0	0	1	1
USA	0	0	1	1
Total	**14**	**14**	**15**	**43**

*includes West Germany

** Argentina and Belgium shared the bronze medal at the 1978 World Cup

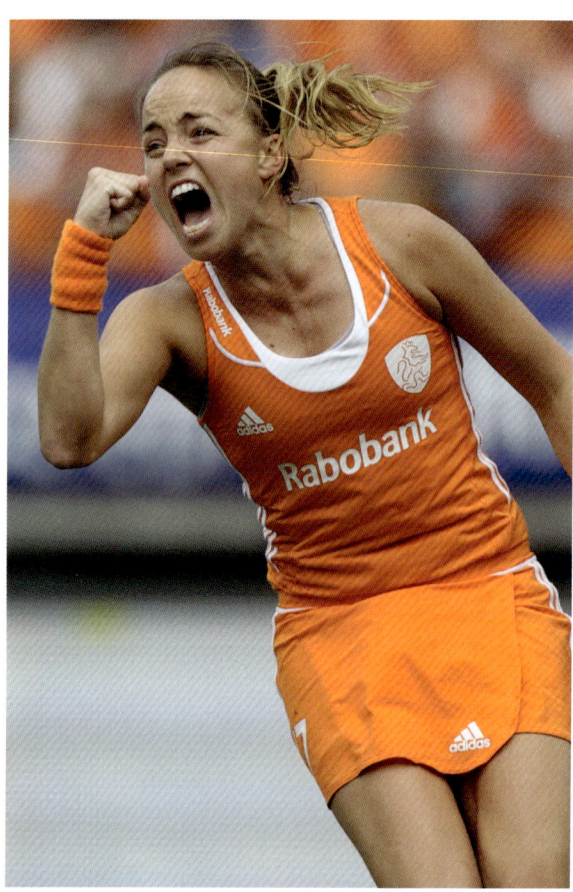

Netherlands captain Maartje Paumen celebrates scoring against Australia in the final of the Rabobank Hockey World Cup 2014. // *Frank Uijlenbroek*

3.5: All-Time Women's Hockey Cup Medal Matches

London 2018
Gold / Silver: Netherlands 6-0 Ireland
Bronze: Australia 1-3 Spain

The Hague 2014
Gold / Silver: Netherlands 2-0 Australia
Bronze: Argentina 2-1 USA

Rosario 2010
Gold / Silver: Netherlands 1-3 Argentina
Bronze: England 2-0 Germany

Madrid 2006
Gold / Silver: Netherlands 3-1 Australia
Bronze: Argentina 5-0 Spain

Perth 2002
Gold / Silver: Argentina 1-1 Netherlands (aps: 4-3)
Bronze: China 2-0 Australia

Utrecht 1998
Gold / Silver: Netherlands 2-3 Australia
Bronze: Germany 3-2 Argentina

Dublin 1994
Gold / Silver: Argentina 0-2 Australia
Bronze: USA 2-1 Germany

Sydney 1990
Gold / Silver: Netherlands 3-1 Australia
Bronze: Korea 3-2 England

Amstelveen 1986
Gold / Silver: Netherlands 3-0 West Germany
Bronze: Canada 3-2 New Zealand (aet)

Kuala Lumpur 1983
Gold / Silver: Netherlands 4-2 Canada
Bronze: Australia 3-1 West Germany

Buenos Aires 1981
Gold / Silver: West Germany 1-1 Netherlands (aps: 3-1)
Bronze: Soviet Union 5-1 Australia

Madrid 1978
Gold / Silver: Netherlands 1-0 West Germany
Bronze: Belgium 0-0 Argentina*

West Berlin 1976
Gold / Silver: West Germany 2-0 Argentina
Bronze: Netherlands 1-0 Belgium

Mandelieu 1974
Gold / Silver: Netherlands 1-0 Argentina (aet)
Bronze: West Germany 2-0 India

Legend: aps – after penalty strokes; aet – after extra time; aso – after shoot-out

* Bronze medal shared.

3.6: Record Breakers at the Vitality Hockey Women's World Cup London 2018
Kindly supplied by hockey statistician B.G. Joshi (Sehore-Bhopal, India).

Most goals by a single team in an FIH Women's Hockey World Cup: Title winners Netherlands scored 35 goals in the Vitality Hockey Women's World Cup London 2018, breaking the record for the highest tally scored by a single team in a women's hockey World Cup. The previous record was also set by Netherlands, having netted 28 goals at the 1981 World Cup in Buenos Aires, Argentina.

Biggest win: the Netherlands' 12-1 victory over Italy in the pool phase set a new record for biggest win in a women's hockey World Cup, surpassing West Germany's 10-1 triumph over Nigeria at the 1978 event in Madrid. Spain were also record breakers in London, with the 7-1 victory over Spain breaking their previous biggest women's hockey World Cup wins of 5-0, a scoreline they achieved against Mexico in 1974 (Mandelieu) and Nigeria in 1976 (West Berlin).

One that got away (just): Frederique Matla needed just 20 seconds to find the target for the Netherlands in their Pool A clash against Korea on 22 July 2018. Remarkably, it was only the second-fastest goal in the history of the women's hockey World Cup. Kim Jong Eun's strike for Korea against England at the 2010 World Cup in Rosario, Argentina was clocked at 14 seconds. The top three can be found below.

Date	Venue	Player	Team	Opponent	Time in seconds
3 Sept 2010	Rosario (ARG)	Kim Jong Eun	Korea	England	14
22 July 2018	London (ENG)	Frederique Matla	Netherlands	Korea	20
6 Dec 2002	Perth (AUS)	Pietie Coetzee	South Africa	Russia	59

3.6: All-Time Medal-Winning Squads – Women's Hockey World Cup

London 2018
Gold – Netherlands: VAN den ASSEM Ireen, DIRKSE van den HEUVEL Carlien (C), van GEFFEN Margot, de GOEDE Eva, JONKER Kelly, KEETELS Marloes, KONING Josine (GK), KOOLEN Sanne, LEURINK Laurien, van MAASAKKER Caia, van MALE Kitty, MATLA Frederique, NUNNINK Laura, PHENINCKX Malou, STAM Lauren, VEENENDAAL Anne (GK), de WAARD Xan, WELTEN Lidewij.

Silver – Ireland: BEATTY Emily, COLVIN Lizzie, DALY Nicola, DUKE Deirdre, EVANS Nicola, FRAZER Megan, MATTHEWS Hannah, McCAY Shirley, McFERRAN Ayeisha (GK), MEEKE Alison, MULLAN Kathryn (C), O'BYRNE Yvonne, O'FLANAGAN Anna, O'FLANAGAN Grace (GK), PINDER Gillian, TICE Elena, UPTON Roisin, WATKINS Chloe, WILSON Zoe.

Bronze – Spain: BONASTRE Berta, CANO Carmen, GARCIA Begoña, GARCIA Maialen, GARCIA Melanie (GK), GINE Xantal, GUINEA Cristina, GUTIERREZ Rocio, JIMENEZ Lucia, LOPEZ Maria, MAGAZ Alicia, OLIVA Georgina (C), PEREZ Beatriz, PETCHAME Carlota, PONS Julia, RIERA Lola, RUIZ Maria (GK), SALVATELLA Carola.

The Hague 2014
Gold – Netherlands: van AS Naomi, BOS Willemijn, DERKX Frederique, DIRKSE van den HEUVEL Carlien, DROST Roos, van GEFFEN Margot, de GOEDE Eva, HOOG Ellen, JONKER Kelly, KEETELS Marloes, LAMMERS Kim, van MAASAKKER Caia, MEIJER Larissa (GK), PAUMEN Maartje (C), SCHOENAKER Jacky, SOMBROEK Joyce (GK), de WAARD Xan, WELTEN Lidewij.

Silver – Australia: BLYTH Madonna (C), BONE Edwina, CLAXTON Jane, DWYER Kirstin, EASTHAM Casey, FLANAGAN Anna, HURTZ Emily, JENNER Kate, KENNY Jodie, LYNCH Rachael (GK), McMAHON Karri, NANSCAWEN Georgia, NELSON Ashleigh, PARKER Georgie, SMITH Emily, TAYLOR Jayde, WELLS Ashlee (GK), WHITE Kellie.

Bronze – Argentina: ALBERTARRIO Agustina, AYMAR Luciana (C), BARRIONUEVO Noel, CAVALLERO Martina, D'ELIA Silvina, HABIF Florencia, JUAREZ Gisele, LUCHETTI Rosario, MERINO Delfina, MUTIO Maria (GK), REBECCHI Carla, RODRIGUEZ Macarena, ROSSI Mariana, SANCHEZ Rocio, SCARONE Mariela, SRUOGA Daniela, SRUOGA Maria, SUCCI Belen (GK).

Rosario 2010:

Gold – Argentina: ALADRO Maria (GK), AYMAR Luciana (C), BARRIONUEVO Noel, BURKART Claudia, D'ELIA Silvina, GARCIA Agustina, GULLA Alejandro, KANEVSKY Giselle, LUCHETTI Rosario, MERINO Delfina, REBECCHI Carla, RODRIGUEZ Macarena, ROSSI Mariana, RUSSO Marine, SCARONE Mariela, SRUOGA Daniela, SUCCI Belen (GK), VATTEONE Romina.

Silver – Netherlands: AGLIOTTI Marilyn, van AS Naomi, DIJKSTRA Wieke, DIRKSE van den HEUVEL Carlien, ENGELS Floortje (GK), GODERIE Maartje, de GOEDE Eva, HOOG Ellen, JONKER Kelly, LAMMERS Kim, PAUMEN Maartje, POLKAMP Sophie, van der POLS Michelle, SCHOPMAN Janneke (C), SMEETS Minke, SOMBROEK Joyce (GK), VEENHOVEN-MATTHEUSSENS Marieke, WELTEN Lidewij.

Bronze – England: BALL Ashleigh, CRADDOCK Charlotte, CULLEN Crista, DANSON Alex, GILBERT Susie, IBLE Gemma (GK), LONG Katie, MACLEOD Hannah, RICHARDSON Helen, ROGERS Chloe, SEYMOUR Natalie, STORRY Beth (GK), TWIGG Georgie, UNSWORTH Laura, WALSH Kate (C), WALTON Sally, WHITE Nicola, WILLIAMS Kerry.

Madrid 2006:

Gold – Netherlands: BOOIJ Minke, DE BRUIJN Chantal, DE HAAN Eveline, DE ROEVER Lisanne, DIJKSTRA Wieke, GODERIE Maartje, HOOG Ellen, KARRES Sylvia, LAMMERS Kim, MOREIRA DE MELO Fatima, MULDER Eefke, PAUMEN Maartje, POLKAMP Sophie, SCHOPMAN Janneke, SMABERS Minke, SNOEKS Jiske, VAN AS Naomi, VAN GEENHUIZEN Miek.

Silver – Australia: ARROLD Nicole, ATTARD Teneal, BEATTIE Wendy, BLYTH Madonna, FAULKNER Suzie, GILBERT De-Anne, HALLIDAY Emily, HUDSON Nikki, IMISON Rachel, LAMBERT Angie, MCGURK Kobie, MUNRO Hope, PATRICK Donna-Lee, SANDERS Rebecca, SMITH Karen, TAYLOR Sarah, TWITT Melanie, WALKER Kim.

Bronze – Argentina: AGUIRRE Gabriela, AICEGA Maria Magdalena, ANTONISKA Mariela, AYMAR Luciana, BOUZA Agustina, BURKART Claudia, DE LA PAZ HERNANDEZ Maria, D'ELIA Maria Florencia, GARCIA Agustina Soledad, GONZALEZ OLIVA Mariana, GULLA Alejandra, KANEVSKY Giselle, LUCHETTI Rosario, MARGALOT Maria Mercedes, REBECCHI Carla, RUSSO Marine, STEPNIK Ayelen, VUKOJICIC Paola.

Perth 2002:

Gold – Argentina: AICEGA Maria Magdalena, ANTONISKA Mariela, ARRONDO Ines, AYMAR Luciana, BURKART Claudia, DE LA PAZ HERNANDEZ Maria, DORESKI Natali, FERRARI Maria Paz, GARCIA Agustina Soledad, GONZALEZ OLIVA Mariana, MARGALOT Maria Mercedes, MASOTTA Karina, ONETO Vanina, PARODI Maria Ines, ROGNONI Cecilia, RUSSO Marine, STEPNIK Ayelen, VUKOJICIC Paola.

Silver – Netherlands: BOOIJ Minke, BOOMGAARDT Ageeth, DE BRUIJN Chantal, DE ROEVER Lisanne, DONNERS Mijntje, KOOIJMAN Femke, LAMMERS Kim, MOREIRA DE MELO Fatima, PETRI Karlijn, SCHEEPSTRA Maartje, SCHOPMAN Janneke, SINNIGE Clarinda, SMABERS Minke, VAN DER VAART Macha, VAN GEENHUIZEN Miek, VAN HEES Aniek, VAN KESSEL Lieve, VERBAKEL Ellis.

Bronze – China: CHEN Qiuqi, CHEN Xiaoling, CHEN Zhaoxia, CHENG Hui, FU Baorong, HOU Xiao Ian, HUANG Junxia, LI Ai Li, LI Shuang, LIU Yanli, LONG Feng Yu, MA Yibo, NIE Yali, PAN Fengzhen, QIU Yingling, TANG Chunling, ZHANG Hai Ying, ZHOU Wanfeng.

Utrecht 1998:

Gold – Australia: ALLEN Katie, ANNAN Alyson, GARARD Renita, HASLAM Juliet, HAWKES Rechelle, LANGHAM Bianca, MAITLAND Clover, MITCHELL-TAVERNER Claire, MOTT Nikki, PEEK Alison, POWELL Katrina, POWELL Lisa, SMITH Karen, SOWRY Justine, STARRE Kate, TOWERS Julie.

Silver – Netherlands: BOOMGAARDT Ageeth, DEITERS Julie, DONNERS Mijntje, DUBBELDAM Ellen, LEWIN Jeannette, MOREIRA DE MELO Fatima, SINNIGE Clarinda, SMABERS Hanneke, SMABERS Minke, TEEUWEN Margje, THATE Carole, TOUW Daphne, VAN DE KIEFT Fleur, VAN DEN BOOGAARD Dillianne, VAN DEN BROEK Inge, VAN DER WIELEN Suzan.

Bronze – Germany: BARTH Friederike, BECKER Britta, CREMER Melanie, DICKENSCHEID Tanja, ERNSTING-KRIENKE Nadine, KAUSCHKE Katrin, KELLER Natascha, KLECKER Denise, LATZSCH Heike, MOLLER Inga, REITER Cornelia, RODEWALD Marion, SUXDORF Philippa, WALTER Louisa, WEISEL Wibke, ZWEHL Julia.

Dublin 1994:

Gold – Australia: ALLEN Katie, ANDREWS Michelle, ANNAN Alyson, CARBON Sally, FARRELL Renita, GHISALBERTI Tammy, HASLAM Juliet, HAWKES Rechelle, MARSDEN Karen, MORRIS Jenny, PEEK Alison, PEREIRA Jackie, PERIS-KNEEBONE Nova, POWELL Lisa, SOWRY Justine, STARRE Kate.

Silver – Argentina: AICEGA Maria Magdalena, ALMADA Valeria, ARNAL Marianna, CASTELLAN Julieta, CASTELLI Maria Paula, FERRARI Maria Paz, FRAGNER Mariana, GAMBERO Anabel, LOPEZ Marisa, MACKENZIE Sofia, MASOTTA Karina, ONETO Vanina, PANDO Gabriela, PERRONE Maria, RIMOLDI Jorgelina, SANCHEZ Gabriela.

Bronze – USA: FILLAT Kris, FUCHS Tracey, HERSHEY Laurel, JAMES Kelli, KELLY Kristen, LUCAS Antoinette, LYNESS Leslie, MAROIS Barb, NEISS Pam, PANKRATZ Marcia, REEVE Jill, SCHUBERT Amy, SHEA Patty, STONE Eleanor, TCHOU Liz, WIELAND Andrea.

Sydney 1990:

Gold – Netherlands: APPELS Ingrid, BENNINGA Carina, BLEEKER Carina, DE RUITER Wietske, FOKKE Annemieke, HOLSBOER Noor, KOENEN Danielle, LEENDERS Caroline, LEJEUNE Lisanne, STEENBERGHE Florentine, THATE Carole, TOXOPEUS Jacqueline, VAN DER BEN Helen, VAN ZENDEREN Isabel, WOLFF Ingrid, WOUTERS Mieketine.

Silver – Australia: BELBIN Tracey, BELL Sally, BUCHANAN Sharon, CAPES Lee, DOBSON Christine, DORMAN Loretta, FISH Maree, HAGER Michelle, HAWKES Rechelle, NAUGHTON Lisa, PEEK Alison, PEREIRA Jackie, POWELL Lisa, PRIDEAUX Clare, SMALL Kim, TOOTH Liane.

Bronze – Korea: CHO Kyu Soon, HAN Keum Sil, JANG Eun Jung, JIN Won Sim, KIM Hyung Soon, KIM Kyung Ae, KIM Soon Duk, KIM Young Sook, KOO Mun Young, KWON Chang Sook, LEE Kyoung Hei, Lee Seon Young, LIM Gae Sook, SON Jeong Im, YANG Hea Sook, YOU Jae Sook.

Amstelveen 1986:

Gold – Netherlands: BOLHUIS-EIJSVOGEL Marjolein, BUTER Yvonne, DE BEUS Det, DE LEEUW Marjolein, HILLEN Elsemieke, LE POOLE Sandra, LEJEUNE Lisanne, NIEUWENHUIZEN Anneloes, OHR Martine, SIBBING Terry, VAN DER BEN Helen, VAN DOORN Marieke, VAN MANEN Aletta, VON WEILER Sophie, WILLEMSE Laurien, WOLFF Ingrid.

Silver – West Germany: APPEL Gabriele, BLUMENBERG Bettina, BREIKEN Dagmar, BURGARD Claudia, HANSMEYER Henrike, HEBERLE Petra, HEGENER Eva, HOFFMANN Carola, JUNGJOHANN Caren, MOSER Christina, OTT Patricia, ROTH Hella, SCHLEY Gabriela, SCHMID Susanne, UHLENBRUCK Gabriele, WOLLSCHLAGER Susanne.

Bronze – Canada: BALLANTYNE Sara, BAYES Sharon, BLAXLAND Jody, BRANCHAUD Laura, CHARLTON Nancy, CONN Michelle, COVEY Deb, CREELMAN Sharon, CZENCZEK Liz, FORSHAW Sheila, LYN Lisa, MACDOUGALL Kathryn, SCHLEPPE Shona.

Kuala Lumpur 1983:

Gold – Netherlands: BENNINGA Carina, BOEKHORST Fieke, BOLHUIS-EIJSVOGEL Marjolein, BROERE Monique, HENDRIKS Irene, HILLEN Elsemieke, HOOGEWEEGEN Yvonne, KAPTEIN Annelies, KUIK Eveline, LE POOLE Sandra, OHR Martine, POS Alette, SEVENS Lisette, VAN DOORN Marieke, VAN MANEN Aletta, ZEGERS Margriet.

Silver – Canada: BEECROFT Lynne, BENSON Heather, BLAXLAND Jody, BOROWY Jan, CHARLTON Nancy, CREELMAN Sharon, ELLIS Phyllis, FORSHAW Sheila, GOURLAY Jean, HEWLETT Karen, LAMBERT Laurie, MAHY Dee, McKINNON Zoe, PALMER Alison, STOYKA Darlene, WINTER Shelley.

Bronze – Australia: AYLMORE Marian, BOTFIELD Evelyn, BUCHANAN Sharon, CLEMENT Elspeth, GLOSSOP Pamela, GRANT-SUNDERLAND Julene, HEBERLE Trisha, IRELAND Kym, LEGGATT Robyn, PEARCE Colleen, PISANI Sandra, SIMPSON Sharyn, SMITH Sharon, WATKINS Susan, WHARTON Kerry, WHARTON Lorraine.

Buenos Aires 1981:

Gold – West Germany: APPEL Gabriele, BIRKENFELD Silke, BRUCKERT Ingrid, BURGER Stefanie, DRÜLL Elke, HAGEN Birgit, HAUDE Karen, KOCH Martina, LANDGRAF Sigrid, LINGNAU Corinna, MANTHEI Doris, MARX Dorothea, MOSER Christina, NEUMANN Gudrun, PAGELS Eva, SCHMID Susanne.

Silver – Netherlands: BAX Anneke, BAX Toos, BELIEN Madelon, BLEIJERVELD Margriet, BOEKHORST Fieke, BOLHUIS-EIJSVOGEL Marjolein, DE BEUS Det, HENDRIKS Irene, HILLEN Elsemieke, KAPTEIN Annelies, LE POOLE Sandra, POELMANS Jose, RAMAER Vib, SEVENS Lisette, VON WEILER Sophie, ZEGERS Margriet.

Bronze – Soviet Union: AKHMEROVA Leyla, BUZUNOVA Natalia, BYKOVA Natalia, CHIZHIK Larisa, CHOTCHAYEVA Tatiana, FILIPPOVA Nadezhda, FROLOVA Lyudmila, GLUBOKOVA Lydia, GORBATKOVA Nelli, GULYAEVA Nadezhda, INZHUVATOVA Galina, KONYUKHOVA Galina, KRASNIKOVA Natella, OVECHKINA Nadezhda, SHVYGANOVA Tatyana, ZAZDRAVNYH Valentina.

Madrid 1978:

Gold – Netherlands: BAX Anneke, BAX Toos, BEKKER Suzan, BELIEN Madelon, BLEIJERVELD Margriet, BOEKHORST Fieke, DE BEUS Det, FIKKERS Maria, HENDRIKS Irene, HILLEN Elsemieke, LE POOLE Sandra, MAHLER Jolien, SEVENS Lisette, VAN KOLLENBURG Nel, VON WEILER Sophie, WOUDENBERG-SCHRODER Cathy.

Silver – West Germany: APPEL Gabriele, BEHR Christel, BRUCKERT Ingrid, ECKERT Evi, GENNERICH Birgit, HAGEN Birgit, HAHN Birgit, KEIMER Uschi, KOCH Martina, LINGNAU Corinna, MARX Dorothea, MOSER Christina, MÜLLER Margit, NEUMANN Gudrun, PAGELS Eva, RELLING Ina.

Bronze – Argentina: ALFONSO A, ALONSO M, DESALVO C, GORINA P, GUTIERREZ C, MAC CORMIK A, MASTRIPIERI G, MEDICI C, MEDINA S, NAZIONALE M, RAJME P, RODRIGUEZ L, RUPAR A, SACCONE V, SCALLY B.

West Berlin 1976:

Gold – West Germany: APPEL Gabriele, BEHR Christel, BRUCKERT Ingrid, DRESCHER Steffi, ECKERT Evi, HAGEN Birgit, HAHN Birgit, KEIMER Uschi, KLIMPEL Heidemarie, LAU Christel, MULLER Margit, NEUMANN Gudrun, SCHOLZ-SCHELLER Gudrun, VON LADIGES Elisabeth, WELZEL Brigitte.

Silver – Argentina: ALFONSO A, ALFONSO V, DAY V, GORINA P, GOYENECHE B, GUTIERREZ C, MAC CORMIK A, MASTRIPIERI G, MEDICI C, NAZIONALE M, RUPAR A, SALICHS C, SCALLY B, STICKFORTH C, TAYLOR D.

Bronze – Netherlands: BAX Anneke, BAX Toos, BEKKER Suzan, DOYER Gonneke, DRAGT Joke, FIKKERS Maria, GOUKA Marjolein, GROEN Mieke, HAGEMANS Marja, JANSEN Marlies, POELMANS Jose, SEVENS Lisette, VAN KOLLENBURG Nel, VAN LIEROP Nicole, WOUDENBERG-SCHRODER Cathy.

Mandelieu 1974:

Gold – Netherlands: BAX Anneke, BAX Toos, BEKKER Suzan, DE GROOTH Cora, HAGEMANS Marja, HOEGEN Helma, KOOPMANN Wilma, KREFT Debbie, LEURS Loes, POELMANS Jose, SEVENS Lisette, VAN KOLLENBURG Nel, VAN LIEROP Nicole, VAN STRATEN Marjo, VAN OOSTERHOUT Tanja.

Silver – Argentina: ALFONSO A, ALFONSO V, BARNADAS R, BEAUCHAMP A, CHAUFEN S, DAY V, FERIOLI M, GUTIERREZ C, KOCOUREK R, LEBR'N M, MAC CORMIK A, MACHIN C, MASTRIPIERI G, SACCONE V, SCALLY B, TAYLOR D, TURCONI S.

Bronze – West Germany: BEHR Christel, REITER Christine, BÜHLER Ilona, DRESCHER Steffi, HEINZ Karin, HIEMISCH Petra, HUTH Ulrike, KEIMER Uschi, KLIMPEL Heidemarie, LAU Christel, MÜLLER Margit, SEIFFERT Barbara, WELZEL Birgitte, WULF Dörte, ZIMMERMANN Edda.

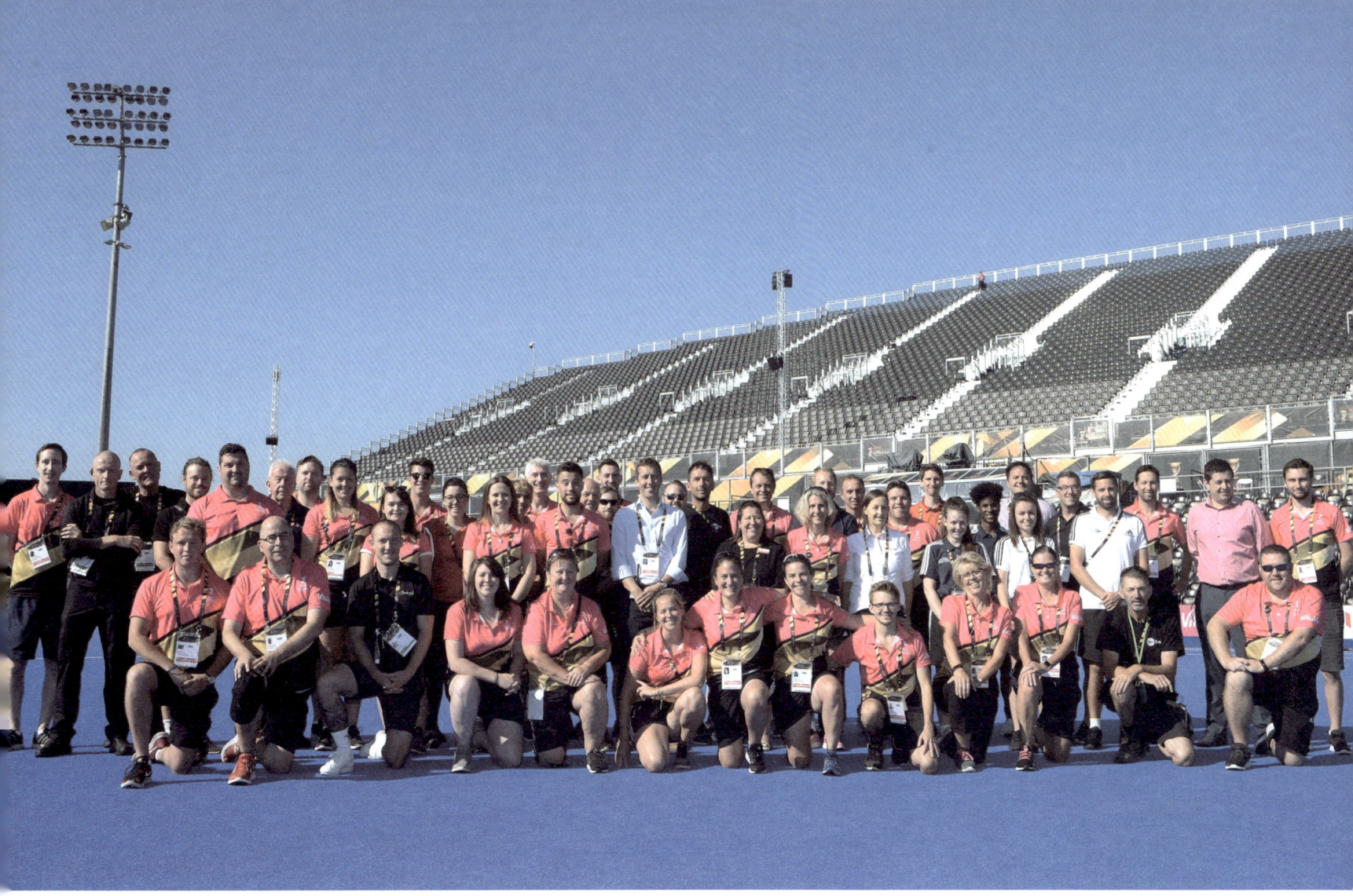

The Vitality Hockey Women's World Cup marked the culmination of five years of work for our team since England Hockey won the bid to host the event back in November 2013. Hosting three major events along the way; the EuroHockey Championships in 2015, the Men's and Women's Champions Trophies in 2016 and the Men's World League Semi-Final in 2017 – meant that we were able to develop a strong team of partners and contractors, and provide valuable experience for England Hockey staff and our wonderful volunteer Hockey Makers. Delivering the event through England Hockey also meant that every part of our business was involved. We couldn't be prouder with the outcome; it was a real privilege to host the event on behalf of the FIH and to welcome the best athletes in the world to London.

Sue Catton, Event Manager VHWWC

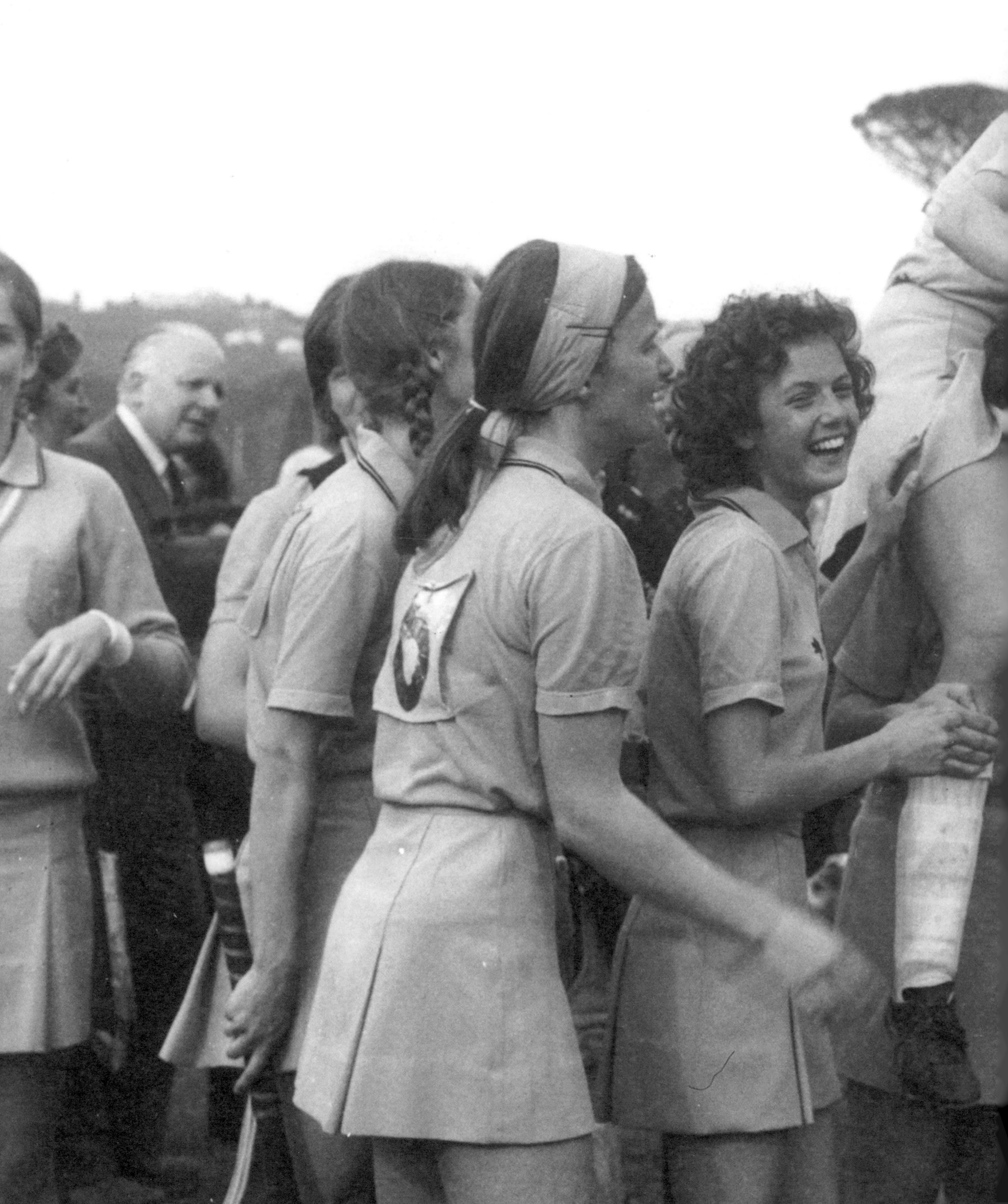